Fifth Edition

PUBLIC PERSONNEL MANAGEMENT

CURRENT CONCERNS, FUTURE CHALLENGES

Norma M. Riccucci

Rutgers University Newark

Routledge

Taylor & Francis Group

LONDON AND NEW YORK

First published 2012, 2006, 2002 by Pearson Education, Inc.

Published 2016 by Routledge
2 Park Square, Milton Park, Abingdon, Oxon OX14 4RN
711 Third Avenue, New York, NY, 10017, USA

Routledge is an imprint of the Taylor & Francis Group, an informa business

ISBN: 9780205012671 (pbk)

Cover Designer: Suzanne Duda
Cover Design: © skvoor/shutterstock

Library of Congress Cataloging-in-Publication Data
Public personnel management / [edited by] Norma M. Riccucci.—5th ed.
    p. cm.
  Includes bibliographical references and index.
  ISBN-13: 978-0-205-01267-1 (alk. paper)
  ISBN-10: 0-205-01267-1 (alk. paper)
  1. Civil service—United States—Personnel management. 2. Civil service—Personnel management. I. Riccucci, Norma.
JK765.P947 2012
352.60973—dc22

                                                          2010037489

For David H. Rosenbloom, whose support and friendship have been invaluable

CONTENTS

Preface *vii*

Chapter 1 **Public Human Resource Management: How We Get Where We Are Today** **1**
Stephen E. Condrey

Chapter 2 **Building Public HRM Capacity in Fragile and Transitional States: Linking Theory, Research, Practice, and Teaching** **14**
Donald E. Klingner

Chapter 3 **Generational Differences and the Public Sector Workforce** **28**
Madinah F. Hamidullah

Chapter 4 **Affirmative Action and the Law** **39**
Norma M. Riccucci

Chapter 5 **Diversity and Cultural Competency** **50**
Norma M. Riccucci

Chapter 6 **Lesbian, Gay, Bisexual, and Transgendered Employees in the Public Sector Workforce** **60**
Charles W. Gossett

Chapter 7 **Chronic Health Issues and the Public Workplace** **77**
James D. Slack, Samuel Douglas Drake Slack, and Sarah Ashley Slack

Chapter 8 **Public Employee Unions in a New Era** **95**
T. Zane Reeves

Chapter 9 **Public Employees' Liability for "Constitutional Torts"** **104**
David H. Rosenbloom

Chapter 10 **Strategic Human Resource Management** **120**
Dennis M. Daley

Chapter 11   Hiring in the Federal Government: Balancing Technical, Managerial, and Political Imperatives   135

Carolyn Ban

Chapter 12   The Challenges of Succession Planning in Turbulent Times   148

Heather Getha-Taylor

Chapter 13   Public Sector Pensions and Benefits: Challenges in a New Environment   157

Albert C. Hyde and Katherine C. Naff

Chapter 14   Managing Human Resources to Improve Organizational Productivity: The Role of Performance Evaluation   173

J. Edward Kellough

Chapter 15   Privatized Prisons and Unions: Personnel Management Implications   186

Trina M. Gordon and Byron E. Price

Chapter 16   Human Resources Management in Nonprofit Organizations   196

Joan E. Pynes

Chapter 17   Ethics Management and Training   213

Jonathan P. West and Evan M. Berman

Index   228

PREFACE

Public personnel management continues to be a dynamic, robust field. This edited volume illustrates the wide-ranging aspects of the field in the most up-to-date fashion. The book is designed to provide readers with a broad understanding of the key policy and management issues facing the field today. As with previous editions, the book is not a "how-to" manual, with detailed instructions on the nuts and bolts of developing and implementing personnel procedures.

NEW TO THIS EDITION

Among the many updates made throughout, this new edition includes eight new readings:

- In Chapter 1, Stephen Condrey presents five models of public human resource management service delivery, and, in the context of four fairly recent events, illustrates how the current practice of public human resource management has been shaped. The chapter points to the enduring tension between efforts to create and sustain a neutrally competent civil service corps and helping to ensure that public bureaucracies are responsive to elected and appointed officials as well as the public they serve. It sets the stage for the field of public personnel management today and why it continues to draw attention from the standpoint of study and practice.
- New and challenging developments in all areas of public personnel management are subsequently addressed. For example, Chapter 2, by Donald Klingner, seeks to close some of the glaring gaps within the global area of human resources management (HRM) through the development of a comprehensive, coherent, and theory-driven research agenda, which would not only help to improve the sustainability of adapted innovations but also draw attention to the professional competencies required of international HRM consultants and practitioners. This chapter will ultimately assist in the maturation of global HRM practices.
- In addition, one of the most critical issues today in public personnel management is how governments will manage their multigenerational workforces. This issue is addressed in Chapter 3 by Madinah Hamidullah.
- Relatedly, governments continue to be challenged by succession planning, which is addressed by Heather Getha-Taylor in Chapter 12, as well as pension and other benefits, which are addressed by Albert Hyde and Katherine Naff in Chapter 13.

Additional issues and ongoing challenges to the field are also addressed in this book. Topics such as affirmative action, HIV/AIDS, public sector labor relations, employees' legal responsibilities, and privatization (see Gordon and Price, Chapter 15) are addressed in this volume. So, too, are topics covering issues such as the importance of building cultural competency in governments (see Riccucci, Chapter 4); human resources in nonprofits (see Pynes, Chapter 16); lesbian, gay, bisexual, and transgendered employees in the public sector workforces (see Gossett, Chapter 6); and government's commitment to ethics training (see West and Berman, Chapter 17). These are the critical issues that will shape and define the field of public personnel management in the years to come.

1

PUBLIC HUMAN RESOURCE MANAGEMENT: HOW WE GET WHERE WE ARE TODAY

Stephen E. Condrey[1]

Stephen E. Condrey, Ph.D., is senior associate and program director for human resource management with the University of Georgia's Carl Vinson Institute of Government. He is also adjunct professor of public administration and policy in the School of Public and International Affairs at the University of Georgia. He has over a quarter of a century of professional experience in human resource management and has consulted nationally and internationally with over 700 organizations concerning personnel-related issues. He presently serves as editor-in-chief of the *Review of Public Personnel Administration* and is the editor of the *Handbook of Human Resource Management in Government,* third edition (2010, Jossey-Bass).

There is perhaps no area of public administration that has experienced greater change, professionalization, and controversy over the past four decades than public human resource management. The purpose of this introductory chapter is to explicate this phenomenon and set the stage for the chapters that follow.

This chapter first describes five models of public human resource management service delivery. The chapter will then discuss four fairly recent events and how the influence of these events shapes the current practice of public human resource management. The four events are as follows:

- The Civil Rights Act of 1964
- The Civil Service Reform Act of 1978
- Radical reform of civil service systems
- The election of President Barack Obama

Underlying each of these events is an enduring tension regarding how to create and sustain a neutrally competent civil service corps while at the same time helping to

---

[1] The author is grateful to Linda Seagraves and Alex Daman of the Carl Vinson Institute of Government at the University of Georgia for their assistance in preparing this chapter.

ensure that public bureaucracies are responsive to elected and appointed officials as well as the public they serve. This constant and seemingly irresolvable tension brings life to the field of public human resource management and makes it an interesting one to study, explore, and practice.

PUBLIC HUMAN RESOURCE MANAGEMENT SERVICE DELIVERY

The most definitive history of the development of the field of public human resource management is Paul Van Riper's *History of the United States Civil Service* (1958). Additionally, all of the leading texts in the field (e.g., Berman, Bowman, Van Wart, and West, 2010; Klingner, Nalbandian, and Llorens, 2009; Nigro, Nigro, and Kellough, 2006; Riccucci and Naff, 2008) provide an excellent historical analysis of the field. Essentially, public human resource management history in the United States began with early elitist tendencies that favored the landed gentry as holders of public jobs. The election of Andrew Jackson in 1828 ushered in an era of spoils politics in which public jobs were considered a commodity to be bartered for political support. In a direct confrontation of spoils politics, the *Pendleton Act of 1883* established the first federal civil service system that slowly expanded its reach over the decades and helped to professionalize the workforce of an increasingly complex bureaucracy. This civil service structure was to stay in place until the *Civil Service Reform Act of 1978*.

Table 1.1 lists five organizing models for public human resource management. What is interesting to this author is that while there are definite historical time periods that each of these models is most closely associated with, all of these can be found today in varying degrees in federal, state, and local governments in the United States. Therefore, rather than a strict historical analysis, the next several pages discuss various organizing strategies for the delivery of human resource management services and how these, in turn, influence the role of the human resource manager.

The *traditional model* of public human resource management is most closely associated with strong civil service systems such as the federal civil service system in existence prior to the *Civil Service Reform Act of 1978* or those employed today by many state and local governments. Under this form of human resource management service delivery, the human resource manager is seen as the gatekeeper of public jobs, an enforcer of "merit," and a by-product of this role, a hindrance to the effective management of public organizations. This role of merit enforcer has helped build professional public bureaucracies but at the same time has diminished the relevance of public human resource managers to the actual functioning of public organizations.

As a direct result of this preoccupation with rule enforcement, the *reform model* emerged. The reform model set out to decentralize human resource management away from central personnel authorities to the actual departments they serve. The intended result of this decentralized approach was to make human resource management systems more closely aligned with the organizations they serve. Now managers would be unfettered by uniform sets of rules promulgated and enforced by central personnel authorities. For example, the 1996 Georgia law that abolished the state's protections for its civil servants also decentralized personnel authority to its various departments (Condrey, 2002; Kellough and Nigro, 2006). Furthermore, demonstration projects allowed by the federal *Civil Service Reform Act of 1978* have allowed federal agencies to develop varying performance appraisal systems, alternative position classification

| Table 1.1 | A Comparison of Five Models of Public Human Resource Management |

Function	Traditional Model	Reform Model	Strategic Model	Privatization or Outsourcing Model	Hybrid Model
Service delivery	Centralized	Decentralized	Collaborative	Contract	Mixed
Goal orientation	Uniform enforcement of rules, policies, and procedures	Manager centered	Respectful of human resource management and organizational goals	Effective contract negotiator and administrator	Mission centered
Communication pattern	Top–down	Two-way	Multidirectional	Reports and contract monitoring	Multi-directional to include contract monitoring
Feedback characteristics	Formal and informal complaints	Muted	Continuous	Muted	Continuous and routine
Value orientation	"Merit"	Immediate responsiveness to organizational mission and goals	Effective organizational functioning coupled with a respect for effective human resource management practices	Efficiency: private sector preference	Mission centered
Role of human resource manager	Enforcer of "merit"	Diminished authority and control	Organizational consultant	Contract negotiator and administrator	Key organizational player
Perception of human resource management	Hindrance to effective organizational functioning	Adjunct collection of skills	Full managerial partner	Diminished	Enhanced
Role of education	Public personnel administration	Adjunct to managerial skills	Human resource management, general management, practical focus	Contract negotiation and administration skills	Characteristics of the strategic and privatization models

Source: Condrey, S. E. (2010). *Handbook of Human Resource Management in Government* (p. xlviii). San Francisco, CA: Jossey-Bass.

systems, and agency-specific pay systems. James Thompson terms this the "disaggregation" of the federal personnel system and points to the difficulty that it poses to the overall coordination of federal personnel management:

> Disaggregation . . . represents a fundamental threat to an institution whose viability is contingent on its inherently collective nature. The existence of a common set of employment practices contributes in an important way to a collective orientation that is integral to the Civil Service as an institution. (2006, p. 497)

The *strategic model* seeks to blend positive features of the traditional and reform models. James Perry (1993) points to the positive space that such an arrangement makes for human resource professionals. Under the strategic model, human resource management is closely aligned with the overall management of an agency. The human resource professional's focus is not preoccupied with enforcing rules and regulations but targeted toward helping management achieve organizational objectives. Theoretically, this role enhances the profile of the human resource professional to that of a managerial consultant who is involved in substantive managerial issues. It may also have the effect of creating a schizophrenic role whereby the human resource manager must sometimes choose between conflicting managerial goals and sound human resource management policy.

The *privatization or outsourcing model* of public human resource management has emerged in the past several decades. Closely associated with new public management (NPM), privatizing or outsourcing seeks to have specific human resource functions performed by private organizations rather than governmental agencies. For example, Bowman and West (2006) point to the state of Florida and its mixed-to-negative experience with the Converysis Corporation (Bowman, West, and Gertz, 2006).A more radical example of outsourcing is the federal Transportation Security Administration (TSA). Here, legislation establishing the TSA outsourced much of its human resource management functions (Naff and Newman, 2004). As can be easily surmised, a continued and focused effort to outsource human resource functions leads to a diminished role for the human resource manager. On the other hand, it creates the need for human resource professionals to become skilled in contract specification, negotiation, and administration—a far cry from their human resource counterparts of generations past. As of this writing, the privatization and outsourcing fervor of the Clinton and Bush administrations is being tempered by the Obama administration's stated call to reverse the outsourcing trend and to "insource" federal functions and jobs (Weigelt, 2010). It remains to be seen if this retrenchment will be substantially sustained in the coming decades.

A fifth and emerging model for public human resource management delivery is the *hybrid model*. Essentially, this model blends positive features of the strategic and the privatization or outsourcing models. This model recognizes that privatization and outsourcing are not only a permanent part of the public human resource management landscape but also create a space for the human resource manager to have an active role in the management of public organizations.

While crystal balls are not readily at hand, it appears that all five of these models will be present to some degree in the practice of public human resource management in the foreseeable future. This fact alone creates a need for enhanced human resource management education, not only for human resource managers but also for public managers in general. The following sections discuss four events that have shaped the practice of public human resource management and the conditions under which it is delivered.

The Civil Rights Act of 1964

The *Civil Rights Act of 1964* as applied to government organizations by the *Equal Employment Opportunity Act of 1972* has had a profound and positive effect on the practice of public human resource management. Prior to 1972, many public human resource selection procedures were accepted on their face as being valid, even though they were sorely lacking in their professional development and application. In the landmark Supreme Court case, *Griggs v. Duke Power Company*, the court held that the burden of proof as to the validity of selection devices lay with the organizations that developed and administered them:

> Since the passage of the *Civil Rights Act of 1964*, case after case brought before the U.S. courts had led to the mandating of objective personnel practices. Although these practices have been exhaustively advocated by personnelists prior to the 1964 Act, the courts have now provided strong and compelling legal support for their employment. The extension of the *Griggs* decision to include performance appraisal systems (*Connecticut v. Teal*, 1982) broadens that mandate. (Daley, 2010, p. 566)

While many public human resource agencies practiced in an aboveboard and professional manner prior to 1972, the *Equal Employment Opportunity Act of 1972* caused increased scrutiny of time-honored techniques and practices arising out of the scientific management movement of the early twentieth century and heretofore applied without serious questioning. Employees and applicants were now free to question and legally challenge selection devices—written tests, oral examinations, training and experience evaluations, and performance appraisal techniques. In many cases, these practices were found to be lacking. This increased scrutiny caused introspection in the field and helped serve to make sure that public sector selection devices were valid and related to the positions for which they were designed to assess.

Since selection devices that had "adverse impact" on minorities and women were now open to legal challenge, many public agencies embraced professionally developed assessment centers that were job related and did not block otherwise qualified minorities and women from the public sector workforce. As a result, human resource practices and techniques were professionalized and state and local government workforces became more diverse and representative of the bureaucracies they served.

An excellent example of how application of federal legislation and court ratings has professionalized public human resource management is the Jefferson County, Alabama, personnel board (Sims, 2009). The personnel board is an example of the traditional model of human resource management discussed earlier and serves the City of Birmingham, Jefferson County, and 21 other jurisdictions in Jefferson County as a central personnel agency. Over three decades of law suits, consent decrees, and, finally, a receivership has resulted in the use of valid selection devices for civil service positions. While structural problems remain with how the personnel board is organized, the resulting workforces are far more diverse and representative of the populations they serve as a result of federal court intervention (Condrey and West, 2011; Sims, 2009).

Civil Service Reform Act of 1978

President Carter's *Civil Service Reform Act of 1978* (CSRA of 1978) set the tone for much of the efforts surrounding public human resource management reform in the following decades. As a former governor and Washington outsider, Carter ran against the federal bureaucracy and used the CSRA of 1978 partially as a means of exerting presidential executive control into the structural and substantive aspects of federal personnel management. It was also a signal that being a civil servant was no longer to be considered a high calling, as under the Kennedy administration, but that "bureaucracy" and the civil servants that inhabited them were in need of control, direction, and the exertion of executive authority and leadership.

Five provisions of the CSRA of 1978 will be discussed here:

- Office of Personnel Management (OPM)
- Merit Systems Protection Board (MSPB)
- Merit pay for managers
- HR demonstration projects
- Senior executive service (SES)

The 1978 act abolished the Civil Service Commission that had been in place since the passage of the *Pendleton Act of 1883*. The Civil Service Commission had been a semi-independent commission that administered the federal civil service system and also held hearings and heard appeals from aggrieved employees (Van Riper, 1958). The commission was now replaced by two agencies: the OPM and the MSPB.

The OPM marked the first time in modern U.S. history that the president would have formal administrative control over the gatekeepers of the federal bureaucracy. With an OPM director appointed by the president and directly accountable for federal human resource management, the means for direct executive influence over the federal bureaucracy was now established. This is in contrast to the semi-independent Civil Service Commission it replaced.

While the establishment of OPM allowed a formal mechanism for executive control and influence, U.S. presidents had long sought to influence federal human resource management policy and exert their influence over the federal bureaucratic corps. An extreme example was the Nixon administration's *Malek Manual* (Thompson, 2003). Developed by the White House Personnel Office, the manual was a step-by-step guide of how to overcome the Civil Service Commission's authority—a prime example of the enduring tension between the desire for executive control and the need for a neutrally competent bureaucracy described earlier.

The second major feature of the CSRA of 1978 is the MSPB. The MSPB retained the adjunctive authority of the formal Civil Service Commission. The MSPB also provides periodic independent assessments of the federal workforce and administers federal whistle-blower protections.

Another major feature of the CSRA of 1978 was merit pay for managers. While the initial merit pay plan for managers was not successful at the federal level, it is important since merit pay has continued to be a recurring and controversial theme across all levels of government in the United States. For example, the National Security Personnel System (NSPS) of the second Bush administration was a version of a merit-based compensation system (*From proposed to final,* 2005; Riccucci and Thompson, 2008, p. 881;). This system was ended by the Obama administration in 2010 when participants returned to the federal General Schedule (O'Keefe, 2010).

Even though the Obama administration has put an end to NSPS, it still holds out the possibility of expanding merit pay in the federal government. One might ask after such a series of failures, why does the desire for merit pay systems still exist? This writer believes that merit pay enjoys popularity with politicians and the public due to its perceived possible effectiveness in influencing recalcitrant bureaucrats. Why is merit pay so difficult to implement and administer? The problem is complex but seems to distill down to a few elements: low organizational trust levels, perceived ineffectiveness of performance appraisal instruments, small monetary rewards, a large and diverse bureaucracy, and lack of union support. While such obstacles may seem insurmountable, it appears that a continuing search for a merit pay system that "works" will continue into the following decades.

The *Civil Service Reform Act of 1978* also allowed for federal human resource management demonstration or pilot projects. This provision allows agencies specific exemptions from the portions of federal civil service law that allow them to develop alternative mechanisms to classify, appraise, and reward employees. Probably the most notable and studied demonstration project was the China Lake project at the naval weapons laboratory (Thompson, 2008, p. 241). While there have been numerous demonstration projects, none of these experiments has proven to be a definitive guide for restructuring federal personnel policy. As James Thompson argues, these projects may have in fact contributed to what he describes as the "disaggregation" of the federal personnel management system. Instead of a uniform human resource management framework, what exists today is far from a coordinated system but rather a patchwork quilt of systems, rules, regulations, and policies (Thompson, 2007). Since such an ad hoc system mitigates against overall executive control of federal personnel management, it would not be surprising to see future presidents retreat toward a more uniform and centralized system for human resource management. This may well have influenced the Obama administration's decision to abolish the NSPS.

A fifth major provision of the CSRA of 1978 is the SES. The SES was designed to create an elite cadre of federal managers that would provide executive expertise and leadership at the highest levels of the federal bureaucracy. As Hugh Heclo (1977) notes in his now classic *A Government of Strangers*, published just prior to the passage of the CSRA of 1978, there was a perceived need to build linkages between the career and appointed bureaucratic leadership to provide for policy articulation and continuity. While the jury is mixed on the true result of the SES, Lah and Perry (2008) report that some variation of the SES has expanded to many state governments as well as to numerous countries around the world.

Radical Reform Enters the Picture

While the *Civil Service Reform Act of 1978* tinkered legislatively with the federal human resource management delivery system, "radical reformers" were to take a quite different and more direct approach: Instead of reforming human resource systems, they would seek, in some instances, to abolish policies, procedures, as well as entire civil service protection systems, making civil servants "at will" employees rather than being protected from adverse political and managerial actions. Thus, it seems that civil service systems had come full circle—created as a result of the *Pendleton Act of 1883* to provide protection for employees and encourage the development of a neutrally competent administration corps—and were now being whittled away and, in some cases, dismantled in the name of executive control and managerial flexibility.

Radical reform found nurture and support in the antigovernment sentiments of the preceding two decades as well as the NPM movement, a global phenomenon. NPM argues that effective government management has been hindered by excessive regulations, particularly in the human resources arena (Kearney and Hays, 1998). Adherents to NPM were encouraged to "let managers manage" and not be constrained by unnecessary and unwieldy rules and regulations. Symbolic of this philosophy, the Clinton/Gore administration "abolished" the federal personnel manual and further decentralized federal human resource management through privatization, outsourcing, and continued "disaggregation" of the federal personnel function.

The second Bush administration did not differ significantly with the Clinton administration's human resource policies and continued with privatization and outsourcing efforts (Riccucci and Thompson, 2008). The most significant difference between the two administrations concerned federal labor relations. Clinton fostered improved labor/management partnerships, while Bush shunned such partnerships. The result was an acrimonious labor/management atmosphere typified by the diminution of employee rights and protections through avenues such as the NSPS discussed earlier (Tobias, 2010).

While a timid version of radical reform efforts occurred at the federal level under the Clinton and second Bush administrations, it would be one state—Georgia—that would signal the start of real radical reform and begin its diffusion (in whole or in part) to many state governments (Battaglio and Condrey, 2007; Hays and Sowa, 2006; West, 2002). Led by the then governor (and later U.S. Senator) Zell Miller, the State of Georgia abolished civil service protections for new employees effective July 1, 1996. Presently, more than 80 percent of the state's employees serve "at will," which means that they effectively serve at the pleasure of the state and may be dismissed without "just cause." Thus, the balance between executive control and employee rights has been weighted heavily toward executive and managerial control. What has been the result of this policy? Battaglio and Condrey (2009) point to evidence of spoils politics creeping back into state human resource management. The most damaging finding is that Georgia's at-will employment system has a tendency to undermine the trusting relationships necessary for effective government management and administration:

> It appears that HR professionals are somewhat receptive to the concept of EAW [employee-at-will] personnel systems. However, HRM does not take place in a vacuum. When the reality of these systems is experienced, abuses are viewed, and evidence of spoils-like activities appears. The results suggest that HR professionals tend to sour on EAW implementation and to, in turn, exhibit less trust in management and in their respective organizations. This phenomenon may indicate that EAW systems have a fundamental flaw in that they undermine trusting workplace relationships necessary for effective public management. (Battaglio and Condrey, 2009)

Evidence of effectiveness to the contrary, it appears that this brand of radical reform is now an accepted part of the public human resource management landscape and should continue to influence the field over the coming years.

The Obama Administration

The election of Barack Obama may have signaled a reversal or, at least, a halting of the antibureaucratic themes of the past four decades. Obama, unlike his recent predecessors, ran for office on a campaign that embraced public service as a high calling. He has also appointed John Berry as OPM Director. Berry is the highest profile director of that office since its initial director, Alan Campbell. While this chapter is written in the second year of Obama's term, Obama's call to public service harkens back to President Kennedy's administration. Also, Obama appears to have an active policy agenda concerning federal human resource management reform. As John Berry states:

> I believe this is an historic opportunity for comprehensive reform of our civil service system. The stars are aligned in a way that occurs only once in a generation. We have a President who deeply values service and wants to restore the dignity and respect for our civil service to what it was during Kennedy's stirring call. We have a Congress that is willing to help and a public that increasingly recognizes that our current approaches to hiring, rewarding, appraising and training our employees are inadequate. (Berry, 2009a)

There are six areas that the Obama administration has addressed, or likely will address, concerning federal human resource management:

- Recruitment
- Pay system reform
- Performance management
- Training and development
- Improved labor/management relations
- In-sourcing

Recruitment

The OPM, and in particular its director, has made the improvement of federal recruitment a top priority. With 1.9 million employees and the need to fill 300,000 positions on an annual basis, the federal government is hiring at a rapid pace, and the need for quality applicants is critical. At this writing, OPM is turning from lengthy essay examinations that probe knowledge, skills, and abilities related to a particular job to a resume-based system. Other priorities are sharing information about applicants from agency to agency as well as limiting the effects of the "rule of three," a rule that requires hiring from the top three ranked applicants for a position. As Berry notes:

> The very procedures that were supposed to ensure job applicants are evaluated based on merit are discouraging applicants from completing the arduous quest of actually getting a civil service job." (Berry, 2009b)

Effective recruitment, and eliminating barriers to such, appears to have been the top priority of OPM in the nascence of the Obama administration.

Pay System Reform

While Obama has approved the abolition of the NSPS and its reintegration into the federal General Schedule, overall pay system reform is still on its policy agenda. The federal pay system has remained virtually structurally unchanged since its creation in the 1940s. Such reform would probably include some form of pay for performance and also feature career ladders and career bands (a rank-in-person system) over the step and grade structure (a rank-in-position system) of the General Schedule. While such ideas percolate, there is natural resistance from employee unions to these reforms. Additionally, other major policy distractions such as a focus on the recovery from the deep recession of 2009–2010, major foreign policy challenges, and the impending ecological disaster caused by the Gulf of Mexico oil spill may lessen the sweeping nature of any possible pay system reform or other human resource management reform proposals of a controversial nature.

Performance Management

The disaggregation of the federal personnel system is perhaps best evident in the system utilized to assess employee performance. Different agencies utilize different performance appraisal systems, and these systems utilize a differing number of performance appraisal categories. Director Berry (2009a) has proposed more closely tying performance appraisal outcomes with overall career development, perhaps linking performance appraisal to movement through the career bands discussed earlier. A uniform federal performance management system would have three levels:

- In good standing
- Outstanding
- Not-in-good standing

A more uniform performance management system could theoretically increase the possibility for overall coordination efforts related to the federal bureaucracy.

Training and Development

Closely linked to career bands and an enhanced and reaggregated performance management system is the need for an increased focus on training and development: "We need to get the best people into the Federal government, and once they're here, we need to get them in the right places" (Berry, 2009a). In combination, these three elements represent a cultural shift in how the federal government attracts, rewards, appraises, and develops its workforce. Such a shift would help build a human resource management system suited to the complex tasks federal civil servants face on a daily basis. If implemented successfully, these structural changes to the federal government's human resources system would most likely diffuse to state and local governments as well.

Improving Labor Management Relations

The "big chill" on labor relations during the second Bush administration is over. The Obama administration is working closely to rebuild positive relations with federal employee labor unions. Robert Tobias (2010) argues that to be effective, human resource managers need to embrace the possibility of positive and productive relations with labor unions. As Obama set out to restructure the labor/management partnership councils of the Clinton Administration, John Gage, President of the American Federation of Government Employees, stated:

> If there's a management team that's HR and labor relations, we're not going to play. (Rosenberg, 2010)

What Gage means is that federal labor unions want a seat at the table when major policy decisions are made—if they are solely dealing with human resources representatives, they are not interested. This attitude is an artifact of decades of union experience in dealing with human resource managers operating under their traditional role as gatekeepers of merit and the uniform enforcers of rules and regulations. If unions view HR in this narrow role, they are unlikely to seek them out unless matters involve interpretation of contracts, regulations, and the like. To this writer, the above statement from federal union leaders should not be dismissed but rather embraced. As a field, public human resource management has as much to learn from its detractors as it does from its supporters.

Where Are We Headed?

Where is the field of public human resource management headed? While the path is not directly clear, this writer believes that public human resource management is on the way toward revitalization and increased importance in the management of public organizations. Human resource management expertise is not only required for those staffing agency human resources offices but is also an essential part of the job of every public manager. As sound human resource management practices are diffused throughout public organizations, the challenge is for central human resources departments to be viewed as credible and viable sources of human resource management expertise.

References

Battaglio, P. R., and S. E. Condrey. 2007. "Framing Civil Service Innovations: Assessing State and Local Government Reforms." In J. S. Bowman & J. P. West, eds. *American Public Service: Radical Reform and the Merit System*. Boca Raton, FL: CRC Press.

Battaglio, P. R., and S. E. Condrey. 2009. "Reforming Public Management: Analyzing the Impact of Public Service Reform on Organizational and Managerial Trust." *Journal of Public Administration Research and Theory* 19: 689–707.

Berman, E. M., J. S. Bowman, J. P. West, and M. R. Van Wart. 2010. *Human Resource Management in Public Service: Paradoxes, Processes, and Problems* (3rd ed.). Thousand Oaks, CA: SAGE Publications, Inc.

Berry, J. 2009a. A Merit System for the 21st Century? Remarks of John Berry, Director of OPM, September 11, 2009.

Berry, J. 2009b. Remarks of OPM Director John Berry at the Human Capital Management Forum, November 17, 2009.

Bowman, J. S., and J. P. West. 2006. "Ending Civil Service Protections in Florida Government." *Review of Public Personnel Administration* 26(2): 139–157.

Bowman, J. S., J. P. West, and S. Gertz. 2006. "Florida's Service First: Radical Reform in the Sunshine State." In J. E. Kellough and L. Nigro, eds. *Civil Service Reform in the States* (pp. 145–170). Albany, NY: SUNY Press.

Condrey, S. E. 2002. "Reinventing State Civil Service Systems: The Georgia Experience." *Review of Public Personnel Administration* 22(2): 114–124.

Condrey, S. E., and J. P. West. 2011, forthcoming. "Civil Service Reform: Past as Prologue?" In D. C. Menzel and H. L. White, eds. *The State of Public Administration: Issues, Challenges, Opportunities*.

Daley, D. M. 2010. "Designing Effective Performance Appraisal Systems." In S. E. Condrey, ed. *Handbook Human Resource Management in Government* (3rd ed., pp. 555–586). San Francisco, CA: Jossey Bass.

From proposed to final: Evaluating regulations for the national security personnel system: Hearings before the U.S. Senate Committee on Homeland Security and Governmental Affairs, 109th Congress, 1, (2005) (testimony of Ronald Ault).

Hays, S. W., and J. E. Sowa. 2006. "A Broader Look at the 'Accountability' Movement: Some Grim Realities in State Civil Service Systems." *Review of Public Personnel Administration* 26(2): 102–117.

Heclo, H. 1977. *A Government of Strangers: Executive Politics in Washington*. Washington, D.C.: The Brookings Institution.

Kearney, R. C., and S. W. Hays. 1998. "Reinventing Government, the New Public Management and Civil Service Systems in International Perspective." *Review of Public Personnel Administration* 28(4): 38–54.

Kellough, J. E., and L. G. Nigro. 2006. *Civil Service Reform in the States: Personnel Policy and Politics at the Subnational Level*. Albany, NY: State University of New York Press.

Klingner, D. E., J. Nalbandian, and J. Llorens. 2009. *Public Personnel Management: Contexts and Strategies* (6th ed.). New York: Prentice Hall.

Lah, T. J., and J. L. Perry. 2008. "The Diffusion of the Civil Service Reform Act of 1978 in OECD Countries: A Tale of Two Paths to Reform." *Review of Public Personnel Administration* 28(3): 282–299.

Naff, K. C., and M. A. Newman. 2004. "Symposium: Federal Civil Service Reform: Another Legacy of 9/11?" *Review of Public Personnel Administration* 24: 191–201.

Nigro, L. G., F. A. Nigro, and J. E. Kellough. 2006. *The New Public Personnel Administration* (6th ed.). Florence, KY: Wadsworth Cengage Learning, Inc.

O'Keefe, E. 2010, April 27. "Thousands of Defense Workers Switching to General Schedule Pay System." *The Washington Post*, p. B3.

Perry, J. L. (1993). "Strategic Human Resource Management." *Review of Public Personnel Administration* 13(4): 59–71.

Riccucci, N., and K. C. Naff. 2008. *Personnel Management in Government: Politics and Process* (6th ed.). Boca Raton, FL: CRC Press.

Riccucci, N. M., and F. J. Thompson. 2008. "The New Public Management, Homeland Security, and the Politics of Civil Service Reform." *Public Administration Review* 68(5): 877–890.

Rosenberg, A. 2010, February 26. "Trust Issues Raised at First Meeting of Labor-Management Council." *The Government Executive Report*.

Sims, R. R. 2009. "Civil Service Reform in Action: The Case of the Personnel Board of Jefferson County, Alabama." *Review of Public Personnel Administration* 29(4): 382–401.

Thompson, F. J. 2003. *Classics of Public Personnel Policy* (3rd ed.). Belmont, CA: Wadsworth/Thompson Learning.

Thompson, J. R. 2006. "The Federal Civil Service: The Demise of an Institution." *Public Administration Review* 66(4): 496–503.

Thompson, J. R. 2007. "Federal Labor-Management Relations Under George W. Bush: Enlightened Management or Political Retribution." In J. S. Bowman and J. P. West, eds. *American Public Service: Radical Reform and the Merit System* (pp. 233–254). Boca Raton, FL: CRC Press.

Thompson, J. R. 2008. "Personnel Demonstration Projects and Human Resource Management Innovation." *Review of Public Personnel Administration* 28(3): 240–262.

Tobias, R. M. 2010. "Working with Employee Unions." In S. E. Condrey, ed. *Handbook of Human Resource Management in Government* (3rd ed., pp. 379–402). San Francisco, CA: Jossey Bass.

Van Riper, P. P. 1958. *History of the United States Civil Service.* Evanston, IL: Row, Peterson.

Weigelt, M. 2010, January 10. "Obama Official Hits Campaign Trail to Sell Insourcing." *WashingtonTechnology Magazine.*

West, J. P. 2002. "Georgia on the Mind of Radical Civil Service Reformers." *Review of Public Personnel Administration* 22(2): 79–93.

2
BUILDING PUBLIC HRM CAPACITY IN FRAGILE AND TRANSITIONAL STATES: LINKING THEORY, RESEARCH, PRACTICE, AND TEACHING

Donald E. Klingner

Donald Klingner is a University of Colorado Distinguished Professor in the School of Public Affairs at the University of Colorado at Colorado Springs. He served as elected president of the American Society for Public Administration in 2008–2009 and is an elected fellow of the National Academy of Public Administration. He is a coauthor of Klingner, Nalbandian, and Llorens, *Public Personnel Management* (6th Ed., 2010), which is also published in Spanish and Chinese. http://sites.google.com/site/donaldklingner

Within the United States, public human resource management (HRM) was viewed for almost a century (from after the Civil War until the social and political upheavals of the 1960s) as civil service ("merit") system principles and defined by its opposition to the inefficiencies and inequities of the political patronage ("spoils") system. This image of "neutral professionalism," derived from its origins in scientific management and based on a presumed politics–administration dichotomy, enhanced its reputation yet delayed its maturation as an academic discipline and field of professional practice until the 1970s. Beginning in that decade, scholars' wider recognition of its underlying value conflicts (Klingner and Nalbandian, 1978) led first to the field's broader reconceptualization as part of public policy and management (around such topics as organizational effectiveness, performance management, social equity, and human relations) and then to defining and implementing a more comprehensive research agenda that affirmed its significance as a field of study and body of professional practice. In sum, U.S. public HRM did not—indeed could not—mature until a broader understanding of the contextual variables affecting practice led to the development of a theory-driven research agenda that defined the competencies it required of practicing HRM professionals.

At the same time, public HRM has also gradually emerged as an international field of study and practice during the past 30 years because of its demonstrated relevance to global economic development and building governance capacity. Although international development has been largely driven by macroeconomics, public administrators have managed to convince international development policy specialists and political leaders that public HRM is important, particularly in fragile and transitional states, for bolstering weak institutions, increasing professionalism, reducing corruption, and enhancing the use of the human resources. But by so effectively advocating public HRM as an apolitical and value-neutral development tool, its proponents have in fact undermined its long-term significance. By presenting public HRM as a uniformly applicable "best practices" global development toolkit, they have downplayed the importance of the contextual and circumstantial variables that profoundly influence the sustainability of adapted innovations. This inadvertent outcome has hampered the development of a comprehensive, coherent, and theory-driven research agenda needed to improve the sustainability of adapted innovations. It has also understated the professional competencies required of international public HRM consultants and practitioners.

Its proponents can correct these negative consequences by (1) developing a body of public HRM theory that focuses on the contextual and circumstantial factors affecting its evolution and application in fragile and transitional states, (2) developing a theory-driven research agenda that illumines and clarifies the dilemmas that confront international public HRM practitioners in the real world, and (3) making sure those responsible for implementing international public HRM on the ground have the knowledge they need to understand and the competencies they need to respond appropriately and effectively to the challenges the field's complexities present, and (4) focusing on "smart practice" innovations that lead to sustainable performance improvement. In sum, international public HRM will mature only by undergoing a similar process to that by which it evolved in the United States.

STRENGTHENING THEORY: TOWARD A COMPARATIVE AND CONTEXTUAL MODEL OF PUBLIC HRM IN FRAGILE AND TRANSITIONAL STATES

In the United States, public HRM can be viewed from several perspectives (Klingner, Nalbandian, and Llorens, 2010). First, it is the functions needed to manage human resources in public agencies. Second, it is the process by which a scarce resource (public jobs) is allocated. Third, it reflects the influence of underlying values over how public jobs should be allocated. Fourth, it has symbiotic and competing systems—the laws, rules, and regulations used to express these abstract values. Conceptually, it can be understood as a historical process, whereby new systems evolve to champion emergent values, are integrated with the mix, and are in turn supplemented—neither supplanted nor replaced—by their successors. In practical terms, this means that U.S. public HRM is complex, laden with contradictions in policy and practice resulting from often unwieldy and unstable combinations of values and systems and fraught with the inherent difficulties of relying on competitive and collaborative systems to achieve diverse goals (Kellough and Nigro, 2006). Table 2.1 describes the evolutionary process for public HRM values and systems in the United States.

There exists a relatively large and diverse body of literature on international public HRM.[1] Heady's (1966) seminal treatment of comparative public administration used public bureaucracies as the basis for comparisons across developed nations. Beginning in the 1990s, international public HRM divided into two intellectual foci,

Table 2.1   The Evolution of Public HRM Systems and Values in the United States

Stage of Evolution	Dominant Value(s)	Dominant System(s)	Pressures for Change
Privilege (1789–1828)	Responsiveness/representation	"Government by founding fathers"	Political parties + patronage
Patronage (1829–1882)	Responsiveness/representation	Patronage	Modernization + democratization
Professionalism (1883–1932)	Efficiency + individual rights	Civil service	Responsiveness + effective government
Performance (1933–1964)	Responsiveness/representation + efficiency + individual rights	Patronage + civil service	Individual rights + social equity
People (1965–1979)	Responsiveness/representation + efficiency + individual rights + social equity	Patronage + civil service + collective bargaining + affirmative action	Dynamic equilibrium among four competing values and systems
Privatization (1980–now)	Responsiveness/representation + efficiency + individual accountability + limited government + community responsibility	Patronage + civil service + collective bargaining + affirmative action + alternative mechanisms + flexible employment relationships	Dynamic equilibrium among four progovernmental values and systems, and three antigovernmental values and systems
Partnerships (2002–now)	Responsiveness/representation + efficiency + individual accountability + limited government + community responsibility + collaboration	Patronage + civil service + collective bargaining + affirmative action + alternative mechanisms + flexible employment relationships	Dynamic equilibrium among four progovernmental values and systems, three antigovernmental values and systems

development and comparative related, paralleling the same more general split within international public administration. Development-related HRM emerged as an outgrowth of development economics and public administration. Its purpose is prescriptive and applied—to improve economic conditions and governance systems in developing countries by replicating the institutional reforms (i.e., HRM systems and structures) that have generally characterized Western democracies. Comparative HRM remained as the more value-neutral study of public administrative systems across countries and cultures (Morgan and Perry, 1988; Raadschelders, Toonen, and Van der Meer, 2007). Its primary purpose is descriptive and conceptually analytical—to understand how comparative HRM systems have evolved and why they function as they do. As NPM became increasingly popular in the West, its proponents also began to extrapolate that movement's characteristic HRM reform strategies (e.g., weakening civil service in favor of managerial flexibility, nonstandard work arrangements, and privatization and service contracting) to developing countries (Kettl, 1997). While these three approaches' conflicting values and objectives preclude scholars from combining or synthesizing them, most edited readers (Dwivedi and Henderson, 1990; Farazmand, 2001; Huque and Zafarullah, 2006) include contributed articles that reflect each approach's assumptions and goals.

Most public HRM research literature focuses on the United States and Western Europe (Hirsch, 1999). Much of the rest focuses on studies of single countries like China (Chou, 2009) or the transitional states that arose following the collapse of the former Soviet Union in 1989 (Baker, 1994; Straussman, 2007). Because most of these are single-country case studies based on some combination of quantitative and qualitative data and/or the author(s)' consultant experience, their underlying theory is often hard to elucidate. Frankly, because these "spin-off" articles are typically donor driven and rarely comparative, there may be no underlying theory at all. Moreover, simplistic models of international public HRM development based on replicating "best practice" Western solutions are not likely to be effective. While problems may seem similar, most analysts conclude that solutions that are effective in one context may not succeed in another. Thus, the term "smart practice" (Bardach, 2000) is better suited to adapting and sustaining exogenous innovations because it is based on the assumption that while we learn much from comparative study, applying what we learn must take into account a number of context-specific variables (Desai and Snavely, 2007; Jabbra and Dwivedi, 2004; Robinson, 2007) to explain why reforms succeed in some nations but not others (Barzelay, 2001). Without such adaptation to contingencies, policy implementers will make little or no progress (Caiden and Sundaram, 2004).

For example, the inadequacies of extrapolating the United States' experience become clear once one considers the differences in context and circumstance between the evolution of public HRM in the United States and in most fragile and transitional states. The United States developed over almost two centuries of democratic government under a single Constitution, within a civil society widely considered to be controlled by laws rather than individuals. By contrast, fragile or transitional states may lack conditions we take for granted (e.g., a national identity, a national language, clear land titles, effective civil and criminal law, and a self-sufficient economy). Even their development of stable patronage systems may be hampered by societal conditions (e.g., chronic underemployment, an inability to meet even minimum standards of education and health care, and overly centralized and authoritarian political systems) that perpetuate political leadership based on "cults of personality" rather than true pluralist political parties. Furthermore, timing is everything. In the United States, public HRM system developed through sequential, successful efforts to first balance a fledgling civil service with the need for continued patronage-based political leadership, to then balance employee rights and social equity with politics and civil service, and, finally, to balance public HRM systems with the market-based values and mechanisms exemplified by nonstandard work arrangements and outsourcing (to both community- or faith-based NGOs and the private sector). By contrast, fledgling civil service systems in developing countries usually face simultaneous intractable, opposing pressures (e.g., political pressure for continued patronage, underpaid and underqualified public employees, institutionally entrenched unions in public or autonomous agencies, and demands from international lenders and corporations to reduce public spending and employment through contracting and divestiture).

Furthermore, having uninformed and unrealistic expectations about presumed similarities between evolving public HRM systems in developed and developing countries only retards the emergence of theory-driven research, practice, and teaching. This is because social sciences traditionally develop based on cumulative, symbiotic relationships among, practice, research, theory, and teaching. Thus, theory advances only as scholars first hypothesize and test the effects of independent variables on behavioral outcomes and then apply the lessons learned to teaching and practice. Table 2.2 shows some of the contextual variables that may affect the evolution of international public HRM systems. These can be used to test and validate hypotheses about the factors most likely to influence the sustainable effectiveness of potentially useful HRM innovations at strengthening institutions and building governance capacity in fragile and transitional states.

Table 2.2   Effects of Context on Evolution of Public HRM in Fragile and Transitional States

1. Transition from Independence to a Functional Patronage System

Negative Indicators	Positive Indicators
• High reliance on charismatic leadership	• Stable political parties
• Restricted freedom of speech and press	• Open information and free media
• High emphasis on export of agricultural products and raw materials	• Balanced, domestically focused economic growth, including professional/technical
• Capital flight	• Domestic reinvestment of capital
• Repression based on race, ethnicity, or class	• Some social justice
• Inadequate electoral process	• Functioning electoral process

2. Transition from Patronage to a Functional Civil Service System

Negative Indicators	Positive Indicators
• Government process considered low on effectiveness, rationality, and transparency	• Government process considered high on effectiveness, rationality, and transparency
• Widespread patronage appointments, and job retention based on salary "kickbacks"	• Civil Service law, public personnel agency, and policies and procedures
• High unemployment or underemployment	• Low unemployment or underemployment
• Public sector the "employer of last resort"	• Balanced economic growth/ development
• Underpaid, underqualified employees	• Adequately paid, qualified civil service

Table 2.2 Continued	
• Widespread employment discrimination based on race, gender, or ethnicity	• Low level of employment discrimination based on race, gender, or ethnicity
• High degree of administrative formalism	• Low degree of administrative formalism
• High role of the military in civil society and government	• Reduced role of the military in civil society and government
• Reforms due mainly by international economic and political pressure	• Reforms due mainly to domestic political, social and economic pressure

3. Transition beyond Civil Service to a Mature Public Personnel System

Negative Indicators	*Positive Indicators*
• Overrigidity, uniformity, and centralization of HRM policies and practice	• Balance of flexibility/rigidity, centralization and decentralization, and uniformity and variation
• Overemphasis on employee rights or on managerial efficiency	• Balance between employee rights and managerial efficiency
• Over- or underemployment in the public sector	• Balanced public and private employment

STRENGTHENING RESEARCH: TOWARD A THEORY-DRIVEN RESEARCH AGENDA FOR INTERNATIONAL PUBLIC HRM IN FRAGILE AND TRANSITIONAL STATES

Public HRM did not emerge as a subdiscipline of public administration in the United States until deeper recognition of its underlying value conflicts led to development and execution of a theory-driven research agenda that resulted in more widespread appreciation for the competencies it requires of HRM professionals. Likewise, international public HRM is unlikely to emerge as a mature subdiscipline of international development studies until deeper recognition of its underlying value conflicts and contextual variables leads to the development and execution of a theory-driven research agenda. This will in turn promote a wider appreciation of the competencies it requires of international development scholars, practitioners, and consultants.

International public HRM's proponents must therefore be cautious about even tacitly supporting an upbeat and comforting—yet essentially illusory—apolitical and value-neutral image of the field. While accepting the field's successes, they should also use its challenges—particularly in failed, fragile, or transitional states—to illustrate why imperfectly understood contextual variables demonstrate the need to develop a focused and comprehensive action research agenda, select appropriate research methods (including participant observation as well as objective data collection and analysis) and performance measures, and disseminate research results effectively. Fortunately, this is already happening. The National Academy of Public Administration (NAPA, 2008), working with Princeton University, Oxford University, and the London School of Economics, has identified and is exploring 32 governance topics affecting fragile and transitional states. Some topics (e.g., civil service reform) are widely recognized as falling within traditional public HRM. Others (such as reintegrating combatants, enabling indigenous leadership, and establishing the rule of law) are more typical of the persistent and underlying issues affecting HRM capacity failed or fragile states.

International development agencies, financial institutions, and NGOs now collect and publish information international public HRM scholars and practitioners can use to benchmark performance on a range of descriptive indicators related to poverty (United Nations, 2009), economic development (World Bank, 2008), political liberty (Freedom House, 2007), and perceived corruption (Transparency International, 2008). However, while aggregated quantitative data can help measure progress and pinpoint areas of concern, they offer little insight into the operational issues that affect policy implementation. Retrospective qualitative evaluations are usually better at this than descriptive and quantitative analysis. Case-based oral histories make information useful operationally and result in insights into successes and failures that are otherwise lost (Yin, 2009).

Nonetheless, collecting and organizing qualitative data so that they are useful to practicing public administrators is challenging. Much of the information and "lessons learned" generated through existing case studies and expert workshops reflect the viewpoints of donors or outside scholars and do not necessarily meet the needs of hard-pressed institution builders (NAPA, 2008). Researchers may overlook or discount the perspectives of practitioners not affiliated with development institutions, associations, and informal professional networks. The objective is to inventory available governance information, distill it, organize it meaningfully, link it for easy access by the users, and add to it whatever information and lessons can be gathered from practitioners on the ground (NAPA, 2008: 5–6). The most effective dissemination strategy is to relate stories of various experiences through a virtual, Web-based network among individuals and organizations around the world that are grappling with similar institution- and capacity-building issues. By opening virtual spaces (e.g., Web sites, videoconferences, "wikis," and "blogs") for knowledge management, information and communications technologies allow users to draw upon, add to, correct, or contribute material to a virtual community.

Numerous political factors and actors complicate the connections between social science research results, outcomes, and policy influences. Methodologies for their assessment are not well developed (Ryan and Garrett, 2003). To be useful, action research ultimately depends on organizational learning, policy influence, and "smart practice" implementation. Organizations and governments must:

- Provide economic and noneconomic incentives that foster competition among governance innovations and innovators (e.g., the Dubai, UN Habitat, Ash Institute, and Ford Foundation awards).
- Use practical approaches pioneered by agencies like the Ash Institute and other awards programs (e.g., the media, producing television programming, teaching- and practice-based case studies, networks of innovators, and global information portals).
- Focus on the values, purposes, and principles underlying innovation diffusion and adaptation and emphasize these in resource material and documentation.
- Use credible and legitimate advocates (individuals and organizations) as intermediaries in the diffusion, adaptation, and adoption process for specific innovations.

- Maintain a facilitative climate (i.e., a supportive policy environment, political leadership, environmental stability, and internal social structure and capacity).
- Share information about innovations and outcomes by using appropriate approaches, guidelines, training, and transfer methodologies (Klingner, 2006).

STRENGTHENING PRACTICE: FOCUSING ON SUSTAINABLE, PERFORMANCE-ORIENTED, "SMART PRACTICE" INTERNATIONAL PUBLIC HRM INNOVATIONS

Sustainability is based on successful organizational learning and knowledge utilization. Organizational learning means that individual insights are transformed into knowledge that helps the organization respond effectively. There are four kinds of organizational learning:

- Tacit to tacit: Individuals share knowledge with each other that cannot necessarily be communicated explicitly (e.g.; socialization or on-the-job training).
- Explicit to explicit: Individuals synthesize disparate information into a new whole.
- Tacit to explicit: Individual employees convert tacit knowledge into a form that can be shared with other employees.
- Explicit to tacit: Employees internalize explicit information so that it automatically affects their perceptions, feelings, and thoughts (Johnson and Thomas, 2007).

Knott and Wildavsky (1980) address the link between organizational learning and knowledge utilization by using six cumulative stages (reception, cognition, discussion, reference, adoption, and influence) to describe the effect of university research on government agencies' policy making. Different types of factors affect knowledge utilization by public officials. First, technical factors like the availability of information and the appropriate rational/technical organizational resources to use it increase the likelihood that agencies will adopt performance measures based on policy research. However, the adoption of performance measures does not necessarily mean that the policy research results will be implemented (Julnes and Holzer, 2001). Second, contextual factors including politics and organizational culture affect adoption and implementation of policy recommendations. Organizational responses toward risk taking, innovation, and policy change mediate the impact of context on knowledge management. Subjective factors (e.g., the perceived relevance of research to their agency and the policy issue in question, its direct applicability to agency policy, and the agency's policy-making power) directly affect policy makers' use of information and hence the organization's knowledge management policies. Differences in the professional cultures of academics and bureaucrats are also an important part of this social context. Measurements of such linkage mechanisms as informal communication, conferences, e-mail, and agencies' reference libraries (Landry, Lamari, and Amara, 2003) lead researchers to conclude that these two groups don't interact well at communicating and sharing knowledge (Lomas, 1997; Oh and Rich, 1996). Third, individual attributes like professionalism and education (Sabet and Klingner, 1993) and decision-making style (Webber, 1992) also influence policy adoption decisions.

Performance measurement and management are critical because decisions on future program and agency funding are likely to involve an evaluation of past performance. Evaluation criteria differ across users (e.g., funding bodies and oversight boards), and vary with the interests involved. In general, performance measures have shifted from audit-based evaluations of expenditures to evaluation of program outcomes by efficiency, effectiveness, or program worthiness. This requires recognizing the differences between rational/economic and political/social policy-making perspectives (Kingdon, 2003; Peters, 2006).

STRENGTHENING TEACHING: TOWARD A COMPETENCY-BASED MODEL FOR INTERNATIONAL PUBLIC HRM EDUCATION AND TRAINING

HRM scholarship in developed countries has already recognized that practitioners need *technical* competencies (i.e., those used to recruit, select, train, evaluate, and motivate employees within the limits of law and policy) they can use to reward good employees and get rid of bad ones: rewriting job descriptions to increase an employee's pay level or giving outstanding performance evaluations to high-quality employees. HRM practitioners must also apply the professional standards and judgment needed to respond adequately to the conflicting demands and expectations of advocates for competing values and systems. They must be sensitive to the need for administrative systems to be responsive to legitimate political values and public participation, especially in local government. Given complex and conflicting laws (e.g., affirmative action, labor relations, professional liability, employee privacy, due process, and pay equity), "merit" can mean different things under different circumstances. Privatization and contracting blur distinctions between public and private.

Historical traditions emphasize the technical side of public HRM, with less emphasis on policy-related analytical work, relationships with outside organizations, and conflicting values. These traditions view both employees and management as clients served through the merit system. A more contemporary view emphasizes different activities and relationships. Modern HR professionals work closely with other officials within their own agency (budget directors, attorneys, collective bargaining negotiators, affirmative action compliance officers, and supervisors) and outside it (legislative staff, union officials, affirmative action agencies, civil service boards, health and life insurance benefit representatives, pension boards, ethics commissions, and employee assistance programs). By performing effectively in a climate of change and uncertainty, they assert their central role in agency management, developing their own professional status and also that of their profession (Klingner, 1979; Nalbandian, 1981).

HR professionals generally welcome the opportunity to move from a traditional, technical view of the field to a modern, professional view involving interpretation and mediation among conflicting interests. This transition includes *ethical* competencies: the ability to balance conflicting expectations like employee rights and organizational effectiveness, reconcile competing systems and values, make complex decisions quickly, and communicate them effectively (Bowman *et al.*, 2004).

Globalization adds another dimension. Depending on context and circumstance, these and other technical and professional competencies will be required of international public HRM practitioners. Multinational corporations promote international assignments not only as an explicit leadership development strategy but also because their leaders share an implicit worldview that "becoming global" is a necessary component for organizational survival in the global economy (Counihan, 2009). As networked governance joins the more traditional concept of authority as the legal exercise of power in a defined geographic area, public agency heads may also come to view global public administrative competence—organizational and individual—as equally essential.

International public HR managers need a range of competencies to provide effective management consultancies and exchanges among countries and cultures. This challenge can be met by interdisciplinary professional training and education, interdisciplinary faculty exchanges, multidisciplinary team projects in MPA degree programs, and collaborative, multidisciplinary research for practitioners, MPA graduates, and researchers. Professional associations like the American Society for Public Administration (ASPA) and the International Public Management Association for Human Resources (IPMA-HR) help develop globally competent international public HR managers because their member services (training and certification, technical assistance, publications, conferences, and virtual networking) increase individual and organizational competencies. Given the key role of U.S. educational institutions and professional associations, U.S. HRM educators should embrace concentrations or full integration of international issues with the regular curriculum or focus on functional areas, tools, or both. They need to consciously enrich students' diversity in their learning, teaching, and research, with greater emphasis placed on interactive experiences for the maximum exposure to different culture and perspectives in the process of learning about specific substantive issues (Rice, 2004). If an action research agenda is to drive public administration education, public administrators need to incorporate research and consulting organizations by changing both their roles and their perspective on knowledge management (Cooley, 2008) so as to share what they have learned about program planning, active participation, and service delivery and to use interactive experiential modalities, simulations, decision situations, technical problem-solving workshops, and other creative means to understand and achieve global connectedness (Thynne, 1998). Since new models pile atop existing ones, new competencies join—but do not supplant—their predecessors. In governance networks, the ability to manage diverse, multidisciplinary, and multiorganizational work teams is critical. As governance networks become increasingly global, the required skill set will expand to encompass the cultural and linguistic competencies required of multinational public HRM (Argyriades and   Pichardo Pagaza, 2009; Rice, 2004).

CONCLUSION: LINKING HRM THEORY, RESEARCH, PRACTICE, AND TEACHING IN FRAGILE AND TRANSITIONAL STATES

By presenting international public HRM as a universally applicable "best practices" global development toolkit, its proponents have inadvertently and understandably de-emphasized the importance of the contextual and circumstantial variables that profoundly influence the sustainability of adapted innovations. Much as it did in the United States a half century ago, emphasizing international public HRM's apolitical and value-neutral nature hinders the development of the comprehensive and coherent (i.e., theory driven) research agenda that would, in the long run, enhance the sustainability of diffused and adopted/adapted innovations in HRM practice. Minimizing the professional competencies required of international public HRM consultants and practitioners thus completes a "vicious circle" that undermines the strategic significance of the field to international development.

Public HRM will mature internationally only by undergoing a process congruent with that by which it evolved in the United States. If this is to happen, its proponents should direct their efforts so as to link theory, research, teaching, and practice by (1) developing a body of public HRM theory that focuses on the factors affecting its evolution and application in fragile and transitional states, (2) developing a theory-driven research agenda that illumines and clarifies the dilemmas that confront international public HRM practitioners in the real world, (3) focusing these insights on implementing "smart practice" innovations that lead to sustainable performance improvement, and (4) making sure those responsible for implementing international public HRM on the ground have the knowledge they need to understand and the competencies they need to respond appropriately and effectively to the challenges the field's complexities present.

References

Argyriades, D., and I. Pichardo Pagaza, eds. 2009. *Winning the Needed Change: Saving our Planet Earth—A Global Public Service*. New York: IOS Press, International Institute of Administrative Sciences Monographs, Volume 30.

Baker, R., ed. 1994. *Comparative Public Management*. Westport, CT: Praeger.

Bardach, E. 2000. *Practical Guide for Policy Analysis: The Eightfold Path to More Effective Problem Solving*. New York: Chatham House.

Barzelay, M. 2001. *The New Public Management*. Berkeley, CA: University of California Press.

Bowman, J., J. West, E. Berman, and M. Van Wart. 2004. *The Professional Edge: Competencies in Public Service*. Armonk, NY: M. E. Sharpe.

Caiden, G., and P. Sundaram. 2004. "The Specificity of Public Service Reform." *Public Administration & Development* 24(5): 373–383.

Chou, B. 2009. "Does 'Good Governance' Matter? Civil Service Reform in China." *International Journal of Public Administration* 31: 54–75.

Cooley, L. 2008. "The State and International Development Management: Commentary from International Development Management Practitioners." *Public Administration Review* 68(s1): 1003–1004.

Counihan, C. 2009. "Going Global: Why Do Multinational Corporations Participate in Highly Skilled Migration?" *Comparative Technology Transfer and Society* 7(1): 19–42.

Desai, U., and K. Snavely. 2007. "Technical Assistance for Institutional Capacity Building: The Transferability of Administrative Structures and Practices." *International Review of Administrative Sciences* 73(1): 133–146.

Dwivedi, O., and K. Henderson, eds. 1990. *Public Administration in World Perspective*. Ames, IA: University of Iowa Press.

Farazmand, A., ed. 2001. *Handbook of Comparative and Development Administration* (2nd ed.). New York: Marcel Dekker.

Freedom House. 2007. *Freedom in the World: The Annual Survey of Civil Rights and Political Liberties*. New York: Rowman & Littlefield.

Heady, F. 1966. *Public Administration: A Comparative Perspective* (1st ed.). Englewood Cliffs, NJ: Prentice-Hall.

Hirsch, D. 1999, November. *Merit Systems in Western Democracies #1: An Introduction to Merit in Canada, the United States, Britain, Australia, and New Zealand*. Ottawa: Research Directorate, the Public Service Commission of Canada.

Huque, A., and H. Zafarullah, eds. 2006. *International Development Governance*. Boca Raton, FL: Taylor & Francis.

Jabbra, J., and O. Dwivedi. 2004. "Globalization, Governance, and Administrative Culture." *International Journal of Public Administration* 27(13/14): 1101–1127.

Johnson, H., and A. Thomas. 2007. "Individual Learning and Building Organisational Capacity for Development." *Public Administration & Development* 27(1): 39–48.

Julnes, P., and M. Holzer. 2001. "Promoting the Utilization of Performance Measures in Public Organizations: An Empirical Study of Factors Affecting Adoption and Implementation." *Public Administration Review* 61(6): 693–708.

Kellough, J., and L. Nigro. 2006. *Civil Service Reform in the States: Personnel Policies and Politics at the Subnational Level*. Albany, NY: State University of New York Press.

Kettl, D. 1997. "The Global Revolution in Public Management: Driving Themes, Missing Links." *Journal of Policy Analysis and Management* 16(3): 446–462.

Kingdon, J. 2003. *Agendas, Alternatives, and Public Policies* (2nd ed.). New York: Addison-Wesley.

Klingner, D. 2006. "Diffusion and Adoption of Innovations: A Development Perspective." In Guido Bertucci, ed. *Innovations in Governance and Public Administration: Replicating What Works* (pp. 55–60). New York: UN/DESA/DPADM.

———.1979, September. "The Changing Role of Public Personnel Management in the 1980s." *The Personnel Administrator* 24: 41–48.

Klingner, D., and J. Nalbandian. 1978. "Personnel Management by Whose Objectives?" *Public Administration Review* 38(4): 366–372.

Klingner, D., J. Nalbandian, and J. Llorens. 2010. *Public Personnel Management: Contexts and Strategies* (6th ed.). New York: Pearson Longman.

Knott, J., and A. Wildavsky. 1980. "If Dissemination is the Solution, What is the Problem?" *Knowledge: Creation, Diffusion, Utilization* 1(4): 537–578.

Landry, R., M. Lamari, and N. Amara. 2003. "The Extent and Determinants of the Utilization of University Research in Government Agencies." *Public Administration Review* 63(2): 192–205.

Lomas, J. 1997. "Research and Evidence-Based Decision Making." *Australian and New Zealand Journal of Public Health* 21(5): 439–441.

Morgan, E., and J. Perry. 1988. "Re-orienting the Comparative Study of Civil Service Systems." *Review of Public Personnel Administration* 6(1): 84–95.

Nalbandian, J. 1981. "From Compliance to Consultation: The Role of the Public Personnel Manager." *Review of Public Personnel Administration* 1(1): 37–51.

NAPA. 2008, May 8. *Building Public Administration in Fragile and Post-Conflict States: Why, What, How and Who?* Washington, DC: National Academy of Public Administration (Interim Report to the International Standing Panel, NAPA, on the Institutions for Fragile States Initiative of Princeton University and NAPA).

Oh, C., and R. Rich. 1996. "Explaining Use of Information in Public Policymaking." *Knowledge and Policy* 9(1): 3–35.

Peters, B. 2006. *American Public Policy: Promise and Performance* (7th ed.). Washington, DC: CQ Press.

Raadschelders, J., T. Toonen, and F. Van der Meer. 2007. *Civil Service in the 21st Century: Comparative Perspectives*. Basingstoke, NY: Palgrave-Macmillan.

Rice, M. 2004. *Diversity and Public Administration: Theory, Issues, and Perspectives*. Armonk, NY: ME Sharpe.

Robinson, M. 2007. "The Politics of Successful Governance Reforms: Lessons of Design and Implementation." *Commonwealth & Comparative Politics* 45(4): 521–548.

Ryan, J., and J. Garrett. 2003. *The Impact of Economic Policy Research: Lessons of Attribution and Evaluation from IFPRI*. Washington, DC: International Food Policy Research Institute. http://purl.umn.edu/16581 (accessed August 9, 2009).

Sabet, G., and D. Klingner. 1993. "Exploring the Impact of Professionalism on Administrative Innovation." *Journal of Public Administration Research and Theory* 3(2): 252–266.

Straussman, J. 2007. "An Essay on the Meaning(s) of 'Capacity Building'—with an Application to Serbia." *International Journal of Public Administration* 30: 1103–1120.

Thynne, I., ed. 1998. "IASIA Symposium on Education and Training for the Public Sector in a Changing World of Government." *International Review of Administrative Sciences* 64: 371–383.

Transparency International. 2008. *The 2008 Transparency International Corruption Perceptions Index*. http://www.transparency.org/policy_research/surveys_indices/cpi/2008.

United Nations. 2009. *The Millennium Development Goals*. New York: UN/DESA/DPADM. http://www.un.org/millenniumgoals (accessed June 16, 2009).

Webber, D. 1992. "The Distribution and Use of Policy Knowledge in the Policy Process." *Knowledge and Policy* 4(4): 6–35.

World Bank. 2008. *World Bank Development Report 2008*. Washington, DC: The World Bank. http://portals.wi.wur.nl/files/docs/File/rethinkingagriculture/Review%20Reports.doc (accessed April 30, 2009).

Yin, R. 2009. *Case Study Research: Design and Methods* (4th ed.). Thousand Oaks, CA: Sage.

Endnote

1. A large and growing body of private-sector HRM literature has followed the same path and reached many of the same conclusions, first questioning the universality of Western HRM models and then affirming the need to test their applicability in a cross-national, cross-cultural and comparative context. This literature, while not directly relevant to this article, will be of great interest to those scholars who seek to generalize HRM theory, research, practice and teaching across public and private sectors. See, for example:

Bowen, D., Galang, C., & Pillai, R. (2002). The role of human resource management: An exploratory study of cross-country variance. *Human Resource Management, 41*(1): 103–122.

Brewster, C., Tregaskis, O., Hegewisch, A., & Mayne, L. (1996). Comparative research in human resource management: A review and an example. *The International Journal of Human Resource Management, 7*(3): 585–604.

Budhwar, P., & Debra, Y. (2001). Rethinking comparative and cross-national human resource management research. *The International Journal of Human Resource Management, 12*(3): 497–515.

Clark, T., Gospel, H., & Montgomery, J. (1999). Running on the spot? A review of twenty years of research on the management of human resources in comparative and international perspective. *The International Journal of Human Resource Management, 10*(3): 520–544.

Clark, T., Grant, D., & Heijltjes, M. (Winter 1999–2000). Researching comparative and international human resource management: Key challenges and contributions. *International Studies of Management & Organization, 29*(4): 6–23.

Drost, E., Frayne, C, Lowe, B., & Geringer, M. (2002). Benchmarking training and development practices: A multi-country comparative analysis. *Human Resource Management, 41*(1): 67–86.

Florkowski, G., & Nath, R. (1993). MNC responses to the legal environment of international human resource management. *The International Journal of Human Resource Management, 4*(2): 305–324.

Geringer, M., Frayne, C., & Milliman, J. (2002). In search of "best practices" in international human resource management: Research design and methodology. *Human Resource Management, 41*(1): 5–30.

Huo, P., Heh, J., & Napier, N. (2002). Divergence or convergence: A crossnational comparison of personnel selection practices. *Human Resource Management, 41*(1): 31–44.

Keating, M., & Thompson, K. (2004). International human resource management: Overcoming disciplinary sectarianism. *Employee Relations, 26*(4): 595–612.

Kiessling, T., & Harvey, M. (2005). Strategic global human resource management in the twenty-first century: An endorsement of the mixed-method research methodology. *International Journal of Human Resource Management, 16*(1): 22–45.

Lowe, K., Milliman, J., De Cieri, H., & Dowling, P. (2002). International compensation practices: A ten-country comparative analysis. *Human Resource Management, 41*(1): 45–66.

Lazarova, M., Morley, M., & Tyson, S. (2008). Introduction: International comparative studies in human resource management—the Cranet data. *The International Journal of Human Resource Management, 19*(11): 1995–2003.

Milliman, J., Nason, S., Zhu, C., & De Cieri, H. (2002). An exploratory assessment of the purposes of performance appraisals in North and Central America and the Pacific Rim. *Human Resource Management 41*(1): 87–102.

Murray, V., Jain, H., & Adams, R. (1976). A framework for the comparative analysis of personnel administration. *Academy of Management Review,* pp. 47–57.

Schuler, R., Budhwar, P., & Florkowski, G. 2002International human resource management: Review and critique. *International Journal of Management Reviews, 4*(1): 41–70.

Sparrow, P., & Hiltrop, J. (1997). Redefining the field of European human resource management: A battle between national mindsets and forces of business transition? *Human Resource Management, 36*(2): 201–219.

Teagarden, M., Von Glinow, M., Bowen, D., Frayne, C., Nason, S., Huo, Y., Milliman, J., Arias, M., Butler, M., Geringer, J., Kim, N., Scullion, H., Lowe, K., & Drost, E. (1995). Toward a theory of comparative management research: An idiographic case study of the best international human resource management project. *Academy of Management Journal, 38*(5): 1261–1287.

Von Glinow, M. (2002). Guest editor's note—Best practices in IHRM: Lessons learned from a tencountry/regional analysis. *Human Resource Management, 41*(1): 3–4.

Varma, A. (2002). Book review editor's note and book reviews. *Human Resource Management, 41* (1): 141–145.

Welch, D. (1994). Determinants of international human resource management approaches and activities: A suggested framework. *Journal of Management Studies, 31*(2): 139–164.

3 GENERATIONAL DIFFERENCES AND THE PUBLIC SECTOR WORKFORCE

Madinah F. Hamidullah

Madinah F. Hamidullah received her Ph.D. from the University of Georgia (May 2009) and joined the faculty at Rutgers University–Newark as an assistant professor in the fall of 2009. She received her BA in Dance and Political Science and MPA from the University of North Carolina at Charlotte. Her research interests include generational differences in the workforce, public management, employee turnover, organizational performance, and executive leadership succession. Her research has appeared in *Public Organization Review*.

The problems presented by an aging workforce have led to increased attention to managing generations in the workforce, partly as a means of effecting smooth transitions of responsibility from older and retiring workers to younger less experienced workers. The public sector will be hit especially hard by aging and possible personnel shortages (Scott, 2004), resulting in intense competition for talented employees. Managing generations in the workforce is becoming an important conversation to have in the contemporary public workforce, due to the rapidly changing and diverse make-up of its employees. Policy-relevant types of diversity include race, gender, sexual orientation, and religion. Lately, individuals have been working longer, and the presence of multiple generations is easily observable in the current workforce. Due to the increased attention paid to these generational differences and the observations that have been made regarding the attitudes of the younger generation, public personnel managers need to know if there are substantive differences in how particular generations approach work.

Observers of popular culture (Lancaster and Stillman, 2002; Mitchell, 2000) contend that individuals belonging to different generational cohorts will approach work differently based on the social and historical conditions associated with their development. Some differences proposed by various human resource consultants suggest that younger generations are more likely to challenge authority, less loyal to their organizations, and looking for promotions based on performance rather than agreeing with promotions based on longevity (Shelton and Shelton, 2005; Smith, 2007). Additionally, researchers who focus on the public sector (e.g., Perry, 1996, 1997; Perry and Wise, 1990) have found that some individuals will have a predisposition to serve the public and therefore will be attracted to public sector work. What is rarely looked at in empirical work is if social and historical factors may influence an individual's desire to work for the public. As individuals grow and mature they may develop different patterns toward work, which may influence the type of work they do and the kind of organization they choose to work for.

Government agencies are seeing their workforce grow older and retire, while at the same time, fewer people are going into the public service (Leibowitz, 2004). The impending demands for suitable replacements for retiring public employees accentuates the need for better understanding of the motives of younger workers. Younger workers will be the future of the workforce, and understanding their values and motives will give managers the necessary information needed for managing them.

Money constraints are often suggested as a major reason for government's lack of ability to attract and retain qualified personnel, because the status of government employment is equally important as the pay that should accompany it. The image created by politicians, civic leaders, voters, and clientele groups all affect the position of government as a competitive employer (Nigro and Nigro, 2000), so civil service reform has tried to address the issue of image as a barrier to recruit talented and qualified individuals into the public sector workforce. One example of such reform has taken place in Georgia with the implementation of "GeorgiaGain." By removing traditional civil service protections, Georgia hoped to reward employees with a pay-for-performance system designed to motive, reward, and retain high-quality public employees (Sanders, 2004).

Recruitment and retention continues to be a top priority for public organizations. One way to address the issue could be to examine the characteristics of individuals based on age, generational affiliation, and time with the organization, so that the data could help assess where managers spend their resources. Managers have the daunting task of organizing a large number of employees in an ever-changing workforce, so understanding how those individuals' age and life experiences affect their life and work could be very beneficial in the larger process. Job behaviors that develop from individual maturation must be separated from those that are a result of the social and historical impacts that make up generational differences (if such differences exist), and plans that are being adopted to help offset the more traditional workforce trends in the public sector should be clear as to what problems they are addressing. Moreover, the need for these aggressive plans in response to these alarming trends that public employers are beginning to face can be improved greatly by looking deeper into the differences between generations and, further, how those differences can be incorporated.

Take for instance the baby boom generation. This generation is a compellation of individuals who were born between 1946 and 1964 and make up approximately 30 percent of the state government workforces who were eligible to retire in 2006 (Scott, 2004). The federal government faced a similar crisis in 2004, when 53 percent of federal civil servants and 71 percent of federal senior executives were eligible to retire (Leibowitz, 2004). In 1999, 42 percent of state and local government employees were between the ages of 45 and 64 years (Pynes, 2003). As the workforce continues to age, agencies need to be aware of the irreplaceable knowledge, experience, and wisdom that will be lost when certain individuals leave the organization (Boath and Smith, 2004).

By learning from those older generations who will be leaving the workforce, agencies can create plans that collect the knowledge needed in order to maintain and then redistribute what works and what does not, to managers and coworkers alike. A way for organizations to do such maintenance is to identify the knowledge that is most at risk and institutionalize it within career-development processes (Boath and Smith, 2004). Additionally, organizations must build knowledge communities that capture expert as well as informal information and insights into how business is done and how that information is transferred from one employee to the next. If agencies do not conduct these knowledge plans, organizational knowledge loss or "brain drain" can become a problem within the entire employment life cycle, including recruiting, hiring, performance, retention, and retirement (Boath and Smith, 2004).

Generations are considered to have different personalities that would explain their behavior in the workplace (Lancaster and Stillman, 2002; Mitchell, 2000). Not only are some groups more concerned with personal achievement, they may be more career committed versus organization committed. This study seeks to use generational profiles as a typology. Popular and more academic-based typologies have often been used to describe individuals within organizations. For example, Downs (1967) suggested that the bureaucracy can be made up of zealots, advocates, statesmen, and climbers, whereas Weber (1947) developed archetypes of leadership into phenotypes like the hero ("heroic charisma"), the father ("paternalistic charisma"), the savior ("missionary charisma") and the king ("majestic charisma"). Bureaucrats, as referred to here, can take on many different personalities, and generational research suggests that each cohort may have distinguishing characteristics.

Because public organizations at all levels of government have begun to plan human resource policies that take into account the differences that generations will bring with them to the workforce (Center for Organizational Research, 2003), public administration research and public management scholars must be able to evaluate the generations in the workforce today. Whether or not generations differ in the ways they approach work, their interest in serving the public, their time spent in jobs, and how they may influence on individual's careers are all important areas to consider.

THE MAKING OF A GENERATION

Generations are defined as recognizable groups of individuals that share a common history and significant life events at critical developmental stages (Lancaster and Stillman, 2002). Generations also form personalities that influence their feelings toward authority and organizations, what work means to them, and how they attempt to satisfy specific desires (Kupperschmidt, 2000). The most prevalent generations in today's workforce are the baby boomers (boomers) and Generation X (Gen-Xers), followed by traditionalists and millennials (Gen-Yers) (Lancaster and Stillman, 2002; Mitchell, 2000).

Background on Generational Research

It has always been thought that generations collided in certain ways, but currently more generations are in the workplace due to longer life expectancies and prolonged retirements (Lancaster and Stillman, 2002). This will be the first time in history that four generations have been in the workplace at the same time. The problem or the challenge is that each generation brings its own set of values, beliefs, life experiences, and attitudes to the workplace. The following profiles are very broad but were developed from survey research by the Bridgeworks Corporation (Lancaster and Stillman, 2002). Each of the four generational cohorts is a typology that explains a group that shares common history (Lancaster and Stillman, 2002). These shared events and conditions determine who they are and how they see the world.

In 1997, a company called the Bridgeworks Corporation formed to help bridge the gap between generations by helping people look beyond their own perspective to understand the events, conditions, values, and behaviors that make each generation unique. In 2000 and 2001, this company conducted a nationwide survey with over 400 respondents to help bring merit to the idea that different generations may have different values and attitudes toward life that may reflect in the workforce. By ignoring such differences they believed that the workplace will have a clash of the generations due to misunderstandings.

Traditionalists (born between the turn of the twentieth century and the end of World War II, i.e., 1900–1945) are considered to have preferences for longtime careers with one company and strong beliefs in hard word and respect for leaders. The generational personality for this cohort is loyal, which should suggest longer durations in each job since job changing carries a stigma for this cohort.

Baby boomers (1946–1964) are considered the most competitive cohort as a result of sheer size, almost 8 million peers. The term "baby boomers" comes from the boom in births from 1946 to 1964. As a generation affected by the Vietnam War, the civil rights movement, Kennedy and King assassinations, and Watergate, it seems only fitting that they would have a lack of respect for and loyalty to authority and social institutions (Adams, 2000; Bradford, 1993; Kupperschmidt, 2000). Boomers are currently feeling the crunch of caring for aging parents and their own children; many are simultaneously working in positions of power in the workplace and carry the modest values of material success and traditional values with them to the workplace (Miniter, 1997; O'Bannon, 2001). This cohort is very motivated to make a change in the world and values money, title, and recognition. The generational personality for this group is optimistic. Baby boomers are least likely to report work as being their most important activity (Mitchell, 2000).

Generation X (1965–1980) is the generation of skeptics. The boomer generation is well known for its loyalty to collectivism. Gen X-ers are often considered a product of financial, family, and societal insecurity (Jurkiewicz and Brown, 1998), leading to a generation that has a sense of individualism rather than collectivism. Based on its great diversity and a lack of solid traditions (Jurkiewicz and Brown, 1998; Smola and Sutton, 2002), often due to witnessing their parents being laid off, Gen X-ers are sometimes considered to be cynical and untrusting (Kupperschmidt, 2000). As a generation that relies on team support, craves mentors, and values stable families, Gen X-ers bring with them to the workplace practical approaches to problem solving (Jurkiewicz and Brown, 1998; Karp, Sirias, and Arnold, 1999; Kupperschmidt, 2000; O'Bannon, 2001). As a technically competent group that is most comfortable with diversity, change, and multitasking, they push for similarities to be emphasized over differences (Kupperschmidt, 2000; O'Bannon 2001). Gen X-ers are often thought to ask, "WIFM, What's in it for me?" (Karp et al., 1999). Gen X-ers are expected to bring various values and attitudes to the traditional workplace, including a different approach to benefits and compensation, along with diverse ideas about work loyalty and commitment (The Singer Group, 1999). Job changing is seen as a necessary condition because faith in institutions was lost as a result of seeing lots of businesses downsize and merge. Individuals in this cohort look for career security versus job security, suggesting a greater likelihood to have more jobs across a particular work history.

Generation Y (1981–1999) is the most recent addition to the workplace. We know very little about Gen X-ers and the millennials (those born between 1981 and present) due to the fact that they are just beginning to enter the workforce. Research suggests that if millennials follow the lead of Gen X-ers, they too will want higher salaries, more financial leverage, and flexible work arrangements (Jennings, 2000; Smola and Sutton, 2002). Millennials are connected to the world 24 hours a day, distrust institutions, and voice their opinions (Ryan, 2000; Smola and Sutton, 2002). Due to the connected nature of this generation, made possible by technology, it is expected that they will be the first generation to be socially active since the 1960s and will have an abundant appetite for work. This realistic generation is classified as seeing job chang-ing as a part of the daily work routines. Younger generations are more likely to have a "work to live" attitude versus the "live to work" attitude of their predecessors. This however does not mean they do value work; it is just more likely that they will seek out employment that will allow them to have the best work–life balance (Mitchell, 2000).

Although this research was conducted based on survey data, it should be noted that Bridgeworks is a consulting firm that needs a product to sell. However, their client lists include several public, private, and professional organizations. Whether or not indi-viduals buy into this idea of generational differences, organizations like the American Management Association, International City/County Management Association (ICMA), International Public Management Association for Human Resources (IPMA-HR), Internal Revenue Service, and several universities have had presentations on how to manage generations in their workforce.

Companies have set cultures and policies that may not fit with new employees entering the work world. Generational collisions at work can result in loss of valuable employees, reduced profitability, poor customer service, derailed careers, wasted human potential, and even health problems caused by stress (Lancaster and Stillman, 2002).

When these characteristics are applied to the development of civil service systems, there could be disconnects when following generations try to fit into the established system. The general idea is that there is a system, set up by traditionalists that may not fit into the ideas and values of more recent generations. Traditionalists generally do not see "job hopping" as a desirable trait in employees. Many Generation X and Y members may see having multiple jobs necessary to achieve desired salary and goals. Rules that were set up and seen as important safeguards at one time may be seen as hindrances to efficient work flow processes by another generation. Generation X members are consid-ered to have more focus on achieving a better work–life balance, whereas Generation Y members are simply more focused on self-gratification (Bowen, 2000).

Responses to Managing Multiple Generations in the Workforce

Government will be one of the first sectors to experience the consequences of an aging national workforce (Scott, 2004). Some of the reasons for this phenomenon include the declining appeal of public service, competition with the private sector for talent, and lower retirement eligibility (Center for Organizational Research , 2003). While this crisis may be mediated by the economic downturn, eligible employees delaying retirement and a renewed interest in public service after September 11, public organizations are preparing themselves for managing an aging and retiring workforce. Public agencies have been urged to find strategic trouble spots by collecting necessary data to forecast for the changing workforce.

Generational Differences and Work Values

Most of the debate about generations in the workplace centers on the difference in generations and life stage development. The Protestant work ethic dates back to the sixteenth century and is described as a belief that hard work, dedication, frugality, and perseverance are both pleasing to God and necessary for salvation (Steiner and Steiner, 2000). While similar work values are prevalent in other cultures, there is no surprise that a common definition of work values is hard to come across. As with any value, work values help individuals define what people believe is right and wrong (Smola and Sutton,

2002). Since the workplace is no longer a place that can easily be separated into right and wrong, it is important that current work values fit with current work conditions. Modern work environments require decision making, problem solving, troubleshooting, and, often, the managing of difficult situations. Due to this, work values could be defined as a structural framework that reflects the central elements of the construct and reduces confusion over its conceptual boundaries (Dose, 1997). Smola and Sutton (2002) use the following definition: "Work values are the evaluative standards relating to work or the environment by which individuals discern what is right or assess the importance of preferences." To really explore generational differences attention must be paid to the changing nature of work along with individuals.

The Singer Group is an organizational consultant firm that gives a popular description of current generations in the workforce to help businesses manage people and their organizations. The term "free-agents" often categorizes the retention of Gen X-ers. Flexible work schedules along with flex time, consulting work, and temporary work are often valued by this younger generation (The Singer Group, 1999). When getting compensated, Gen X-ers are often "Independent Contractors" with a need for rapid results and broader roles rather than specialized jobs (The Singer Group, 1999). Attitudes toward retirement include "pay me now and I'll take care of myself," and X-ers often don't see Social Security as anything that they will receive (The Singer Group, 1999). Overall, workplace policies for Gen X-ers include work flexibility, and they will not sacrifice personal or family-related goals for their careers (Gerkovich, 2005).

Interest to Serve the Public

In recent years theoretical development and empirical work has been used to operationalize what public interest means for employees, why they develop a strong sense of public service, and how it influences their behavior (e.g., Alonso and Lewis, 2001; Brewer and Selden, 1998; Brewer, Selden, and Facer, 2000; Crewson, 1997; Houston, 2000; Perry, 1996, 1997). Brewer et al. (2000) noted that public service motivation (PSM) is important not just to motivation but also to productivity, improved management practices, accountability, and trust in government, making it one of the major current topics of investigation in public administration. The appearance of PSM is not limited to the public sector. While PSM tends to be particularly high for government employees, those in the private and non-profit sectors also exhibit PSM to varying degrees (Wittmer, 1991).

Perry (2000) asserts the importance of PSM as an alternative to rational and self-interested theories of motivation that tend to focus on pecuniary rewards. PSM can also explain the shape of beliefs and behavioral outcomes. The theory argues that individual behavior is not just the product of rational self-interested choices but is rooted in normative and affective motives as well. If we only study motivation from a rational incentive-driven perspective, we will only have a partial understanding of motivation. To fully grasp the concept we must study social processes that shape an individual's normative beliefs and emotional understandings of the world. This should be an interesting place to include the idea of generational cohorts.

Brewer (2002) stated that public administration researchers have long believed that some individuals have a strong public service ethic that attracts them to government employment and promotes work-related attitudes and behaviors that advance the public interest. Social factors have not been completely ignored in the exploration of PSM. It has been proposed that PSM depends on how individuals are socialized via sociohistorical institutions, primary parental relations, religion, observational learning and modeling during the course of their life events, education, and professional training (Perry, 2000).

This could also be expanded to include the common history that generations may have experienced. Memories of downsizing may be familiar to those in the baby boomer generational cohort. Generation X and Generation Y may have witnessed the dislocation of parents and relatives, which could make the idea of being loyal to a particular firm foreign and less appealing (Bowen, 2000). Knowing the timelines in which each cohort grew up it is proposed that they will share some similar reference points and attitudes when applied to work.

Members of Generation X are described as not being as attached to the employer–employee contract and have a higher need for recruitment and rewards. Members of this generation may not be as socially developed as older generations but are more concerned with making money and are looking for career security rather than job security. The experiences of this generation would not align cohort members with traditional values included in PSM. As described by Lancaster and Stillman (2000), this generation will look to put faith in themselves versus institutions. As a cohort it seems that Generation X members will be more concerned with self-survival versus a sense of public commitment and involvement, thereby having lower levels of PSM.

Difference Between Age and Generation

We cannot ignore the connection between age and generational differences. The life cycle of stability concept suggests that generations really don't matter, but rather each generation will act a certain way based on when they are observed. In the life cycle of stability, model traditionalists only appear to have preferences for long jobs because they are at a point in their life where job-hopping is not desirable. Because of these competing hypotheses, it is important to examine if there is any reason to continue to give attention to this notion of generational differences in the workplace.

Life course research is an area that is rarely studied in the field of public administration. Sociology and psychology often pull from work based in this area. Glen Elder is a leading researcher in life course theory, and his work emphasizes the value of linking life stages and examining transitions into research aging (1998). Life course research challenges researchers to look at aging as a continuing, lifelong process that can have turning points, start and end points, as well as a holistic impact on an individual's development (Elder and Johnson, 2002).

The life cycle approach to understanding aging suggests that individuals will have different values and experiences throughout the aging process. Young adults could be considered to have less stable values compared to older adults (Johnson, 2001). Booth, Francesconi, and Garcia-Serrano (1999) used the British Household Panel Survey and found that men and women held an average of five jobs in the course of their work lives, with half of these jobs occurring in the first 10 years. Younger cohorts were found to have more separation hazards, which suggests they may have an increase in job instability. As the number of jobs an individual held increased, the tenure in a particular job lengthened (Booth et al., 1999). In the United States, the number of jobs held by men and women is nearly double that held by British men and women (Booth et al., 1999; Hall, 1982; Topel and Ward, 1992).

Social psychology has informed much of the research on job values and the aging process, which suggests that job values and the rewards obtained on a job grow more important over time (Kohn and Schooler, 1983; Lindsay and Knox, 1984; Mortimer and Lorence, 1979). Job tenure and job mobility are topics that need further exploration in public administration. In the case of U.S. federal employees, it was found that tenure matters not only in the likelihood of quits but also in an individual's dependence on the job (Black, Moffitt, and Warner, 1990). Based on work in this area, it is expected that older-generational cohorts will have longer job durations than younger cohorts.

Previous studies have found that less experienced workers and those that feel poorly compensated for their jobs are more likely to leave (Mor Barak, Nissly, and Levin, 2001). Organizations that invest in training and job-related education may help lessen the likelihood of individuals leaving their organization. The finding in the human services field suggests that individuals are not leaving their jobs for personal reasons but more because they are not satisfied with their jobs, and feel excessive burnout and that their supervisors do not support them. Some of the behaviors witnessed by different generations could merely be a function of life stage or career stage.

Conclusion

This chapter contributes to the literature on generations in the workplace and interest in public sector work. There are many public organizations adopting plans and investing resources to deal with generational differences in the workplace with very little empirical evidence that these differences really exist and produce conflict in the work environment. Work in this area should address the fact that what appears to be a conflict of the generations could be the natural expectations of individuals at particular stages in the life cycle. For the first time in history, there are four generations in the workplace at the same time. People are working longer and may not retire when they first become eligible. What may appear to be generational differences may be life stage differences that have not had to be dealt with in the past.

Since the public sector is at a time where recruitment and retention are of the utmost importance, public managers must understand the needs of the individuals they wish to employ. As public agencies try to develop new methods of recruitment and retention, it may be the case that younger generations will prefer different items in a benefits package. Younger generations are described as trying to find better work–life balance, so compressed work schedules, job sharing, and telecommuting may be items public agencies may adopt in response to employee demand. It is also expected that baby boomers will approach retirement in a different way than the generations before them (The Singer Group, 1999). Not only are baby boomers working longer, they may favor different retirement options like phased retirement or part-time work. It may not be the case that Generation X is different than those that came before them based on shared experiences, but the current life stage that those individuals are in may make some jobs more attractive than others.

Generational differences and their possible impacts on public management and personnel policies have and will remain a hot topic of debate in both popular literature and human resource management. Ultimately, generational differences will remain to be discussed because the prevalence of multiple generations will be visible in and outside the workplace for the indefinite future. If generations do indeed differ, managers living 25 years apart should have different work values and be attracted to different aspects of work. The argument that generational researchers are making suggests that work values will be influenced by life events and socialization more than by age and maturity. It seems commonplace for one generation to complain about the work ethic or behaviors of the generations that follow. The obvious questions are as follows: If each subsequent generation is in fact lazy or self-centered, do individuals become more conscientious and less self-centered with maturity (Smola and Sutton, 2002)? Do previous generations forget how they used to be when they were young and stereotype younger generations for going through a natural stage in development?

This chapter explores the common stereotypes in order to inform public managers about engaging in generational-specific policies and programs without fully understanding if the differences are fact or fiction. Previous work in public administration simply controls for age and does not take into account the social and historical connections that generations might have that would affect the way in which they operate in the workplace. Since this is the first time four generations have been present in the workforce, it seems to be the case that information on how these generations are approaching work might be a helpful addition to public management literature.

References

Adams, S. J. 2000. "Generation X: How Understanding This Population Leads to Better Safety Programs." *Professional Safety* 45(1): 26–29.

Alonso, P., and G. B. Lewis. 2001. "Public Service Motivation and Job Performance: Evidence from the Federal Sector." *American Review of Public Administration* 31(4): 363–380.

Black, M., R. Moffit, and J. T. Warner. 1990. "The Dynamics of Job Separation: The Case of Federal Employees." *Journal of Applied Econometrics* 5(3): 245–262.

Boath, D., and D. Y. Smith. 2004. "When Your Best People Leave, Will Their Knowledge Leave, Too?" *Harvard Management Update* 9(9): 6–7.

Booth, A. L., M. Francesconi, and C. Garcia-Serrano. 1999. "Job Tenure and Job Mobility." *Industrial and Labor Relations Review* 53(1): 43–70.

Bowen, R. B. 2000. *Recognizing and Rewarding Employees.* New York, NY: McGraw-Hill.

Bradford, F. W. 1993. "Understanding 'Generation X.' " *Marketing Research* 5: 54.

Brewer, G. A. 2002. "Public Service Motivation: Theory, Evidence, and Prospects for Research." Paper presented at the Annual Meeting of the American Political Science Association. Boston, MA, p. 1.

Brewer, G. A., and S. C. Selden. 1998. "Whistleblowers in the Federal Civil Service: New Evidence of the Public Service Ethic." *Journal of Public Administration Research and Theory* 8(3): 413–439.

Brewer, G. A., S. C. Selden, and R. Facer. 2000. "Individual Conceptions of Public Service Motivation." *Public Administration Review* 60(3): 254–264.

Center for Organizational Research. 2003. *The Aging-and-Retiring Government Workforce: How Serious is the Challenge? What are Jurisdictions Doing about It?* In Partnership with the International Personnel Management Association, the Council of State Governments, and the National Association of State Personnel Executives. The Center for Organizational Research, a division of Linkage, Inc.

Crewson, P. E. 1997. "Public-Service Motivation: Building Empirical Evidence of Incidence and Effect." *Journal of Public Administration Research and Theory* 7(4): 499–518.

Dose, J. J. 1997. "Work Values: An Integrative Framework and Illustrative Application to Organizational Socialization." *Journal of Occupational and Organizational Psychology* 70(3): 219–240.

Downs, A. 1967. *Inside the Bureaucracy.* Santa Monica, CA: RAND Corporation.

Elder, G. H. 1998. "Life Course and Human Development." In W. Damon, ed. *Handbook of Child Psychology* (pp. 939–991). New York, NY: Wiley.

Elder, G. H., and M. K. Johnson. 2002. "The Life Course and Human Development: Challenges, Lessons, and New Directions." In R. A. Settersten, ed. *Invitation to the Life Course: Toward New Understandings of Later Life.* Amityville, New York, NY: Baywood.

Gerkovich, P. 2005. "Generations X and Work/Life Values." *The Network News, A Work-Family News Publication* 7(2): 1–5.

Hall, R. E. 1982. "The Importance of Lifetime Jobs in the United States Economy." *American Economic Review* 72(4): 716–724.

Houston, D. J. 2000. "Public-Service Motivation: A Multivariate Test." *Journal of Public Administration Research and Theory* 10(4): 713–727.

Jennings, A. 2000. "Hiring Generation X." *Journal of Accountancy* 189(2): 55–59.

Johnson, M. K. 2001. "Job Values in the Young Adult Transition: Change and Stability with Age." *Social Psychology Quarterly* 64(4): 297–317.

Jurkiewicz, C. E., and R. C. Brown. 1998. "GenXers vs. Boomers vs. Matures: Generational Comparisons of Public Employee Motivation." *Review of Public Personnel Administration* 18: 18–37.

Karp, H., D. Sirias, and K. Arnold. 1999. "Teams: Why Generation X Marks the Spot." *The Journal for Quality & Participation* 22(4), 30–33.

Kohn, M., and C. Schooler. 1983. *Work and Personality: An Inquiry into the Impact of Social Stratification.* Norwood, NJ: Ablex Press.

Kupperschmidt, B. 2000. "Multi-generation Employees: Strategies for Effective Management." *Health Care Manager* 19: 65–76.

Lancaster, L. C., and D. Stillman. 2002. *When Generations Collide.* New York, Harper Collins Publishers Inc.

Leibowitz, J. 2004. "Bridging the Knowledge and Skills Gap: Tapping Federal Retirees." *Public Personnel Management* 33(4): 421–448.

Lindsay, P., and W. E. Knox. 1984. "Continuity and Change in Work Values Among Young Adults." *American Journal of Sociology* 89(4): 918–931.

Miniter, R. 1997. Generation X Does Business. *The American Enterprise* 8: 38–40.

Mitchell, S. 2000. *American Generations: Who They Are. How They Live. What They Think* (3rd ed.). Ithaca, NY: New Strategist Publications, Inc.

Mor Barak, M. E., J. A. Nissly, and A. Levin. 2001. "Antecedents to Retention and Turnover among Child Welfare, Social Work, and Other Human Service Employees: What Can We Learn from Past Research? A Review and Metanalysis." *Social Service Review* 75(4): 625–661.

Mortimer, J. T., and J. Lorence. 1979. "Work and Experience and Occupational Value Socialization: A Longitudinal Study." *American Journal of Sociology* 84(6): 1361–1385.

Nigro, L. G., and F. A. Nigro. 2000. *The New Public Personnel Administration* (5th ed.). Itasca, IL: F.E. Peacock Publishers.

O'Bannon, G. 2001. "Managing Our Future: The Generation X Factor." *Public Personnel Management* 30: 95–109.

Perry, J. L. 1996. "Measuring Public Service Motivation: An Assessment of Construct Reliability and Validity." *Journal of Public Administration Research and Theory* 6(1): 5–22.

Perry, J. L. 1997. "Antecedents of Public Service Motivation." *Journal of Public Administration Research and Theory* 7(2): 181–197.

Perry, J. L. 2000. "Bringing Society In: Toward a Theory of Public-Service Motivation." *Journal of Public Administration Research and Theory* 10(2): 471–488.

Perry, J. L., and L. R. Wise. 1990. "The Motivational Bases of Public Service." *Public Administration Review* 50(3): 367–373.

Pynes, J. E. 2003. "Strategic Human Resource Management." In S. W. H. a. R. C. Kearney, ed. *Public Personnel Administration: Problems and Prospects* (4th ed., pp. 93–105). Uppers Saddle River, NJ: Prentice Hall.

Ryan, M. 2000, September 10. "Gerald Celente: He Reveals What Lies Ahead." *Parade Magazine*, pp. 22–23.

Sanders, R. M. 2004. "GeorgiaGain or GeorgiaLoss? The Great Experiment in State Civil service Reform." *Public Personnel Management* 33(2): 151–164.

Scott, L. 2004. "Trends in State Personnel Administration." In K. S. Chin, ed. *The Book of the States 2004* (Vol. 36, pp. 401–404). Lexington, KY: The Council of State Governments.

Shelton, C., and L. Shelton. 2005. *The Next Revolution: What Gen X Women Want at Work and How Their Boomer Bosses Can Help Them to Get It.* Mountain View, CA: Davies-Black Publishing.

Singer Group, Inc. 1999, May 5. *Arrival of Generation X in the Workforce: Implications for Compensation and Benefits*. Annual Benefits and Compensation Update WEB Baltimore Chapter. http://www.singergrp.com/presentations/karens-genx.pdf (accessed August 1, 2007).

Smith, G. P. 2007. "Baby Boomer Versus Generation X, Managing the New Workforce." http://www.chartcourse.com/articlebabyvsgenx.html (accessed December 12, 2008).

Smola, K. W., and C. D. Sutton. 2002. "Generational Differences: Revisiting Generational Work Values for the New Millennium." *Journal of Organizational Behavior* 23(4): 363–382.

Steiner, G. A., and J. F. Steiner. 2000. *Business, Government, and Society: A Managerial Perspective* (9th ed.). New York, NY: Irwin McGraw-Hill.

Topel, R. H., and M. P. Ward. 1992. "Job Mobility and The Careers of Young Men." *Quarterly Journal of Economics* 107(2): 439–479.

Weber, M. 1947. *The Theory of Social and Economic Organizations* (T. Parsons, Trans.). New York, NY: Free Press.

Wittmer, D. 1991. "Serving the People or Serving for Pay: Reward Preferences Among Government, Hybrid Sector, and Business Managers." *Public Productivity and Management Review* 14(4): 369–383.

4 AFFIRMATIVE ACTION AND THE LAW

Norma M. Riccucci

Norma M. Riccucci is a professor at the School of Public Affairs and Administration at Rutgers University, Newark. She is the author of several books in the areas of public personnel administration and public management. She has received a number of national awards including the American Society of Public Administration's Charles H. Levine Award for excellence in teaching, research, and service. She is a fellow of the National Academy of Public Administration.

One of the most polemical and polarizing personnel issues over the past several decades has been affirmative action. Scholars, practitioners, and policy makers have debated its appropriateness and potential effectiveness since its inception. After decades of legal wrangling and uncertainties, the U.S. Supreme Court issued a ruling, in 2003, that paved the way for not only universities but also public and private sector employers to rely on affirmative action policies in order to redress past discrimination as well as to promote or enhance diversity in the classroom and the workplace.

The purpose of this chapter is to provide a legal snapshot of the use of affirmative action in the workplace. It examines the U.S. Supreme Court's *Bakke* decision, as well as the Court's 2003 decisions in two University of Michigan cases. Although not an affirmative action case per se, the chapter also addresses the most recent Supreme Court decision, *Ricci v. DeStefano* (2009), which has ramifications for affirmative action or, more broadly, diversity programs. These decisions have major implications for the continued use of affirmative action not only in education but in the workforce as well.

THE *BAKKE* RULING

First employed as a tool to promote equal employment opportunity (i.e., to prevent discrimination), affirmative action has evolved into a more proactive tool to not only redress past discrimination against persons based on such factors as race and gender but also correct racial and gender imbalances in the workplace. Most recently, affirmative action has been viewed as a tool to create diversity in the workplace. And, at least at the entry levels of employment, affirmative action has proven to be effective. (See, for example, Riccucci, 2002, 2009; Naff, 2001; Kellough, 2006; Cornwell and Kellough, 1994.)

The U.S. Supreme Court issued its first substantive ruling on affirmative action in 1978 with its *Regents of the University of California v. Bakke* decision. The *Bakke* ruling upheld the general principle of affirmative action but struck down its use by the University of California under the Fourteenth Amendment of the U.S. Constitution and Title VI of the Civil Rights Act of 1964. A closely divided Court objected to the use of what it labeled "quotas" in admission decisions. The University of California's Davis Medical School was reserving 16 spaces out of a possible 100 for students of color. In actuality, the school was not operating a strict "quota" system but instead was setting a goal or benchmark for the admissions of students of color. A quota implies sanctions if not met; courts have the power to impose sanctions, but universities as well as employers do not sanction themselves with, for example, fines, if they don't meet their goals. The misuse of the term "quota" here has not only galvanized the debate over affirmative action but, as will be seen later in this chapter, continues to serve as a yardstick in gauging the legality of affirmative action programs.

The Supreme Court's *Bakke* decision was so fractured that it created a split among lower federal courts over the use of affirmative action and, in effect, whether the ruling could actually serve as legal precedent. After a number of subsequent Supreme Court rulings, the Court's decision in *Grutter v. Bollinger* (2003) reconciles this critical problem.

THE *UNIVERSITY OF MICHIGAN* RULINGS

In 2003, marking the 25th anniversary of the *Bakke* decision, the U.S. Supreme Court ruled on two affirmative action cases involving the University of Michigan. In one case, *Grutter v. Bollinger*, the Court was asked to rule on the constitutionality, under the Fourteenth Amendment's Equal Protection Clause, of affirmative action at the University of Michigan's Law School. In a 5-4 ruling, the Court majority opined that the racial diversity of a study body can be a sufficiently compelling interest on the part of a state university to warrant its use of racial preference in its admissions decisions. The Court ruled that the Fourteenth Amendment's Equal Protection Clause allows for the "Law School's narrowly tailored use of race in admissions decisions to further a compelling interest in obtaining the educational benefits that flow from a diverse student body" (*Grutter v. Bollinger*, 2003, p. 342).

Since *Bakke*, the courts have judged the constitutionality of affirmative against the strict scrutiny test. This two-pronged test asks (1) there is a compelling governmental interest for the program and (2) whether the program is sufficiently narrowly tailored to meet its specified goals (e.g., whether race is only one factor among many). In the context of *Grutter*, the U.S. Supreme Court ruled that the

> Law School's admissions program bears the hallmarks of a narrowly tailored plan. To be narrowly tailored, a race-conscious admissions program cannot "insulat[e] each category of applicants with certain desired qualifications from competition with all other applicants" .... Instead, it may consider race or ethnicity only as a "'plus' in a particular applicant's file"; i.e., it must be "flexible enough to consider all pertinent elements of diversity in light of the particular qualifications of each applicant, and to place them on the same footing for consideration, although not necessarily according them the

same weight" . . . . It follows that universities cannot establish quotas for members of certain racial or ethnic groups or put them on separate admissions tracks . . . 40. Moreover, the program is flexible enough to ensure that each applicant is evaluated as an individual and not in a way that makes race or ethnicity the defining feature of the application. (*Grutter v. Bollinger*, 2003, p. 322)

This decision, in effect, states that diversity, which is a goal of affirmative action, serves as a compelling government interest. And, if the programs are narrowly tailored, they can survive legal challenges. The program at the University of Michigan's law school met the two prongs of the strict scrutiny test.

The second Supreme Court decision provides further clarification around what constitutes "narrowly tailored." In *Gratz v. Bollinger* (2003), the Supreme Court struck down the use of affirmative action in admissions at the University of Michigan's undergraduate programs in the College of Literature, Sciences, and Art. This program awarded 20 points on a scale of 150 for membership in an underrepresented group, such as African American, Latino, or American Indian. An applicant could be automatically admitted with 100 points. The Court, in a 6-3 decision, ruled that the program was "not narrowly tailored to achieve the assertedly compelling interest in educational diversity [and] the admissions policy did not provide individualized consideration of each characteristic of a particular applicant" (*Gratz v. Bollinger*, 2003, p. 268).

In short, the Supreme Court would not support a point system such as the one used by the undergraduate program at the University of Michigan. This point system has been likened to, even by the district court ruling in *Gratz*, to a quota system (see *Gratz v. Bollinger*, 2000).

Parenthetically, as many have argued, the assignment of 20 points for race is no different from awarding points for other "nonacademic" criteria. For example, under the undergraduate program in question at the University of Michigan, points were awarded for a variety of factors including the following:

1. Up to 20 points could be awarded at the Provost's discretion.
2. Up to 5 points could be awarded to children or grandchildren of alumni.
3. Up to 5 points could be awarded for male students choosing to enroll in the nursing program.
4. Up to 10 points could be awarded for residents of Michigan.

Ultimately, the awarding of 20 points for race may not necessarily give students of color a "competitive" edge in the admissions process.

These two University of Michigan decisions form a critical basis of law around affirmative action. Moreover, they are significant not only in university admissions but for public employment as well. As Naylor and Rosenbloom (2004, p. 151) point out: "Post-*Grutter*, there is greater reason to believe that narrowly tailored affirmative action to promote diversity in public employment can survive constitutional challenge." Thus, if government employers are seeking to promote diversity in the workplace, and the programs do not assign points based on such factors as race, affirmative action will be deemed legal.

It is worth noting that over 100 *amicus curiae* (friend of the court) briefs were filed in support of the University of Michigan's use of affirmative action including briefs from former president Gerald Ford, government, several state governments, elected officials, the military, major corporations, leading colleges and universities, civil rights organizations, and academic and research associations. The Bush administration, however, filed a brief urging the Court to find the University of Michigan's use of affirmative action unconstitutional.

Since the *Gratz* and *Grutter* rulings, Michigan Civil Rights Initiative or Proposal 2, a ballot initiative by the Michigan voters, passed in 2006. Proposal 2 is patterned after California's Proposition 209 and others (e.g., Nebraska's I-424 and Washington's I-200) which bar the use of affirmative action in government contracting and universities. However, legal analysts have stated that Proposal 2 would not nullify the *Grutter* ruling. Indeed, the Michigan's Civil Rights Commission (MCRC) issued a directive to this effect, stating first that:

> "Proposal 2 does not end equal opportunity or the critical pursuit of diversity and inclusion in the State of Michigan. Neither does it mean that the terms "race" or "sex" are banished from the official state vocabulary, as it relates to the state's decision-making process." (MCRC, 2007, p. 2)

The MCRC (2007, p. 3) went on to say that:

> "There is legal precedent from the U.S. Supreme Court that race and sex may be used as one of a number of factors in the state's decision-making process, if the objective serves a compelling state interest, such as diversity in higher education, and is narrowly tailored to achieve the objective sought. We do not believe that Proposal 2 has overturned the referenced U.S. Supreme Court precedent."

This indicates that despite voter initiatives to end affirmative action, government entities will develop measures to pursue diversity, the end result of affirmative action. It may be that governments recognize that making progress toward diversity is a long, hard battle that they do not wish to raze. Moreover, governments may also recognize the positive benefits that come with diversity in employment and in the classroom and are therefore not willing to abandon affirmative action programs and policies. However, as will be discussed below with the *Ricci v. DeStefano* (2009) case, courts will continue to monitor how programs aimed at promoting diversity are implemented.

THE *RICCI* CASE

In 2009, the U.S. Supreme Court issued a ruling in *Ricci v. DeStefano* (2009), which involved not affirmative action per se, but rather, more broadly, employment discrimination law. More specifically, the ruling has implications for the goal of affirmative action—diversity. Briefly, in 2003, the New Haven, Connecticut, fire department administered a promotion exam for the posts of lieutenant and captain. Out of 77 candidates taking the lieutenant exam, 43 were white, 19 were African American, and 15 Latino. Twenty-five whites (58 percent) passed the exam along with only 6 African Americans (32 percent) and 3 Latinos (20 percent). Because the top 10 scorers were white, and there were only 8 vacancies for lieutenant, under the rule of three,[1] no African Americans or Latinos would be eligible for promotion.

Of the 41 applicants who took the captain examination, 25 were white, 8 were African American, and 8 Latino. Of the 22 candidates who passed the exam, 16 (64 percent) were white, 3 (38 percent) were African American, and 3 (38 percent) were Latino. There were seven captain vacancies, but under the rule of three, no African Americans and at most two Latinos would be eligible for promotion. The city determined, given the statistical outcome, that the exam had an adverse impact on the African American and Latino candidates and, fearing litigation from them, refused to certify the results of the exam. Seventeen white firefighters and one Latino firefighter who passed the exam filed suit against the city alleging disparate treatment under Title VII of the Civil Rights Act, as well as discrimination under the Equal Protection Clause of the Fourteenth Amendment to the U.S. Constitution. Both the federal district court and the U.S. Appeals Court for the Second Circuit ruled against Ricci and for the city of New Haven. Ricci appealed to the High Court, which addressed the statutory claim under Title VII first (Peffer, 2009).

The Supreme Court in a 5-4 ruling reversed the lower court decisions and ruled for the white and Latino firefighters, stating that "Fear of litigation alone cannot justify the City's reliance on race to the detriment of individuals who passed the . . . examinations and qualified for promotions. Discarding the test results was impermissible under Title VII" (*Ricci v. DeStefano*, 2009, online). The Court instead argued that there must be a "strong basis" in evidence for concluding that the tests might be vulnerable to a disparate impact claim. The statistical imbalance alone, stated the Court, was not enough. According to the Court, without this showing, the city engaged in "express, race-based decision-making," resulting in disparate treatment, which, along with disparate impact, is also prohibited by Title VII. Because the court ruled for the plaintiffs on statutory grounds, it did not render a ruling on the equal protection claim.

The Court's *Ricci* decision, in effect, sets the two provisions of Title VII—disparate treatment and disparate impact—in an endless battle for primacy which can only deter employers' efforts to promote equal opportunity and end discriminatory practices. For example, according to the majority ruling, if the city could have demonstrated that the exams were not job related, the city may have prevailed.[2] But subjecting the tests to validity studies would have been very costly to the city. And, if the validity studies revealed that the tests were job related, the strong-basis-in-evidence standard created by the *Ricci* Court would have been satisfied, thereby clearing the way for the use of the promotional exams. But this would have defeated the city's express purpose of seeking to diversify the upper levels of its fire department.

A viable solution to this challenge in any government agency would be to provide a battery of tests for promotion to upper-level jobs. Oral exams, for example, are critical, and could be weighted more heavily than written exams. Other assessment tools such as computer simulations or group exercises might also be deemed more important than written exams. These types of arrangements may facilitate an employer's goal to diversify its upper echelons, while staving off possible litigation. Indeed, a recent study by the Merit Systems Protection Board (MSPB 2009) found that, although not used extensively in the federal government, job simulations are associated with lower rates of adverse impact, have higher predictive ability, and are more likely to be perceived as fair and job related among job candidates.

It is also worth noting the experiences in Bridgeport, Connecticut, as Justice Ginsberg offered in her dissenting opinion in the *Ricci* ruling. She pointed to evidence offered by Donald Day of the Northeast Region of the International Association of Black Professional Firefighters. Ginsberg wrote that

Day contrasted New Haven's experience with that of nearby Bridgeport, where minority firefighters held one-third of lieutenant and captain positions. Bridgeport . . . . had once used a testing process similar to New Haven's, with a written exam accounting for 70 percent of an applicant's score, an oral exam for 25 percent, and seniority for the remaining five percent . . . Bridgeport recognized, however, that the oral component, more so than the written component, addressed the sort of "real-life scenarios" fire officers encounter on the job. . . .Accordingly, that city "changed the relative weights" to give primacy to the oral exam . . . Since that time. . . . Bridgeport had seen minorities "fairly represented" in its exam results. (*Ricci v. DeStefano*, 2009, online)

The full impact of Ricci is yet to be seen. But, as Peffer (2009, p. 410) points out:

Congress could step in and overrule *Ricci* by amending the Civil Rights Act. We can only hope that amid all this litigation and lawmaking that the importance and original intent of civil rights and of diversity in the workplace is not forgotten.

WHAT DOES THE FUTURE HOLD?

The *Grutter* decision in conjunction with previous Supreme Court precedents ensures the legality of affirmative action not only in university admissions but also in hiring and promotions when certain conditions are met. But, to be sure, the Court will closely monitor how diversity initiatives will be implemented in light of the *Ricci* case.

Table 4.1 provides a summary of the Court's decisions around the use of affirmative action in employment. As can be seen, after *Bakke*, the U.S. Supreme Court

Table 4.1   Key U.S. Supreme Court Actions or Decisions on Affirmative Action

1978   *Regents of the University of California v. Bakke*, 438 U.S. 265
U.S. Supreme Court upholds the principle of affirmative action, but strikes down its operation by the University at California under the Fourteenth Amendment and Title VI of the Civil Rights Act of 1964.

1979   *United Steelworkers of America v. Weber*, 443 U.S. 193
U.S. Supreme Court upholds legality of voluntarily developed affirmative action plan under Title VII of Civil Rights Act of 1964.

1980   *Fullilove v. Klutznick*, 448 U.S. 448
U.S. Supreme Court upholds constitutionality (under Fifth and Fourteenth Amendments) of federal set-aside programs enacted by the U.S. Congress.

1984   *Firefighters Local Union and Memphis Fire Department v. Stotts*, 467 U.S. 561
U.S. Supreme Court upholds, under Title VII of the Civil Rights Act, as amended, the use of a seniority system in layoff decisions, despite its negative impact on affirmative action.

1986   *Wygant v. Jackson Bd. of Education*, 476 U.S. 267
U.S. Supreme Court strikes down, under the Fourteenth Amendment to the U.S. Constitution, the use of affirmative action in layoff decisions.

1986 *Sheet Metal Workers' International Association v. EEOC*, **478 U.S. 421**

U.S. Supreme Court upholds, under Title VII and Fifth Amendment to the U.S. Constitution, a court-ordered affirmative action program to remedy past discrimination by a union and apprenticeship committee against people of color.

1986 *Int'l Assoc. of Firefighters v. City of Cleveland*, **478 U.S. 501**

U.S. Supreme Court upholds, under Title VII, affirmative action consent decree that provided for the use of race-conscious relief in promotion decisions.

1987 *Johnson v. Transportation Agency, Santa Clara County*, **480 U.S. 616**

U.S. Supreme Court upholds, under Title VII, voluntarily developed affirmative action program intended to correct gender and racial imbalances in traditionally segregated job categories.

1987 *U.S. v. Paradise*, **480 U.S. 149**

U.S. Supreme Court upholds, under the Fourteenth Amendment to the U.S. Constitution, a court-ordered affirmative action plan aimed at remedying discrimination against African Americans in hiring and promotion decisions in Alabama Public Safety Department.

1989 *City of Richmond v. Croson*, **488 U.S. 469**

U.S. Supreme Court strikes down the constitutionality, under the Fourteenth Amendment, of a local government's set-aside program because it could not satisfy the criteria of the strict scrutiny test.

1989 *Martin v. Wilks*, **490 U.S. 755**

U.S. Supreme Court allowed white firefighters to challenge, under Title VII, a consent decree, to which they were not a party, years after it had been approved by a lower court.

1995 *Adarand v. Peña*, **515 U.S. 200**

U.S. Supreme Court rules that the Equal Protection Clause of the Fifth Amendment requires that racial classifications used in federal set-aside programs must undergo strict scrutiny analysis.

1996 *Hopwood v. State of Texas*, **518 U.S. 1033**

U.S. Supreme Court let stand a ruling by the U.S. Court of Appeals for the Fifth Circuit, which struck down the constitutionality of an affirmative action program at the University of Texas Law School.

1999 *Lesage v. Texas*, **528 U.S. 18**

U.S. Supreme Court throws out a reverse discrimination suit filed under the Equal Protection Clause of the Fourteenth Amendment against the University of Texas' Department of Education.

2003 *Grutter v. Bollinger*, **539 U.S. 306**

The U.S Supreme Court upheld affirmative action at the University of Michigan's Law School under the Fourteenth Amendment, arguing that there is a compelling state interest in "racial diversity." Race was one factor considered among many other factors.

2003 *Gratz v. Bollinger*, **539 U.S. 244**

The U.S. Supreme Court struck down the use of affirmative action in the University of Michigan's undergraduate program under the Equal Protection Clause of the Fourteenth Amendment and Title VI of the Civil Rights Act. The Court stated that the program was based on a formula or "quota" system, giving, extra points for race.

issued a number of rulings upholding the use of affirmative action, under both the U.S. Constitution and Title VII of the Civil Rights Act of 1964 as amended. In 1989, however, the U.S. Supreme Court issued a number of regressive rulings not only to affirmative action but also to equal employment opportunity precedents. The Civil Rights Act of 1991 overturned every single negative Court ruling issued in 1989. In effect, affirmative action can be relied upon in hiring and promotion decisions. However, the Court has not upheld its use when layoffs are involved.

Layoffs, downsizing, "rightsizing," and reductions-in-force (RIFS) tend to be based on seniority, so that the last persons hired are the first fired. These systems are sometimes referred to as "last in, first out," or LIFO systems. Because women and people of color are systematically the last to be hired—due to, for example, past discrimination—they are generally the first in line to be fired when layoffs are instituted. In effect, layoff systems based on seniority tend to have a disproportionately harsh impact on women and people of color. The first U.S. Supreme Court case to examine this issue, albeit obliquely, was *Firefighters Local and Memphis Fire Department v. Stotts* (1984).

In 1980, the city of Memphis entered into a consent decree—to settle a lawsuit filed by Carl Stotts—to increase the representation of persons of color in uniformed jobs in the fire department. When fiscal problems ensued the following year and layoffs were necessary, RIFS were made on the basis of a collectively bargained LIFO seniority system. Carl Stotts filed suit arguing that the layoffs would eviscerate the consent decree as well as any gains made pursuant to the decree. The *Stotts* Supreme Court did not make a ruling directly on affirmative action in this case, but rather on the legality of the seniority system. The Court opined that because the seniority system did not *intend* to discriminate against persons of color, it therefore was bona fide or legal under Title VII of the Civil Rights Act. The city's affirmative action efforts were effectively abrogated.

Two years after *Stotts*, the U.S. Supreme Court issued a ruling that squarely addressed the use of affirmative action in conjunction with layoffs. In *Wygant v. Jackson Board of Education* (1986), a local school district along with a labor union sought to maintain racial diversity in its workforce during a period of layoffs. The school district and union negotiated a layoff plan that required the use of seniority as well as preserving racial balance of the teaching faculty. Specifically, the contract stipulated that, in the event of layoffs, the most senior teachers would be retained

> except that at no time will there be a greater percentage of minority personnel laid off than the current percentage of minority personnel employed at the time of the layoff. (*Wygant v. Jackson Board of Education*, 1986, p. 1845)

When it became necessary, layoffs were made in accordance with the collective bargaining provision. Consequently, persons of color with less seniority were retained and white teachers with greater seniority were laid off. White teachers affected by the layoffs challenged the constitutionality of the collective bargaining provision. The U.S. Supreme Court struck down the constitutionality of the layoff plan, on the grounds that the use of racial classifications in the layoff plan was not justified by a "compelling state interest," the first prong of the strict scrutiny test, discussed earlier. The Court began by stating that

[t]his Court never has upheld that societal discrimination alone is sufficient to justify a racial classification. Rather, the Court has insisted upon some showing of prior discrimination by the governmental unit involved before allowing limited use of racial classifications in order to remedy such discrimination. (*Wygant v. Jackson Board of Education*, 1986, p. 1847)

The Court went on to say that even if the school board's purpose was to remedy its own past discrimination, the means selected (i.e., the layoff plan) to achieve that goal were not "sufficiently narrowly tailored." The Court stated that "Other, less intrusive means of accomplishing similar purposes—such as the adoption of hiring goals—are available" (*Wygant v. Jackson Board of Education*, 1986, p. 1852).

Finally, the Court argued that the use of affirmative action may not be appropriate in layoffs because of its impact on "innocent" parties. The Court argued that affirmative action is appropriate in hiring decisions, since the burden to be borne by "innocent parties" is diffused among society. In contrast, the *Wygant* Court stated, when affirmative action is employed during layoffs, the

entire burden of achieving racial equally [is placed on] particular individuals, often resulting in serious disruption of their lives. That burden is too intrusive. (*Wygant v. Jackson Board of Education*, 1986, pp. 1851–1852)

In sum, while the U.S. Supreme Court finds affirmative action legally permissible in hiring and promotions when certain conditions are met, it has been unwilling to balance affirmative action against seniority rights.

Conclusion

The U.S. Supreme Court's ruling in the University of Michigan's Law School case has major implications for the continued use of affirmative action in the workplace. But, it should be noted that the ruling is based on a close 5-4 majority. The Court's conservative members, Justices Kennedy, Scalia, and Thomas and Chief Justice Rehnquist, ruled against the use of affirmative action in admissions. Justices Stevens, Souter, Ginsburg, and Breyer, and an important swing vote in affirmative action cases, Justice O'Connor, voted in the majority. However, the balance of power on the Court has shifted since 2003. The conservative Chief Justice William Rehnquist was replaced by a conservative Bush appointee in 2005, John Roberts, who assumed the Chief Justice position. David Souter, considered part of the liberal wing of the Court, was replaced by the liberal-leaning Sonia Sotomayor, President Obama's appointee, in 2009. The shift in power that leaves future affirmative action rulings in doubt is Bush's appointment of Samuel A. Alito, confirmed to the Court in 2006. Justice Alito replaced Justice O'Connor, the pivotal vote in affirmative action cases as well as others (e.g., civil liberties ranging from race to family leave to reproductive freedom). Alito tipped the balance of the High Court in a conservative direction, which was evidenced in the *Ricci v. DeStefano* ruling.[3] This may be prophetic vis-à-vis the legal landscape of affirmative action.

But, for now, the University of Michigan decisions clearly support the continued use of affirmative action when, as outlined in this chapter, certain criteria are met.

References

Cornwell, Christopher, and J. Edward Kellough. 1994. "Women and Minorities in Federal Government Agencies: Examining New Evidence from Panel Data." *Public Administration Review* 54(3): 265–270.

Firefighters Local Union No. 1784 and Memphis Fire Department v. Stotts. 1984. 467 U.S. 561.

Gratz v. Bollinger. 2000. 122 F. Supp. 2d 811.

Gratz v. Bollinger. 2003. 539 U.S. 244.

Grutter v. Bollinger. 2003. 539 U.S. 306.

Kellough, J. Edward. 2006. *Understanding Affirmative Action: Politics, Discrimination, and the Search for Justice.* Washington, DC: Georgetown University Press.

Memphis v. Stotts. 1984. 104 S.Ct. 582.

Meredith v. Jefferson County Board of Education. 2007. 551 U.S. 701.

Michigan Civil Rights Commission (MCRC). 2007, March 7. " 'One Michigan' at the Crossroads: An Assessment of the Impact of Proposal 06-02." http://www.michigan.gov/documents/mdcr/FinalCommissionReport3-07_1_189266_7.pdf (accessed January 21, 2010).

Naff, Katherine C. 2001. *To Look Like America: Dismantling Barriers for Women and Minorities in Government.* Boulder, CO: Westview Press.

Naylor, Lorenda A., and David H. Rosenbloom. 2004. "*Adarand, Grutter,* and *Gratz*: Does Affirmative Action in Federal Employment Matter?" *Review of Public Personnel Administration* 24(2): 150–174.

Parents Involved in Community Schools v. Seattle School District. 2007. 551 U.S. 701.

Peffer, Shelly L. 2009. "Title VII and Disparate-Treatment Discrimination Versus Disparate-Impact Discrimination: The Supreme Court's Decision in *Ricci v. DeStefano.*" *Review of Public Personnel Administration* 29(4): 402–410.

Regents of the University of California v. Bakke. 1978. 438 U.S. 265.

Ricci v. DeStefano. 2009. 557 U.S. _____,online.

Riccucci, Norma M. 2002. *Managing Diversity in Public Sector Workforces.* Boulder, CO: Westview Press.

Riccucci, Norma M. 2009. "The Pursuit of Social Equity in the Federal Government: A Road Less Traveled?" *Public Administration Review* 69(3): 373–382.

Wygant v. Jackson Board of Education. 1986. 476 U.S. 267.

Endnotes

1. The rule of three requires that vacant positions be filled by the top three scorers on an exam.
2. Under Title VII of the Civil Rights Act as amended, if an exam on its face has a statistically adverse impact against, for example, African Americans or Latinos, the aggrieved group could file suit challenging its legality under Title VII. Before a court, if the employer could demonstrate that it was relying on the exam for business necessity (i.e., that it could prove the exam was job related), the burden of proof would shift back to the plaintiffs to demonstrate that another employment tool with less adverse impact could be substituted. If the employer could not demonstrate that the exam was job related, adverse or disparate impact would be found, and the employer would be prohibited from using the exam results.

3. The presence of Justice Alito on the Court can also be seen in the consolidated 2007 cases, *Parents Involved in Community Schools v. Seattle School District* and *Meredith v. Jefferson County Board of Education*, where affirmative action suffered a setback when a divided Supreme Court ruled, 5-4, that programs in Seattle and Louisville, Kentucky, seeking to maintain diversity in schools by considering race when assigning students to schools are unconstitutional. In the majority in that case were Chief Justice Roberts and Justices Alito, Kennedy, Scalia, and Thomas. In the dissent where Justices Ginsberg, Stevens, Breyer, and Souter.

DIVERSITY AND CULTURAL COMPETENCY

Norma M. Riccucci

Norma M. Riccucci is a professor at the School of Public Affairs and Administration at Rutgers University, Newark. She is the author of several books in the areas of public personnel administration and public management. She has received a number of national awards including the American Society of Public Administration's Charles H. Levine Award for excellence in teaching, research, and service. She is a fellow of the National Academy of Public Administration.

In response to the changing demography in this nation over the past few decades, the public and private sectors have worked to create more diversity in their workplaces. (Pitts and Wise, 2010). Diversity management programs were developed to ensure that organizations ran smoothly as they continued to grow more heterogeneous. These programs continue to be vital to the performance of public organizations (Choi and Rainey, 2010). More recently, there have been calls for cultural competency—a critical component of diversity management—in public as well as private sector workforces. Cultural competency, according to Bailey (2010, p. 171), requires " 'respect for, and understanding of, diverse ethnic and cultural groups, their histories, traditions, beliefs, and value systems' in the provision and delivery of services." It is an area within public personnel, and more broadly public management that has gone grossly understudied (Rice, 2010).

The purpose of this chapter is to examine the topic of cultural competency in the context of public personnel or human resources management. The chapter begins with a brief review of diversity efforts by government workforces and areas where progress is still needed. It then addresses the importance of cultural competency for governments. Given the increased diversity not only within government workplaces but in society as well, the effectiveness of governments at every level will hinge upon their ability to become more culturally astute.

DIVERSITY IN GOVERNMENT WORKFORCES

The demographics of the United States began to shift over the past few decades, leading to growth in the Asian, African American, and, particularly, Latino populations. The U.S. Census Bureau reports that non-Latino whites have been the slowest growing group in this country. As seen in Table 5.1, by 2006, the proportion of whites decreased to about 74 percent of the population, with a little over 12 percent African American, 15 percent Latino (all races), over 4 percent Asian and Pacific Islander, and close to 1 percent American Indian or Alaskan Native. By 2050, the Census Bureau predicts that not even 53 percent will be non-Latino white. The proportion of the population is projected to be

Table 5.1 U.S. Population Change, 1980 and 2006–2008 (estimates).

	1980		2006–2008		Percent Change
	Number	**Percent**	**Number**	**Percent**	
White	188,371,622	83.1	223,965,009	74.3	−8.8
African American	26,495,025	11.6	37,131,771	12.3	0.7
Latino (any race)	14,608,673	6.5	45,432,158	15.1	8.6
Asian/Pacific Islander	3,500,439	1.5	13,164,169	4.4	2.9
American Indian and Alaskan Native	1,420,400	0.6	2,419,895	0.7	0.1
Other	6,758,319	2.9	na	na	na

Note: Totals may not equal 100 due to rounding errors and overlap in Latino population (e.g., black latinos are counted as Latino).

Sources: U.S. Census Bureau, 2006–2008 American Community Survey 3-Year Estimates, http://factfinder.census.gov/servlet/IPCharIterationServlet?_ts=286976022359; http://www.census.gov/population/www/documentation/twps0056/tab01.pdf, date accessed, March 18, 2009.

16 percent African American, 23 percent Latino origin, 10 percent Asian and Pacific Islander, and about 1 percent American Indian or Alaskan Native.[1] Today, there are higher percentages of people of color in our society than ever before.

As a result of these shifts, the labor pools of these groups have risen, ultimately changing the landscape of both public and private sector workforces. Today, these groups represent a large share of government and private sector jobs. At the federal level, for example, as Table 5.2 shows, white women and people of color increased their share of civilian, nonpostal jobs between the two time periods presented. This is one indication that the federal government has had some success in promoting overall diversity of the federal workforce. As the workplace became more diverse, governments at every level began to develop and implement programs to manage diversity in their workforces. To be sure, some governments simply relabeled their affirmative action programs "diversity" or "diversity management" programs (Naff and Kellough, 2001), thus not making a serious effort to manage diversity.

At the upper, higher-paying, policy-making positions, governments have been less successful in their diversity efforts (see, e.g., Riccucci, 2009; Naff, 2001). For instance, as seen in Table 5.3, higher-level posts in the federal government—the senior executive service or SES—continue to be dominated by white males. Ensuring that white women and people of color reach the upper echelons of all government workforces continues to remain a challenge. Successful diversity management programs are key.

Aside from efforts to promote women and people of color to upper levels, diversity programs in general, must go further. For example, a number of studies have pointed to such factors as supportive leadership and training programs as potentially contributing to effective diversity management programs (see, e.g., White and Rice, 2010; Berry-James, 2010; Riccucci, 2002).[2] In addition, a component of diversity management that continues to be absent is cultural competency (see, Rice, 2010; Mathews, 2010). As public organizations strive to improve their performance and enhance their democratic accountability in an ever-changing social climate, building cultural competence is integral.

Table 5.2 Federal Civilian Employment by Race, Ethnicity and Gender, All Grades, 1984 and 2004.				
		Number Percent 1984	**Number Percent 2004**	**Percent Change**
Total Executive Branch		**2,023,373**	**1,851,349**	
	Women	809,095	822,345	
		40.2	44.4	+ 4.2
	Men	1,214,238	1,029,004	
		59.7	55.6	− 4.1
African American	Women	177,718	192,482	
		8.5	10.4	+ 1.9
	Men	140,157	120,617	
		6.7	6.5	− 0.2
Latino	Women	33,623	57,344	
		1.7	3.1	+ 1.4
	Men	61,957	78,189	
		3.1	4.2	+ 1.1
Asian or Pacific Islander	Women	20,052	41,884	
		1.0	2.3	+ 1.3
	Men	35,966	51,328	
		1.8	2.7	+ 0.9
American Indian or Alaskan Native	Women	16,493	21,314	
		0.8	1.2	+.04
	Men	16,922	17,825	
		0.9	1.0	+ 0.1
White	Women	561,209	509,321	
		27.7	27.5	− 0.2
	Men	959,236	761,045	
		46.9	41.1	− 5.8

Sources: Calculated from U.S. Office of Personnel Management, Demographic Profile of the Federal Workforce (2004 data), http://www.opm.gov/feddata/demograp/demograp.asp#RNOData, date accessed, March 11, 2008. For 1984 data, U. S. Office of Personnel Management (OPM),Central Personnel Data File (CPDF), provided by OPM.

Table 5.3	Senior Executive Service (SES) by Race, Ethnicity and Gender, 1985 and 2007.

		Number Percent 1985	Number Percent 2007	Percent change
Total SES		**6,710**	**7,473**	
	Women	514	2,141	
		7.6	30.0	+22.4
	Men	6,196	5,332	
		92.3	70.0	−22.3
African American	Women	49	251	
		0.73	3.4	+2.7
	Men	253	342	
		3.7	4.6	+0.9
Latino	Women	10	72	
		0.15	1.0	+0.9
	Men	59	206	
		0.88	2.8	+1.9
Asian or Pacific Islander	Women	5	67	
		0.07	0.9	+0.8
	Men	54	111	
		0.8	1.5	+0.7
American Indian or Alaskan Native	Women	0	30	
			0.4	+0.4
	Men	29	60	
		0.43	0.8	+0.4
White	Women	447	1,713	
		6.7	23.0	+16.3
	Men	5,788	4,597	
		86.3	62.0	−24.3
Unspecified or More than 1 Race	Women	3	8	
		0.04	0.1	+0.06
	Men	13	16	
		0.19	0.2	+0.01

Note: Totals may not equal 100 due to rounding errors.

Source: Calculated from data provided by the U.S. Office of Personnel Management (OPM).

STRIVING FOR CULTURAL COMPETENCY IN THE GOVERNMENT WORKPLACE

The health care profession has long championed the creation of culturally competent organizations and personnel. As Weech-Maldonado and colleagues point out (2002, p. 111), the main purpose here is to provide "culturally appropriate care" and ensure that it is reflected in official policies and practices. Quoting Brach and Fraser (2000, p. 183), they say that "Cultural competency has been defined as an 'ongoing commitment or institutionalization of appropriate practice and policies for diverse populations' . . . While cultural competence is the goal, diversity management is the process leading to culturally competent organizations" (Weech-Maldonado et al., 2002, p. 112).

A number of different definitions have emerged for cultural competency, but the cornerstone, as Brach and Fraser (2000, p. 183) point out, is as follows: "It includes not only possession of cultural knowledge and respect for different cultural perspectives but also having skills and being able to use them effectively in cross-cultural situations." Mathews (2010, p. 214) goes on to say that

> Culture, just like diversity, is defined as the totality of ways that shape how individuals see and respond to the world and community around them. For instance, people's personal, family, and group values, views, and culture are shaped by education, gender, income level, religious background, geographic location and residence, place of birth, age, and individual experiences. Furthermore, culture also affects views toward health, poverty, welfare, crime, and other social and human services areas.

There is also an ethical component or value to cultural competency. If public servants are to genuinely serve the needs and interests of their clients, they have an ethical obligation to effectively interact and communicate with them. In the context of care ethics, Burnier (2003, p. 533) points out that public servants work with "actual people, [who] have concrete, specific needs that. . . . must be taken into account by those responsible for their well being." She states that there is a "compelling moral salience of attending to and meeting the needs of the particular others for whom we take responsibility" (Burnier, 2003, p. 533).

In the context of human resources, building culturally competent workers at every level within the organization is essential, particularly at the street level, where face-to-face interactions between government employees and clients occur. That is, not only health care professionals, but social workers, police officers, youth and vocational counselors, juvenile justice workers, department of motor vehicle employees, and all other types of workers who come into direct contact with the public must demonstrate cultural competence in order to effectively serve them. Moreover, as public sector workforces have become more culturally diverse, the ability of supervisors, managers, and coworkers to demonstrate competencies across all cultural landscapes is critical for effective organizational performance.

CULTURAL COMPETENCY WITHIN ORGANIZATIONS

As noted, government workforces at every level have become increasingly diverse. Along with this diversity has come a need for cultural competency. In fact, early research on diversity management called for a form of cultural competency within organizations. Loden and Rosener (1991), for example, stressed the importance of cultural change within organizations so that the needs and interests of *all* workers could be met. They and others suggested that managers, supervisors, and workers themselves should be equipped with the tools necessary to interact and engage with persons from all cultural backgrounds. Worker productivity may depend upon the ability of organizations to demonstrate cultural competence. In addition, it may help to diversify the upper levels of government workforces. Organizations that accommodate the needs and interests of all workers, male and female of all races and ethnicities, and celebrate differences, rather than eschew them are more likely to value the contributions diverse groups can make at the upper levels of organizations. Indeed, this is evidenced in the plethora of research on representative bureaucracy, which illustrates that women and people of color in key posts in government will push for the needs and interests of their counterparts in the general population (see, e.g., Meier, 1993; Meier and Nicholson-Crotty, 2006; Naff and Crum, 2000).

CULTURALLY COMPETENT STREET-LEVEL WORKERS

Street-level workers or bureaucrats come into daily contact with the general citizenry. And the U.S. citizenry, particularly in such states as California, Texas, Florida, and New York with high immigrant rates, has become increasingly diverse. This is perhaps a partial explanation for health care being one of the most progressive in terms of building culturally competent personnel and more broadly institutions. In their research, Betancourt and colleagues (2005, pp. 502–503) found that "minorities . . . have difficulty getting appropriate, timely, high-quality care because of linguistic and cultural barriers. As such cultural competence aims to change a 'one size fits all' health care system to one that is more responsive to the needs of an increasingly diverse patient population." They go on to say that cultural competence helps to eradicate racial and ethnic disparities in health care.

Table 5.1 presented data on the changing demographics in this nation. Tables 5.4 and 5.5 provide data on the growth of immigrant populations in the United States, which also has implications for cultural competency in street-level work. Localities in particular offer a variety of services to both legal and illegal immigrants, including linking new immigrants to health and social services. Cultural competency training for government workers can help improve the delivery of those services.

In fact, a number of governments have embraced cultural competency, especially at the local level where clients as well as the general public are most likely to interact with street-level workers in a host of areas from social services to recreational facilities.[3] As Benavides and Hernández (2007) found in their research, effective governance hinges on responsiveness to the citizenry. They point to a number of examples, including those that require very little capital. For example, they note that in Latin American communities, it is common for a driver being pulled over for a traffic violation to step out of the vehicle and approach the police car. In Seattle, Washington, police officers, as part of cultural competency training, are taught to be cognizant of this cultural behavior and to expect it, thus helping to avoid any mishap or misunderstandings.

A number of others have reported progress that localities have made with cultural competency programs (see, e.g., McKibben, 2008; Kellar, 2005; Long, 2004). From small cities such as Woodburn, Oregon, to larger cities such as Stockton, California, local governments are developing ways to insure that the needs of their culturally diverse communities are met. Woodburn, for example, has a population of 22,000, of which over 50 percent is Latino. Russians also represent a sizable proportion of the city's population. In an effort to be more responsive to their diverse population, the city established a

Table 5.4 Foreign-Born Population by World Region of Birth, U.S. Citizenship Status, and Year of Entry (percentages; numbers in thousands).

World Region of Birth and U.S. Citizenship Status	Foreign Born	Year of Entry				
		2000–2004	1990–1999	1980–1989	1970–1979	Before 1970
Total Foreign-Born Population	34,244	6,052	11,968	7,865	4,499	3,861
Naturalized U.S. Citizen	38.3	4.6	21.4	49.7	70.8	82.7
Not a U.S. Citizen	61.7	95.4	78.6	50.3	29.2	17.3
Foreign Born from Europe	4,661					
Naturalized U.S. Citizen	54.9	8.7	30.4	63.1	70.2	86.2
Not a U.S. Citizen	45.1	91.3	69.6	36.9	29.8	13.8
Foreign Born from Asia	8,685					
Naturalized U.S. Citizen	52.4	6.9	36.3	68.9	89	91.5
Not a U.S. Citizen	47.6	93.1	63.7	31.1	11	8.5
Foreign Born From Latin America (majority are from Mexico)	18,314					
Naturalized U.S. Citizen	27.4	2.7	12.4	37.2	59.2	77.8
Not a U.S. Citizen	72.6	97.3	87.6	62.8	40.8	22.2
Foreign Born, Other (Africa, Oceania, and North America)	2,584					
Naturalized U.S. Citizen	38.8	7	23.9	57.6	69.8	76.2
Not a U.S. Citizen	61.2	93	76.1	42.4	30.2	23.8

Source: U.S. Census Bureau, Current Population Survey, Annual Social and Economic Supplement, 2004 Immigration Statistics Staff, Population Division, http://www.census.gov/population/socdemo/foreign/ppl-176/tab02-6.pdf, date accessed, March 22, 2010.

community relations officer (CRO) in 2002, who is responsible for providing oral and written translation services; ombudsman services, producing a bilingual quarterly newsletter, coordinating cultural events through local merchants, and promoting city services and activities via multiple media outlets (Hernández, Brown, and Tien, 2007).

In Stockton, California, where 37 percent of its population is Latino and 23 percent is Asian, the city has made great strides in serving its multicultural community. One example can be seen in the city's partnering with a local community organization, the Lao Khmu Association (LKA), to provide outreach services to its Southeast Asian refugee community. The program, funded by the LKA and the U.S. Department of Health and Human Services' Office of Refugee Resettlement, seeks to break down barriers between the city government and the Asian community and provide them with job skills to enhance their employability (Hernández, Brown, and Tien, 2007).

Table 5.5	Estimated Unauthorized Immigrant Population in the United States, 2000–2009 (millions).
2000	8.5
2005	10.5
2006	11.3
2007	11.8
2008	11.6
2009	10.8

Source: U.S. Department of Homeland Security, http://www.dhs.gov/xlibrary/ assets/statistics/ publications/ois_ill_pe_2009.pdf, date accessed, March 22, 2010.

Other cities have taken steps to ensure cultural competency in their police departments. Rubaii-Barrett (2009, p. 25) reports, for example, the following efforts:

The Chicago Police Department coordinates regular community forums for immigrant groups; Bellingham, Washington, uses special liaisons for ethnic groups; Delray Beach, Florida, established a Haitian Police Academy; Corcoran, California, offers a Spanish-language citizen's police academy; and police in Orange, New Jersey, and Dallas, Texas, help immigrants become citizens.

The results of a survey administered by the ICMA in 2008 to 517 local government officials are presented in Table 5.6. From this small sample, it appears that cities are making some efforts to promote cultural competency in their communities. Providing local government materials in languages other than English seems to be most prevalent, having been reported by over half of the respondents. Other efforts such as requirements for cultural competency were also reported. Future research on the pervasiveness of such efforts more broadly throughout governments at every level is certainly needed.

Table 5.6	Local Government's Efforts to Promote Cultural Competency, 2008	
Local Government Leaders Reporting that they:		
Hold/held community events to promote immigrant contributions to the community and/or celebrate community diversity		30.7%
Referred immigrants to religious and nonprofit organizations for services		39.6%
Provide/provided local government materials (print or electronic) in languages other than English		54.8%
Encouraged or required local government employees to obtain cultural competencies		29.5%

Source: International City/County Management Association, http://icma.org/upload/bc/attach/%7B2B 1FF4FF-01EA-4CDC-B9F1-52952A6BCACF%7DImmigration.pdf, date accessed, March 24, 2009.

Conclusion

The changing demographics of this nation have enriched society at any number of levels. If the diversity is to be genuinely embraced, cultural competency programs, whether part of broader diversity management efforts or as stand-alone programs, are imperative. As seen in this chapter, some governments are developing such programs, particularly those that have become more diverse over the past several decades. As we move into the second decade of the twenty-first century, local governments will be challenged to develop or strengthen existing cultural competency programs in order to fully and effectively serve their culturally diverse communities.

References

Bailey, Margo L. 2010. "Cultural Competency and the Practice of Public Administration." In Mitchell F. Rice, ed. *Diversity and Public Administration: Theory, Issues, and Perspectives*, 2nd ed. Armonk, NY: M.E. Sharpe, pp. 171–188.

Benavides, Abraham David, and Julie C. T. Hernández. 2007. "Serving Diverse Communities—Cultural Competency." *Public Management* 89(6): 14–18.

Berry-James, RaJade M. 2010. "Managing Diversity: Moving Beyond Organizational Conflict." In Mitchell F. Rice, ed. *Diversity and Public Administration: Theory, Issues, and Perspectives*, 2nd ed. Armonk, NY: M.E. Sharpe, pp. 61–80.

Betancourt, Joseph R., Alexander R. Green, J. Emilio Carriilo, and Elyse R. Park. 2005. "Cultural Competence and Health Care Disparities: Key Perspectives and Trends." *Health Affairs* 24(2): 499–505.

Brach, Cindy, and Irene Fraser. 2000. "Can Cultural Competency Reduce Racial and Ethnic Racial Health Disparities? A Review and Conceptual Model." *Medicare Care Research and Review* 57(Supplement 1): 181–217.

Burnier, DeLysa. 2003. "Other Voices/Other Rooms: Towards a Care-Centered Public Administration." *Administrative Theory & Praxis* 25(4): 529–544.

Choi, Sungjoo, and Hal G. Rainey. 2010. "Managing Diversity in U.S. Federal Agencies: Effects of Diversity and Diversity Management on Employee Perceptions of Organizational Performance." *Public Administration Review* 70(1): 109–121.

Hernández, Julie C. T., John C. Brown, and Christine C. Tien. 2007. "Serving Diverse Communities: Best Practices." *Public Management* 89(5): 12–17.

Kellar, Elizabeth. 2005. "Wanted: Language and Cultural Competence." *Public Management* 87(1): 6–9.

Loden, Marilyn, and Judy B. Rosener. 1991. *Workforce America!* Homewood, IL: Business One Irwin.

Long, Donna. 2004. "Providing Outstanding Service to Diverse Customers and Citizens." *Public Management* 86(10): 33–35.

Mathews, Audrey L. 2010. "Diversity Management and Cultural Competency." In Mitchell F. Rice, ed. *Diversity and Public Administration: Theory, Issues, and Perspectives*, 2nd ed. Armonk, NY: M.E. Sharpe, pp. 210–263.

McKibben, Carol Lynn. 2008. "Seaside is Embracing Diversity, Creating Opportunity." *Public Management* 90(7): 24–28.

Meier, Kenneth J. 1993. "Latinos and Representative Bureaucracy: Testing the Thompson and Henderson Hypotheses." *Journal of Public Administration Research and Theory* 3(4): 393–415.

Meier, Kenneth J., and Jill Nicholson-Crotty. 2006. "Gender, Representative Bureaucracy, and Law Enforcement: The Case of Sexual Assault." *Public Administration Review* 66(6): 850–860.

Naff, Katherine C. 2001. *To Look Like America: Dismantling Barriers for Women and Minorities in Government.* Boulder, CO: Westview Press.

Naff, Katherine C., and John Crum. 2000. "The President and Representative Bureaucracy: Rhetoric and Reality." *Public Administration Review* 60(2): 98–110.

Naff, Katherine C., and J. Edward Kellough. 2001. *A Changing Workforce: Understanding Diversity Programs in the Federal Government.* Washington, DC: Price Waterhouse Coopers, The Business of Government (December).

Pitts, David W., and Lois Recascino Wise. 2010. "Workforce Diversity in the New Millennium: Prospects for Research." *Review of Public Personnel Administration* 30(1): 44–69.

Riccucci, Norma M. 2002. *Managing Diversity in Public Sector Workforces.* Boulder, CO: Westview Press.

Riccucci, Norma M. 2009. "The Pursuit of Social Equity in the Federal Government: A Road Less Traveled?" *Public Administration Review* 69(3): 373–382.

Rice, Mitchell F. 2010. "Cultural Competency, Public Administration, and Public Service Delivery in an Era of Diversity." In Mitchell F. Rice, ed. *Diversity and Public Administration: Theory, Issues, and Perspectives*, 2nd ed. Armonk, NY: M.E. Sharpe, pp. 189–209.

Rubaii-Barrett, Nadia. 2009. "The Case for Immigrant Integration." *Public Management* 91(4): 22–26.

Weech-Maldonado, Robert, Janice L. Dreachslin, Kathryn H. Dansky, Gita De Souza, and Maria Gatto. 2002. "Racial/ethnic Diversity Management and Cultural Competency: The Case of Pennsylvania Hospitals." *Journal of Healthcare Management* 47(2): 111–124.

White, Harvey L., and Mitchell R. Rice. 2010. "The Multiple Dimensions of Diversity and Culture." In Mitchell F. Rice, ed. *Diversity and Public Administration: Theory, Issues, and Perspectives*, 2nd ed. Armonk, NY: M.E. Sharpe, pp. 3–23.

Endnotes

1. See, U.S. Census Bureau, http://www.census.gov/population/www/pop-profile/natproj.html, date accessed, March 18, 2010.

2. Some have called for greater efforts to examine the effects of diversity programs. See for example, Pitts and Wise (2010) and Choi and Rainey (2010).

3. At the federal level, the U.S. Defense Department has initiated some cultural competency training. However, it would seem that after 9/11, there may have been a suspension of these efforts especially where Middle Easterners are concerned, as evidenced in the U.S. government's sanctioning, under the Bush Administration, such practices as extraordinary rendition and waterboarding.

6

LESBIAN, GAY, BISEXUAL, AND TRANSGENDERED EMPLOYEES IN THE PUBLIC SECTOR WORKFORCE

Charles W. Gossett

Charles Gossett is currently dean of the College of Social Sciences and Interdisciplinary Studies at California State University, Sacramento. He is also a professor in the departments of Government and Public Policy and Administration. His recent publications have addressed legal challenges to domestic partnership laws, public opinion on same-sex marriage, and the impact of HIV/AIDS on the Botswana civil service.

If one can characterize the 1960s through the 1980s as periods in which human resource professionals were highly focused on the issues of better incorporating members of underrepresented racial groups and women into the public sector workforce, it would seem fair to say that from the 1990s till the current period, HR focus has expanded, if not shifted, to how best to recruit and make use of lesbian, gay, bisexual, and transgendered (LGBT) employees. This chapter will introduce the reader to a number of issues facing HR managers with respect to some of the unique issues involved in effectively managing LGBT members of the workforce.

TERMINOLOGY

Before proceeding, a brief word about terminology may be useful. When talking about lesbians, gay men, and bisexuals, we are identifying people on the basis of what is called *sexual orientation*. Homosexuality, bisexuality, heterosexuality, and asexuality are generally included whenever reference is made in laws to a person's sexual orientation. Early on laws tended to use the term *sexual preference* or *affectional preference*. Advocates for gay rights, however, object to the use of the word "preference" because it represents a conclusion that one's sexual orientation is a choice. Since they see the question as to the nature and origins of homosexuality, and, for that matter, of heterosexuality, as one that is still unresolved, they prefer the term "orientation," which does not imply a conscious choice.

Opponents of laws that prohibit discrimination on the basis of sexual orientation often claim that pedophilia and bestiality are also sexual orientations, and, historically, many state laws grouped homosexuality with those behaviors. However, in recent decades, and especially since 1973, when the American Psychiatric Association removed homosexuality from its list of mental disorders (Bayer, 1987), the common use of the term *sexual orientation* has not included behaviors still classified as mental or psychological disorders.

Transgendered refers to persons whose biological sex at the time of birth does not match their psychological gender identity (Califia, 1997). This group includes transsexuals (i.e., persons who have had or are preparing to have surgical alteration of their biological sex to match their gender identity or, occasionally, persons who have decided not to have surgery but rely on hormone therapies and live their lives in a manner consistent with their gender identity) and cross-dressers or transvestites (i.e., persons who choose to dress as a member of the opposite sex, either on a regular basis or only occasionally, but do not plan to surgically alter their bodies) (Currah and Minter, 2000; Garber, 1992; Green, 2000). Transgendered persons may or may not also be lesbian or gay males. If so, they face many of the same problems as other lesbians and gay men. In recent years, it has become more common to see the two following acronyms—MTF and FTM, respectively, male-to-female and female-to-male—to describe the direction of the sex reassignment, a process often referred to as "transitioning."

Unlike homosexuality, however, transgendered individuals are still considered to be suffering from a mental disorder by the medical profession. "Gender identity disorder (GID)" and "gender dysphoria" are terms with which the American Psychiatric Association characterizes the illness of those who are transgendered (American Psychiatric Association, 2000). It is important to note that, although transgenderism remains classified as a medical disorder and homosexuality is no longer classified as such, the principal legal tool for protecting people with physical or mental impairments, the Americans with Disabilities Act, specifically *excludes* use of the act to protect their rights. On the other hand, some state laws prohibiting disability discrimination, like New Jersey, have found that transgendered people are covered (*Enriquez v. West Jersey Health Systems*, 2001). Transgender activists would like to see the disease classification issue resolved in a way that would avoid classifying transgenderism as a "disease" yet still recognize it as a condition requiring certain types of medical treatment in much the same way that the condition of being pregnant requires medical care, yet it is not a disease.

HISTORICAL OVERVIEW

Although the written record of sexual relations between persons of the same sex indicates that such practices are hardly a new phenomenon, the concept of such persons as a "class" different from persons who have sexual relations with persons of the opposite sex is usually traced to the latter half of the nineteenth century. At that time, homosexual behavior moved from being a "sinful" act to being viewed as an "illness," more specifically a psychiatric abnormality (Katz, 1995). Despite the characterization of homosexuality as a disease, however, it retained an identity as a sin as evidenced by the fact that, in the United States, all states had laws that criminalized same-sex sexual relationships (Nice, 1994), though between 1960 and 2000, 34 states and the District of Columbia decriminalized such behaviors. In 2003, the U.S. Supreme Court ruled, in *Lawrence v. Texas*, that states could not criminalize private and consensual homosexual activity.

Recently, scientific investigations into biological origin for homosexuality have become prominent in discussions of whether or not sexual orientation is a personal characteristic more appropriately compared to race, ethnicity, or gender or whether comparison to some voluntary behaviors like religious choice is more suitable. The very fact that the term "sexual orientation" has replaced "sexual preference" in the discussion of this topic suggests that the arguments in favor of at least a partial biological explanation have gained fairly wide acceptance (Burr, 1993; Hamer and Copeland, 1994; LeVay, 1993). This brief discussion of how homosexuality has been conceptualized is important because, as in all policy matters, how the "problem" is stated has great influence on how "solutions" are developed.

Until recently, governments at all levels exhibited hostility toward employing lesbians and gay men. Purging gay men and lesbians from federal and state civil services in the 1950s and beyond, along with dismissing homosexuals from military service, which continues to this day, have meant that public sector employers never devoted any resources to thinking about how to recruit and incorporate members of this minority group into the workforce. (For histories of gay people in civil and military service (see Johnson, 2004; Lewis, 1997; Katz, 1992, pp. 91–105; Shilts, 1993; Berube, 1990; Meyer, 1996; Dyer, 1990; Wolinsky and Sherrill, 1993; Gossett, 2006).)

FEDERAL GOVERNMENT

As the social climate changed, particularly in the period following the historic 1969 Stonewall rebellion, which is often cited as the beginning of the current press for equal rights for lesbians and gay men (Duberman, 1993), the former Civil Service Commission (CSC) began to modify its official policies in response to both court decisions and political pressure. In the mid-1970s, the CSC advised agencies that "merely" because a person is a homosexual, absent a showing that conduct affects ability to perform the job, there were insufficient grounds for a finding of "unsuitability." In 1980, the first Director of the Office of Personnel Management, Alan Campbell, reemphasizing the importance of a nexus between off-duty behavior and job performance, issued a memorandum that stated, "applicants and employees are to be protected against inquiries into, or actions based upon, non-job-related conduct, such as religious, community or social affiliations, or sexual orientation" (Lewis, 1997). This policy was also consistent with language in the 1978 Civil Service Reform Act that outlined "merit principles" that required selections to be made "solely on the basis of relative ability, knowledge, and skills" and that employee retention should be based only on "the adequacy of their performance" (P.L. 95-454, §2301(b)(1) and (6), 1978). Despite a change in administration, this policy remained in effect throughout the 1980s. In 1998, President Clinton amended the executive branch's equal employment policy statement originally issued in 1969, Executive Order 11478, by adding the words "sexual orientation" to the list of categories protected from discrimination in federal civilian agencies (Executive Order 13087). Presidents George W. Bush and Barack Obama continued to leave the executive order in effect during their terms.

In 1995, a bill known as the Employment Non-Discrimination Act (ENDA) was introduced into the U.S. Congress. Beginning in 1974, congressional supporters of equal rights for gay men and lesbians had simply tried to amend the Civil Rights Act of 1964 to prohibit discrimination on the basis of sexual orientation. Gay activists changed strategies with the election of Bill Clinton and decided to focus exclusively on the issue of employment discrimination and developed ENDA as the legislative tool for doing so

(Feldblum, 2000). The bill was reintroduced in each subsequent Congress with more sponsors each time—46 Senators and 203 representatives in May 2010. This bill would prohibit employment discrimination in the public and private sectors on the basis of sexual orientation in a manner similar to, but more restricted than, the way such discrimination is prohibited by the Civil Rights Acts of 1964 and 1991.

In the most recent controversies concerning ENDA, pressure has been brought to bear on those gay rights advocacy organizations lobbying most heavily for the law to include the phrase "gender identity" along with "sexual orientation" when talking about the bases for prohibiting discrimination against transgendered persons. The 2010 version of the bill does include protection on the basis of gender identity and language that requires employers to allow employees who have transitioned or are transitioning under medical supervision to dress in a manner appropriate to the "new" sexual identity.

The other major debate over federal employment and sexual orientation has concerned the military (D'Amico, 2000). Traditionally, homosexuality was a prohibition to military service. In 1993, President Clinton proposed repealing that prohibition, but a majority of Congress opposed the move and adopted a policy known as "Don't Ask, Don't Tell," which, theoretically, allowed gay men and lesbians to serve in the armed forces provided their sexual orientation never became known to their comrades or superior officers.

STATE AND LOCAL GOVERNMENT

Although no legal protections against discrimination based on sexual orientation have been enacted at the federal level, 140 local governments had passed laws or adopted personnel policies covering public employees by 1994 (Riccucci and Gossett, 1996, and over 200 local jurisdictions had such policies in place by 2005 (Cahill, 2005). Additionally, over 100 local governments prohibited discrimination on the basis of gender identity (NGLTF, 2008). By 2009, 21 states and the District of Columbia had sexual orientation antidiscrimination laws, of which 13 states and D.C. also prohibited discrimination on the basis of gender identity (NGLTF, 2008).

IMPLICATIONS OF NONDISCRIMINATION LAWS FOR PERSONNEL FUNCTIONS

If a jurisdiction adopts a law that prohibits discrimination on the basis of sexual orientation and/or gender identity, there are a number of corollary issues that must be faced by personnel administrators. These include issues involving recruitment, selection, and affirmative action; discrimination complaints; terminations; sexual harassment; diversity training; compensation and employee benefits; and several miscellaneous related tasks.

RECRUITMENT, SELECTION, AND AFFIRMATIVE ACTION

For many people, two of the most important contributions to personnel management coming out of the movements for civil rights for African Americans and women have been the focus on (1) expanding the variety of sources from which job applicants are recruited and (2) improving personnel selection methods by insisting that jobs be carefully defined and that the methods for selecting people be validly related to identifying the necessary skills for each job. Expanded outreach helps organizations attract previously underutilized or overlooked talent, while better selection tools are supposed to weed out "irrelevant" considerations such as race or sex or religion in determining whether or not a person was qualified for a particular job. In jurisdictions that prohibit sexual orientation and/or gender identity discrimination, those characteristics are also to be treated as irrelevant.

Because the sexual orientation of a job applicant or an employee is not usually apparent, most lesbians and gay men do not face the blatant discrimination faced historically and currently by persons of color and women. This is particularly true withrespect to recruitment and access to job information since sexual orientation is a characteristic that overlays other demographic (and legally protected) characteristics such as race, ethnicity, sex, and religion. To the extent that information and recruitment activities are targeted toward one of those groups, many lesbians and gay men will receive the information as well. However, organizations that have historically discriminated against lesbians and gay men may find that positive, specifically targeted, recruitment efforts are necessary to overcome reluctance to working for previously hostile organizations. Thus, police departments in some cities have set up recruitment booths at lesbian and gay festival sites or established community liaisons to overcome negative perceptions earned after years of antigay harassment (Belkin and McNichol, 2002).

There are, however, two specific situations in which discrimination against homosexuals may occur at the selection stage. First, popular stereotypes often associate certain physical and behavioral characteristics with homosexuality, for example, men who exhibit mannerisms society views as feminine and women considered too masculine. Such persons may or may not be a homosexual, but they are much more likely to face discrimination based on perceived sexual orientation than lesbians and gay men who exhibit socially defined gender-appropriate behaviors. This is also a major area of concern for transgendered employees who may be in the process of transitioning or who, even after transitioning, retain certain physical markers of their former gender that make it more or less obvious to an interviewing official that the job candidate's gender presentation is not the same as their biological sex at birth. The principle identifying gender stereotyping as a basis for employment decisions as illegal discrimination was first established in *Price Waterhouse v. Hopkins* (1989). This argument has successfully applied to a transgendered employee in the case of *Smith v. City of Salem* (2004). The second exception is for applicants who make known to potential employers their sexual orientation or their intention to transition from one gender to the other. Application forms provide a number of opportunities for people to reveal their sexual orientation. Perhaps the most obvious is when application forms ask about organizational member-ships. Required listings of organizational memberships have been used by public employers to screen out certain job applicants (*Shelton v. Tucker*, 1960). Failure to list a particular organizational membership became grounds for dismissal on the basis of having submitted a fraudulent application. This catch-22 scenario has been replicated with respect to the hiring of lesbians and gay men (*Acanfora v. Board of Education of Montgomery County*, 1974), although in the absence of a nondiscrimination law this may be legal. Lesbian and gay male employees may also reveal their sexual orientation informally, though not inadvertently, in the course of an interview (McNaught, 1993; Woods, 1993).

For transgendered job applicants, the question on many application forms asking a person to identify his or her sex may pose a dilemma as to whether the response should be the biological sex at birth or the sex appropriate to one's gender identity. Also, applications for positions requiring background checks ask a person to list all the names ever used, and a combination of both male and female names is likely to raise questions (Chapman, 2008). In at least one case, an FTM transitioning job applicant was selected for a position after passing a background check and drug screening, only to be told later that the offer was withdrawn on the basis of the applicant "misrepresenting" herself as a woman when she was, in their opinion, a man (Lambda Legal, 2008). That a person's driver's license or birth certificate may also be inconsistent with the job applicant's gender identity poses yet an additional hurdle. The Library of Congress was found guilty of violating Title VII of the 1964 Civil Rights Act by discriminating on the basis of gender when they withdrew an offer of employment to an applicant who informed them before the first day on the job of an intention to transition from male to female (*Schroer v. Billington*, 2008).

Another feature of the application form relevant here is the marital status box. Marriage is both a legal and a religious ceremony, and, until 2004, no American jurisdictions legally recognized marriages between two people of the same sex.[1] However, some religious denominations do perform unions between same-sex partners (Sherman, 1992; Sullivan, 1997). In any event, a person who *considers* himself or herself married to someone of the same sex may very well choose to indicate that by checking the "Married" box on an application form as the most honest representation of his or her relationship status (*Shahar v. Bowers*, 1993). The issue of affirmative action in the context of sexual orientation is somewhat more complex than it is in the case of race or gender. First, there is no reliable statistical way to determine whether or not lesbians and gay men are proportionally represented, overrepresented, or underrepresented in a particular type or level of a government job. This is not surprising given that there continues be a dispute over what proportions of the total population should be classified as homosexual, bisexual, and heterosexual (Singer and Deschamps, 1994). And while there have been very few people calling for affirmative action programs similar to those in place for historically underrepresented groups, there have been regular calls by activists for the appointment of "openly gay" officials at the highest levels of each political jurisdiction. Organizations like the Victory Fund have major recruiting efforts underway to identify openly gay and lesbian candidates for presidential appointments, and many state and local organizations refer people for public sector jobs to political office holders they have supported (O'Bryan, 2010). Similarly, the number of transgendered persons in the United States is unknown, and such information is not collected by any government agencies. Thus, while public employers who wish to specifically recruit the transgendered will find organizations that can help them reach such people, there is little concern about developing affirmative action programs. President Obama appointed the first openly transgendered woman to a position in the Commerce Department at the beginning of 2010 (Keen, 2010).

DISCRIMINATION COMPLAINTS

For most employees, bringing a complaint of discrimination to the attention of the appropriate authorities is not easy. Such a complaint formalizes a conflict by bringing in a third party, often from the personnel department in the form of an employee relations specialist or an equal employment opportunity officer. Employees who believe they are being treated in a discriminatory manner because of their race, gender, age, or disability must reach a point where the personal psychic and physical costs of the discriminatory behavior outweigh the costs of the tension in the work environment that are likely to result from filing a formal complaint. But for many lesbian and gay male employees, particularly those who have not discussed their sexual orientation in the workplace but receive discriminatory treatment based on people's perceptions that they are gay, the decision also involves making a public record of their sexual orientation. This is an additional cost not usually borne by people for whom the discriminatory treatment is based on a visible characteristic such as skin color or gender. As a consequence, it was not surprising that in the early years in jurisdictions with sexual orientation nondiscrimination laws, the use of such protective provisions was relatively low (Button, Rienzo, and Wald, 1997; Riccucci and Gossett, 1996). A more recent study, however, suggests that sexual orientation discrimination complaints are filed in roughly the same relative proportions as complaints about gender and race discrimination (Ramos, Badgett, and Sears, 2008).

Determining what constitutes discrimination against the transgendered is not always easy, and it often comes down to some rather mundane issues of office policy. If there is a dress code, are transgendered persons required to dress in accordance with their biological sex or gender identity? Which toilet facilities should a transgendered person use? Are there positions with bona fide occupational qualifications related to gender (e.g., a prison guard who conducts body searches), and how do those apply to transgendered employees? And if the employer makes a decision that is different from the decision the transgendered person would like to have made, is it discrimination? (Harris and Minter, 2002).

In the past few decades, as noted earlier, the courts have been forcing public employers to demonstrate how any particular off-duty behavior has an impact on the job performance of an individual employee before using that off-duty behavior as justification for a termination of employment. At the federal level, *Norton v. Macy* (1969) was the first case involving homosexual activity to apply this standard in a way that overturned the agency's decision to terminate. Although this standard is now fairly well entrenched, application of the standard does not automatically lead to a finding of no relationship between sexual orientation (or a related aspect, such as a declaration of sexual orientation) and the requirements of a particular job. Several cases, for example, *Singer v. United States Civil Service Commission* (1976), and *Shahar v. Bowers* (1995), have found that an individual could be denied a job because of some factor closely related to his or her sexual orientation. With the decision in the *Lawrence v. Texas* case, however, it is much less likely to find the courts upholding the denials or terminations of employment.

SEXUAL HARASSMENT

The distinction that courts make between *quid pro quo* sexual harassment and harassment created by a "hostile environment" is proving to be particularly important to lesbians and gay men as the federal courts develop case law in this area. In *Oncale v. Sundowner Offshore Services* (1998), the U.S. Supreme Court unanimously found that Title VII of the Civil Rights Acts of 1964 and 1991 included protection against being sexually harassed by a person of the same sex. Previously, lower courts had been divided with some saying same-sex sexual harassment was not covered, some saying it was only covered if the harasser were a homosexual, and others saying that the issue was the sexual nature of the harassment regardless of the orientation of the harasser (Paetzold, 1999; Turner, 2000).

Even though the Supreme Court has made clear that same-sex sexual harassment is possible, federal courts have been equally clear that the discrimination must be on the basis of sex and not the sexual orientation of the victim (Zalesne, 2001). Specific claims of sexual orientation discrimination in the U.S. Postal Service were rejected by the U.S.

Court of Appeals (*Simonton v. Runyon*, 2000). Applying the principle from *Price Waterhouse*, however, a different U.S. Court of Appeals has found that sex stereotyping of male appearances and behaviors may have led to the sexual harassment of a summer youth employee (he wore an earring) in a municipal public works program (*Doe v. City of Belleville*, 1997). On the other hand, establishing that the person accused of sexually harassing someone of the same sex was a homosexual could be used to support a charge of sexual harassment (Zalesne, 2001).

In what many consider a rather bizarre twist, federal courts have created what amounts to a "bisexual safe harbor," when the person accused of harassment sexually harasses men and women equally, or, in the words of the court, the victims are subject to an "equal opportunity harasser" (*Holman v. Indiana*, 2000). The reasoning is that because both sexes suffer ill-treatment, there is no discrimination against one sex or the other, hence no violation of Title VII. It should be noted, however, that discrimination *against* an employee because of his or her bisexuality is not prohibited by Title VII (Colker, 1993).

Some state and local governments prohibit discrimination in employment based on sexual orientation and gender identity. However, state courts are making different decisions because if sexual orientation or gender identity discrimination is prohibited and if creation of a hostile environment is a form of discrimination, then an antigay or antitransgendered hostile environment would not be defensible (*Murray v. Oceanside Unified School District*, 2000). Similarly, New York state courts interpret the term "sex" more broadly than the federal courts do and found that transgendered employees who are harassed are protected by state nondiscrimination laws, even when they don't specifically mention gender identity (*Maffei v. Kolaeton Industry*, 1995).

COMPENSATION AND EMPLOYEE BENEFITS

Government entities, like private businesses, are governed by the Equal Pay Act of 1963. Lesbians, gay men, bisexuals, and the transgendered are not paid different wages or salaries based specifically on their sexual orientation or gender identity, though there is some evidence that earnings of gay men are somewhat lower than comparable heterosexual men in society at large (Badgett, 1995) and that lesbians earn more than straight women (Black et al., 2003). Of more immediate relevance, however, is the fact that the concept of "compensation" has, in recent years, been broadened beyond the idea of base pay and take-home pay to an idea called "total compensation" (McCaffery, 1992). Total compensation attempts to recognize that the value an employee receives from his or her employer in exchange for work include not just wages and salary, but a variety of monetary and nonmonetary benefits as well. While 30 or 40 years ago, such benefits made up a relatively small proportion of total payroll expenses, by the 1980s, such benefits comprised up to 40 percent of payroll costs (Gossett, 1994). Unlike actual wages and salaries, however, many employers distribute benefits of different value to different types of employees. The most common distinction made, which results in differential benefit treatment, is between married and unmarried employees. While technically this is a distinction between single and married employees, the fact that gay male and lesbian employees are prohibited in most states from marrying a same-sex partner makes this an issue of particular concern. Differences in treatment can be seen in a wide variety of benefits including sick leave, bereavement leave, life insurance, health insurance, disability compensation, and retirement benefits.

Leave benefits are important because they usually include allowances for an employee to take leave to care for an ill family member or attend the funeral of a deceased family member. "Family member," however, is usually defined as a blood relative or someone related by marriage. Even when lesbian and gay male employees are willing to make known that they are in a relationship with someone of the same sex, existing rules may not enable an employee to take leave to care for or grieve for such partners (or the children or the parents of such partners). Employee life insurance programs often permit employees to purchase additional coverage on the lives of their spouses and children. Disability (or workers') compensation in some jurisdictions provides different levels of benefits for employees with a spouse and/or dependent children than it provides for "single" employees. And pension programs, particularly defined benefit programs, usually include an option for an employee to elect a reduced annuity in order to provide a survivor's annuity for his or her spouse or minor children, another benefit denied to unmarried employees except in unusual circumstances (District of Columbia, 1990).[2]

For gay male and lesbian activists, equal access to health benefits for the same-sex partners of homosexual employees is sought once legal protection against employment discrimination has been obtained. In the United States, access to health insurance for adults is, for all practical purposes, tied to employment. Most government employers offer their permanent employees the opportunity to purchase subsidized health insurance for themselves and for certain members of their family, namely their legal spouse and their own children and any children of their spouse. Given that employers may subsidize family health benefit plans at a higher dollar value (even if it is at the same percentage rate of the premium cost) than the subsidy given to single employees, an argument can be made that single and married employees are receiving unequal pay for equal work. More common, however, are complaints that the partners of heterosexual employees are being treated differently from the partners of homosexual employees. Technically, however, courts and human relations commissions that receive such complaints usually rule that the distinction made is not on the basis of sexual orientation but on the basis of marital status. That is, the difference in treatment is not because the employee is homosexual, but because he or she is not legally married to his or her partner; the fact that the law prevents the partners from marrying is not a concern of the employer (Riccucci and Gossett, 1996). An exception to this trend occurred in Oregon where state courts found that the denial of health benefit coverage for the domestic partners of gay men and lesbian state employees violated the state constitution's guarantee of equal treatment of all citizens (*Tanner v. Oregon Health Sciences University*, 1998). In addition to seeking redress through the legal system, lesbians and gay men have also used the political process to secure such benefits. In many local governments (municipalities, counties, school boards, and special districts), laws have been passed, collective bargaining agreements negotiated, or executive orders issued that provide for access to health benefits and various leave benefits by employees with same-sex partners on the same or similar terms available to employees who have opposite-sex partners (Gossett, 1994). These programs are usually referred to as "domestic partnership" benefit programs. Opposition to such programs often turns on the fear of significant increases in costs to the employer, although, in practice, cost increases have been very limited (Badgett, 2000; Hostetler and Pynes, 1995).

Though most of the jurisdictions adopting the domestic partnership benefit programs treat unmarried opposite-sex partnerships the same way they treat same-sex partnerships, a few have proposed limiting access to benefits only to same-sex partners on the theory that opposite-sex partners have the option of marriage while same-sex partners do not. Private corporations that offer domestic partnership benefits to their employees often limit such benefits to only same-sex couples. While there is some logic in this latter position, a public entity that adopts it is open to criticism as discriminating against heterosexuals and creating "special rights" for homosexuals alone. Of course, this argument can be countered by saying that this different treatment is only offered because civil marriage is a "special right" only available to opposite-sex partners (Donovan, 1998; Horne, 1994).

In recent developments, following the decision to allow same-sex marriages in Massachusetts, Vermont, New Hampshire, Connecticut, Iowa, and the District of Columbia, employers in those states are wrestling with the question of whether or not to continue providing benefits to domestic partners who choose not to marry or to require that any couple, opposite sex or same sex, must be married in order to receive benefits. While a decision to condition benefits solely on marriage may seem reasonable in these circumstances, others have pointed out that the decision to marry may not be practical for all same-sex couples since a variety of federal laws and rules might disadvantage them in a way that heterosexual couples are not disadvantaged. Also, not all employees in an organization necessarily live in a state that allows same-sex couples to marry (Blanton, 2004).

At the federal level there has been activity on the issue of benefits for the domestic partners of employees involving all three branches of government. In the last several sessions of Congress, a bill has been introduced to extend various benefits, but especially health benefits, to the same-sex partners of federal workers. While there have been hearings on the bill, passage has not been secured. A major concern is whether or not granting such benefits would run afoul of the Defense of Marriage Act of 1996, which prohibits the federal government from recognizing same-sex marriages (Ginsberg, 2010). In 2010, President Obama issued a memorandum that authorized a number of benefits (e.g., sick leave, access to family medical leave for partner care, and long-term care insurance, but not basic health benefits) for the same-sex partners, but not opposite-sex unmarried partners, of federal employees (Berry, 2010; Obama, 2009; Shoop, 2010). And the federal courts are addressing this issue from two different directions. First, advocates have filed suit on behalf of same-sex legally married citizens of Massachusetts who work for the federal government and are denied access to federal employee family benefit programs (specifically, health benefits), though that case is in its early stages. This is a direct challenge to the Defense of Marriage Act claiming that the failure of the national government to recognize as legally married couples that the state of Massachusetts says are, in fact, married is a violation of the equal protection clause of the U.S. Constitution (Seelye, 2010). In a different manner, two federal courts in California have made internal administrative rulings that court system employees who are in legal same-sex marriages (including those that took place in California between May and November of 2008) *must* be provided access to health benefit coverage for their spouses and dependents. The U.S. Office of Personnel Management (OPM) refused to obey the court's instruction to enroll the same-sex spouse, arguing the agency could not act while the Defense of Marriage Act was valid; the employee has now filed suit in the federal courts seeking to force OPM to obey administrative orders of the federal judges (Roth, 2010).

There is one benefits issue that is of special concern to transgendered employees. Such employees often have extensive and expensive medical needs as a result of their transgendered status, and many employer-sponsored health plans exclude coverage for the specific psychological, medical, surgical, and prescription services needed. San

Francisco gained a great deal of attention when, in 2001, in response to a recommendation of its Human Rights Commission, it specifically incorporated into its health plan the medical benefits needed by transgendered employees (Gordon, 2001; San Francisco Human Rights Commission, 2006).

DIVERSITY TRAINING

In recognition of the changing composition of the American workforce, a number of employers, public as well as private, have begun to focus on ways of utilizing workforce diversity to facilitate achievement of the organization's goals. "Diversity training" is one approach that employers take to teach workers and supervisors to deal with cultural and value differences among their coworkers and subordinates. Such training hopes to eliminate dysfunctional friction at the worksite and to train supervisors to recognize, avoid, or properly handle discriminatory treatment so as to minimize legal actions against the employer. Sexual orientation and gender identity, however, were topics ignored in many discussions of diversity until recently (Caudron, 1995; Cox, 1993).

In organizations governed by laws or policies that prohibit discrimination on the basis of sexual orientation and/or gender identity, inclusion of these issues in diversity training courses flows naturally from the official policy. This does not mean, however, that sexual orientation or gender identity will be a particularly comfortable or easy topic to address in such training. When there is no protection against discrimination, handling these issues can be quite explosive and even threatening, given that self-revelation by lesbians, gay men, bisexuals, or the transgendered may lead to dismissal or harassment. Some employees feel that diversity training "promotes" a point of view that infringes on their rights to personal religious beliefs intolerant of homosexuality (Kaplan, 2006). On the other hand, avoiding the topic may defeat the purpose of much diversity training, which is aimed at making people tolerant and understanding of important differences among coworkers, which, in turn, builds trust and facilitates the work of the organization (McNaught, 1993; Winfeld and Spielman, 1995; Zuckerman and Simons, 1996).

OTHER ISSUES

Personnel offices are frequently assigned responsibility for addressing a variety of other workplace-related issues in addition to the core personnel functions. Many of these tasks can be grouped under the very broad heading "Quality of Work Life" (QWL). The presence of lesbian, gay male, bisexual, and transgendered employees in the workforce is not often addressed in the existing QWL literature, but personnel officials who wish to ensure inclusive work environments need to be aware of how certain actions affect nonheterosexual employees.

Lesbians and gay men are often accused of "flaunting" their sexuality whenever it becomes known to other workers; they have violated the presumption of hetero-sexuality (sometimes called "heteronormativity") that pervades most organizations. Whether the employee simply made a statement about his or her sexual orientation, discussed his or her social activities over the weekend, displayed a picture of his or her family on the desk, or appeared at an office function with the person he or she lives with, some employees are offended and find such behavior inappropriate in a work setting. Yet, if any of these situations had involved a heterosexual employee, little notice would have been taken. If the organization is committed to equal treatment regardless of sexual orientation, managers and their advisers in the personnel office must be able to distinguish *unacceptable* behavior from *unexpected* behavior. Standards concerning appropriate levels of discussion or knowledge about an individual's life outside the office need to be consistent, although, of course, every employee is entitled to determine the amount of personal information shared for himself or herself.

"Celebrating diversity" is somewhat a recent addition to the responsibilities of the personnel office and is considered part of maintaining organizational morale. In the public sector, events such as Black History Month may be even more important than in the private sector because they also reinforce the idea that the government is there to serve all of the people. For several years, October 11 has been celebrated as "Coming Out Day" when lesbians, gay men, and bisexual people are encouraged to identify themselves in some way to their families, friends, and coworkers (http://www.hrc.org/ncod/). Late June is traditionally the time for Gay Pride celebrations. Again, to the extent that personnel offices are responsible for making all employees feel that the organization respects and values the contributions any group makes, they must be knowledgeable about events and times of the year that have special meaning to each particular group.

Employee recognition is often an important part of an organization's traditions. Annual award dinners, employee appreciation picnics and parties, holiday parties, and other similar activities frequently fall to the personnel office to organize. Many times these events are designed to include family members in appreciation of the important role that family life plays in support of the productivity of each worker. Invitations to "husbands" and "wives" are likely viewed as limited to only legally married partners of employees; more inclusive invitations to "your guest" or "your partner" will indicate that the partners and family members of lesbian and gay male employees are welcome. One can also imagine that the retirement of a long-time employee who, in the course of employment, transitioned from one sex to the other might require that the employee be consulted about the best way to construct the review of their career in any speeches or video presentations or the use of old photographs.

Occupational safety and health is another responsibility often assigned to the personnel office. Although there are no occupational injuries or diseases that are unique to lesbian and gay male employees, the public association of acquired immunodeficiency syndrome (AIDS) with gay men has created a volatile workplace issue that must be addressed by personnel officers.

A related, but important, health issue for transgendered employees concerns access to proper toilet facilities while on the job. This is one of the first issues raised by coworkers of a transgendered person and one of the most emotionally charged ones that managers have to resolve immediately in order to prevent unnecessary disruptions in the workplace. Most transgendered employees would prefer to use the restroom facilities consistent with their gender identity, but nontransgendered employees are often extremely uncomfortable in such situations (*Goins v. West Group*, 2001; Smith, 2003). Some employers have resolved this dilemma by designating at least one facility as a "unisex" facility, a practice that is not uncommon in very small offices even when there are no transgendered employees. Many organizations have antinepotism provisions in their personnel policies, and the question of how these policies apply to lesbian and gay male partners who work for the same organization presents a quandary. In organizations that provide for the registration of domestic partners and treat such partnerships in a manner similar to the way marital partnerships are treated with respect to employee benefits, for example, application of antinepotism rules to homosexual partners would be appropriate. But if the organization does not recognize such partnerships in any other way, "legitimizing" the relationship through the application of antinepotism rules would undercut the rationale for not recognizing the partners for other purposes.

Conclusion

Public sector organizations have three options available for addressing issues pertaining to lesbians, gay men, bisexuals, and the transgendered who currently, or may potentially, work for them. Historically, government agencies actively sought to identify and remove such employees. A second option is to simply ignore the fact that the organization has nonheterosexual and transgendered employees and omit these issues from personnel policies or practices. This probably describes the current situation in many, albeit a decreasing number of, public sector organizations. Finally, governments can choose to recognize, appreciate, and attempt to find advantages in the diversity of sexual orientations and gender identities to be found in its workforce. A small, but increasing, proportion of the 83,000 governmental units found in the United States have chosen this strategy. Every year, more states, cities, and counties have adopted this approach. The National Gay and Lesbian Task Force estimated that nearly 52 percent of all Americans lived or worked in a jurisdiction that prohibited discrimination on the basis of sexual orientation (NGLTF, 2007) and that almost 40 percent of the population was covered by laws prohibiting gender identity discrimination (NGLTF, 2008).

Regardless of which strategy any particular organization currently applies to the issue of sexual orientation and the workplace, the pressures for a policy change will confront every public sector organization in the next few years. Whether it is to remove a policy of automatic exclusion of homosexuals as in the military, or provide the protection of a nondiscrimination law, or treat domestic partnerships in the same way that marriages are treated for employee benefits, or make health benefit plans inclusive of the services needed by transgendered employees, the demands for change are unlikely to subside.

References

Acanfora v. Board of Education of Montgomery County. 1974. 491 F. 2d 498.

American Psychiatric Association. 2000. *Diagnostic and Statistical Manual of Mental Disorders*, 4th ed. Washington, D.C.: Task Force.

Badgett, M. V. Lee. 1995. "The Wage Effects of Sexual Orientation Discrimination." *Industrial & Labor Relations Review* 48(4): 726–739.

———. 2000. "Calculating Costs with Credibility: Health Care Benefits for Domestic Partners." *Angles: Journal of the Institute for Gay and Lesbian Strategic Studies* 5(1):1–8. http://www.iglss.org/media/files/Angles_51.pdf

Bayer, Ronald. 1987. *Homosexuality and American Psychiatry: The Politics of Diagnosis.* Princeton, NJ: Princeton University Press.

Belkin, Aaron, and Jason McNichol. 2002. "Pink and Blue: Outcomes Associated with the Integration of Open Gay and Lesbian Personnel in the San Diego Police Department." *Police Quarterly* 5(1): 63–95.

Berry, J. 2010, June 2. "Implementation of the President's Memorandum Regarding Extension of Benefits to Same-Sex Domestic Partners of Federal Employees." http://www.chcoc.gov/transmittals/TransmittalDetails.aspx?TransmittalID=2982 (accessed June 2, 2010).

Berube, Allan. 1990. *Coming Out Under Fire: The History of Gay Men and Women in World War Two*. New York: Penguin Books.

Black, Dan A., Hoda R. Makar, Seth G. Sanders, and Lowell J. Taylor. 2003. "The Earnings Effects of Sexual Orientation." *Industrial and Labor Relations Review* 56(3): 449–469.

Blanton, Kimberly. 2004, August 22. "Benefits for Domestic Partners Maintained." *Boston Globe*.

Burr, Chandler. 1993, March. "Homosexuality and Biology." *The Atlantic Monthly*, pp. 47–65.

Button, James W., Barbara A. Rienzo, and Kenneth D. Wald. 1997. *Private Lives, Public Choices: Battles over Gay Rights in American Communities*. Washington, D.C.: Congressional Quarterly Press.

Cahill, Sean. 2005. *The Glass Nearly Half Full*. Washington, D.C.: The National Gay and Lesbian Task Force Policy Institute. http://www.thetaskforce.org/downloads/GlassHalfFull.pdf

Califia, Pat. 1997. *Sex Changes: The Politics of Transgenderism*. San Francisco, CA: Cleis Press.

Caudron, Shari. 1995, August. "Open the Corporate Closet to Sexual Orientation Issues." *Personnel Journal* 74: 42–55.

Chapman, M. 2008, April 24. "How Do You Interview Transgendered Job Applicants?" *Business Management Daily*. http://www.businessmanagementdaily.com/articles/15943/1/How-do-you-interview-transgender-job-applicants/Page1.html# (accessed June 3, 2010).

Chibbaro, Jr., Lou. 1993, September 17. "Sodomy Law Repealed." *The Washington Blade* [Washington, D.C.], p. 1.+

———. 1995, August 4. "Clinton: Being Gay Is 'Not a Security Risk.' " *The Washington Blade* [Washington, D.C.], p. 1+.

Colker, Ruth. 1993. "A Bisexual Jurisprudence." *Law & Sexuality* 3: 127–137.

Cox, Jr., Taylor. 1993. *Cultural Diversity in Organizations: Theory, Research & Practice*. San Francisco, CA: Barrett-Koehler Publishers.

Currah, Paisley, and Shannon Minter. 2000. *Transgender Equality*. Washington, D.C.: National Gay and Lesbian Task Force. http://www.thetaskforce.org/

D'Amico, Francine. 2000. "Sex/uality and Military Service." In Craig A. Rimmerman, Kenneth D. Wald, and Clyde Wilcox, eds. *The Politics of Gay Rights*. Chicago, IL: University of Chicago Press.

Doe v. City of Belleville. 1997. 119 F. 3d 563; 1997 U.S. App. LEXIS 17940.

Donovan, James M. 1998. "An Ethical Argument to Restrict Domestic Partnerships to Same-Sex Couples." *Law & Sexuality* 8: 649–670.

Duberman, Martin. 1993. *Stonewall*. New York: Dutton.

Dyer, Kate, ed. 1990. *Gays in Uniform: The Pentagon's Secret Reports*. Boston, MA: Alyson Publications.

Enriquez v. West Jersey Health Systems. 2001. 342 N.J. Super. 501; 777 A.2d 365; 2001 N.J. Super. LEXIS 283.

Feldblum, Chai. 2000. "The Federal Gay Rights Bill: From Bella to ENDA." In John D'Emilio, William B. Turner, and Urvashi Vaid, eds. *Creating Change: Sexuality, Public Policy and Civil Rights*. New York: St. Martin's Press.

Garber, Marjorie. 1992. *Vested Interests: Cross-Dressing and Cultural Anxiety*. New York: HarperPerennial.

Ginsberg, W. R. 2010. *Federal Employee Benefits and Same-Sex Partnerships*. Report No. 41030. Washington, D.C.: Congressional Research Service. http://assets.opencrs.com/rpts/R41030_20100121.pdf (accessed June 5, 2010).

Goins v. West Group. 2001. 635 N.W.2d 717; 2001 Minn. LEXIS 789.

Gordon, Rachel. 2001, May 1. "S.F. to Finance Staff Sex Changes." *San Francisco Chronicle*, p. A1.

Gossett, Charles W. 1994, Winter. "Domestic Partnership Benefits: Public Sector Patterns." *Review of Public Personnel Administration* 14: 64–84.

———. 2006. "Lesbians and Gay Men in the Public Sector Workforce." In Norma M. Riccucci, ed. *Public Personnel Management: Current Concerns, Future Challenges*, 4th ed. New York: Longman.

Green, Jamison. 2000. "Introduction to Transgender Issues." In Paisley Currah and Shannon Minter, eds. *Transgender Equality*. New York: National Gay and Lesbian Task Force.

Hamer, Dean, and Peter Copeland. 1994, July 11. *The Science of Desire*. New York: Simon & Schuster.

Harris, Sheryl I., and Shannon Minter. 2002, July 11. "Employment Rights for Transgendered People." *Bay Area Reporter*. http://www.las-elc.org/arch-020711-transgender.html

Holman v. Indiana. 2000. 211 F. 3d 399; U.S. App. LEXIS 8532.

Horne, Philip S. 1994. "Challenging Public- and Private-Sector Schemes Which Discriminate against Unmarried Opposite-Sex and Same-Sex Partners." *Law & Sexuality* 4: 35–52.

Hostetler, Dennis, and Joan E. Pynes. 1995, Winter. "Domestic Partnership Benefits: Dispelling the Myths." *Review of Public Personnel Administration* 15: 41–59.

Johnson, David K. 2004. *The Lavender Scare: The Cold War Persecution of Gays and Lesbians in the Federal Government*. Chicago, IL: University of Chicago Press.

Katz, Jonathon Ned. 1992. *Gay American History: Lesbians and Gay Men in the U.S.A.* Revised Edition. New York: Meridian.

Katz, Jonathon Ned. 1995. *The Invention of Heterosexuality*. New York: Dutton.

Kaplan, D. M. 2006. "Can Diversity Training Discriminate? Backlash to Lesbian, Gay, and Bisexual Initiatives." *Employee Responsibilities and Rights Journal* 18(1): 61–72.

Keen, L. 2010, January 4. "Obama appoints first openly transgender person to post." *365Gay*. http://www.365gay.com/news/obama-appoints-first-openly-transgender-person-to-post/ (accessed June 2, 2010).

Lambda Legal. 2008. "Court Recognizes Viability of Lambda Legal's Sex Discrimination Claim on Behalf of Transgender Woman." http://www.lambdalegal.org/news/pr/court-recognizes-sex-discrimination.html (accessed June 2, 2010).

Lawrence v. Texas. 2003. 539 U.S. 558.

LeVay, Simon. 1993. *The Sexual Brain*. Cambridge, MA: MIT Press.

Lewis, Gregory B. 1997. "Lifting the Ban on Gays in the Civil Service: Federal Policy Towards Gay and Lesbian Employees since the Cold War." *Public Administration Review* 57(5): 387–395.

Maffei v. Kolaeton Industry. 1995. 164 Misc. 2d 547; 626 N.Y.S.2d 391; 1995 N.Y. Misc. LEXIS 115.

McCaffery, Robert M. 1992. *Employee Benefit Programs: A Total Compensation Perspective*, 2nd ed. Boston, MA: PWS-Kent Publishing Company.

McNaught, Brian. 1993. *Gay Issues in the Workplace*. New York: St. Martin's Press.

Meyer, Leisa D. 1996. *Creating GI Jane: Sexuality and Power in the Women's Army Corps During WW I*. New York: Columbia University Press.

Murray v. Oceanside Unified School District. 2000. 79 Cal. App. 4th 1338; 2000 Cal. Appl LEXIS 298.

National Gay and Lesbian Task Force (NGLTF). 2007. "Percentage of U.S. Population Covered by a State, County, and/or City Nondiscrimination Law and/or a Broad Family Recognition Law Over Time." http://www.thetaskforce.org/downloads/reports/fact_sheets/CoveredBy NondiscrimLaws0507Color.pdf (accessed June 5, 2010)

———. 2008. "Jurisdictions with Explicitly Transgender-Inclusive Nondiscrimination Laws. http://www.thetaskforce.org/downloads/reports/fact_sheets/all_jurisdictions_w_pop_8_08.pdf (accessed June 5, 2010).

Nice, David C. 1994. *Policy Innovation in State Government*. Ames, IA: Iowa State University Press.

Norton v. Macy. 1969. 417 F. 2d 1161.

Obama, B. 2009, June 17. "Memorandum for the Heads of Executive Departments and Agencies on Federal Benefits and Nondiscrimination." http://www.whitehouse.gov/the-press-office/memorandum-heads-executive-departments-and-agencies-federal-benefits-and-non-discri (accessed June 2, 2010).

O'Bryan, W. 2010, May 6. "Commissions Calling: Presidential Appointments Project's New Push Promotes LGBT Candidates for Unpaid Positions." *MetroWeekly*. http://www.metroweekly.com/news/?ak=5173 (accessed June 2, 2010).

Oncale v. Sundowner Offshore Services. 1998. 479 U.S. 806.

Paetzold, Ramona. 1999. "Same-Sex Sexual Harassment Revisited." *Employee Rights and Employment Policy Journal* 3: 251.

Price Waterhouse v. Hopkins. 1989. 490 U.S. 228, 104 L. Ed. 2d 268, 109 S. Ct. 1775.

Ramos, C., M. V. Lee Badgett, and Brad Sears. 2008. *Evidence of Employment Discrimination on the Basis of Sexual Orientation and Gender Identity: Complaints Filed with State Enforcement Agencies 1999–2007*, University of California Los Angeles—The Williams Institute. http://www.escholarship.org/uc/item/7j0413pd (accessed June 2, 2010).

Riccucci, Norma M., and Charles W. Gossett. 1996. "Employment Discrimination in State and Local Government: The Lesbian and Gay Male Experience." *American Review of Public Administration* 26(2): 175–200.

Roth, T. 2010, January 22. "Federal Employee Sues Obama Admin for Same Sex Benefits." *Law & Daily Live*, FindLaw. http://blogs.findlaw.com/law_and_life/2010/01/federal-employee-sues-obama-admin-for-same-sex-benefits.html (accessed June 5, 2010).

San Francisco Human Rights Commission. 2006, April 1. "San Francisco City and County Transgender Health Benefit—Letter from Human Rights Commission." http://www.hrc.org/issues/7782.htm (accessed June 3, 2010).

Schroer v. Billington. 2008. 577 F. Supp. 2d 293.

Seelye, K. Q. 2010, May 6. "Marriage Law is Challenged as Equaling Discrimination." *New York Times*, p. A16.

Shahar v. Bowers. 1993. 836 F. Supp. 869.

Shahar v. Bowers. 1995. 70 F.3d 1218.

Shelton v. Tucker. 1960. 364 U.S. 479.

Sherman, Suzanne, ed. 1992. *Lesbian and Gay Marriage.* Philadelphia, PA: Temple University Press.

Shilts, Randy. 1993. *Conduct Unbecoming: Lesbians and Gays in the U.S. Military: Vietnam to the Persian Gulf.* New York: St. Martin's Press.

Shoop, T. 2010, June 2. "Obama Extends Benefits to Same-Sex Partners of Federal Employees." *GovernmentExecutive.com.* http://www.govexec.com/story_page.cfm?articleid=45412&dcn=e_gvet (accessed June 3, 2010).

Simonton v. Runyon. 2000. 232 F. 3d 33; 2000 U.S. App. LEXIS 21139.

Singer, Bennett L., and David Deschamps, eds. 1994. *Gay and Lesbian Stats: A Pocket Guide to Facts and Figures.* New York: The New Press.

Singer v. United States Civil Service Commission. 1976. 530 F.2d 247 (1976); *vacated,* 429 U.S. 1034.

Smith, Jennifer. 2003, July 4. "Employee Sues over Transgender Bathroom Use." *Southern Voice.* http://www.sovo.com/2003/7-4/news/localnews/transbath.cfm

Smith v. City of Salem. 2004. 378 F.3d 566; 2004 U.S. App. LEXIS 16114. (Amended Opinion).

Sullivan, Andrew, ed. 1997. *Same Sex Marriage: Pro and Con.* New York City: Vintage Books.

Tanner v. Oregon Health Sciences University. 1998. 157 Ore. App. 502; 971 P.2d 435; 1998 Ore. App. LEXIS 2183.

Turner, Ronald. 2000. "The Unenvisaged Case, Interpretive Progression, and Justiciability of Title VII Same-Sex Sexual Harassment Claims." *Duke Journal of Gender Law and Policy* 7: 57.

Winfeld, Liz, and Susan Spielman. 1995. *Straight Talk about Gays in the Workplace.* New York: American Management Association.

Wolinsky, Marc, and Kenneth Sherrill. 1993. *Gays and the Military: Joseph Steffan versus the United States.* Princeton, NJ: Princeton University Press.

Woods, James D. 1993. *The Corporate Closet.* New York City: The Free Press.

Zalesne, Deborah. 2001. "When Your Harasser is Another Man." *The Gay and Lesbian Review* 8(1): 19–21.

Zuckerman, Amy J., and George F. Simons. 1996. *Sexual Orientation in the Workplace.* Thousand Oaks, CA: Sage Publications.

Endnotes

1. In 2003 (*Goodridge v. Department of Public Health*), the highest state court of Massachusetts found that there was no state constitutional basis for denying marriage rights and benefits to two people just because they were the same sex. In 2000 (*Baker v. State*), the Vermont Supreme Court ruled that same-sex couples should be eligible to receive the same state-provided benefits available to opposite sex couples.

2. The federal Civil Service Retirement System, for example, allows an unmarried employee to show that a third party is financially dependent on the retiree and provision for a survivor annuity can be made for that person. However, if the employee died before actually retiring, such a dependent third party, unlike a spouse and/or minor children, would not, by right, be eligible for an annuity. There is no requirement that spouses or children actually be financially dependent on the retiree in order to receive a survivor's annuity.

7 CHRONIC HEALTH ISSUES AND THE PUBLIC WORKPLACE

James D. Slack, Samuel Douglas Drake Slack, and Sarah Ashley Slack

James D. Slack is a professor in the Department of Government at the University of Alabama at Birmingham (UAB). His most recent book is *Abortion, Execution and the Consequences of Taking Life* (Transaction Publishers, 2009).
Samuel Douglas Drake Slack is a senior at Hoover High School, Hoover, Alabama. His interests lie in workplace management issues.
Sarah Ashley Slack is an undergraduate at Auburn University. Her interests lie in health care delivery issues.

In both the public and the private sectors, the American workplace faces two kinds of health challenges.[1] First, there are acute health issues, short-term problems like colds and influenza, as well as reparable damages to the body like broken bones, ergonomics, and migraines. These certainly play havoc in the workplace. For instance, in 2009, as many as 26 million working-age Americans contracted the H1N1 virus—of which, the Centers for Disease Control and Prevention (CDC) estimates, 213,000 were hospitalized and 12,720 died (U.S. Department of Health and Human Services, "H1N1 Study," 2010).

While acute issues are problematic, the second kinds of health challenge—those that are chronic in nature—represent far greater burdens for the workplace. Chronic health issues include long-term and reoccurring conditions that, in many cases, are either irreparable or terminal. These include physical impairments like cancers, dysfunctional organs, and paralysis, as well as mental impairments like depression, schizophrenia, and anxiety disorders. Nearly 50 percent of adults in America have at least one chronic condition, resulting in more than 75 percent of all health care expenditures (U.S. Department of Health and Human Services, "Power of Prevention," 2009). By law, chronic health conditions are disabilities, and one in five Americans have classified themselves as having such.

Because chronic health issues do not always present a healing remedy, they tend to place a greater burden on the organization's benefit package. They also require greater investments in thought and resources in finding acceptable responses to the resulting workflow disruption. Moreover, the challenge of chronic health issues is that management must find ways to protect the workplace rights of affected employees as well as maintain the collective health rights of the entire workforce. Consequently chronic health issues tend to be increasingly subject to litigation, and this represents the greatest workplace cost.

This chapter focuses on what public personnel managers need to know about the challenges surrounding chronic health issues that affect the workplace.

THE CONSEQUENCES OF POOR HEALTH IN THE AMERICAN WORKPLACE

Perhaps as a result of government regulations and oversight, the American workplace remains reasonably safe. "Only" 5,214 deaths occurred in 2008 as a result of workplace accidents (U.S. Department of Labor, Bureau of Labor Statistics, 2010). In that year, the private sector fatality rate (per 100,000) was just 3.7, while the public workplace fatality rate was 2.4. This is the lowest level of workplace fatalities in either sector since these data were first collected in 1992.

Poor health, however, escapes government regulations and oversight. Obesity (defined by body mass index > 30) and overweight (body mass index = 25–29) are catalysts to a variety of chronic illnesses, including stroke, heart disease, diabetes, and arthritis. These can also lead to, and be symptomatic of, mental health problems. According to the CDC ("Power of Prevention," 2009), 34 percent of American adults are overweight and another 33 percent are obese. As illustrated in Table 7.1, no state can boast less than 55 percent of its population falling in either of these two categories. A minimum of 60 percent of most states' populations are either overweight or

Table 7.1   Obese and Overweight American Adults by State

<55%	55–<60%	60–<65%		65% or more
none	District of Columbia	Rhode Island	Virginia	Delaware
	Colorado			Georgia
	Hawaii	New Mexico	Maine	Alaska
	Utah	Montana	Illinois	Oklahoma
	Vermont	New Hampshire	Nevada	Louisiana
	Massachusetts	New York	Missouri	South Carolina
	California	Oregon	Idaho	Arkansas
	Connecticut	Minnesota	Indiana	South Dakota
		Florida	Ohio	Texas
		Washington	Kansas	Alabama
		Wyoming	Michigan	Tennessee
		Wisconsin	North Carolina	West Virginia
		New Jersey	Nebraska	Mississippi
		Arizona	Iowa	Kentucky
		Maryland	North Dakota	
		Pennsylvania		

Note: Mississippi has the highest obesity percentage at 32.6.

Source: U.S. Department of Health and Human Services, Centers for Disease Control and Prevention, "Behavioral Risk Factor Surveillance System" data base, http://caolorielab.com/

Table 7.2	Most Common Causes of Disabilities in the United States

Ranking	Cause of Disability
1	Arthritis/rheumatism
2	Back or spine problems
3	Heart disease
4	Lung or respiratory problems
5	Mental/emotional problems
6	Diabetes
7	Deafness/hearing problems
8	Stiffness/deformity in limbs
9	Stroke
10	Cancer

Source: U.S. Department of Health and Human Services, Center for Disease Control and Prevention. 2009. "The Power of Prevention." http://www.nimh.nih.gov.

obese, with Kentucky at the bottom approaching 70 percent. Obesity appears most pronounced in southern states, and this could be due to the region's tradition of heavy meals that are mostly fried. The least obese states seem to be those with an abundance of outdoor sports and recreation opportunities, such as prolonged seasons for skiing, surfing, swimming, or skating. Whether in the more "health conscious" Pacific Rim and New England or the more "deep fried" South, the threat of obesity and overweight damages the American worker and hinders his or her productivity.

Chronic health issues reduce workers' ability to perform essential job functions; hence, they cause disabilities. As shown in Table 7.2, the most common cause of disability in the United States is arthritis/rheumatism—due to aging baby boomers and longevity in work years. Table 7.3 reports that these illnesses are much more prevalent in older employees. Some chronic conditions—heart disease, high blood pressure, and arthritis/chronic joint disease—approach or surpass quadrupling with age. Diabetes increases by nearly a factor of 6 as the worker gets older. Table 7.4 shows that black workers are affected by more chronic diseases at higher rates than white workers, with diabetes being the most pronounced example. Whites suffer more than blacks from heart disease. Men and women are much more evenly affected by each chronic disease.

The National Institute of Mental Health (2010) estimates that more than 26 percent of adult Americans suffer from at least one form of mental impairment. Within this total, 45 percent suffer from more than one disorder. Minorities are less likely to gain access to mental health services. They are also less likely to receive quality mental health services (U.S. Department of Human Services, Office of the Surgeon General, 2010). By the year 2020, major depressive disorders are expected to become the number one cause of disabilities among adults in the United States and other developed nations (Murray, 1996). Work-related factors—such as economic hardship, role conflict, work overload, and stress—are expected to contribute greatly to the rise in depressive disorders among adult men and women (McCurry, 2000).

Table 7.3   Percentage of Selected Chronic Diseases by Age

Disability	18–44 Years in Age	45–64 Years in Age
Diabetes	2.3	12.1
Prostrate cancer	—	1.7
Cervical cancer	1.3	1.8
Heart disease	5.7	18.9
High blood pressure	8.7	32.4
Arthritis/joint disease	7.5	30.9
Visual impairment	7.2	13.8
Hearing impairment	6.9	18.4
Stroke	0.6	2.9
Asthma	13.6	12.0

Source: U.S. Department of Health and Human Services, Centers for Disease Control and Prevention, National Health Interview Study, 2008.

Table 7.4   Percentage of Selected Reported Chronic Diseases by Race and Gender

Disability	Race		Gender	
	White	Black	Male	Female
Diabetes	7.6	11.4	8.3	7.9
Prostrate cancer	2.2	2.3	2.2	—
Cervical cancer	1.6	0.6	—	1.4
Heart disease	19.5	13.9	19.9	16.6
High blood pressure	24.6	29.5	23.9	25.8
Arthritis/joint disease	22.5	21.8	18.5	25.0
Visual impairment	10.9	11.7	9.3	12.5
Hearing impairment	16.2	8.9	18.2	12.4
Stroke	2.9	3.1	2.7	3.0
Asthma	12.5	13.5	10.8	14.3

Source: U.S. Department of Health and Human Services, Centers for Disease Control and Prevention, National Health Intervention Study, 2008.

WORKPLACE COST

The cost of poor health is substantial and rising, tripling since 1990. Averaging $7,000 per American born, it is twice the average found in most developed nations (U.S. Department of Health and Human Services, "Power of Prevention," 2009). While changing as the Health Care and Education Reconciliation Act becomes fully implemented in 2014, currently slightly less than 70 percent of all American workers ages 45–64 years have health insurance coverage through the workplace, so do just a little more than 60 percent of those between the ages of 18 and 44. Perhaps due to less than adequate workplace health insurance, the average number of work-loss days is 5 per year for older employees, and the average number of bed days is 5.5 per year. This amounts to more than 800 million work-loss days and more than 1 billion bed days. The numbers rise as education declines and personal stress increases. For instance, workers with high school degrees average eight bed days per year, as do employees who are divorced or separated (U.S. Department of Health and Human Services, National Health Interview Study, 2008).

Employer cost for health care coverage is also substantial and, in the public sector, that means substantial taxes. Eleven percent of employer costs in state and local governments are dedicated to health insurance, or $4.52 per hour for a public servant making an average of $39.81 per hour (U.S. Department of Labor, June 2010). Given that there are more than 3.8 million state employees, health insurance costs taxpayers over $17 million per hour. With more than 11 million local government workers, health insurance costs over $49 million per hour. If other health-related items are included—sick and personal days, life insurance, short-term and long-term disability insurance—state and local governments spend $5.66 per hour, or 14 percent of the $39.81 average total compensation. Hence, the total taxpayer cost for all health care line items comes to over $21.5 million for state employees and over $62.2 million for local government employees—*per hour!* In one work year, this translates to over $44 billion for state government and $129 billion for local government.

Through the Federal Employees Health Benefits Program, the federal government pays two-thirds of all insurance costs for its workers. Federal employees can choose, depending on location, a variety of health insurance plans ranging from HMOs to fee-for-service options. Using the Washington Aetna Health Fund, a typical HMO, the monthly family premium rate is $1,004.62, of which the government pays $753. For Blue Cross, a typical fee-for-service plan, the monthly family standard premium rate is $1,215.72, of which the government pays $814.75. With more than 2 million civilian workers in nonpostal grade, the federal government could pay approximately $1.6 billion per month for health insurance—over $19 billion per year (U.S. Office of Personnel Management, June 2010).

As shown in Table 7.5, productivity costs associated with chronic health conditions are approaching $800 billion annually, with the cost of cardiovascular disease and stroke leading the way at 42 percent. Moreover, the annual productivity costs arising from chronic risk factors are also staggering: $96 billion from smoking, $80 billion from physical inactivity, and $15 billion from poor nutrition (U.S. Department of Health and Human Services, "Power of Prevention," 2009).

Table 7.5 Productivity Costs of Selected Diseases, 2009	
Disease	**Costs (in $billions)**
Cardiovascular disease/stroke	$313.8
Diabetes	$116.0
Smoking	$ 96.0
Cancer	$ 89.0
Arthritis	$ 80.8
Obesity	$ 61.0

Source: U.S. Department of Health and Human Services, Center for Disease Control and Prevention. 2009. "The Power of Prevention."

While estimates vary, workplace costs associated with chronic mental health issues are staggering. According to Mental Health America (2010), this amounts to over $34 billion, annually. However, this estimate may be conservative. The National Mental Health Association (2010), for instance, estimates that yearly workplace costs surpass $105 billion. According to *Time Magazine* (Kingsbury, May 9, 2008), as much as $193.2 billion may be lost in productivity each year. Peter Greenberg et al. (2003) estimate that absenteeism due to mental health issues costs the American workplace over $36 billion. The University of Michigan Health System's Depression Center (Carli, 2004) estimates absenteeism at $52 billion.

Other costs are also associated with chronic mental health challenges. The National Mental Health Association (2010) estimates that more than 200 million sick days per year are taken by adults with mental health symptoms, nearly 75 percent of whom are women. University of Michigan surveys (Carli, 2004) indicate that over 80 percent of employees suffering from depression also lack motivation and have difficulty in concentration, while nearly one in four experience chronic physical pain. According to Greenberg et al. (2003), these symptoms exacerbate the costly phenomenon of "presenteeism"—being present at work but not fully functional—by more than $15 billion, annually.

PROTECTING DISABLED WORKERS

Disabled Americans can be found in all segments of society; they are rich and poor, Anglo and non-Anglo, and men and women. Some have chronic conditions that are very apparent to everyone, others suffer from conditions that are not so immediately apparent, and still others have disabilities that may not be evident at all. Whether or not one can actually see the infliction, people with chronic physical or mental impairments are considered to be disabled and, hence, have access to protection in the workplace.

Disabled Americans need protection because society makes them vulnerable in at least three ways. First, historically we have neglected the needs of disabled people. It was not until the early 1970s that the first piece of legislation was enacted in the United States that actually dealt with the issue of providing disabled people with access to fundamental social and community activities, such as entering public buildings or using the bathrooms in those buildings. By ignoring their needs for nearly 200 years, we also denied them meaningful participation in society. Second, various disabilities are often misunderstood and, as a result, the capabilities of disabled individuals are frequently underestimated. Our initial tendency is to assist the paraplegic person in the wheelchair or to refrain from directing too many questions to the person with a speech impairment. By wanting to help them, we often make the assumption that disabled people cannot participate meaningfully in our society. Third, disabilities can make us feel uncomfortable, and therefore we tend not to want disabled individuals around us. The history of cancer certainly reflects this feeling. Discomfort is sometimes pronounced when it comes to being around people with contagious diseases, such as hepatitis or the human immunodeficiency virus (HIV) that causes acquired immunodeficiency syndrome (AIDS). Our own fears about disabilities can block opportunities for meaningful participation on the part of the disabled person.

Two pieces of federal legislation, the 1973 Rehabilitation (Rehab) Act and the 1990 Americans with Disabilities Act (ADA), protect the workplace rights of disabled employees. While the two laws have many similarities, there are four factors that separate them (Slack, 1998). The first difference is jurisdiction. Rehab protects individuals employed in federal programs or those employed in agencies that either receive federal contracts or direct federal funding. Hence, state and local governments, as well as many nonprofit organizations, are covered by Rehab. The ADA, on the other hand, is much broader in jurisdiction because it covers organizations that affect commerce and do not receive federal funding. Congress defined "affecting commerce" broadly to include the public and private sectors. While the vast majority of businesses are covered under ADA—organizations that employ 15 or more full-time employees for most of the year— state and local governments and nonprofit organizations may also fall under the jurisdiction of the ADA if they have programs that do not receive federal funding.[2] Hence, public human resource specialists must be aware that employees in their organizations may be protected by both Rehab and the ADA.

The second difference deals with selection expectations. Rehab requires management to be "disability sensitive." It mandates managers to take affirmative action with disabled individuals in the hiring, promotion, and retention processes. The ADA, on the other hand, requires management to be "disability-blind" when it comes to those matters. It prohibits managers from using affirmative action practices in selecting disabled individuals. Public and nonprofit human resource specialists must, therefore, be aware as to which law applies to which selection process because Rehab can invite litigation from disabled persons and the ADA can invite litigation from those who are not.

The third difference between Rehab and ADA deals with enforcement mechanisms. Seeking remedy against an employer is a bit more complex under Rehab, requiring the involvement of the EEOC, the federal department responsible for funding the particular program, and the U.S. Department of Justice. The ADA, however, simply requires notification through the EEOC.

Fourth, the laws differ in terms of permanent physical modification expectations, with architectural requirements being much stricter under Rehab. Employers "must accommodate" the disabled in removing office barriers. Hence, the organization is expected, regardless of cost and inconvenience, to do such things as install wheelchair ramps, provide Braille instructions in elevators, and make restrooms handicap accessible. In contrast, the ADA requires permanent structural modifications to be made only when those accommodations are "readily achievable" in terms of expense and effort.

From all other perspectives, Rehab and the ADA are identical. Each is designed to protect the workplace rights of disabled Americans. An employer cannot discriminate against a disabled employee if the employee is otherwise qualified to perform the essential functions of the job with or without reasonable accommodations. In providing protection from workplace discrimination, both Rehab and the ADA use the same three-pronged definition of "disability." A person can claim to be protected under either law if he or she[3]

1. has a physical or mental impairment that substantially limits one or more of the major life activities, or
2. has a record of such an impairment, or
3. is regarded as having such an impairment.

The second and third prongs of the definition are intended to prevent speculation on the part of the employer as to what employee-related costs the future might bring to the organization. They are especially important in combating subtle and clever disability-based discrimination in the workplace. The second prong protects a person from either being denied employment or being terminated from employment as a result of fear that additional costs might be borne at the end of the impairment's remission. *Cleveland v. Policy Management System* (1999) and *Sheehan v. Marr* (1st Cir. 2000) underscore that, while an employee may be deemed as "totally disabled" through another law (such as the Disabled Veterans Act), management is prevented from presuming automatically that the employee cannot perform the essential functions of the job and, hence, is unprotected under Rehab and the ADA.

The third prong protects those individuals with impairments that might never manifest, yet present the possibility of someday adding to the organization's health care and workplace expenses. A series of court decisions (*Murphy v. United Parcel Services, Inc.*, 1999; *School Board of Nassau County v. Arline*, 1987; *Sullivan v. River Valley School District*, 1999) make it very clear that employees must be judged on actual abilities to perform the essential functions of the job. They cannot be judged on the basis of financial fears or social bigotry.

DISABILITIES COVERED AND NOT COVERED

While all chronic health conditions are viewed as disabilities, the federal government has been relatively careful in delineating specifically which disabilities are protected under the ADA and Rehab. Physical impairments include physiological disorders, cosmetic disfigurements, and anatomical losses or dysfunctions, which affect at least one of the major body systems. Mental impairments include psychological disorders like emotional or mental illness, specific learning disabilities, mental retardation, and organic brain syndrome. Asymptomatic chronic conditions, especially workers with HIV, are protected under both Rehab and the ADA, as affirmed in *Bragdon v. Abbott* (1998).

Some physical and mental impairments are not protected. For instance, EEOC guidelines do not recognize certain physical characteristics, such as age, pregnancy, normal ranges of weight and muscle tone, height, and hair color. Personality traits, like poor judgment and hot tempers, are also not considered impairments. Congress made it very clear that certain lifestyles and behaviors are not protected under either Rehab or the ADA: homosexuality, transsexualism, transvestism, pedophilia, exhibitionism, voyeurism, kleptomania, compulsive gambling, and pyromania, to name a few.

Past abuse of addictive drugs and alcohol is considered a protected disability, but *current* abuse is not protected under either Rehab or the ADA. In *Collings v. Longview Fibre* (9th Cir. 1995), "current" use of addictive drugs was defined as being a matter of months prior to detection and discharge. In *Conley v. Village of Bedford Park* (7th Cir. 2000), the court ruled that recovering alcoholics are protected under Rehab and the ADA as long as they are actually "recovering" and can perform the essential functions of the job. The reason for distinguishing between "past" and "current" problems with drugs and alcohol is that Congress acknowledges the right of employers to maintain a safe workplace. Employers can demand that employees' blood and urine be free from drugs and alcohol at the workplace (Colbridge, 2000). In *Newland v. Dalton* (9th Cir. 1996) and *Williams v. Widnall* (9th Cir. 1996), the courts ruled that employers do not have to tolerate disruptive behavior or insubordination of recovering addicts (drugs or alcohol) even if the behavior is the result of the addiction.

For a period of time, an increasingly conservative Supreme Court started to limit access to disability protection that Congress had intended to be covered under the ADA and Rehab. The Court specifically focused on limited correctable chronic health conditions. In *Sutton v. United Airlines* (1999) and *Murphy* (1999), the Supreme Court determined that many correctable impairments—such as poor eyesight and high blood pressure—were not protected because they were considered to have "mitigating measures" that basically eliminated the disability. As Justice Sandra Day O'Connor noted in *Sutton*, "If the impairment is corrected it does not 'substantially limit' a major life activity." In *Toyota v. Williams* (2002), the Supreme Court rejected a claim that the employer should have provided reasonable accommodation for an employee with carpel tunnel syndrome because the impairment substantially limited only one of many major life activities. Hence, the Supreme Court moved down a path of stricter standards for determining both disability and reasonable accommodation. In doing so, the Court reversed *Bragdon* (1998) where it had underscored that protection under ADA and Rehab did not necessitate a "total" limitation but only a "substantial" limitation.

ADA AMENDMENTS ACT OF 2008

In response to the Supreme Court's path, Congress passed the ADA Amendments Act (ADAAA) of 2008, which came into effect on January 1, 2009. The ADAAA returned the ADA and Rehab to the original congressional intent: a broad interpretation of "disability" and a broad net for being "disabled." Hence, the Court (as in its recent decisions) could not assume that just because the original legislation stated that 43 million Americans were disabled, that group consisted of a discrete minority. The congressional intent was reestablished to cover as many people who can document a disability and to prohibit courts from using "mitigating measures," such as medication or corrective apparatuses, in determining who is protected by law. Perhaps most importantly, the laws no longer require employees to demonstrate a perception of disability when using the third ("regarded as") prong of the disability definition. As per the original intention of Congress, disabled Americans only have to document the fact that discrimination had occurred.

SUBSTANTIALLY LIMITING MAJOR LIFE ACTIVITIES

As affirmed in *Sutton* (1999) and *Murphy* (1999), disabilities covered by both Rehab and the ADA must substantially limit major life activities. Rehab and the ADA take a broad view on what constitutes "major life activities": walking, seeing, hearing, performing manual tasks, or caring for oneself. All or a combination of these activities are central to performing anyone's job. In *Bragdon* (1998), the court underscored that protection under these two laws does not necessitate a "total" limitation but only a "substantial" limitation. However, in *Sutton* (1999), the court ruled that decisions regarding substantial limitations must be made on a case-by-case basis and not simply on a diagnosis of an impairment. In order to be deemed "substantially limiting," Rehab and the ADA (reaffirmed by ADAAA) require the disability to be severe, long term, and permanent in terms of impact on major life activities.

NOTIFICATION AND DOCUMENTATION REQUIREMENT

The ADA and Rehab are similar to other pieces of civil rights legislation in that the burden of proving membership within the protected class belongs solely to the individual seeking protection. Hence, it is the responsibility of the disabled employee to provide management with clear notification and accurate documentation about the chronic health condition. Because many kinds of disabilities are not readily apparent, this requirement typically means the submission of a note or report from either a physician or a mental health counselor.

While the notification and documentation requirement may seem benign *albeit* "bureaucratic," it can have serious impact on persons with certain kinds of disabilities. People tend not to want to "publicize" personal health conditions, and, given the social stigma attached to some chronic illnesses, many employees are afraid of ridicule or retribution. Mental depression or past drug abuse, for instance, may not be issues about which one wants to talk with a supervisor. And given the stigma that still surrounds HIV/AIDS, providing documentation remains risky business for many people infected with the retrovirus (Slack, 2001a, 2001b). For employees with HIV/AIDS, the requirement means presenting *official* documentation that directly links the retrovirus to himself or herself. An anonymous blood test will not satisfy the notification requirement.

The fact is that Rehab and the ADA make the topic of chronic health conditions far less personal and change the very nature of confidentiality in the workplace (Slack, 1996, 1998). Especially in circumstances where reasonable accommodations are requested, the circle of entities that may need to know *something* (yet *not necessarily everything*) about an employee's health condition may extend well beyond the confidence of the immediate supervisor: human resource specialists, other supervisors (in case of job transfer), coworkers and union stewards (in case of job modifications), the legal staff (for guidance on applying Rehab and the ADA), the insurance staff (for purposes of benefit consultation and processing pharmaceutical claims), the organization's first-aid staff (in case of emergencies), the medical staff (for purposes of verifying the disability), and the Employee Assistance Program (EAP) staff (for counseling, intervention, and crisis management). Confidentiality remains, but the need-to-know-something boundaries are expanded significantly.

Ultimately the employee is faced with the dilemma of either not notifying the employer—out of fear of ridicule, ostracization, or discrimination—or trust that the employer will comply with the tenets of either law and be sensitive to the changing nature of confidentiality as well as reactions to social stigmas that may be attached to specific chronic conditions. In both the private (Scheid, 1998) and public (Slack, 1998) sectors, management's compliance *with* the law tends to come part and parcel with understanding *of* the law. Similarly, it appears that disabled employees' tendency to exercise rights covered by both laws increases with added education and training about protections provided by the laws (Granger, 2000). Without proper notification and documentation, however, disabled workers cannot make claims, and management bears no responsibility in protecting workplace rights.

MANAGEMENT'S RESPONSIBILITIES

Chronic health conditions present tremendous challenges to workplace and personnel managers. Some of the more critical issues include (1) redefining job descriptions, (2) determining the agency's capacity to provide reasonable accommodations, (3) controlling costs, and (4) acquiring information and developing strategies to train staff and employees to better prepare them to handle effectively situations involving disabilities.

JOB DESCRIPTIONS

Rehab and the ADA protect disabled workers as long as they can perform the essential functions of their jobs. Although required in neither Rehab nor the ADA, it is wise to reanalyze each job description within the organization so that tasks deemed to be "essential" in nature can be distinguished from tasks that are "marginal." Doing so permits management to determine—and document in court, if necessary—whether a disabled job applicant or employee is otherwise qualified to perform the essential functions of a job. It is especially important to modify job descriptions prior to beginning the selection process, since they are the basis for most job announcements and will be central to counter litigation.

REASONABLE ACCOMMODATIONS

Federal courts have placed limitations on what employers are expected to do on behalf of disabled workers and disabled applicants. In *Board of Trustees of University of Alabama v. Garrett* (2001), the court ruled that state employees cannot sue the state in federal court for violations of Title I of Rehab and the ADA. This ruling was affirmed in *Tennessee v. Lane et al.* (2004). In *Raytheon Co. v. Hernandez* (2003), the court ruled that organizations do not have to consider rehiring former disabled workers who were discharged for violating workplace conduct rules.

Nevertheless, Rehab and the ADA require management to provide reasonable accommodations to otherwise qualified employees and job applicants with disabilities if such accommodations are needed in performing the essential functions of the job. Both laws also require management to do so only in response to requests by the employees for such accommodations. Although management cannot impose reasonable accommodations on employees or job applicants, it should be prepared to enter into a discussion about specific workplace accommodations.

What is reasonable accommodation? From management's point of view, it is important to provide disabled employees with reasonable accommodations for at least two reasons. First, reasonable accommodation constitutes a significant form of health intervention. *Early intervention* can keep disabled employees healthier and, therefore, more productive for a longer period of time. Second, adoption of reasonable accommodation strategies can be submitted in court as evidence that the organization is attempting to comply with both the letter and spirit of Rehab and the ADA. As shown in Figure 7.1, the Job Accommodation Network (JAN) suggests a four-step strategy.

But what constitutes a reasonable accommodation? Reasonable accommodations can and should take a variety of forms. Recognizing that reasonable accommodation is very much in the eye of the beholder, Congress suggests three types: (1) physical or structural changes, such as modifying buildings to ensure wheelchair accessibility; (2) job modification, such as removing marginal tasks from the job description, acquiring assistive technology devises (ATDs), flextime utilization, job transfer, or filling of vacancies; and (3) modification of selection and training materials and processes, such as using special readers or interpreters or changing the size of print on examinations.

Management must recognize that each worksite—indeed, each set of essential functions, type of disability, stage and level of disability, and individual capability—constitutes a unique situation and, thereby, calls for unique accommodations. Hence, what is needed for one disabled American to perform the essential functions of a particular job in a specific workplace will not be identical to what is needed for another disabled American in either the same or different place of employment. A case-by-case approach is required, and this means that human resource specialists and workplace supervisors must gain familiarity with chronic health conditions present in the particular workforce.

In many ways, devising reasonable accommodations for physical disabilities is more straightforward than building strategies to deal with employees with mental disabilities. Certainly there are exceptions; some physical disabilities, especially those with few outward manifestations, can be very problematic in finding accommodations that are acceptable and reasonable. Contagious physical illnesses, such as hepatitis or HIV-related illnesses, are causes for concern especially in improperly trained workforces or ill-equipped workplaces. For the most part, however, it is somewhat simpler to deal with an employee who is paraplegic or perhaps one who has a hearing or sight loss.

FIGURE 7.1 A Sample Process For Determining Effective Accommodation Options

---

Step 1: Determine Why the Employee Needs an Accommodation

When trying to determine effective accommodation options, employers first have to determine why the employee needs an accommodation. For example, if an employee says he is having difficulty using his computer because of a medical condition and needs an accommodation, does the employer have enough information to know why an accommodation is needed? No, the employee did not say why he cannot use his computer. Is he having trouble typing because of a motor impairment? Is he having trouble seeing the screen because of a vision impairment? Or is he having trouble reading because of a learning disability? As you might guess, accommodation options can be very different for a motor impairment versus a vision impairment versus a learning disability. Before an employer can explore accommodation options, the employer must determine why the employee needs an accommodation, the employer must determine why the employee needs an accommodation. Usually the employee or the employee's medical provider can explain why the accommodation is needed.

Step 2: Explore Options

Once the employer determines why the accommodation is needed, the employer is ready to explore accommodation options. Again, the employee, or the employee's medical provider, is often the best starting point. However, if the employee or the employee's medical provider cannot suggest options, JAN offers serveral methods for exploring accommodation options, including One-on-one consultation, JAN's Accommodation and Compliance Series publications and fact sheets, and the Searchable Online Accommodation Resource (SOAR). For more information, visit JAN's Website at http://askjan/org.

Step 3: Choose Option

Once the employer determines effective accommodation options, the employer is ready to choose the accommodation that will be implemented. At this point, the employer should discuss the options with the employee who requested the accommodation. Although the employer is free to choose among effective accommodation options, the EEOC recommends that employers consider the preference of the employee. If the goal is to provide effective accommodations, it makes sense to try to provide the accommodation that the employee prefers when possible.

Step 4: Provide Effective Training

Once an accommodation option is chosen, an often overlooked step in the process is to provide effective training if needed. In some cases, employees and their supervisors or managers must learn how to use new equipment or new methods of doing things. Without effective training, accommodation may fail.

Source: Job Accommodation Network (JAN). 2010. "Five Practical Tips for Providing and Maintaining Effective Job Accommodations," P.O. Box 6080, Morgantown, West Virginia 26506-6080. E-mail: Jan@askjan.org. Website: http://askjan.org

Assuming the necessary reexamination of job descriptions, one can determine if the employee is otherwise qualified to perform the essential functions of the job. One can also determine whether reasonable accommodations are needed to enable the employee to perform the essential functions.

Providing reasonable accommodations for mental impairments is often a much harder task. Stephen Sonnenberg (2000a, 2000b) offers a variety of suggestions on how to deal effectively with employees who suffer from mental disabilities. Five of his suggestions are listed in Figure 7.2. Concerning Suggestion 1, the job description should protect both the organization and the employee. If stressful activities are central to the job, coping with stress should be listed as an essential function. Suggestion 2 reminds us that much of the organizational headaches from mental impairments result from managers and human resource specialists attempting to solve mental health problems on their own. Management should have in place a referral system to handle these issues. Suggestion 3 helps protect the organization from litigation. However, neither Rehab nor the ADA requires reasonable accommodation, in this case a job transfer, simply because of difficulty in working with either a supervisor or coworker (Goldman, 1999). Reasonable accommodation is permitted only in cases where the employee is substantially limited in his or her ability to perform the essential functions of the job. The organization is further protected if the job description includes the statement of "ability to work in stressful conditions" as an essential function. Suggestion 4 underscores that the request for reasonable accommodation may not always be clear and precise. This is especially true in the case of employees with mental health conditions (Noe, 1997). Because reasonable accommodations are always on a case-by-case basis, the employee may not even know what is needed to keep him or her able to perform the essential job tasks. *Management must listen closely.* Suggestion 5 affirms that the decision to provide reasonable accommodation is never a function of a medical opinion. It is always a function of law. Rehab and the ADA, and subsequent court decisions, are the basis for determining who is protected and who is accommodated. The psychiatric diagnosis is only the first step in making these determinations.

FIGURE 7.2   Five Suggestions for Reasonable Accommodations for Mental Impairments

Suggestion 1	Review and revise job descriptions to include references to employees' ability to cope with stressful circumstances.
Suggestion 2	If an employee appears or claims to have a mental impairment, scrupulously avoid generalizations or stereotypes about mental illness. Resist the temptation to play armchair psychologist.
Suggestion 3	If an employee complains that working with his supervisor is too stressful and causes emotional problems, elicit a written admission that he will be able to perform essential job duties only if he has a different supervisor or works in a different location.
Suggestion 4	Consider even vague requests for accommodation from employees, their family members, or their representatives as triggering a duty to engage in an interactive process with the employee.
Suggestion 5	A psychiatric diagnosis is not determinative

CONTROLLING COSTS

If employers dislike Rehab and ADA, it is primarily because of a fear of cost. With few exceptions, however, providing individualized and reasonable accommodations prove to be one of the least expensive activities. In a survey conducted by JAN (2010), 56 percent of employers reported that reasonable accommodations provided to employees cost nothing. Typical accommodations for disabled employees cost around $600 per case. When employer respondents were asked the amount to which they "paid for an employee without a disability who was in the same position," the cost reduced to $320.

Some examples of relatively inexpensive accommodations might include flextime for medical appointments or work breaks to apply medication. For employees with suppressed immune systems or mental disabilities, a relatively inexpensive accommodation might involve an occasional five-minute "stress break." For employees with special diet needs, especially diets needed for specific medication, vendors can provide specialized machine foods at no cost to the employer.

The expense of accommodation is a legitimate concern for the work organization, and so the question remains: How far do you have to go to provide reasonable accommodation? Rehab and the ADA call for accommodations to be *reasonable*, and this has long been affirmed by the courts (*Alexander v. Choate*, 1985). Organizations do not have to endure undue hardships in providing accommodations. They do not have to operate in the red nor do they have to lay off employees. Private businesses are expected to make profit, and public and nonprofit organizations are expected to continue service productivity.

What determines undue hardship? As in the case of accommodations, undue hardship is seen through the eye of the beholder and is determined on a case-by-case basis. Rehab and the ADA provide the following guidelines to assist organizations and the courts in determining whether specific accommodations are "reasonable" in particular work organizations: (1) the nature and cost of the specific accommodation, (2) the financial resources of the specific organization, (3) whether the organization is a part of a larger organization with greater financial resources, and (4) the nature (indoor/outdoor and temporary/permanent) of the worksite.[4]

The cost of group insurance packages is a continuing concern of employers and a primary issue in the area of undue hardship. Unlike other kinds of accommodations, the group health package represents a "collective" accommodation and, therefore, the cost of which is not eased terribly by the size of the organization. For several decades, federal courts searched for a balance between protecting disabled Americans in the workforce and ensuring that the workplace did not suffer unduly. In a series of decisions (*Chrysler v. DILHR*, 1976; *McDermott v. Xerox*, 1985; *Western Weighing Bureau v. DILHR*, 1977) rendered even before the passage of the ADA, the courts ruled consistently that a work organization could not discriminate against employees based on either knowledge about current costs or speculation about future costs. Yet the courts also recognized the right of work organizations to consider the issue of expense in purchasing insurance policies and health care packages for employees. This seemed especially true in the case of mental impairments (Serritella, 2000). In *Weyer v. Twentieth Century Fox Film Corp.* (2000), the court held that a more limited plan of coverage, specifically a shorter term of coverage, for mental disabilities was permissible to help reduce costs and thereby avoid undue hardship. In *Hess v. Allstate Ins. Co.* (2000), the court found that work organizations and insurers could not be held liable for offering less health care coverage for mental disabilities than it does for physical disabilities.

All this is likely to be reconsidered in the courts, based on the passage of the Health Care and Education Reconciliation Act of 2010. Signed by President Barack Obama, this act requires private and nonprofit organizations (with more than 50 full-time workers) to provide group health insurances to all full-time employees by the year 2014. By that year, there can be no maximum limit on coverage for either physical or mental health coverage, and employees cannot be denied coverage based on preexisting conditions. Further, employees will be protected from being dropped from coverage once they get sick.

The impact on undue hardship is yet to be determined under President Obama's health care reform, and a new round of court challenges is expected. According to JAN's recent survey, employers believe the benefits to providing reasonable accommodations far surpass the cost of doing so. Three direct benefits were highlighted: (1) retaining qualified employees, (2) increasing productivity, and (3) eliminating training costs for new employees (2010: 3).

INFORMATION AND TRAINING

It is quintessential for management to acquire current and realistic information regarding medical, legal, and application dimensions of chronic health issues facing the workplace. For instance, a fundamental fear is the transmission of contagious physical impairments, particularly blood-borne pathogens like HIV and hepatitis, through workplace activities. The Occupational Safety and Health Administration (OSHA) and the National Institute for Occupational Safety and Health (NIOSH) provide employers both procedural regulations and technical assistance in meeting this responsibility.[5] General updates on disability issues can be found in *Report on Disability Programs*.[6] As indicated in Figure 7.1, JAN's Web page provides a wide variety of information, including the Searchable Online Accommodation Resource (SOAR), that can be helpful in developing reasonable accommodations for specific chronic impairments. The Disability Rights Section of the Department of Justice's Civil Rights Division offers a variety of documents designed to assist state, county, and municipal governments in complying with the ADA. These documents can be accessed through JAN's Web site. Routine staff meetings should include relevant topics, such as updates on pertinent court cases, Web-based information, and circulation of relevant information.

It is also management's responsibility to develop and implement strategies to train staff and employees in order to better prepare the workplace to handle effectively situations involving chronic health conditions. This involves training on how to implement Rehab and ADA, as well as on how to protect the health of all employees. It also entails acquiring a basic and preliminary understanding of the types of mental and physical impairments found in the particular workplace. Not providing such training simply increases vulnerability to litigation as a result of inappropriate workplace actions and behavior. Litigation is always the most expensive workplace cost.

Especially in the public sector, employee and staff training tends to take a back seat to other budgetary priorities. Richard L. Schott (1999) notes that this is especially true when it comes to providing training programs in the area of mental health. Stephen Sonnenberg (2000a, 2000b) reminds us that the effectiveness of mental health training depends on developing relationships with mental health professionals. In order to gain a better understanding of both physical and mental impairments, it is quintessential to incorporate a variety of external expertise into the training strategy.

For management to send an unambiguous message as to the importance of employee disabilities, training must be mandatory, workplace specific, and periodic. It should include such topics as (1) Rehab, ADA, and OSHA regulations; (2) workplace-specific procedures that management will follow when an employee seeks to provide notification and documentation about a disability, (3) the changing nature of confidentiality under Rehab and the ADA, and its application to the specific workplace; (4) services provided by the organization, including concrete but preliminary sketches of possible "individualized" reasonable accommodations; (5) undue hardship issues pertaining to the specific workplace; and (6) with the help of external experts, familiarization with disabilities and health issues potentially facing the organization.

Conclusion

One thing is abundantly clear about the American workplace: Healthy people are less expensive and more productive than sick people. Two things are equally evident about the American workforce: Individually, we are aging and thereby incrementally becoming less healthy; collectively, we are facing a greater number (and a wider variety of kinds) of chronic health challenges. Since Rehab and the ADA prohibit the exclusion of persons with many types of mental and physical impairments from the workplace, management must do whatever it can to keep them healthy and productive. Whether it is a result of humanitarian feelings of compassion for the employee or businesslike concerns about profit and productivity, it is in management's best interest to develop a workplace environment that supports the needs of disabled employees as well as guards the health of all employees. Building a positive workplace environment—one where employees with chronic health conditions feel comfortable in exercising their rights under the law and where supervisors feel encouraged in the application of those rights—remains a challenge for the next generation of public and nonprofit managers and human resource specialists.

References

Alexander v. Choate. 1985. 469 U.S. 287.
Board of Trustees of University of Alabama v. Garrett. 2001. 531 U.S. 356.
Bragdon v. Abbott. 1998. 524 U.S. 624.
Carli, Thomas. 2004. "Depression-in-the-Workplace-Survey." University of Michigan Health System, Depression Center. www.med.umich.edu/opm/
Chrysler v. DILHR. 1976. 14 Fair Empl. Prac. Cases (BNA) 344. Wis.Cir.Ct.
Cleveland v. Policy Management Systems et al. 1999. 526 U.S. 795.
Colbridge, Thomas D. 2000, October. "Defining Disability Under the Americans with Disabilities Act." *FBI Law Enforcement Bulletin* 69(10): 28–32.
Collings v. Longview Fibre. 1995. 63 F 3d 828 (9th Cir. 1995), cert. denied, 116 S. Ct. 711 (1996).
Conley v. Village of Bedford Park. 2000. WL703806 (7th Cir. Ill.).
Goldman, Charles. 1999, July. "Recognizing When Stress Results from Covered Disability." *ADA Compliance Guide.*
Granger, Barbara. 2000, Winter. "The Role of Psychiatric Rehabilitation Practitioners in Assisting People in Understanding How to Best Assert Their ADA Rights and Arrange Job Accommodations." *Psychiatric Rehabilitation Journal* 23(3): 215–214.
Greenberg, P. E., R. C. Kessler, H. G. Birnbaum, S. A. Leong, S. U. Lowe, P. A. Berglund, and P. K. Corey-Lisle. 2003, December. "The Economic Burden of Depression in the United States." *Journal of Clinical Psychology* 64(12): 1465–1475.
Hess v. Allstate Ins. Co. 2000. 19 NDLR 28. D. Me. 2000. No. 99-384-P-C.
Job Accommodation Network. 2010. "Workplace Accommodations: Loc Cost, High Impact," and "Five Practical Tips for Providing and Maintaining Effective Job Accommodations."

http://askjan.org. P.O. Box 6080, Morgantown, WV 26506-6080. phone: (800) 526-7234. E-mail: jan@askjan.org.

Kingsbury, Kathleen. 2008, May 09. "Tallying Mental Illness' Costs." *Time Magazine.* http://www.time.com/time/health/article/0,8599,1738804,00.html

McCurry, Patrick. 2000, September. "Disabling Depression." *Director* 54(2): 34–38.

McDermott v. Xerox. 1985. 65 N.Y.2d 213, 480 N.E. 2d 695,491 N.Y.S. 2d 106.

Mental Health America. 2010. www.mentalhealthamerica.net/go/information/get-info/depression/depression-in-the-workplace.

Murphy v. United Parcel Service, Inc. 1999. 527 U.S. 516.

Murray, Christopher J. L., and Alan D. Lopez, eds. 1996. *Summary: The Global Burden of Disease: A Comprehensive Assessment of Mortality and Disability from Diseases, Injuries, and Risk Factors in 1990 and Projected to 2020.* Cambridge, MA: Harvard School of Public Health, Harvard University Press.

National Institute of Mental Health, U.S. National Institutes of Health. 2010, January. http://www.nimh.nih.gov/health/topics/statistics/index.shtml

National Mental Health Association. 2010. www.nmha.org.

Newland v. Dalton. 1996. 81 F.3d 904. 9th Cir.

Noe, Samuel R. 1997, January–March. "Discrimination Against Individuals with Mental Illness." *Journal of Rehabilitation*, pp. 20–26.

Raytheon Co. v. Hernandez. 2003. 9th Cir. No. 02-749.

Scheid, Teressa L. 1998. "The Americans with Disabilities Act, Mental Disability, and Employment Practices." *Journal of Behavioral Health Services and Research* 25(3): 312–325.

School Board of Nassau County v. Arline. 1987. 480 U.S. 273 at 284.

Schott, Richard L. 1999, Summer. "Managers and Mental Health: Mental Illness and the Workplace." *Public Personnel Management* 28(2): 161–184.

Serritella, Diane. 2000. "Disability and ADA: Employers and Insurers Not Obligated by the ADA to Provide Equal Benefit Plans for Physical and Mental Disabilities." *American Journal of Law and Medicine* 26(4): 112–115.

Sheehan v. Marr. 2000. 207 F.3d 35. 1st Cir.

Slack, James D. 1996, March/April. "Workplace Preparedness and the Americans with Disabilities Act: Lessons from Municipal Government's Management of HIV/AIDS." *Public Administration Review* 56(2): 159–167.

Slack, James D. 1998. *HIV/AIDS and the Public Workplace: Local Government Preparedness in the 1990s.* Tuscaloosa, AL: University of Alabama Press.

Slack, James D. 2001a. "The Americans with Disabilities Act and Reasonable Accommodations: The View from Persons with HIV/AIDS." *Policy Studies Journal* 29(4): 649.

Slack, James D. 2001b. "Zones of Indifference and the American Workplace: The Case of Persons with HIV/AIDS." *Public Administration Quarterly* 25(3): 247–269.

Sonnenberg, Stephen P. 2000a, June. "Coping with Mental Disabilities in the Workplace: Tips for Employers." *Employee Benefit News* 14(7): 78–81.

Sonnenberg, Stephen P. 2000b. "Mental Disabilities in the Workplace." *Workforce* 79(6): 142–144.

Sullivan v. River Valley School District. 1999. 194 F.3d 1084. 10th Cir.

Sutton v. United Air Lines, Inc. 1999. 527 U.S. 471.

Tennessee v. Lane et al. 2004. 6th Cir. No. 02-1667.

Toyota v. Williams. 2002. 224 F.3d 840.

U.S. Department of Health and Human Services, Centers for Disease Control and Prevention. 2010. "H1N1 Cases and Related Hospitalizations and Deaths of Working Age." http://www.cdc.gov/h1n1flu/estimates_2009_h1n1.htm (accessed June 2010).

U.S. Department of Health and Human Services, Centers for Disease Control and Prevention, National Center for Chronic Disease Prevention and Health Promotion. 2009. "Power of Prevention." http://www.cdc.gov/chronicdisease/pdf/2009-Power-of-Prevention.pdf (accessed June 2010).

U.S. Department of Health and Human Services, National Health Interview Study. 2008. www.cdc.gov/nchs/nhis.

U.S. Department of Health and Human Services, Office of the Surgeon General. 2010. "Culture, Race, and Ethnicity." www.surgeongeneral.gov/library/mentalhealth/cre/.

U.S. Department of Labor, Bureau of Labor Statistics, Census of Fatal Occupational Injuries. 2010. http://www.bls.gov/iif/oshcfoi1.htm (accessed June 2010).

U.S. Department of Labor, Bureau of Labor Statistics. 2010, June. "Employer Costs for Employee Compensation." http://www.bls.gov/news.release/pdf/ecec.pdf (accessed June 2010).

U.S. Office of Personnel Management, Insurance Operations. 2010, June 20. www.opm.gov/insure/index/aspx.

Western Weighing Bureau v. DILHR. 1977. 21 Fair Empl. Prac. Cases (BA) 344. Wis.Cir.Ct.

Weyer v. Twentieth Century Fox Film Corp. 2000. 198 F.3d 1104. 9th Cir.

Williams v. Widnall. 1996. 79 F. 3d 1003. 10th Cir.

Endnotes

1. The authors thank Susan McCarroll, a graduate assistant in the Master of Public Administration (MPA) Program at the University of Alabama at Birmingham, for assistance with this manuscript.
2. Several types of organizations are exempt from both pieces of legislation: the federal government, Native American tribes, private clubs, and, in certain situations, religious organizations.
3. 29 CFR section 1630.2 (h)(1).
4. 42 U.S.C. 12111 section 101(10)(B) (1995).
5. OSHA's Web site: http://www.osha.gov/. NIOSH's Web site: www.cdc.gov/niosh.
6. *Report on Disability Programs* is a newsletter published by Business Publishers, Inc., 8737 Colesville Road, Suite 1100, Silver Spring, MD 20910-3928. (301) 589-5103. Web site: www.bpinews.com.

8 | PUBLIC EMPLOYEE UNIONS IN A NEW ERA

T. Zane Reeves

T. Zane Reeves is Regents' Professor Emeritus of Public Administration at the University of New Mexico. His authored and coauthored books include *Case Studies in Human Resource Management* (2nd ed.), *Personnel Management in the Public Sector*, and *Collective Bargaining in the Public Sector*. Dr. Reeves is a member of the National Academy of Arbitrators and is on several labor arbitration panels including the American Arbitration Association, Federal Mediation and Conciliation Service, and the Association of Conflict Resolution Advanced Arbitration Panel. He also serves as a personnel hearing officer for the City of Albuquerque.

> *I will make it [Employee Free Choice Act]*
> *the law of the land when I'm President of the United States*
>
> SENATOR BARACK OBAMA (APRIL 2008)

Labor unions were major supporters and contributors to the electoral victory of presidential candidate Barack Obama in 2008. Most union members and leaders expected that President Obama would push federal legislation to encourage union organizing and membership growth. Supposedly, it would be a *new era* of opportunity for public and private employee unions in the United States. To understand why this has yet to happen and to assess the future prospects for unions, it is important to clearly appreciate the union movement and the political environment at the end of the first decade of the twenty-first century.

PUBLIC AND PRIVATE EMPLOYEE UNIONS

The U.S. Bureau of Labor Statistics in 2010 marked a critical milestone in its annual summary of union membership. For the first time in the United States, more public sector employees (7.9 million) belonged to a union than did private sector employees (7.4 million), despite the fact that there are five times more workers in the private sector (2010). And this difference between the two sectors is unlikely ever to be reversed as the percentage of private sector union members continued to decline to an all-time low of 7.2 percent, while the rate for public sector workers edged up to 37.4 percent. Of course, actual union members comprise only part of the total employees represented in a bargaining unit; another 781,000 government employees at all levels were covered by a collective bargaining agreement (CBA) and represented by unions, but were not dues-paying union members (U.S. Bureau of Labor Statistics, 2010).

Reasons for the continued decline in union membership in the private sector are due to several combined factors, such as sharp growth in unemployment in 2009, shrinkage of union-dominated manufacturing industries, and the expansion of more transient service and professional jobs where workers are traditionally more difficult to organize. Even so, there are signs that unions are making some in-roads among workers in low-paying jobs in retail and elder health care (MacGillis, 2010). Even with preliminary indications of an economic upturn in 2010, union leadership and rank-and-file members continued to advocate for more favorable legislation that they believe will encourage a resurgence of union growth in the public and private sectors.

Indeed, much of the attraction by unions for candidate Barack Obama lay in the promises of new labor legislation that seemed attainable with the election of Democratic majorities in both houses of Congress. It was in several pieces of proposed federal legislation in 2009–2010 that union leaders pinned their hopes for a union organizing renewal: (1) Employee Free Choice Act (EFCA, 2010), (2) Public Safety Employer–Employee Cooperation Act of 2009 (PSEECA), and (3) an amendment of the 2001 Aviation and Transportation Security Act (ATSA). If enacted, the EFCA would directly affect unions in the private sector, while the PSEECA targeted state, and local employees in law enforcement, and ATSA would encourage unionization of federal transportation security administration (TSA) security screeners in airports. By mid-2010, each of these pieces of legislation had not been reported out of congressional committees for a full vote, and unions were becoming increasingly restive with the Obama administration and Democratic legislators. Indeed, prospects for passage of each piece of legislation seemed mixed at best. The reasons for the unions' pessimistic prospects underscore the inability of unions to translate their perceived political clout into concrete legislation, despite electing a Democratic president and a legislative majority in both the Senate and House of Representatives.

EMPLOYEE FREE CHOICE ACT OF 2009

The EFCA of 2009 (H.R. 1409, S. 560) was introduced into both houses of the 111th Congress on March 19, 2009. The bill's intent was (Losey, 2010):

> "To amend the National Labor Relations Act to establish an efficient system to enable employees to form, join, or assist labor organizations, to provide for mandatory injunctions for unfair labor practices during the organizing efforts, and for other purposes."

The EFCA was originally intended to amend the National Labor Relations Act (NLRA) to accomplish three major changes:

- To allow a union to be certified as the exclusive bargaining agent with an employer if union officials collect signatures of a majority of workers on cards or a petition. The EFCA would remove the present right of the employer to demand an additional, secret ballot where over half of employees have already given their signature supporting the union.
- Secondly, if the employer and union are unable to negotiate a CBA within 90 days, either side may take the impasse to the Federal Mediation and Conciliation Service (FMCS), which would provide mediation free of charge. If after 30 days of mediation, the parties are unable to conclude a CBA, the FMCS will provide a list of arbitrators,

who will select an arbitrator to perform interest arbitration. The results of the arbitration shall be binding on the parties for two years.

• The EFCA would increase penalties on employers who discriminate against workers for union involvement.

Throughout the 2008 presidential campaign, both sides hotly debated the supposed merits and demerits of the EFCA. Proponents argued that companies are often able to intimidate workers before voting in a secret ballot. Secondly, union advocates cited a research study covering more than 22,000 organizing drives by Professor John-Paul Ferguson at the MIT Sloan School of Management that found, "Only one-seventh of organizing drives that filed an election petition with the NLRB managed to reach a first contract within a year of certification," a fact that Professor Ferguson attributes in large part to stalling tactics in negotiations by management (2008, p. 1).

Opponents of the EFCA argued that authorization cards are not in the interest of workers because they are not confidential, whereas the existing law allows the certification election to be confidential. These critics contend that the openness of the cards subject workers to peer pressure, harassment, coercion, and misrepresentation ("NAWER," 2007). Furthermore, management advocates assert that the required binding arbitration at impasse leaves unions and employers at the unpredictable whims of an arbitration panel (Sherk and Kersey, 2007).

The modified version of the EFCA, without the card check, was not passed by Congress in 2010, even though the Democrats had a 60-40 vote advantage in the Senate, and President Obama supported the measure. Several "moderate" Democrats opposed the card-check provision as undemocratic because it eliminated the secret ballot. Union leaders were also told to wait until health care reform was completed (MacGillis, 2010). As Steven Greenhouse (2009, p. A-1) observed, "The abandonment of card check was another example of the power of moderate Democrats to constrain their party's more liberal legislative efforts."

It is not clear that the decision of the Obama administration to abandon the card-check provision of EFCA was a serious setback to organized labor, even though it was perceived as such by some labor leaders (Greenhouse, 2009). First of all, the EFCA is an amendment to the NLRA and would not affect public employee unions in their organizing efforts. Secondly, as the Ferguson (2008) research on union organizing drives underscores, the greater problem has not been in winning certification elections but in successfully negotiating the first CBA with employers. As long as the EFCA retains the mandatory interest arbitration provision as an option for addressing employers who do not negotiate in good faith toward a CBA, unions will have retained an important weapon.

PUBLIC SAFETY EMPLOYER–EMPLOYEE COOPERATION ACT

Compared to the brouhaha surrounding the debate around the EFCA, the PSEECA of 2009 SEECA, introduced in the U.S. House of Representatives as HR 413 and the U.S. Senate as SB 1611, was relatively unnoticed by the media and public, although it has the potential to completely reshape the framework of public sector labor–management relations among states and local jurisdictions. Identical legislation had passed the House of Representatives in 2007 on a bipartisan vote of 314 to 97.

The goal of PSEECA is simple, even though it represents a monumental change in labor–management relations because it "would require all state and local governments to bargain collectively with public safety officers, which includes any . . . police officer, firefighter, emergency medical services personnel (excluding permanent supervisory or management employees)" (Barsook and Eanet, 2009).

Historically and currently, laws governing labor–management relations between public employers and their unions at the state and local levels have been governed by state laws exclusively, unlike the private sector where federal legislation, that is, the NLRA and Railway Act, impose uniform guidelines throughout the states. However, the PSEECA would supersede state law by empowering the Federal Labor Relations Authority (FLRA) to determine whether state law provides specified rights and responsibilities for public safety officers, including (Congressional Research Service, 2009) the following:

1. The right to form and join a labor organization (excluding management and supervisory employees)
2. Requiring employers to recognize and bargain in good faith

The approximately 23 states with comprehensive enabling legislation for all public employees would automatically comply with these guidelines, as would states such as Oklahoma that provide collective bargaining rights specifically to public safety employees.

In states without collective bargaining legislation, the FLRA would be mandated to

1. determine the appropriateness of bargaining units;
2. supervise or conduct elections to determine if a union has been elected by a majority of employees;
3. resolve issues related to duty of bargaining in good faith;
4. conduct hearings and resolve complaints of unfair labor practices; and
5. resolve exceptions to arbitrator's awards.

The political impetus for the PSEECA stems from the fact that public safety employees and their unions have been unsuccessful in efforts to gain statewide collective bargaining rights in about half of the states, located primarily in the South, Southwest, and Rocky Mountain West regions. For example, public safety employees in Oklahoma have long had collective bargaining rights, while officers in neighboring Texas are consistently denied the same rights on a statewide level. The political realities and culture of Texas do not bode well for ever achieving these rights for public law enforcement employees. Thus, an alternative for unions in states without enabling legislation is to work toward gaining through federal legislation what thus far has not been attainable in the state legislatures. Not surprisingly, such legislation has been vigorously opposed by public employers in these same states.

AVIATION AND TRANSPORTATION SECURITY ACT OF 2001 (ATSA)

The Transportation Workforce Security Enhancement Act of 2009 was an amendment to the ATSA, which would formally bring TSA employees under Title V discrimination and whistle-blower protections. It also seeks to provide TSA screeners with full collective bargaining rights and end PASS, the agency's current pay system, moving them to the General Schedule (GS) system. Advocates such as National Treasury Employees Union (NTEU) President Colleen Kelley (2009) contended:

> Fairness demands that they be given the same rights as other federal employees. Providing these rights will lead to a more stable and independent professional workforce, which will be better able to ensure the safety of the traveling public.

Although approved by the House Government and Oversight Reform Committee and House Security Committee in 2009, the bill was not brought to the full House for a vote because of White House focus on health care reform.

Chances for gaining collective bargaining for TSA screeners were further blocked during 2009–2010 by the adamant opposition of Senator Jim DeMint (R-South Carolina), who held up confirmation of two successive presidential nominees for a TSA director, both of whom subsequently withdrew their nominations. Senator DeMint contended that organizing TSA employees into bargaining units would hurt national security (2010):

> Consider how the TSA system works now. When the plot by terrorists from the UK was uncovered in 2006, new rules on carrying liquids onboard went into effect within 12 hours. If TSA had been unionized then, officials would have had to first ask permission of union bosses. And if the unions decided the changes were too burdensome on their employees, weeks of months of negotiations could have ensued, before any changes were made. Even the recent response to the attempt by Abdulmutallab, TSA officials reassigned staff and changed screening procedures within hours, a quick move that would be nearly impossible under collective bargaining with union bosses.

Despite Senator DeMint's opposition, President Obama announced on May 17, 2010, that he would nominate a third person, FBI Deputy Director John S. Pistole, as the new head of the TSA (Lim, 2010).

Despite the opposition of Senator DeMint and other Republican leaders in Congress, the American Federation of Government Employees (AFGE) and NTEU continue their intensive efforts to organize the 40,000-plus airport screeners. On May 28, 2010, the Chicago regional director of the FLRA denied a bid by the AFGE to hold a certification election to decide which union should represent TSA employees (Rosenberg, 2010). The regional FLRA upheld its previous determination that because TSA screeners do not have collective bargaining rights, it has no jurisdiction to process the petition for an election. AFGE appealed the regional director's decision to the full FLRA. NTEU has filed a similar petition with FLRA.

Frustration by the unions, especially the NTEU and AFGE, with the inability or unwillingness of the Obama administration to push for legislation guaranteeing the collective bargaining rights of TSA employees remains high. The unions also urged President Obama to grant TSA employees collective bargaining rights through an executive order or other administrative action as had historically occurred in executive orders going back to President Kennedy. Union leaders also had sharp words for the Obama administration. As a candidate for president, Obama promised to restore collective bargaining rights to TSA employees, and Janet Napolitano, his choice for Homeland Security secretary, said early in her tenure that she was looking into whether she had the authority to grant them those rights. When TSA was established in 2002, Congress gave the agency's administrator authority to extend or deny collective bargaining rights to the workforce. Neither Napolitano nor Obama have moved to extend those rights.

AFGE President John Gage threatened (Rosenberg, 2010, p. 1):

> We're telling them to get the hell out of our way while we exercise our rights . . . whether it's the Senate, DHS or the White House, get out of our way.

AFGE and the NTEU are each seeking to represent roughly 40,000 TSA screeners and are bracing for a fierce organizing battle, should representation be authorized. The rivalry between AFGE and NTEU is aggravated by the fact that AFGE is affiliated with the AFL-CIO, and NTEU is an unaffiliated, independent union. Clearly, the resources of the AFL-CIO would weigh in behind AFGE in an organizing fight with NTEU, but it is not clear who would win this showdown, or whether TSA employees might vote not to be represented by either union (Rosenberg, 2010).

THE *NEW ERA*

In 2009, most public and private employee union leaders, with a few exceptions, undoubtedly believed that a *new era* of labor relations would be ushered in with the election of Barack Obama as president and a Democratically controlled Congress. This new era would be one of union rebirth and growth, supported by favorable legislation and the Democratic Party.

However, that has not happened and at least part of the reason has nothing to do with who controls federal policy making in Washington, DC. The new mood, one which union strategists have not anticipated, is exemplified by the following indicators of a changed political climate that is hardly favorable to union growth:

- The Central Falls School Board in Rhode Island voted to fire 88 teachers because of low performance on test scores, even though its teachers' salaries are among the highest in the country. Houston, Texas, teachers were threatened with a similar fate if student test scores did not improve (www.mahalo.com/rhode-island-teachers-fired).
- In 2009, state government in California was $20 billion in deficit, even though it had closed a similar budgetary deficit the previous year. Since 2000, pension costs for public employees have increased 2,000 percent, while state revenues have gone up by only 24 percent. Over $3 billion was diverted to pension costs from other programs. Many retirees are former police officers, firefighters, and prison guards who could retire at age 50 with a pension equal to 90 percent of their final year's salary (Greenhut, 2010).
- New Jersey governor Chris Christie inherited a $2.2 billion deficit in 2009, with a projected deficit of $10.7 billion and an operating budget of $29.3 billion. Christie was able to close the immediate budget gap but was confronted with government health benefits that he asserted were "41 percent more expensive than those of the average Fortune 500 Company." Without changes in current law, Christie asserted that "spending will have increased 322 percent in 20 years—over 16 percent a year" (Will, 2010).

By early 2010, an increasing number of states had ordered employee furloughs or layoffs, and many states had enacted both measures. No city, county, or state is seemingly immune from drastic budget-cutting measures (Greenblatt, 2010):

> Major cities across the country have taken difficult steps, particularly with regard to personnel, to combat budget shortfalls that in the largest cities are topping the billion-dollar mark. San Francisco Mayor Gavin Newsom in March sent pink slips to 17,000 of the city's 26,000 workers, laying them off with the intention of offering them a shorter work week. Newsom backed down when the unions balked, instead imposing 12 unpaid furlough days. The move was expected to save the city, which faces a $522 million shortfall in the coming fiscal year, about $100 million.

Chicago, which faced a $520 million shortfall for FY 2010, used more than $200 million from a reserve fund created by its long-term lease of parking meters. City workers also accepted 24 unpaid furlough days and the elimination of paid city holidays and overtime pay. In Dallas, which has a budget gap of $100 million, most departments are looking at a 30 percent cut, while police and firefighters face a 5 percent cut.

Almost every large city is shedding jobs, but smaller localities are making deep cuts as well. When Bossier City, La., faced a shortfall of $6.5 million in its $50.3 million budget last year, Mayor Lorenz "Lo" Walker proposed eliminating 117 of 897 city positions, including 80 in the police and fire departments. Dover, Del., closed its shortfall of $10.5 million in part by requiring all city employees to take 12 furlough days. Springfield, Ill., projects a shortfall of up to $12 million in its coming fiscal year and anticipates eliminating up to 192 positions.

What is being recognized by a growing number of observers from all political persuasions was succinctly stated by former California Assembly Speaker and San Francisco Mayor Willie Brown, Jr., in his weekly column in the *San Francisco Chronicle* (2010) about the "Civil Service":

The system was set up so politicians like me couldn't come in and fire the people (relatives) hired by the guy they beat and replace them with their own friends and relatives. Over the years, however, the civil service system has changed from one that protects jobs to one that runs the show.

The deal used to be that civil servants were paid less than private sector workers in exchange for an understanding that they had job security for life. But we politicians, pushed by our friends in labor, gradually expanded pay and benefits to private-sector levels while keeping the job protections and layering on incredibly generous retirement packages that pay ex-workers almost as much as current workers.

Talking about this is politically unpopular and potentially even career suicide for most officeholders. But at some point, someone is going to have to get honest about the fact that 80 percent of the state, county and city budget deficits are due to employee costs. Either we do something about it at the ballot box, or a judge will do something about in Bankruptcy Court. And if you think I'm kidding, just look at Vallejo.

Willie Brown's final reference is to the City of Vallejo, California, which on May 23, 2008, filed a case seeking bankruptcy protection and the adjustment of its debts under Chapter 9 of the United States Bankruptcy Code and became the largest California city to do so. Stephanie Gomes, Vallejo City councilwoman, described the causes of bankruptcy thus (2008):

We don't hate police officers and firefighters. We hate the tactics their unions are using against our city and our community. We hate the fact that nearly 80 percent of our general fund goes to public safety and unsustainably high salaries and benefits, leaving only approximately 20 percent for other necessary city services. We hate the fact that our streets are riddled with potholes, our trees are overgrown, our libraries are closing and our senior centers are reducing programs and services to seniors in need. We hate the fact that we want our city back, and we can't do that until we regain control of our own city checkbook again.

Such is the real *new era* of labor–management relations in the public sector. It is an era marked by fiscal constraints and scarce budgetary resources.

It undoubtedly will be tempting for many elected officials and employers to blame public employees and their unions for spiraling costs in health care premiums and pension plans, even though there is no evidence that such costs are caused by public employee unions. Both are consequences of policy-maker decisions made in more affluent eras. Health care costs are more effectively addressed at the national policy level than at the bargaining table between public managers and local union representatives. Pension investment councils for public governments have sometimes made imprudent and careless investments. The "blame game" for which side caused high costs is endless and unproductive; unions blame management for waste, and politicians see unions as the "bad guys" rather than asking the soul-searching questions regarding which management practices might be contributing to union organizing.

The "*new era*" in labor–management relations is here, and policy solutions are needed to alter the present decline of public revenue sources and mixed priorities in public spending. Rather than pushing Congress to radically alter the nature of public labor–management relations in the states, it might be more worthwhile for unions to focus on organizing unorganized workers instead of fighting to protect the status quo at all costs. Perhaps it is time to reconsider whether it is really fiscally prudent to allow public employees to retire after 20 years of service. Greater coverage of employee health care benefits might be provided in lieu of salary increases. Finally, rather than raising the gravamen of "national security" to prevent airport screeners from organizing, the public interest would be better served by allowing these employees to have the same rights as other employees of the Department of Homeland Security.

These ideas are not offered as policy recommendations, merely as suggestions for consideration so that solutions may be found in cooperative negotiations rather than posturing by unions, employers, and politicians. One thing is certain; the old era of neither side bargaining in good faith to solve mutual problems is no longer working, if it ever did. Willie Brown, Jr., is right; these are hard problems of our own making that need honest assessment, and tough choices must be made. Making the union the scapegoat for past decisions is pointless in the *new era*.

References

Barsook, B., and D. Eanet. 2009. "Would the Public Safety Employer-Employee Cooperation Act of 2009 Impact California Cities?" http://www.westerncity.com/.

Brown, W. 2010. "Homeland Security Chief Takes Responsibility." *The San Francisco Chronicle*. http://articles.sfgate.com/2010-01-03/bay-area/17466406_1_civil-service-job-security-president-obama-s-first-year (accessed January 3, 2010).

Congressional Research Service. 2009. "H.R. 413: Public Safety Employer-Employee Cooperation Act of 2009." *GovTrack.us*.

Gomes, S. 2008, June 28. sgomes@ci.vallejo.ca.us.

Greenblatt, A. 2010. "The Budget Pain Felt by State Lawmakers for the Past Two Years Has Made Its Way to Cities and Counties." National Conference of State Legislatures. http://www.ncsl.org/?tabid=20180.

DeMint, J. 2010, January 5. "Sen. DeMint's Argument Against Collective Bargaining for TSA Officers." Quoted by Joe Davidson, *The Washington Post*, p. A-13.

Employee Free Choice Act. 2010. http://www.GovTrack.us/.

Ferguson, J. P. 2008. "The Eyes of Needles: A Sequential Model of Union Organizing Drives in Workers' Right to Organize: 1999–2004." *Industrial and Labor Relations* 62(1): 1–21.

Greenhouse, S. 2009, July 16. "Democrats Drop Key Part of Bill to Assist Unions." *The New York Times*, p. A-1.

Greenhut, S. 2010. "Public Employee Unions Are Sinking California." *The Wall Street Journal. WSJ.com.* http://online.wsj.com/article/SB10001424052748703699204575017182296077118.html (accessed June 2010).

Kelley, C. 2009, September 9. "Kelley Urges House Committee Members to Approve TSA Collective Bargaining Rights Measure." Press release by the National Treasury Employees Union. http://cbpunion.org/PressRelease/PressRelease.aspx?ID=1473.

Lim, D. 2010, May 17. "White House to Name FBI Deputy Director as New TSA Head." *Government Executive.* dlim@govexec.com.

Losey, S. 2010, May 28. "FLRA Denies Bid for TSA Union Election." *Federal Times* http://blogs.federaltimes.com/federal-times-blog/2010/05/28/flra-denies-bid-for-tsa-union-election/.

MacGillis, A. 2010, February 26. "Five Myths About the Labor Movement." *Press Democrat.* www.pressdemocrat.com/article/20100226/OPINION/100229684?Title=Five-myths-about-the-labor.

"NAWER." 2007, January 17. "Reasons to Oppose the Employee Free Choice Act Now." http://againstcardcheck.blogtownhall.com/default.aspx?mode=post&g=eaab1a6c-ef4f-4244-9f9a-9dd01213d37a.

"Remarks for Senator Barack Obama: AFL-CIO." 2008. http://www.barackobama.com/2008/04/02/remarks_for_senator_barack_oba_3.php.

Rosenberg, A. 2010, February 23. "National Labor Leaders Back AFGE in Effort to Organize Screeners." *Federal Executive.* arosenberg@govexec.com.

Sherk, J., and P. Kersey. 2007, April 23. "How the Employee Free Choice Act Takes Away Workers' Rights." *The Heritage Foundation.* http://www.heritage.org/Issues/Labor.

U.S. Bureau of Labor Statistics, Division of Labor Force Statistics. 2010, February 19. "Economic News Release." Washington, D.C. www.bls.gov/CPS.

Will, G. F. 2010, April 22. "Bringing Thunder-ous Change to New Jersey." georgewill@washpost.com.

9 | PUBLIC EMPLOYEES' LIABILITY FOR "CONSTITUTIONAL TORTS"

David H. Rosenbloom

David H. Rosenbloom is Distinguished Professor of Public Administration at American University (Washington, DC) and Chair Professor of Public Management at City University of Hong Kong. A member of the National Academy of Public Administration, he is recipient of the Levine, Waldo, Gaus, Brownlow, and Mosher Awards, among others, for his scholarly contributions to the field of public administration. Rosenbloom's competing perspectives model of public administration as management, politics, and law is widely used internationally.

Every person who, under color of any statute, ordinance, regulation, custom, or usage, of any State or Territory or the District of Columbia, subjects, or causes to be subjected, any citizen of the United States or other person within the jurisdiction thereof to the deprivation of any rights, privileges, or immunities secured by the Constitution and laws, shall be liable to the party injured in an action at law, suit in equity, or other proper proceeding for redress. For the purposes of this section, any Act of Congress applicable exclusively to the District of Columbia shall be considered to be a statute of the District of Columbia.

CIVIL RIGHTS ACT OF 1871, AS AMENDED AND CODIFIED IN 42 U.S. CODE, SECTION 1983 (1982).

INTRODUCTION

Ever since the establishment of the republic, public employment in the United States has been considered a "public trust." The concept that public employees have special obligations to the political community has prompted a variety of restrictions on their constitutional rights. For instance, the Constitution prohibits federal employees from being electors in the electoral college and from accepting gifts, offices, emoluments, or titles from foreign governments without the consent of Congress. The document also requires them to swear or affirm their support for it. As early as 1801, President Jefferson sought to restrict the First Amendment rights of federal employees to engage in electioneering because he deemed such activities " . . . inconsistent with the spirit of the Constitution and [their] duties to it" (Rosenbloom, 1971, pp. 39–40). Over the years, public employees have faced limitations not only on their political and economic activities but also on their residency, privacy, speech and association, and general liberties (Riccucci and Naff, 2007, chapter 3; Rosenbloom, 1971; Rosenbloom and Carroll, 1995; Rosenbloom, O'Leary, and Chanin, 2010, chapter 6). Beginning in the 1970s, public employees also became potentially liable for "constitutional torts," which has had the effect of requiring public administration to comport more fully with constitutional law and values. The development of this additional legal obligation, its scope, and its consequences for public personnel management in the United States are the subject of this chapter.

Constitutional torts are acts committed by public officials or employees, within the frameworks of their jobs, which violate individuals' constitutional rights in ways that can be appropriately remedied by civil suits for money damages. For instance, the violation of an individual's Fourth Amendment right to privacy through an unconstitutional search is such a tort. So is a public employee's unconstitutional act of racial discrimination. Most federal, state, and local government employees potentially face civil liability for money damages for constitutional torts. In general, they are vulnerable to both compensatory and punitive or exemplary damages. Under Eleventh Amendment interpretation, state governments and agencies cannot be sued in federal court for money damages for their constitutional torts (though other remedies for their unconstitutional acts are available). By extension, state employees cannot be sued as surrogates for state governments in such cases (*Will v. Michigan Department of State Police*, 1989). However, state employees can be sued in their *personal* capacities for constitutional torts committed while exercising official authority (*Hafer v. Melo*, 1991). Similarly, federal employees, but not agencies, can be sued for money damages in constitutional tort suits (*FDIC v. Meyer*, 1994). Local governments do not have Eleventh Amendment immunity. They are treated as "persons" in this area of the law, can be sued for compensatory, but not punitive or exemplary, damages for constitutional torts caused directly by their policies (*City of Newport v. Fact Concerts*, 1981; *Pembaur v. City of Cincinnati*, 1986). Even public employees who never deal directly with members of the public may face liabilities for violations of their subordinates' constitutional rights.

This chapter focuses on public employees' *personal* liability for constitutional torts, which makes "constitutional competence" a matter of basic job competence by requiring public personnel to know the constitutional law that governs their official actions (Rosenbloom and Carroll, 1990; Rosenbloom, Carroll, and Carroll, 2000, chapter 2). For human resource managers, avoidance of personal liability for constitutional torts necessitates the following: (1) understanding how the Constitution pertains to public employment and (2) building constitutionally required protections and procedures into administrative systems for recruitment, selection, employee development, promotion, adverse actions, reductions in force, equal opportunity, labor relations, background investigations, drug testing, and assisting employees with substance abuse and other problems that may jeopardize privacy rights.

PUBLIC OFFICIALS' ABSOLUTE IMMUNITY: THE TRADITIONAL APPROACH

Until the 1970s, under federal judicial interpretations, public employees at all levels of government generally held absolute immunity from civil suits for constitutional torts stemming from the exercise of their official functions. Under this approach, when public employees acted within the outer perimeter of their authority, they could not be sued personally for violating individuals' constitutional rights. For example, in *Stump v. Sparkman* (1978), a state judge enjoying absolute immunity was shielded from a damage suit even though he authorized the sterilization of a "mildly retarded" female high school student under circumstances that failed to protect her constitutional right to due process of law. Moreover, the judge acted without specific legal authorization, but not beyond the ultimate scope of his office. The rationales for granting legislators, judges, executive branch officials, and rank-and-file employees absolute immunity are all somewhat different. But at their root is the belief, developed in common law interpretations, that the activities of governmental functionaries should not be controlled or impeded by individuals' actual or threatened lawsuits. The Supreme Court stated the principle in *Spalding v. Vilas* (1896), the first case on official executive immunity to reach it:

> In exercising the functions of his office, the head of an Executive Department, keeping within the limits of his authority, should not be under an apprehension that the motives that control his official conduct may, at any time, become the subject of inquiry in a civil suit for damages. It would seriously cripple the proper and effective administration of public affairs as entrusted to the executive branch of the government, if he were subjected to any such restraint. (*Spalding v. Vilas*, 1896, p. 498)

This approach drew some of its legal strength from the centuries-old common law principle of "sovereign immunity." In English law, sovereign immunity rests on the premise that "the king can do no wrong," and, consequently, it would be pointless to allow suits against him. Precisely why sovereign immunity was incorporated into U.S. constitutional law has never been wholly clear (*United States v. Lee*, 1882). However, it precludes suing the federal and state governments in some types of cases unless they have given their permission to be sued through a tort claims act or other legal device.

GENERAL LEGAL TRENDS RELATED TO OFFICIAL LIABILITY

Whatever the strength of the legal rationales for public employees' absolute immunity, by the 1970s, there was clearly weaker judicial support for precluding civil suits against public employees for money damages. The changing attitude toward absolute immunity was related to two major legal trends. First, civil liability was expanding throughout the American legal system. As Peter Schuck (1988, p. 4) reflected toward the end of the 1980s, "On almost all fronts and in almost all jurisdictions, liability has dramatically expanded. It does not seem to matter what kind of party is being sued. Doctor or public official, landlord or social host, government agency or product manufacturer—all are more likely to be held liable today." Although the number of suits initiated per capita may be no larger at present than in colonial times and other periods in U.S. history (Galanter, 1988, p. 19), plaintiffs appeared more apt to win or receive satisfactory settlements because of changing judicial interpretations. Schuck (1982), a leading student of "suing government," summarized the underpinnings of the emerging tort law:

> Although the new judicial ideology of tort law is complex and multifaceted, four elements stand out: (1) a profound skepticism about the role of markets in allocating risk; (2) a shift in the dominant paradigm of causation [from determinant to probabilistic causal relationships]; (3) a tendency to broaden jury discretion; and (4) a preoccupation with achieving broad social goals instead of the narrower, more traditional purpose of corrective justice between the litigants. (Schuck, 1988, p. 6)

The second trend affecting the liability of public administrators for constitutional torts was the expansion of individual constitutional rights. Headed by the Supreme Court under Chief Justice Earl Warren (1953–1969), the federal judiciary demonstrated a new propensity to afford individuals greater constitutional protections vis-à-vis public administrative action (Rosenbloom, O'Leary, and Chanin, 2010). Whole categories of persons who formerly had very few constitutional protections when interacting with public bureaucracies were granted greater substantive, privacy, procedural, and equal protection rights under the First, Fourth, Fifth, Eighth, and Fourteenth Amendments. For instance, public employees were afforded substantial procedural due process protections in dismissals, greater freedom of speech and association rights (including such activities as whistle-blowing and joining labor unions), and much stronger claims to equal protection of the laws. Clients or customers receiving welfare or public housing gained clear procedural due process protections of these benefits for the first time. The courts reinterpreted the equal protection clause to over-turn the "separate but equal" doctrine that had previously permitted public services, such as education, to be racially segregated. Prisons were also desegregated under the Fourteenth Amendment and drastically reformed, via the Eighth and Fourteenth Amendments, to reduce overcrowding and brutal conditions. Individuals confined to public mental health facilities were granted a constitutional right to treatment or habilitation. The constitutional rights of persons interrogated about their alleged criminal behavior were expanded to include "Miranda warnings" (*Miranda v. Arizona*, 1966) and other safeguards. The privacy and due process rights of persons engaged in "street-level" encounters were also enhanced, though somewhat modestly (*Delaware v. Prouse*, 1979; *Kolender v. Lawson*, 1983; Lipsky, 1980; *Terry v. Ohio*, 1968).

For the most part, the trend toward greater constitutional rights for individuals in their encounters with public administration continued during the tenures of Chief Justice Warren Burger (1969–1986) and, to a somewhat lesser extent, Chief Justice William Rehnquist (1986–2005). For example, in the 1990s, property rights were strengthened against administrative zoning regulations that effectively deprived individuals of legiti-mate uses of their land (*Dolan v. City of Tigard*, 1994; *Lucas v. South Carolina Coastal Council*, 1992). New procedural due process protections were applied to civil forfeitures of real property (*United States v. James Daniel Good Real Property*, 1994). Contractors' free speech rights were also strengthened (*Board of County Commissioners, Wabaunsee County v. Umbehr*, 1996; *O'Hare Truck Service, Inc. v. City of Northlake*, 1996). Constitutional equal protection also became more salient to contracting out (*Adarand Constructors, Inc. v. Pena*, 1995; *City of Richmond v. J. A. Croson Co.*, 1989). Under the Rehnquist Court, a major exception to the general expansion of constitutional rights occurred with regard to the Fourth Amendment's protection against unreasonable searches and seizures. Today, one can be arrested for a nonjailable (i.e., "fine only") offense, such as not wearing a seat belt, police may use any traffic offense—no matter how minor—as a pretext for stopping a motorist whom they suspect of criminal wrong-doing, and individuals can face criminal penalties for refusing to identify themselves to police officers (*Atwater v. City of Lago Vista*, 2001; *Hiibel v. Sixth Judicial District Court of Nevada, Humboldt County*, 2004; *Whren v. United States*, 1996). Headed by Chief Justice John Roberts since 2005, the Court continued to reduce rights in some areas of central importance to public administration. For instance in *Garcetti v. Ceballos* (2006), the Court held that public employees' work product speech is not constitutionally protected even when it is on a matter of importance to the general public. It also made it more difficult for prisoners to bring suits in federal court for alleged maltreatment in state penal systems (*Woodford v. Ngo*, 2006).

Taken together, the expansion of liability and constitutional rights brought about a revolution in the relationship of the federal courts to public administration at all levels of government. Federal judges became deeply involved in the management of prisons, jails, public mental health facilities, and public schools. The courts also became far more salient to such public administrative matters as budgeting and personnel (Horowitz, 1983; *Missouri v. Jenkins*, 1990, 1995; Rosenbloom, O'Leary, and Chanin, 2010). The intervention of federal courts in state administrative systems added a substantial "juridical" element to federalism (Carroll, 1982).

When individuals possessed few constitutional rights in their encounters with public administrators, constitutional torts would necessarily be limited in number. Certainly, police brutality or violations of the Fifteenth Amendment's guarantee of the right to vote regardless of race might have been the basis of suits, but by and large it was difficult for public administrators to violate individuals' constitutional rights simply because the public held so few substantive, procedural, and equal protection guarantees in their interactions with government agencies. As the courts expanded the constitutional rights of public employees, clients/customers, prisoners, public mental health patients, individuals engaged in street-level encounters, property owners, and government contractors, the potential number and scope of constitutional violations became substantial. Consequently, it was desirable to develop an enforcement mechanism that would protect individuals against unconstitutional administrative action and enable them to vindicate their rights. Enter liability.

FROM ABSOLUTE TO QUALIFIED IMMUNITY: THE RISE OF LIABILITY

As late as 1959, a plurality on the Supreme Court continued to adhere to the following principle:

> It has been thought important that officials of government should be free to exercise their duties unembarrassed by the fear of damage suits in respect of acts done in the course of those duties—suits which would consume time and energies which would otherwise be devoted to governmental service and the threat of which might appreciably inhibit the . . . administration of policies of government. (*Barr v. Matteo*, 1959, p. 571)

However, once the public was gaining an array of constitutional protections in their dealings with administrators and liability law was becoming more expansive, the courts sought to establish a better balance between the governmental requirement of efficient and effective administration, on the one hand, and the need to deter violations of individuals' rights and compensate for them, on the other. So remarkable had the changes in liability and constitutional law been that, by the 1970s, the concept of "absolute" immunity for most public officials was clearly out of place.

During the 1970s, the Supreme Court used two legal vehicles to redefine the liability of public administrators. First, in *Bivens v. Six Unknown Named Federal Narcotics Agents* (1971), the Court held that federal officials could be liable, directly under the Constitution, for breaches of individuals' Fourth Amendment rights. The Court reasoned that the Fourth Amendment gives victims of unconstitutional federal searches and seizures a constitutional right to sue the officials involved for money damages. Subsequently, the Court ruled that similar rights to redress exist under the Fifth and Eighth Amendments (*Carlson v. Green*, 1980; *Davis v. Passman*, 1979). Although the Supreme Court has not directly held that individuals can sue federal officials for violations of the First Amendment, under ordinary circumstances such suits can go forward as well (Lee and Rosenbloom, 2005, chapter 2; see *Bush v. Lucas*, 1983, for an exception).

Second, the Supreme Court dramatically reinterpreted the standards for liability regarding state and local public administrators and officials. The Court resurrected the Civil Rights Act of 1871, which is now codified as 42 U.S. Code section 1983, and generally called "section 1983." The relevant portion of the act is quoted in the epigraph to this chapter. Although well conceived in the Reconstruction Era (1865–1877) as a means of providing federal judicial protection to former slaves, the act was rendered virtually moribund by a number of judicial interpretations and doctrines that drastically restricted its coverage (Rosenbloom, O'Leary, and Chanin, 2010, chapter 8; "Section 1983 and Federalism," 1977). In terms of liability, the courts refused to interpret literally the act's explicit application to "every person who." Instead, the judiciary reasoned that in writing "every person," Congress did not intended to override the long-standing absolute immunity at common law enjoyed by many state and local government officials, such as legislators and judges, from civil suits for damages. Consequently, even though such officials might be directly responsible for the violation of individuals' federally protected rights, they could not be sued for money damages under the act. It was through the redefinition of official immunity during the 1970s that the act became a major force in public administration and U.S. law.

The Supreme Court departed from past interpretations in *Scheuer v. Rhodes* (1974) when it abandoned the concept of absolute immunity for officials exercising executive functions. Instead, it opted for a "qualified immunity" that afforded many public officials immunity from civil suits for money damages only if they acted in good faith and reasonably. A year later, in *Wood v. Strickland* (1975, pp. 321–322), "reasonably" was interpreted to mean whether the official "knew or reasonably should have known that the action he took within his sphere of official responsibility would violate the constitutional rights" of the individuals affected.

Bivens, Scheuer, and *Wood* opened the door to many suits against public administrators by individuals seeking money damages for alleged violations of their constitutional rights. Under the standard for qualified immunity these cases developed, suits could allege that the administrators failed to act in good faith by displaying malice or a reckless disregard of individuals' rights. In practice, defending against such a charge proved burdensome for the public officials involved. The issue of "good faith" is considered a matter of fact that may be submitted to a jury for determination. Consequently, suits could be drawn out and very expensive to defend. Under such conditions, the process itself could be punishment, and public officials were consequently under substantial pressure to settle out of court, without strict regard to the merits of the charges against them. In an age of crowded dockets, elaborate trials in liability suits against public officials also took a toll on the courts.

The Supreme Court sought to reduce these pressures in *Harlow v. Fitzgerald* (1982), which made it easier for public officials to defend themselves against constitutional tort suits.

The *Harlow* decision "completely reformulated qualified immunity along principles not at all embodied in the common law" (*Anderson v. Creighton*, 1987, 645). The new standard for qualified immunity relies on a procedure called "summary judgment" as means of determining whether a suit can proceed to a full trial. A district court judge's decision regarding summary judgment can be appealed. However, once a decision to grant summary judgment to the defendant public employee or official is final, the case ends. It cannot proceed to a full-fledged trial. *Harlow* established the following standard for determining whether summary judgment should be granted: "government officials performing discretionary functions generally are shielded from liability for civil damages insofar as their conduct does not violate clearly established statutory or constitutional rights of which a reasonable person would have known" (1982, p. 818). The defendant's motives and good faith are irrelevant at this stage. The key questions are whether the facts of what happened are sufficiently clear to make it unnecessary to determine them through a trial, and, if so, whether the alleged conduct violated clearly established constitutional rights of which the administrator should reasonably have known. The judge grants qualified immunity if he or she concludes (1) that based on the facts, there was no violation of the Constitution; (2) if the Constitution was violated, the law at the time was not clearly established; or (3) even if the law was clearly established, an administrator could not reasonably have known that the conduct involved would violate a constitutional right.

The great advantage of the *Harlow* approach is that summary judgments are far quicker and much less burdensome than jury rials. The immunity is from suit, not just a defense against liability (*Mitchell v. Forsyth*, 1985). The *Harlow* construction applies to federal officials and employees directly under the Constitution and to state and local personnel under section 1983.

THE LOGIC OF LIABILITY: DETERRENCE AND JUDICIAL INFLUENCE ON PUBLIC ADMINISTRATION

When the courts do something as dramatic as overturning the effects of centuries of common law, one is impelled to consider their rationale and the effects of the change. The logic of rejecting absolute immunity in favor of qualified immunity (or liability) is clear. First, the liability under consideration here is personal liability, not the liability of agencies or government entities. Personal liability is viewed by the Supreme Court as an excellent enforcement mechanism. In the Court's words, " . . . the *Bivens* remedy [that is, official liability], in addition to compensating victims, serves a deterrent purpose" (*Carlson v. Green*, 1980, p. 21), and the general point has been to "create an incentive for officials who may harbor doubts about the lawfulness of their intended actions to err on the side of protecting citizens' constitutional rights" (*Owen v. City of Independence*, 1980, pp. 651–652).

The deterrent effect of liability is magnified greatly by the potential assessment of punitive or exemplary damages against public administrators. In *Smith v. Wade* (1983), the Supreme Court had an opportunity to permit the federal courts to apply a tough standard for subjecting public administrators to such damages. Historically, there have been two general standards for these damages. One is whether the individual found liable acted with malice in violating the other party's rights, that is, displayed "ill will, spite, or intent to injure" (*Smith v. Wade*, 1983, p. 37). The other standard is recklessness, or a "callous disregard of, or indifference to, the rights or safety of others" (*Smith v. Wade*, 1983, p. 37).

The Supreme Court allowed the lower courts to use recklessness, which is the weaker of the two. It reasoned that "the conscientious officer who desires . . . [to] avoid lawsuits can and should look to the standard for actionability in the first instance," that is, whether the action violated clearly established rights of which a reasonable person would have known (*Smith v. Wade*, 1983, p. 50). In other words, a finding that compensatory damages are appropriate will often support the assessment of punitive or exemplary damages as well because conduct at issue will manifest at least an indifference to the rights of the injured party. Reliance on recklessness rather than malice makes it easier to use damages to punish public administrators financially and to deter similar unconstitutional behavior on the part of others. Although punitive damages may trigger due process concerns, they are largely open-ended and not technically required to be tightly related to the injury involved (*BMW of North America v. Gore*, 1996). Consequently, in cases where qualified immunity is not granted, plaintiffs may allege malice (as well as recklessness) in the hope of recovering greater damages.

A second aspect of the logic of liability is more complex. The way that the courts constructed public officials' qualified immunity enables them to exercise considerable direction over public administration. In effect, the Supreme Court has made knowledge of constitutional law a matter of job competence for public administrators. As it stated in *Harlow* (1982, p. 819), "a reasonably competent public official should know the law governing his conduct." But what is that law? In the words of former Supreme Court Justice Lewis Powell, "Constitutional law is what the courts say it is" (*Owen v. City of Independence*, 1980, p. 669). Consequently, public administrators must take direction from judges, who determine how the Constitution bears upon their jobs.

Moreover, despite the qualifier in *Harlow* that the rights involved must be "clearly established," the Supreme Court has not limited liability to instances in which a materially similar or identical administrative action was already ruled unconstitutional (*Hope v. Pelzer*, 2002). Rather, the concept of "clearly established" extends to constitutional values and principles that should be known by a reasonably competent public official. Even if the constitutionality of some particular act has never been litigated, a public administrator engaging in it may be liable if the state of the law gives him or her "fair warning" that it violates the Constitution (*Hope v. Pelzer*, 2002). This standard makes it possible to compensate victims of altogether new administrative violations of their constitutional rights.

Overall, therefore, public administrators' liability promotes two judicial objectives. It is a strong tool for enforcing the constitutional rights established by the judiciary for individuals in their interactions with public administrators. It also enables the courts to exercise greater direction over public administration. The latter judicial interest is also manifested in the courts' willingness to entertain suits seeking very broad reforms of administrative institutions or processes, such as prisons, public mental health facilities, public schools, and public personnel systems (Chayes, 1976; Horowitz, 1977, 1983; *Plata v. Schwarzenegger*, 2005; Rosenbloom, O'Leary, and Chanin, 2010).

THE IMPACT OF LIABILITY

It is difficult to assess comprehensively the impact of the change from absolute to qualified immunity. There is a lack of systematic knowledge about this area of the law. It is clear that thousands of suits have been brought against public employees, but less is known about their resolution (Farley, 1989; Lee, 1987; Lee and Rosenbloom, 2005, chapters 2–3). The likelihood of a public administrator losing a constitutional tort suit and paying damages personally appears relatively slim.[1] Nevertheless, public managers have been very concerned with potential liability and the costs of legal defense, settlements, and judgments (Friel, 1998; Rivenbark, 1998).

Even if more were known about case resolutions, settlements, and damages, however, it would still be very difficult to assess the overall impact of liability upon public administrative practices. Part of the intent of liability is to change public administrators' behavior to assure that it complies with constitutional requirements. To the extent that qualified immunity is successful, public administrators will be less likely to violate constitutional rights, and there will be fewer grounds for suing them. For example, police today routinely do recite "Miranda warnings," and social service and personnel agencies have built constitutional due process into their standard operating practices. It would be surprising to find many constitutional violations in these areas. Nevertheless, there are surely many instances in which individuals whose rights are violated by public administrators fail, for one reason or another, to sue. Consequently, only limited inferences can be drawn from the number of cases filed, the absence of more filings, and the outcomes of cases. But, clearly, liability law is not a dead letter, and the best defense is to know and respect individuals' constitutional rights (Lee, 2004; Lee and Rosenbloom, 2005).

VARIATION WITHIN THE GENERAL PATTERN OF PUBLIC OFFICIALS' LIABILITY

EXCEPTIONS

There are some exceptions to the current standard for qualified immunity and to the availability of compensatory damages as a remedy for injuries. When public employees are engaged in adjudicatory or legislative functions, they are likely to retain absolute immunity, as do judges and elected legislators (*Bogan v. Scott-Harris*, 1998; *Butz v. Economou*, 1978). It is important to remember that absolute immunity pertains to the function, not the official position description. For instance, an administrative law judge will have qualified, rather than absolute, immunity when hiring or disciplining subordinate employees. Necessarily, the functional approach results in some ambiguity, and even some public employees engaged in adjudicatory functions, such as public defenders and members of prison disciplinary committees, do not enjoy absolute immunity (*Cleavinger v. Saxner*, 1985; *Tower v. Glover*, 1984).

In *Bush v. Lucas* (1983), the Supreme Court held that liability suits were an inappropriate remedy for federal employees claiming to have been subject to illegal or unconstitutional personnel actions in retaliation for their exercise of freedom of speech. The Court reasoned that federal personnel law provides for elaborate remedies, including hearings before the Merit Systems Protection Board, for such employees. Therefore, in the Court's view, because Congress explicitly created these remedies, it would be improper for the judiciary to fashion additional ones through constitutional interpretation. *Bush's* broad reasoning precludes constitutional tort suits in federal personnel administration in a wide range of matters. However, where there is no alternative remedy for the violation of constitutional rights, such suits may be appropriate. For example, in *Collins v. Bender* (1999), the U.S. Court of Appeals for the Ninth Circuit held that a former drug enforcement agent could bring a constitutional tort suit against fellow agents who violated his Fourth Amendment rights by seizing personal firearms from his house without a warrant while he was on administrative leave. The seizure was not a personnel action subject to an administrative remedy. The *Collins* holding suggests that more viable constitutional tort suits by federal personnel may emerge as an unintended consequence of measures that reduce the civil service and administrative appeals rights of employees engaged in national security, defense, or other functions. *Bush*, of course, does nothing to prevent nonfederal government employees from using section 1983 as a means of seeking compensatory and punitive damages for personnel actions taken against them in violation of any of their constitutional rights.

VARIANTS

Some aspects of qualified immunity are relatively specific to the functions public employees perform. For example, the Supreme Court has been reluctant to trench on police discretion. Consequently, police are unlikely to face constitutional tort liability for conducting high-speed vehicle chases, even when these end in tragedy (*County of Sacramento v. Lewis*, 1998; *Scott v. Harris*, 2007), and, as mentioned earlier, making arrests for nonjailable (fine only) minor offenses (*Atwater v. City of Lago Vista*, 2001; see also *Brosseau v. Haugen*, 2004, regarding discretion in the use of deadly force). Prison guards also have considerable discretion and, unless they are deliberately indifferent to a prisoner's safety, are unlikely to be liable for injuries caused by prisoner-on-prisoner violence (*Farmer v. Brennan*, 1994; Rosenbloom, O'Leary, and Chanin, 2010, chapter 7). More generally, in *Wilkie v. Robbins* (2007), a case involving federal employees of the Bureau of Land Management, the Court declined to create a "a general provision for tort-like liability when Government employees are unduly zealous in pressing a governmental interest affecting property" because it would invite constitutional tort suits and require the courts to determine when public employees "demanded too much and went too far" (*Wilkie v. Robbins*, 2007, p. 557).

THE CONSTITUTIONAL RIGHT TO DISOBEY

Public administrators' potential liability for constitutional torts has generated a concomitant nascent constitutional right to disobey unconstitutional directives. In *Harley v. Schuylkill County* (1979, p. 194), a federal district court explained that:

> The duty to refrain from acting in a manner which would deprive another of constitutional rights is a duty created and imposed by the constitution itself. It is logical to believe that the concurrent right is also one which is created and secured by the constitution. Therefore, we hold that the right to refuse to perform an unconstitutional act is a right "secured by the Constitution . . . ."

The Supreme Court has not had occasion to consider the constitutional right of public employees to disobey unconstitutional orders. However, the district court's conclusion appears to be supported by strong policy reasons as well as by constitutional imperative. As Robert Vaughn (1977, pp. 294–295) points out: "Congress and the courts have already adopted the concept of personal responsibility by providing penalties for the wrongful acts of public employees. The courts now have the opportunity to vindicate the concept of personal responsibility by accepting the right of public employees to disobey under appropriate circumstances." To prevail in asserting a constitutional right to disobey unconstitutional directives, the employee may have to show (1) that the refusal to obey was based on a sincere belief that the action at issue was unconstitutional and (2) that he or she is correct in his or her legal assessment.

In practice, of course, disobedience is likely to be a last resort. Public employees also have a constitutional right to seek to eliminate unconstitutional practices through whistle blowing (*Givhan v. Western Line Consolidated School District*, 1979; *Pickering v.*

Board of Education, 1968). In modern personnel and management systems, employees will also have the opportunity to discuss their reasons for not wanting to carry out an order with a supervisor, and some resolution short of litigation is highly likely.

CONSEQUENCES FOR PUBLIC PERSONNEL ADMINISTRATION

Public employees' liabilities for constitutional torts have several important consequences for public personnel administration. First, although such liability conveys great benefits by helping to protect constitutional rights, it also adds to the cost of government. The potential to face suit for constitutional torts makes public employment less desirable. Public personnel management is now infused with constitutional law and potential liability. In the past three decades or so, the Supreme Court decided several cases involving public employees' challenges to personnel actions allegedly violating freedom of speech or association, Fourth Amendment privacy rights, procedural due process, and equal protection.[2] The government plainly could have avoided some of the suits it lost by paying greater attention to clear constitutional doctrines in the first place.[3] However, in some cases the law may appear clear to a judge but not necessarily so to a personnel manager. For example, affirmative action became deeply ingrained in the 1980s and 1990s and may still be widely practiced in one form or another in public personnel systems, even though judges relying on the Supreme Court's reasoning in *Adarand Constructors, Inc. v. Pena* (1995) and *Gratz v. Bollinger* (2003) might well find many instances of it unconstitutional (see Naylor and Rosenbloom, 2004).[4] In other cases, the law itself may be so unclear that it affords little or no useful guidance. *Waters v. Churchill* (1994), which involved public employees' freedom of speech, is probably the preeminent example of just how fuzzy constitutional law can be (Rosenbloom, 1994). The key standard in Justice Sandra Day O'Connor's plurality opinion is that "only procedure outside the range of what a reasonable manager would use may be condemned as unreasonable" (*Waters v. Churchill*, 1994, p. 678). To this, Justice Antonin Scalia responded that "it remains entirely unclear what the employer's judgment *must* be based on" (*Waters v. Churchill*, 1994, p. 693).[5] Although such a lack of clarity would seem to relieve public personnelists of liability under the *Harlow* standard, they nevertheless need to follow the case law as it develops in lower court decisions, which may provide "fair warning" that a contemplated action is unconstitutional (*Hope v. Pelzer*, 2002).

Many public personnel systems protect their employees in liability suits by providing them with legal representation, legal insurance, and/or indemnification. These approaches go a long way toward eliminating the risk of being harmed financially in a lawsuit arising out of one's performance in public office. Nevertheless, sufficient insurance can be costly, the availability of legal representation may depend upon the specific circumstances involved, and indemnification may be incomplete or unavailable for punitive or exemplary damages. Moreover, any significant lawsuit will engulf one's time, attention, and energy. Consequently, liability remains an aspect of the public service that may be viewed as a drawback by prospective and current public employees.

Outsourcing public personnel functions and other government work may not reduce this problem. With the exception of the Thirteenth Amendment's ban on slavery and involuntary servitude, the Constitution does not ordinarily apply to interactions between private parties. However, the Constitution may control the behavior of private organizations and individuals when they engage in public functions or become so deeply entwined with government that they are indistinct from it (i.e., when they engage in "state action").[6] For instance, private physicians on part-time contracts to provide health care to prisoners and privately employed prison guards can be held liable for violating the Eighth Amendment's ban on cruel and unusual punishment (*Richardson v. McKnight*, 1997; *West v. Atkins*, 1988). Moreover, they have no immunity—either absolute or qualified—in such suits (*Richardson v. McKnight*, 1997).[7]

Unfortunately for those making human resource management decisions in areas of outsourced government work, the law regarding state action is notoriously unclear (*Brentwood Academy v. Tennessee Secondary School Athletic Association*, 2001; *Lebron v. National Railroad Passenger Corporation*, 1995). There is a great deal of uncertainty regarding the specific characteristics of personnel functions or public–private partnerships that might make the Constitution apply to outsourcing arrangements. Perhaps the leading candidates for triggering state action doctrine are background investigations, which can involve Fourth Amendment privacy concerns, and designing promotional exams for public employees, which can potentially raise equal protection concerns.[8]

Second, public personnel systems will have to take greater responsibility for teaching public servants to be constitutionally competent (Rosenbloom, Carroll, and Carroll, 2000). This is especially true if more variation in constitutional tort law continues to develop as a result of judicial efforts to tailor qualified immunity to the specific functions performed by categories of public employees, such as police and prison guards. The public administrator's best defense against liability for constitutional torts is reasonable knowledge of the constitutional rights of those individuals upon whom his or her official actions bear. Universities can teach broad constitutional principles, values, and reasoning in their Master of Public Administration programs, but they are not well suited for teaching the detailed constitutional law that controls specific jobs, such as that of a social worker or Bureau of Land Management employee. Constance Horner, former director of the U.S. Office of Personnel Management (OPM), recognized the important role that personnel agencies can play in constitutional education by calling for "constitutional literacy" among higher-level federal employees (Horner, 1988). In 2004, OPM director, Kay Coles James, followed suit by highlighting the importance of the oath that federal employees take to support the Constitution (Barr, 2004). Local governments, in particular, should systematically follow constitutional law cases and integrate new rulings into their training and operational manuals. In *City of Canton v. Harris* (1989, p. 390), the Supreme Court held that a local government may be held liable for violations of constitutional rights caused by its failure to take "reasonable steps to train its employees."

Finally, education and training in personnel and human resources management for the public sector should specifically and comprehensively cover the constitutional rights of public employees and applicants. Public servants have extensive constitutional rights to freedom of speech, association, privacy, procedural due process, equal protection, and liberty (Rosenbloom, 1971; Rosenbloom and Carroll, 1995; Rosenbloom, O'Leary, and Chanin, 2010). Therefore, virtually any public administrator who engages in hiring, promoting, disciplining, or evaluating subordinates may potentially violate an individual employee's constitutional rights. Traditional personnel policies as well as those of the new public management and reinventing government movements, which heavily emphasize cost-effectiveness, should be tempered by substantial attention to public employees' constitutional rights. Personnelists who are poorly trained in the constitutional aspects of public employment will not be well positioned to develop policies that secure the due process, equal protection, privacy, and other constitutional rights of public employees.

References

Adarand Constructors, Inc. v. Pena. 1995. 515 U.S. 200.

Anderson v. Creighton. 1987. 482 U.S. 635.

Atwater v. City of Lago Vista. 2001. 532 U.S. 318.

Barr, Stephen. 2004, November 12. "Federal Diary: OPM's Constitutional Confab." *Washington Post*, p. B2.

Barr v. Matteo. 1959. 360 U.S. 564.

Bivens v. Six Unknown Named Federal Narcotics Agents. 1971. 403 U.S. 388.

BMW of North America v. Gore. 1996. 517 U.S. 559.

Board of County Commissioners, Wabaunsee County v. Umbehr. 1996. 518 U.S. 668.

Bogan v. Scott-Harris. 1998. 523 U.S. 44.

Brentwood Academy v. Tennessee Secondary School Athletic Association. 2001. 531 U.S. 288.

Brosseau v. Haugen. 2004. 543 U.S. 194.

Bush v. Lucas. 1983. 462 U.S. 367.

Butz v. Economou. 1978. 438 U.S. 478.

Carlson v. Green. 1980. 446 U.S. 14.

Carroll, James D. 1982, Spring. "The New Juridical Federalism and the Alienation of Public Policy and Administration." *American Review of Public Administration* 16: 89–105.

Chayes, Abram. 1976. "The Role of the Judge in Public Law Litigation." *Harvard Law Review* 89: 1281–1316.

Chicago Teachers Union v. Hudson. 1986. 475 U.S. 292.

City of Canton v. Harris. 1989. 489 U.S. 378.

City of Newport v. Fact Concerts. 1981. 453 U.S. 247.

City of Richmond v. J. A. Croson Co. 1989. 488 U.S. 469.

Cleavinger v. Saxner. 1985. 474 U.S. 193.

Cleveland Board of Education v. Loudermill. 1985. 470 U.S. 532.

Collins v. Bender. 1999. 195 F.3d 1076.

Correctional Services Corporation v. Malesko. 2001. 534 U.S. 61.

County of Sacramento v. Lewis. 1998. 523 U.S. 833.

Davis v. Passman. 1979. 422 U.S. 228.

Delaware v. Prouse. 1979. 440 U.S. 648.

Dolan v. City of Tigard. 1994. 512 U.S. 374.

Farley, John J. 1989, Spring. "The Representation and Defense of the Federal Employee by the Department of Justice." *U.S. Department of Justice* (mimeograph).

Farmer v. Brennan. 1994. 511 U.S. 825.

FDIC v. Meyer. 1994. 510 U.S. 471.

Friel, Brian. 1998, May 19. "Managers Rarely Found Liable in Lawsuits." *Government Executive (The Daily Fed)*, p. 1.

Galanter, Marc. 1988. "Beyond the Litigation Panic." In Walter Olson, ed., *New Directions in Liability Law* (pp. 18–30). New York: Academy of Political Science.

Garcetti v. Ceballos. 2006. 547 U.S. 510.

Givhan v. Western Line Consolidated School District. 1979. 349 U.S. 410.

Gratz v. Bollinger. 2003. 539 U.S. 244.

Grutter v. Bollinger. 2003. 539 U.S. 306.

Harley v. Schuylkill County. 1979. 476 F. Supp. 191.

Harlow v. Fitzgerald. 1982. 457 U.S. 800.

Hafer v. Melo. 1991. 502 U.S. 21.

Hiibel v. Sixth Judicial District Court of Nevada, Humboldt County. 2004. 542 U.S. 177.

Hope v. Pelzer. 2002. 536 U.S. 730.

Horner, Constance. 1988, October 14. "Remarks on FEI's [Federal Executive Institute's] 20th Anniversary Dinner." Charlottesville, VA, p. 14.

Horowitz, Donald. 1977. *The Courts and Social Policy.* Washington, D.C.: Brookings Institution.

____. 1983. "Decreeing Organizational Change: Judicial Supervision of Public Institutions." *Duke Law Journal* 88(3): 1265–1307.

Kolender v. Lawson. 1983. 461 U.S. 352.

Lebron v. National Railroad Passenger Corporation. 1995. 513 U.S. 374.

Lee, Yong. 1987, March/April. "Civil Liability of State and Local Governments: Myths and Reality." *Public Administration Review* 47: 160–170.

____. 2004, July/August. "The Judicial Theory of a Reasonable Public Servant." *Public Administration Review* 64: 425–437.

____ and David H. Rosenbloom. 2005. *A Reasonable Public Servant.* Armonk, NY: M. E. Sharpe.

Lipsky, Michael. 1980. *Street-Level Bureaucracy.* New York: Russell Sage.

Lucas v. South Carolina Coastal Council. 1992. 505 U.S. 1003.

Miranda v. Arizona. 1966. 384 U.S. 436.

Missouri v. Jenkins. 1990. 494 U.S. 33.

Missouri v. Jenkins. 1995. 515 U.S. 70.

Mitchell v. Forsyth. 1985. 472 U.S. 511.

National Treasury Employees Union v. Von Raab. 1989. 489 U.S. 656.

Naylor, Lorenda A., and David H. Rosenbloom. 2004, June. "*Adarand, Grutter,* and *Gratz*: Does Affirmative Action in Federal Employment Matter?" *Review of Public Personnel Administration* 24: 150–174.

O'Connor v. Ortega. 1987. 480 U.S. 709.

O'Hare Truck Service, Inc. v. City of Northlake. 1996. 518 U.S. 712.

Owen v. City of Independence. 1980. 445 U.S. 622.

Pembaur v. City of Cincinnati. 1986. 475 U.S. 469.

Pickering v. Board of Education. 1968. 391 U.S. 563.

Plata v. Schwarzenegger. 2005. Dist. Lexis 43796.

Rankin v. McPherson. 1987. 483 U.S. 378.

Ricci v. DeStefano. 2009. 557 U.S.___; 129 S.Ct. 2658; 174 L.Ed. 2d 490.

Riccucci, Norma, and Katherine Naff. 2007. *Personnel Management in Government* (6th ed.). Boca Raton, FL: Taylor and Francis.

Richardson v. McKnight. 1997. 521 U.S. 399.

Rivenbark, Leigh. 1998, July 20. "Protection Needed Against Lawsuits." *Federal Times,* p. 3.

Rosenbloom, David H. 1971. *Federal Service and the Constitution.* Ithaca, NY: Cornell University Press.

____ 1994, November/December. "Fuzzy Law from the High Court." *Public Administration Review* 54: 503–506.

____ and James D. Carroll. 1990. *Toward Constitutional Competence: A Casebook for Public Administrators.* Englewood Cliffs, NJ: Prentice Hall.

____ and James D. Carroll. 1995. "Public Personnel Administration and Law." In Jack Rabin, Thomas Vocino, W. B. Hildreth, and Gerald Miller, eds. *Handbook of Public Personnel Administration* (pp. 71–113). New York: Marcel Dekker.

____ James Carroll, and Jonathan Carroll. 2000. *Constitutional Competence for Public Managers: Cases and Commentary.* Itasca, IL: F. E. Peacock Publishers.

____ Rosemary O'Leary, and Joshua Chanin. 2010. *Public Administration and Law* (3rd ed.). Boca Raton, FL: Taylor and Francis.

Rutan v. Republican Party of Illinois. 1990. 497 U.S. 62.

Scheuer v. Rhodes. 1974. 416 U.S. 232.

Schuck, Peter. 1982. *Suing Government: Citizen Remedies for Official Wrongs.* New Haven, CT: Yale University Press.

____ 1988. "The New Judicial Ideology of Tort Law." In Walter Olson, ed. *New Directions in Liability Law* (pp. 4–14). New York: Academy of Political Science.

Scott v. Harris. 2007. 550 U.S. 372.

"Section 1983 and Federalism." 1977. *Harvard Law Review* 90: 1133–1361.

Smith v. Wade. 1983. 461 U.S. 31.

Spalding v. Vilas. 1896. 161 U.S. 483.

Stump v. Sparkman. 1978. 435 U.S. 349.

Terry v. Ohio. 1968. 392 U.S. I.
Tower v. Glover. 1984. 467 U.S. 914.
United States v. James Daniel Good Real Property. 1994. 510 U.S. 471.
United States v. Lee. 1882. 106 U.S. 196.
United States v. National Treasury Employees Union. 1995. 513 U.S. 454.
Vaughn, Robert. 1977. "Public Employees and the Right to Disobey." *Hastings Law Journal* 29: 261–295.
Waters v. Churchill. 1994. 511 U.S. 661.
West v. Atkins. 1988. 487 U.S. 42.
Whren v. United States. 1996. 517 U.S. 806.
Wilkie v. Robbins. 2007. 551 U.S. 537.
Will v. Michigan Department of State Police. 1989. 491 U.S. 59.
Wood v. Strickland. 1975. 420 U.S. 308.
Woodford v. Ngo. 2006. 548 U.S. 81.
Wygant v. Jackson. 1986. 478 U.S. 267.

Endnotes

1. Yong Lee (1987) identified approximately 1,700 cases in the odd years from 1977 to 1983. This figure pertains only to reported cases. The number of unreported federal district court decisions in official liability cases is unknown, but presumably substantial. From 1993 to 1998, 7,000 federal employees sought legal representation by the Department of Justice, but only 14 were ultimately found personally liable in court (Friel, 1998, p. 1). Lee (1987, p. 169) lists the mean awards as follows: 1977, $48,552; 1979, $14,711; 1981, $63,031; 1983, $92,411. See also Yong Lee (2004) and Yong Lee and David H. Rosenbloom (2005).

2. Successful First Amendment challenges include *Chicago Teachers Union v. Hudson* (1986) (nonunion employees in bargaining unit cannot be coerced to pay for a union's nonrepresentational activities, including political activities, and a procedure for resolving amounts in dispute is required); *Rankin v. McPherson* (1987) (remark by probationary employee in constable's office expressing hope that next assassination attempt on President Ronald Reagan is successful is constitutionally protected and cannot be the basis for dismissal of a low-level probationary employee with data entry responsibilities and little or no contact with the public); *Rutan v. Republican Party of Illinois* (1990) (partisan affiliation or support is an unconstitutional basis for personnel actions involving ordinary public employees' promotion, training, assignment, and similar actions, as well as hiring and firing); *Waters v. Churchill* (1994) (speech-related dismissals require reasonable belief that employee made alleged remarks); *United States v. National Treasury Employees Union* (1995) (provision banning federal employee acceptance of pay for nonjob related published and other expression violates free speech/press). Fourth Amendment decisions include *O'Connor v. Ortega* (1987) (administrative searches and seizures in public workplace must be reasonable in inception and scope if employee meets threshold test of having a reasonable expectation of privacy under the circumstances involved); *National Treasury Employees Union v. Von Raab* (1989) (suspicionless drug testing of some categories of customs employees is constitutional). Procedural due process violated by dismissal from civil service job without prior notice and opportunity to respond (*Cleveland Board of Education v. Loudermill*, 1985). Equal Protection Clause prohibits dismissal of nonminority in violation of seniority rights to further equal employment opportunity/affirmative action (*Wygant v. Jackson*, 1986).

3. *Cleveland Board of Education v. Loudermill* (1985), is perhaps the clearest example of an instance in which a minimal, almost costless, procedure could have obviated a suit. *Wygant v. Jackson* (1986), occurred because a school board agreed to race-based dismissals that would almost certainly result in litigation and, in high probability, loss as well. The statutory ban in *United States v. National Treasury Employees Union* (1995), was exceptionally broad and the administrative rules pursuant to it were so complex as to appear irrational and arbitrary.

4. In *Adarand Constructors, Inc. v. Pena* (1995), the Supreme Court held that all racial classifications are constitutionally suspect and subject to strict judicial scrutiny. To be constitutional they must serve a compelling governmental interest in a narrowly tailored fashion. See also *Grutter v. Bollinger* (2003) and *Gratz v. Bollinger* (2003).

5. The question was whether a public employee could be disciplined for what her supervisor thought she said or only for what she actually said. There was no majority opinion on the Supreme Court, but the guiding principles appear to be that (1) the employer must reasonably investigate what the employee may have said, and (2) the employer must really believe the employee said it before imposing discipline.

6. "State action" means governmental action, regardless of whether at the federal, state, or local governmental levels.

7. Private organizations that become state actors by working for federal agencies are not subject to constitutional tort suits for money damages (*Correctional Services Corporation v. Malesko*, 2001). At the state and local levels, private organizations that are state actors can be sued under section 1983.

8. See *Ricci v. DeStefano* (2009), which involved equal employment opportunity law that closely tracked equal protection analysis in constitutional law.

10 STRATEGIC HUMAN RESOURCE MANAGEMENT

Dennis M. Daley

Dennis M. Daley is a professor of Public Administration at North Carolina State University. He is the author of *Performance Appraisal in the Public Sector: Techniques and Applications* (1992) and *Strategic Human Resource Management* (2002) along with over 50 refereed articles and book chapters. He teaches classes in Human Resource/Personnel Management, Organizational Behavior, and Negotiations and Mediation. He has served as the Chair of the Faculty (2003–2005) at North Carolina State University.

The modern public service is a professional service. Professions are built on knowledge and expertise. This is not a matter that lends itself to a temporary workforce. Knowledge is not gained overnight. It's earned the old fashion way—by hard work. Professional workers must be sought out and guaranteed an environment in which their careers can prosper and be nurtured.

While good human resource practices can be introduced without being linked to a strategic objective, that is a rather foolish, if not faddish, option. An organization must know what its mission is and have some notion of how to tell if it is succeeding. This is more complicated in the public sector. In addition to the generic E3 (economy, efficiency, and effectiveness) requirement, public purpose governments and nonprofit organizations must also be responsive to their citizens and responsible to society or the public interest.

A prerequisite for strategic human resource management lies in the ability of an organization to define what its mission is and how it will go about achieving it. Strategy is dependent on the target. The more precise and accurate this is the more focused can be the human resource practices employed to achieve it. A vague mission or one inaccurately measured will not succeed. The pursuit of measurable objectives that encompass the entire mission (i.e., do not leave out or ignore essential aspects due to their difficulty in measurement) is crucial. Given human limitations, these should also compose no more than 6–12 measures. Any scorecard or dashboard entailing more will likely overload the human element or distract effort from that which is indeed most important.

All of these pose difficult measurement issues. Yet, long lists of various "Returns on Investment" (ROIs) and "customer satisfaction" measures are readily available. However, there is often a tendency to load up on these, in fact, creating an overload. A scoreboard or dashboard needs to focus on only a few, key measures. This enables the organization and its individuals to focus and concentrate their efforts on what is seen as most mattering.

For motivation and incentives to work, they must first be tied to a goal. An organization must employ needs assessment and human resource development strategies in pursuit of its vision or mission. Needs assessment (of where an organization wants to go) and human resources development (of those who are to get it there) focus on the specific organizational and individual needs whose satisfaction will lead to enhanced productivity. The vision and path for fulfilling it derived from strategic planning is put into practical perspective using macro tools such as total quality management (TQM; at the group level) and management by objectives (MBO; at the individual level).

Strategic planning is rational analysis (Berry, 1994; Bryson, 1996; Klingner, 1993; Ledvinka, 1995; Mintzberg, 1994; Nutt and Backoff, 1992; Perry, 1993). It takes "what is" and develops ideas of "what should be" along with plans for "how to get there." With a realistic organizational strategy focused on what the future should look like, strategic planning provides the "road map" for fulfilling that future.

Through environmental scanning strategic planning helps size up what the existing organization's capabilities are and what the real world it exists in is. The planning process explores alternatives—both in terms of the vision involved and the courses of action necessary to accomplish them. Finally, strategic planning helps an organization settle on one choice of direction and mesh it with the appropriate objectives and action plans. Strategic planning should also incorporate the human resources necessary for accomplishing its goals (Mesch, Perry, and Wise, 1995; Perry and Mesch, 1997).

The foremost advantage derived from strategic planning is that it helps improve organizational performance. Strategic planning focuses on the future—what should be. As such, it serves as a guiding star by which to steer the organization's development. Individual and team effort can be devoted to accomplishing the organization's goals (Keen, 1994).

Strategic planning also helps to concentrate individual efforts into a team effort. It can assist in developing TQM and objective-based performance appraisal systems. Accountability for results can be assigned. The strategic planning process itself can serve as a team-building exercise. Finally, the process itself transforms perceptions away from separate and distinct projects and toward systemic viewpoints (Keen, 1994).

It is perhaps the primary task of an organization's leadership to provide vision. Organizations are often large, cumbersome entities with only vague, general notions of what it is they are suppose to do (i.e., the individuals assembled under its rubric have only vague, general notions as to what they hope to do and accomplish). It is the job of those individuals occupying top management positions to provide detail and substantive direction to those notions. Here is where Osborne and Gaebler's (1992) analogy of "steering rather than rowing" is called for. It is the vision that serves to bring together and reinforce people's sense of belonging to an organization. It makes them stakeholders and active, contributing participants.

In addition to leadership support, those engaged in strategic planning need to be aware of other potential problems. As occurs with all management techniques, individuals will need extensive training and refresher training (to answer unforeseen questions that arise in response to implementation). Conflict, confusion, and chaos will prevail initially and for some time thereafter. Only as individuals learn how to do it and see its value will the benefits of strategic planning be realized (Merjanian, 1997).

The value of strategic planning is highly dependent upon those in the agencies who assemble and provide the data, seeing that the data also help them do their jobs better. Excessive requests for information and data unconnected to an organization's mission undermine the strategic planning process. While such information is useful in a command-and-control environment, strategic planning is essential for the more complex, knowledge-based organization's coaching and coordination. However, in such complex organizations the nonlinear nature of management is recognized. Strategic planning serves to define boundaries (Kiel, 1994). Planning is successful because it is useful (Merjanian, 1997).

Resource-based theory (Barney, 1991, 2001; Wernerfelt, 1984) argues that the techniques and practices that an organization possesses (along with the human knowledge base for its use) can provide it with a substantial competitive advantage and ultimately contributes to its effectiveness. Resource-based theory, specifically research on human resource management, notes that human resource techniques and practices do indeed make a difference (Boxall, 1991; Delaney and Huselid, 1996; Delery and Doty, 1996).

In the modern, knowledge-based organization, strategic planning is quite clearly strategic human resources planning. In noting the impact of strategic human resource management on organizational performance, John E. Delery and D. Jarold Doty (1996) identify seven general employment practices. To these are added three candidate, *italicized* items that I feel are well worth previewing. These strategic techniques cover the gamut of the human resource process from organizational position management (broadly defined jobs and *competencies*), staffing (internal career ladders and employment security), and compensation (performance-based compensation and *efficiency wage*) to performance management (results-oriented performance appraisal and formal training systems) and employee relations (*goal setting motivation* and employee voice).

POSITION MANAGEMENT

BROADLY DEFINED JOBS

The "triumph of technique over purpose" is also evident here. The rigidity invested in the use of pay scales (and the commitant job analyses upon which they are based) denies organizations the flexibility to adjust to and meet change. Individuals cannot readily be reassigned duties. This is especially a problem if those duties are from jobs officially designated as having lower grades. Even if pay remains constant, a lower-grade assignment might be seen psychologically as a career setback. Reward for exceptional performance is thwarted by the formal attachment of pay ceilings or maximum salaries to specific job grades.

Broadbanding has been introduced as a means to cut through the Gordian knot of classification. Whether "broad grades" or "career bands" are used, management obtains greater flexibility. The employee is seen to benefit from both more challenging and meaningful work assignments and the possibility of pay increases (Fox Lawson & Associates, 2008; Risher and Schay, 1994).

Broad grades are simply a recalibration of the existing pay scales. Under broad grades, a system of say 50 pay grades is collapsed into 1 of 10 or 12 grades. The range for each broad grade is from 50 to 100 percent of the minimum, starting salary. These new grades are subsequently divided into steps. The advantage of this simple, incremental approach is twofold. First, within each broad grade individuals can take on any of the previously lower-grade duties without loss of pay or prestige. Second, for all but the formerly top-rung employees in each of the broad grades, there is now more "head room" between them and the pay ceilings. However, this flexibility introduces a higher degree of uncertainty or fussiness in the calculation of appropriate pay.

Career bands are more innovative and dynamic. While career bands also reduce the number of pay grades from, for example, 50 to 10 or 12, they do not impose any internal step structure onto this new system. Managers are given the flexibility to freely assign (and reassign) duties and salaries (limited only by overall budget figures). Individuals need not begin at the minimum, starting salary nor serve their time prior to receiving increases. Managers are often permitted to hire at any salary between the minimum and range midpoint; offers above the midpoint would be permitted but require approval. Ideally, salary determination within broadbanding is calculated from a midpoint base. The base is set by the market or competitive salary, which should be the median or average salary.

Employees who are use to rapid promotion through the traditional narrow-grade and step systems may suffer from a sense of stagnation. Additionally, it is necessary to carefully monitor the salary adjustments made by supervisors and managers within these broader bands to make sure that they are being equitably applied based on job performance (Fox Lawson & Associates, 2008).

COMPETENCIES Competencies have much in common with personality traits or attitudes. The important difference that transforms a trait or attitude into a competency is job relatedness. Unfortunately, many organizations do not make the effort to carry out the validation studies that establish the competency link to performance. Hence, competencies remain a candidate for inclusion in strategic human resource management rather than as a proven factor.

By highlighting skills and competencies instead of tasks and behaviors, the organization is targeting the very things it needs to do to succeed. Competencies encompass results; specifically, they indicate the effort necessary for a task or activity to be performed successfully. Individuals think of achieving goals and results rather than narrowly focusing on one specific means of accomplishing an often vaguely defined task. By assuring that the competencies [skills, knowledge, and abilities (SKAs)] necessary for fulfilling the strategic plan are possessed or provided for through employee training and development, the organization's managers and supervisors concentrate their efforts on the factors essential for success (Pickett, 1998; Raja, Johns, and Ntalianis, 2004; Sullivan, 1996).

The documentation of the SKAs necessary to perform a job successfully is a key element in planning for training and for individual career advancement (Wooten, 1993). The identification of similar SKAs also enables organizations to recognize jobs with comparable work and aids in the job evaluation process. In as much as SKAs focus on characteristics and traits (including efforts to validate their use), they are centering in on the very core requirements in the knowledge organization.

SKAs designate the minimum competencies required for a job. However, they can also include advanced SKAs that can lead to greater proficiency (and, ultimately, to advancement). While these would not be required for an individual to assume a position, they would indicate that the minimum expected standards were not also the maximum effort expected.

While research is promising, its focus is primarily on establishing the validity of competency instruments. The definition of competencies also remains open. In addition to the narrower SKAs I discuss, some suggest including characteristics, attitudes, and traits. I fear such a definition expands the concept of competency into meaninglessness. There is little research linking competencies to performance outcomes, especially within the context of a performance appraisal system. Research is also necessary, indicating that a mixture of 6–10 differently weighted competencies can adequately account for a myriad of job classes. Otherwise, one is faced with the problem that has plagued traits. While traits are valid indicators, they provide no advantage over using individual task responsibilities. The advantage promised by competencies is the development of effective and economical measures.

STAFFING

INTERNAL CAREER LADDERS

For government career ladders mean that a balance between inside and outside selection must be struck. Career services such as those associated with rank-in-person approaches virtually limit their recruitment to internal selection. The ideal of the rank-in-position approach, on the other hand, invokes images of external selection. Reality lies somewhere in between. Even rank-in-position career systems (e.g., the elite French *grands corps*) have discovered the benefit of importing talented outsiders (or providing their members with significant outside, sabbatical experiences).

A career system is necessary to focus individual attention on the strategic issues facing an organization over the long term. Objectives and reward systems tied to the short term lead to dysfunctional behavior and goal displacement. Government with its 2-year, 4-year, and 6-year electoral cycles has always suffered from this myopia.

A long-term perspective induces organizational commitment and loyalty. It enables individuals and organizations to invest in training and productivity improvements knowing that they will reap the benefits from that enhanced knowledge and technique. Internal selection is also easier. The employee has already been attracted. The questions on whether an individual will fit in and adapt to an organization's culture are now moot. The problems of orientation and socialization (which are fraught with disappointment and turnover) have been overcome. The not so inconsequential costs of recruitment (which are often an unfortunate, limiting factor among governments) are dramatically reduced.

However, internal selection exposes an organization to the dangers of "inbreeding." While it promotes a more harmonious, homogeneous workforce, it can also blind the organization to what is going on in the world at large. Outside selection stirs up an organization. All the problems mentioned above that are avoided by internal selection are also lost opportunities.

EMPLOYMENT SECURITY   Providing employees with job rights, especially regarding security of tenure, is a major productivity enhancement. Guaranteeing that employees have administrative due process protections in regard to grievances and disciplinary matters creates a sense of organizational justice. This employment security allows individuals to focus their attention on performance, especially that entailing long-term consequences.

The knowledge-based environment also heightens the importance attached to employee rights along with the instrumental grievance and discipline system. Employees are human beings and work better when their humanity is recognized and respected.

The employer–employee relationship is not that of master and servant (although much of the legal system is based on that design). Foreshadowed by the work of Mary Parker Follett and commencing with the Hawthorne studies in the late 1920s, motivational research has clearly pointed this out. With the transformation of the organization into an entity based on the skills of its employees rather than the efficiency of its machinery, this lesson becomes even more important.

Employee rights and the mechanism for enforcing them (i.e., the grievance process) serve as a safeguard for assuring that employees are accorded the basic dignity that every human being is entitled to have. Like similar safety devices, we hope that we never will really need to use them. While most organizations would prefer to do without such legal and formal systems, reality requires them. If there were no past abuses, there would be no need for laws prohibiting such practices.

While all employees possess legal rights vis-à-vis the employment relationship or "contract," those in the public sector are afforded even greater protections. Public employees are both employees and citizens. As citizens, they are extended the basic protections that the federal and state constitutions provide citizens against the abuse of government power. In essence, the Bill of Rights becomes part of the employment contract.

Counterpoised to the greater legal rights that public sector employees possess is a greater difficulty in using them. Legal rights and real rights are not the same thing. Public officials possess greater standing in the eyes of the courts than business managers do, and the public coffers run deeper than those of a business do. Because public officials are viewed as agents administering the public interest, American courts only reluctantly cast them in the role of the "villain." The evidence must indeed be quite substantial for the courts to overcome their presumption of official good conduct. While a business must calculate the costs of litigation against company profits, litigation involving government officials draws on the general public purse. Since litigation is not charged against an agency's operating budget and a court "loss" could damage an official's career, the incentive is to pursue a Dickensian strategy of legal exhaustion.

This legal dilemma underlies the trend for employment-at-will provisions, which abolish administrative due process protections (i.e., require firing for cause that is backed up by objective documentation). While there are serious restrictions on this legal doctrine, remedies are available only through expensive and slow litigation. Neither the employee nor the organization is provided adequate safeguards against administrative abuse. Dependence on administrative caprice and whim stifles employee engagement.

The fad for downsizing also undermines employee productivity. Other than serving as a rearguard action temporarily buying time for restructuring during a crisis, downsizing does not contribute to productivity. Employment security is sacrificed merely to appear au courant.

COMPENSATION

PERFORMANCE-BASED COMPENSATION

Strategic pay requires that all decisions relative to compensation and benefits be designed to attract, retain, or motivate employees. As such, the entire organization's reward structure is designed to serve fully its mission or purpose. In reality, most organizations limit incentive pay to only a portion of the compensation package. All employees who perform satisfactorily are guaranteed a set base pay and benefits package. Even so, this guarantee serves to calm fears with regard to financial security and, hence, helps attract and retain individuals.

Extrinsic incentives primarily use monetary rewards as their motivating factor. Career development and training opportunities that can lead to promotion or interesting, fulfilling assignments (which also provide intrinsic motivation through their recognition of merit) are another source of extrinsic motivation in the sense that in addition to higher compensation levels they pay individuals in terms of power and responsibility.

Pay for performance is an application of expectancy theory. Employee motivation is deemed to be extrinsic and follow the outlines of B. F. Skinner's (1904–1993) operant conditioning models. Expectancy theory posits that employees will be motivated to the extent to which their calculation of the desirability of rewards, the effort required to perform a task, and the probability of successful performance (and of the organizations paying off) are viewed favorably. While not theoretically dependent upon human cognition, goal-setting theory also posits a similar relationship. Pay-for-performance schemes concentrate on providing or determining the right balance between extrinsic reward (pay) and required effort (performance).

A wide array of extrinsic pay-for-performance schemes exist. The modern pay-for-performance scheme builds upon a base pay system. The salary or wage put "at risk" is such to encourage or motivate the worker without jeopardizing his or her basic financial security. One can address overall individual performance or specific instances; focus can be on group performance at the organizational or team level. Individual systems based on merit pay step increases, annuities, bonuses, and suggestion awards as well as skill- or competency-based approaches abound. In addition, group or organization rewards are the focus of gain- or goal-sharing programs. Performance appraisal systems are the trigger instrument for operationalizing pay for performance. The individual performance rating is used to determine which employees are eligible for individual and group awards as well as the amount of reward an individual is entitled to receive. MBO systems may also serve as the measurement instrument for a pay-for-performance system (appraisal by objectives formally incorporates MBO into the performance appraisal process).

Merit step increases, even in systems that are primarily across-the-board longevity awards, are today often modified by the requirement that an employee obtain a minimum (average or fully satisfactory) performance rating in order to be eligible. Mild as such requirements are (less than 5 percent of covered employees are likely to be ineligible), they serve as an incentive encouraging poor performers to improve or to seek opportunities elsewhere.

Merit pay annuities reward the individual's overall performance by an addition to their base salary (hence, the term "annuity"). Because the increased base salary pays dividends throughout the employee's future years, the amount of the pay-for-performance award need be only half that associated with lump-sum bonuses. Currently, a minimum figure of 2.5 percent is suggested (although 5 percent was widely advocated only a few years ago). However, there is little in the way of empirical evidence supporting these figures; they remain, for the most part, the guesses of compensation and benefits experts. What is essential is that the amount be substantial enough from the employee's perspective to serve as a motivating factor. This is likely to depend on both the economic situation and the individual's relevant equity comparisons. Merit pay annuities may be applied as a set percentage (or dollar) increase added to all who achieve a specified performance rating. On the other hand, different performance rating levels may trigger different percentage (or dollar) increases.

The bonus (like the single-event suggestion award) is a lump-sum payment. Its advantage is that it recognizes exceptional performance occurring during the year without entailing a commitment to continuous future payments. Because they are one-time rewards, bonuses need to be more substantial than merit pay annuities. A minimum figure of 5 percent is currently suggested; however, results are more likely if bonuses are, at least, approximately 10 percent or 1-month's salary.

Bonuses, like merit pay annuities, can also be prorated to correspond with differing performance rating levels. Skill- and competency-based pay rewards employees more for organizational potential than for actual performance. In a way, it is an expanded variation of "on-call" pay. Employees are paid extra for possessing the ability to step in and use their acquired skills or competencies. In fact, they are paid even if they are never called upon to use their additional skills and competencies. As personnel technicians have narrowly defined "skills," the broader term "competency" has been introduced to represent desired capabilities. The organizational advantage is that needed talent is on call in case of emergency or special circumstances. It allows the organization the ability to transfer temporarily (or permanently) individuals to more needed tasks. In addition to the extra pay, individuals benefit in the intrinsic motivation and revitalization inherent in the learning process and job rotation. They are also able to explore career options without having to abandon their current jobs. Skill- and competency-based pay is also associated with the broadbanding of jobs. An organization's management determines what extra skills or competencies the organization wants or needs. It then pays those employees extra who have acquired those skills or competencies; the organization is also very much likely to assist employees in acquiring the designated skills or competencies. To continue receiving the extra pay, employees are required to demonstrate periodically proficiency in their skills or competencies; the list of needed skills and competencies are also periodically reevaluated by the organization.

One serious problem faced by most pay-for-performance schemes in the public sector is the tendency to cap awards. Locked into older notions of classification pay grades, individuals who have obtained the maximum pay allowed within their official pay grade may be deemed ineligible for merit annuities or bonuses. Since these awards are touted as being earned through meritorious performance, their denial greatly undermines perceptions not only of the programs efficacy but of organizational fairness as well.

Most pay-for-performance systems focus primarily on the individual; however, growing concern for the group or team aspects of the work processes is directing attention to group incentives. TQM movements have brought these concerns to the forefront in recent years. While W. Edwards Deming (1900–1994) insisted that the only rewards necessary for TQM were intrinsic, other advocates also embrace the use of extrinsic group rewards.

Gain sharing or goal sharing is the primary group or team incentive system employed to measure and reward organizational performance. It is an outgrowth or refinement of the profit-sharing plans (such as Scanlon, Rucker, or Improshare). Profit sharing focuses on the entire organization and rewards individuals based on its overall performance. Since individual employees materially share in creating the organization's success, sharing the resultant profits or gains would serve to motivate their performance.

However, for large or diversified organizations, individuals often did not see how their individual efforts could influence the overall results. Individuals in internal services or staff units also had difficulty in related their efforts to the overall organization's purpose. Gain sharing addresses those concerns by focusing on organizational subunits instead of the overall organization. Using the organization's budget process and performance management system, savings, or productivity gains (in addition to profits) can be used as the basis for group rewards. This enables rewards to be dispensed for staff and service units that reduce costs as well as for units that have made improvements in productivity even if they are still technically losing money.

Gain sharing is quite appealing to public sector organizations. It capitalizes on both the public sector's lack of a profit system and its greater reliance on group processes. As such, gain sharing complements TQM efforts by providing a mechanism for extrinsic rewards.

A recent refinement to gain sharing has been the notion of goal sharing. Instead of rewards being based on documented budget savings they are tied to the achievement of specified group or team goals. Goals derived from TQM (or strategic planning or MBO) programs are thereby linked to extrinsic rewards for the individual. This serves to assure the individual's attention and motivation.

For gain sharing or goal sharing to be effective, the goals or savings gains must be based on measurable factors under control of employees in unit. Individual employees must understand what the goals are and feel that they are indeed obtainable through their group's combined teamwork. Employee participation in the selection of the goals is an added means for ensuring that understanding and a sense of stakeholder status.

Related to this is the requirement that payout pools for gain-sharing or goal-sharing rewards also be readily understood. Complex or the manipulation of payout formulas undermines confidence in the system's efficacy. Upward adjustments or the ratcheting of expected performance rates or goals also undermines employee confidence.

Payout pools should link together an identifiable "community of interest." Employees must see the people in their pool as being part of a team. The distribution of gain-sharing or goal-sharing rewards can be across the board (in terms of actual dollars or percentages). It can be linked to individual performance appraisals as an eligibility factor or as a prorating device. It can even be left for the employees themselves to decide.

The above-described limitations along with sustained, long-term funding of such proposals have hindered the successful implementation of merit pay schemes. With few exceptions, merit pay has failed in the public sector (Bowman, 2010; Ingraham, 1993; Perry, Engbers, and Jun, 2009; Perry, Petrakis, and Miller, 1989).

EFFICIENCY WAGE   The efficiency wage notion (i.e., paying high wages in order to attract the best qualified employees) is drawing interest. While not widely used or fully vetted, it suggests an alternative approach to the employment contract. The use of an efficiency wage approach has been noted in St. Charles, Illinois (suspended with the advent of the Great Recession). In essence, annual salary surveys are conducted with all positions being funded at a 75 percentile level.

A number of advantages are associated with the efficient wage model. Above-average pay attracts higher-quality employees. To be effective an efficiency wage needs to be closely aligned with the hiring process. Whether responsibility or competency based, it is essential that positions be filled by individuals fully capable of achieving the results expected. While the high pay serves to attract individuals, it is the pride in their work, more than fear of losing this higher pay, motivates these employees. In addition, less expense and effort are subsequently required to monitor employee performance (Davis and Gabris, 2008).

PERFORMANCE MANAGEMENT

RESULTS-ORIENTED PERFORMANCE APPRAISAL

Since we are unable to test them, motivation theories (e.g., Maslow's hierarchy of needs, Herzberg's two factors, Adam's equity theory, or Vroom's expectancy theory) are primarily heuristic devices. As such, they still serve to inform and provide useful insights. However, goal-setting theory (Latham, 2007) has been subject to empirical verification. While influenced by a priori mediators (direction, effort, persistence, and task strategies) along with intervening moderators (feedback, commitment, ability, and task complexity), goal setting can, most definitely, influence individual performance. This is essentially the basis of objective performance appraisal systems.

While goal setting has empirical support for its effectiveness, its incorporation within merit pay schemes has been quite disappointing. Evidence exists that merit pay does not work in the public sector. This is perhaps more due to the failure to fund such programs and to maintain them over a long term than to any failure in goal setting (Ingraham, 1993; Perry, Engbers, and Jun, 2009; Perry, Petrakis, and Miller, 1989).

Performance appraisal is used as an aid in making judgment decisions pertaining to promotion, demotion, retention, transfer, and pay. It is also employed as a developmental guide for training needs assessment and employee feedback. Performance appraisal also aids with a number of more general organizational functions as a means for validating selection and hiring procedures, promoting employee–supervisor understanding, and supporting an organization's culture. Modern performance appraisal systems combine an objective appraisal instrument with supervisory and employee training in its proper use.

Two formats dominate the arena of objective appraisal techniques: behaviorally anchored rating scales (BARS) and MBO. BARS and MBO approaches essentially involve the same components; however, the objective components that are common in both approaches are introduced into the appraisal process in a somewhat different order. BARS appraisals work best with large groups and subgroups of individuals whose job descriptions can be standardized; MBO, on the other hand, is more suited to cases that can be tailored to each individual job. MBO is best when it is focused on the results to be expected from job performance; BARS handles behavioral processes where outputs are more identifiable and assurable than outcomes. Both employ variations on participative management in order to guarantee their effectiveness. A somewhat more passive approach to participation guides BARS, while a more proactive style is found in MBO.

While the use of objective appraisal instruments is recommended, many jurisdictions still employ subjective graphic rating scales. Although invalid, for the most part, they are relatively inexpensive and prove adequate "paper systems" for jurisdictions, wherein performance appraisal is not realistically relied upon as an aid in decision making. Often effective and trusted supervisors can compensate for the shortcomings of inadequate systems. Unfortunately, supervisory (and employee) training in the proper use of the appraisal process tends to lag significantly. This often results in systems failures in that the advantages of an objective appraisal are dissipated thorough assorted managerial mistakes and rater errors.

FORMAL TRAINING SYSTEMS Training and development is the philosopher's stone. The modern organization is indeed its people and the knowledge they possess. We must recognize that this knowledge is, at best, only the beginning of the mystery. It can no longer be taken for granted that employees will arrive at work with all the requisite skills. Too much of what goes on in today's organization requires specific adaptation. The most knowledgeable and skilled worker still requires training so as to fit into the organization and become a valuable contributor to the team (Quinn, Anderson, and Finkelstein, 1996). The chief function of the supervisor is the development of the people in their unit. Managers who have often been promoted from a technical position must remember that they are now the coaches; others have the responsibility of carrying out the plays on the field. The manager/coach can have the greatest effect only by assuring that the employee/player is truly prepared for action.

Training and development are an important complement, if not indeed necessary, within a career system. Using an on-the-job approach (with 1-year assignments), the Roman *cursus honourum—quaestor* (finance), *aedile* (public works), *praetor* (judicial), and *consul* (executive)—focused on developing a pool of talented individuals from which each successive level could be staffed.

Unfortunately, training and development is one of the most neglected aspects of government. Well into the 1950s and 1960s, governments denied the value of training and development. Individuals were hired for specific jobs and were assumed to already possess all the skills that would be needed. While the importance of training and development is now recognized, it remains a neglected area. Beginning employees, like the buildings and equipment of government, are allowed to depreciate through an underinvestment in maintenance (Elmore, 1991; Gray, Hall, Miller, and Shasky, 1997).

EMPLOYEE RELATIONS

GOAL-SETTING MOTIVATION

The need theories describing what motivates individuals from Frederick Taylor's money through Abraham Maslow's Hierarchy of Needs (along with Clayton Alderfer Existence-Relatedness-Growth adaptation) and Frederick Herzberg's Hygiene-Motivators to David McCelland's nAch, nAff, and nPwr all fail to meet social science criteria for testing. They rely on human cognitive behavior that cannot be discerned. Yet, they serve as a useful heuristic guiding our notions of motivation. A similar cognitive behavior situation exists with respect to process theories on how motivation works such as Victor Vroom's Expectancy Theory and J. Stacy Adams' Equity Theory. The calculation of values and probabilities for success as well as the benchmark or reference against which that value is measured are cognitive processes.

However, goal setting bypasses these problems simply by ignoring the cognitive dimension. Goal setting focuses on observable actions and cares little for why they were pursued. That they were indeed pursued by an individual is sufficient in itself (Edwin Locke and Gary Latham). Goal setting shares with scientific management (especially in its training of workers) and MBO (and TQM concepts) a focus on measurable objectives or goals. It differs in that these goals are seen as being associated or inherent with the organizational employee rather than the employer. Goals Setting works because the employee sees the goals as an inherent component in the wage–effort bargain. The work relationship is one predicated on a fair exchange of an employee's labor and knowledge for an organization's (employer's) intrinsic and extrinsic rewards. In addition, individuals internalize the goals that are set as indicators of their own professional competence.

Goal setting is subject to various mediators (direction, effort, persistence, and task strategies) that are preconditions in its successful application. Direction reflects the priority or importance attached to a specific goal. Effort registers the amount of "work" put into this task. Persistence focuses on both the long-term (proximate vs. distal) nature of the task and the ability to handle and overcome setbacks and errors. Task strategy notes conditions that require learning which techniques work and how to apply them.

Moderators (feedback, commitment, ability, and task complexity) can act as a dampening agent. Feedback, especially on distal, long-term goals, is important for both correcting the trajectory and encouraging continued action (MBO system incorporates milestones to achieve this purpose). Commitment reflects the continued value placed in the goal. In the public sector with its wavering political fads, this can often prove difficult. Ability measures the inherent competence of those tasked with achieving a goal. Task complexity focuses on whether the problem is tame or wicked. How independent of other problems and players is it?

EMPLOYEE VOICE   J. Stacy Adams (1963) suggests in his equity theory that employee assessments are comparative. In evaluating the balance in the reward–effort nexus, an individual employee while cognizant of the work performed and the reward received for it assesses their worth cognitively. The objective situation is analyzed through subjective, comparative lenses. Each individual decides the extent to which the reward–effort balance is fair. While situations in which an imbalance is deemed to exist can be adjusted for through increasing (or decreasing) the work effort to accord with a perceived higher (or lower) reward, they can also be psychologically adjusted by reassessing the balance as indeed fair (or, in cases previously seen as fair, unfair). The crucial fulcrum on which this balance rests is the comparative referent employed by the individual. Fairness is perceived because of general principles or specific instances guiding how others are treated. An employee most likely will compare their wage–effort arrangement with that of fellow workers. The amount of reward received is thrown into the scales with the perceived effort expended by each colleague. An external referent can also be employed where some social or industrial standard exists. Since referents as well as workload can be adjusted, the cognitive responses guarantee no simple bottom-line equation for balancing the reward–effort bargain.

As such, it is imperative that the organization make a concerted effort in demonstrating the fairness of its motivation and reward structure. This is an underlying precept in the use of both internal job evaluation and external market wage determination techniques. Job evaluation constructs an elaborate and integrated system of what each job contributes or is worth to the organization and rewards it accordingly. The market technique focuses on external factors and anchors pay and benefits in the global supply and demand.

Consistent standards are essential for success. Pay-for-performance schemes often fail this test. While performance or productivity demands makes extensive reference to the market and real-world practices, salary and wage practices rely on internal measures or political whim. The rewards and risks of the external market system are not included along with the demands for businesslike efficiencies.

In Exit, Voice, and Loyalty Albert O. Hirschman (1970) propose a typology of responses to dissatisfaction. A theory of individual self-interest that not only operates in terms of the economic market but with respect to sociopolitical values is primarily an attempt to explain an organization's survival. Although Hirschman's theory focuses on decisions regarding the acceptance/rejection of an organization's products or services, it can also be interpreted with regard to similar decisions by an organization's own personnel vis-à-vis the organization itself.

Exit is a conceptual representation of the market or economic system. The individual consumer chooses to buy or not buy; that is, to stay or exit. By exiting a product line or service, individuals register their market judgment. Similarly, an employee can express dissatisfaction with the organization by leaving it.

For such a market system to work, basic economic assumptions need to be met. The consumer or employee must have viable alternatives from which to choose (as well as the knowledge of the situation). Even so, Hirschman notes that the exit option, as such, is not made lightly. Hence, he suggests that prior to such a step being taken a consumer or employee is likely to make other attempts to rectify the perceived problems or dissatisfactions.

It is this effort to change the situation that gives rise to voice. Voice is seen to represent a political dimension that can encompass a gamut of behaviors ranging from grumbling through participative management to full-scale democracy. It represents a viable, nonmarket means for assuring organizational survival.

While voice focuses internally on the advocacy of reform, loyalty represents the employee's willingness to "stand up" for the organization. In this instance advocacy is in response to outside criticism and an expression of confidence in the organization.

In a series of articles, Farrell and Rusbult (Farrell, 1983; Farrell and Rusbult, 1981; Rusbult, 1980; Rusbult, 1983; Rusbult and Farrell, 1983; Rusbult, Farrell, Rogers, and Mainous, 1988) explicitly extend Hirschman's concept to personnel matters. Because of a multidimensional scaling of job dissatisfaction, Farrell (1983) was able to demonstrate support for a modified version of Hirschman's typology. To the categories of exit, voice, and loyalty, Farrell added one for neglect. Neglect indicates a condition in which employees give up but stay to draw a paycheck. Neglect may involve absenteeism and obstructionism or merely a passive "I don't care" attitude.

Farrell arranges these four categories into a two-dimensional structure: (1) constructive versus destructive and (2) active versus passive. Voice and loyalty are constructive, while exit and neglect are destructive of the organization. Crosscutting this, we find that voice and exit are active.

Rusbult and Farrell identify motivation as being affected by previous job satisfaction, investment in the job, and job alternatives. These lead to different dissatisfaction responses. Specifically, high levels of job satisfaction are linked to constructive voice and loyalty responses (and retard exit and neglect). A high degree of job investment also encourages constructive voice and loyalty responses while retarding destructive exit and neglect tendencies. Finally, the presence of job alternatives is linked to active exit and voice options (while inhibiting loyalty but not neglect).

References

Adams, J. Stacy. 1963, November. "Toward an Understanding of Inequity." *Journal of Abnormal and Social Psychology* 67: 422–426.

Barney, Jay B. 1991. "Firm Resource and Sustained Competitive Advantage." *Journal of Management* 17: 99–120.

Barney, Jay B. 2001, January. "Is the Resource-Based 'View' a Useful Perspective for Strategic Management Research? Yes." *Academy of Management Review* 26(1): 41–56.

Berry, Frances Stokes. 1994, July/August. "Innovation in Public Management: The Adoption of Strategic Planning." *Public Administration Review* 54(4): 322–330.

Bowman, James S. 2010, March. "The Success of Failure: The Paradox of Merit Pay." *Review of Public Personnel Administration* 30(1): 70–88.

Boxall, Peter. 1991. "The Strategic HRM Debate and the Resource-Based View of the Firm." *Human Resource Management Journal* 6(3): 59–75.

Bryson, John M. 1996. *Strategic Planning for Public and Nonprofit Organizations*. San Francisco, CA: Jossey Bass.

Davis, T. J., and G. T. Gabris. 2008. "Strategic Compensation: Utilizing Efficiency Wages in the Public Sector to Achieve Desirable Organizational Outcomes." *Review of Public Personnel Administration* 28(4): 327–348.

Delaney, John T., and Mark A. Huselid. 1996, August. "The Impact of Human Resource Management Practices on Perceptions of Organizational Performance." *Academy of Management Journal* 39(4): 949–969.

Delery, John E., and D. Harold Doty. 1996, August. "Modes of Theorizing in Strategic Human Resource Management: Tests of Universalistic, Contingency, and Configurational Performance Predictions." *Academy of Management Journal* 39(4): 802–835.

Elmore, Richard. 1991. "Teaching, Learning, and Education for the Public Service." *Journal of Policy Analysis and Management* 10(2): 167–180.

Farrell, Dan. 1983. "Exit, Voice, Loyalty, and Neglect as Responses to Job Dissatisfaction: A Multidimensional Scaling Study." *Academy of Management Journal* 26: 596–606.

Farrell, Dan, and Caryl E. Rusbult. 1981. "Exchange Variables as Predictors of Job Satisfaction, Job Commitment, and Turnover: The Impact of Rewards, Costs, Alternatives, and Investments." *Organizational Behavior and Human Performance* 27: 78–95.

Fox Lawson & Associates. 2008, January. "Report on the State of Personnel Management and Career Bands in the State of North Carolina." North Carolina Government Performance Audit Committee.

Gray, George R., McKenzie E. Hall, Marianne Miller, and Charles Shasky. 1997, Summer. "Training Practices in State Government Agencies." *Public Personnel Management* 26(2): 187–202.

Hirschman, Albert. 1970. *Exit, Voice, and Loyalty: Responses to Decline in Firms, Organizations and States*. Cambridge, MA: Harvard Press.

Ingraham, Patricia W. 1993. "Of Pigs in Pokes and Policy Diffusion: Another Look at Pay-for-Performance." *Public Administration Review* 53(4): 348–356.

Keen, Christine D. 1994, August. "Tips for Effective Strategic Planning." *HRMagazine*, pp. 84–87.

Kiel, L. D. 1994. *Managing Chaos and Complexity in Government*. San Francisco, CA: Jossey Bass.

Klingner, Donald. 1993, Winter. "Developing a Strategic Human Resources Management Capability in Public Agencies." *Public Personnel Management* 22(4): 565–578.

Latham, Gary P. 2007. *Work Motivation*. Thousand Oaks, CA: Sage.

Ledvinka, James. 1995. "Human Resources Planning." In Jack Rabin, Thomas Vocino, W. Bartley Hildreth, and Gerald Miller, eds. *Handbook of Public Personnel Administration* (pp. 217–240). New York, NY: Marcel Dekker.

Merjanian, Ara. 1997, June. "Striving to Make Performance Measurement Work: Texas Implements Systems Approach to Planning, Budgeting." *PA Times* 20(6): 1, 19–20.

Mesch, Debra J., James L. Perry, and Lois R. Wise. 1995. "Bureaucratic and Strategic Human Resource Management: An Empirical Comparison in the Federal Government." *Journal of Public Administration Theory and Research* 5: 385–402.

Mintzberg, Henry. 1994. *The Rise and Fall of Strategic Planning*. New York, NY: Free Press.

Nutt, Paul C., and Robert W. Backoff. 1992. *Strategic Management of Public and Third Sector Organizations*. San Francisco, CA: Jossey-Bass.

Osborne, David, and Ted Gaebler. 1992. *Reinventing Government How the Entrepreneurial Spirit is Transforming the Public Sector from Schoolhouse to State House, City Hall to Pentagon*. Reading, MA: Addison-Wesley.

Perry, James L. 1993, Fall. "Strategic Human Resource Management." *Review of Public Personnel Administration* 13(4): 59–71.

Perry, James L., Beth Ann Petrakis, and Theodore K. Miller. 1989. "Federal Merit Pay, Round II: An Analysis of the Performance Management and Recognition System." *Public Administration Review* 49(1): 29–37.

Perry, James L., and Debra J. Mesch. 1997. "Strategic Human Resources Management." In Carolyn Ban and Norma Riccucci, eds. *Public Personnel Management: Current Concerns, Future Challenges* (pp. 21–34). New York, NY: Longman.

Perry, James L., Trent Engbers, and So Yun Jun. 2009. "Back to the Future? Performance-Related Pay, Empirical Research, and the Perils of Persistence." *Public Administration Review* 69(1): 1–31.

Pickett, Les. 1998, Spring. "Competencies and Managerial Effectiveness: Putting Competencies to Work." *Public Personnel Management* 27(1): 103–115.

Quinn, James Brian, Philip Anderson, and Sydney Finkelstein. 1996, August. "Leveraging Intellect." *Academy of Management Executive* 10(3): 7–27.

Raja, Usman, Gary Johns, and Filatheos Ntalianis. 2004, June. "The Impact of Personality on Psychological Contracts." *Academy of Management Journal* 47(3): 350–367.

Risher, Howard, and Brigitte W. Schay. 1994, Summer. "Grade Banding: The Model for Future Salary Programs?" *Public Personnel Management* 23(2): 187–199.

Rusbult, Caryl E. 1980. "Commitment and Satisfaction in Romantic Associations: A Test of the Investment Model." *Journal of Experimental Social Psychology* 16: 172–186.

Rusbult, Cayrl E. 1983. "A Longitudinal Test of the Investment Model: The Development (and Deterioration) of Satisfaction and Commitment in Heterosexual Involvements." *Journal of Personality and Social Psychology* 45: 101–117.

Rusbult, Caryl E., and Dan Farrell. 1983. "A Longitudinal Test of the Investment Model: The Impact on Job Satisfaction, Job Commitment, and Turnover of Variations in Reward, Costs, Alternatives, and Investments." *Journal of Applied Psychology* 68: 429–438.

Rusbult, Caryl E., Dan Farrell, Glen Rogers, and Arch G. Mainous, III. 1988, September. "Impact of Exchange Variables on Exit, Voice, Loyalty, and Neglect: An Integrative Model of Responses to Declining Job Satisfaction." *Academy of Management Journal* 31(3): 559–627.

Sullivan, John. 1966, October 30. "What is Superior to Job Descriptions? Try a Position Expectation Description!" HRNET@cornell.edu listserve.

Wernerfelt, Birger. 1984. "A Resource-Based View of the Firm." *Strategic Management Journal* 5: 171–180.

Wooten, William. 1993, Winter. "Using Knowledge, Skill, and Ability (KSA) Data to Identify Career Path Opportunities: An Application of Job Analysis to Internal Manpower Planning." *Public Personnel Management* 22(4): 551–563.

11

HIRING IN THE FEDERAL GOVERNMENT: BALANCING TECHNICAL, MANAGERIAL, AND POLITICAL IMPERATIVES[1]

Carolyn Ban

Carolyn Ban is a professor and former dean of the Graduate School of Public and International Affairs at the University of Pittsburgh. She has written extensively on administrative reform, organizational culture, and human resources in the United States and is currently studying the management of the European Commission. Her current and much of her past research can be found on her Web site, www.carolynban.net.

Hiring is one of the most critical personnel functions in any organization. Each hiring decision is a major commitment of organizational resources, and that is particularly true in the public sector, where turnover is low and getting rid of poor performers is difficult. And all organizations, whatever the sector, face the challenge of adapting to changes in the workforce and new technology, as they try to meet the needs of the organization. But change in the public sector is particularly difficult, because of the complex trade-offs among competing values. This chapter will review the conflicts between values that continue to make "getting it right" so difficult and show how those conflicts, which have played out in several policy arenas, have led to a system that is far from ideal. It concludes with a discussion of the current reforms introduced by the Obama administration.

HIRING AS A COMPLEX BALANCING ACT

In theory, hiring should be quite straightforward: An organization determines how many people it needs to hire and with what set of skills or experience. It then recruits candidates through a range of methods, determines a reasonably effective way to evaluate whether candidates have those skills, and then makes a final selection and offers positions to the best candidates. Ideally, this process would be simple, fast, effective in identifying high-quality candidates, and transparent. In the federal government, however, each step is fraught with potential problems and conflicts. I summarize here some of the most important trade-offs.

OPEN COMPETITION VERSUS SPEED

In the private sector, organizations can limit their recruitment efforts so as to get a pool of candidates large enough to ensure adequate choice; screen them sequentially; and, as soon as they find someone who fits, hire that person. They can even identify a single candidate who has the needed competencies and hire the person immediately. But federal hiring system is based on the core value of open access, so that all citizens have the right to know about and apply for any job, which is very much at odds with the managerial imperative of a fast and efficient hiring system. Because vacancies are posted online, anyone with computer access can apply to multiple positions with relatively little effort, and the agency may be inundated with thousands of applicants so that the process of initial screening becomes very costly and time consuming (US GAO, 2009; US MSPB, 2006).

CENTRALIZATION VERSUS DECENTRALIZATION

Every large organization faces the challenge of whether to centralize or decentralize key functions. In the area of hiring, centralization may bring economies of scale and simplify life for job applicants, who need only to make one application to be considered for multiple positions. Depending on the method used, centralized systems may (especially with modern technology) even be faster and cheaper. But individual agencies argue that centralized hiring makes it more difficult for them to find applicants who fit their specific needs and are interested in working for them. Decentralization, on the other hand, can lead to widely divergent practices and can undermine the sense of the federal government as a unitary employer, leading, instead, to a situation where agencies that have the flexibility to set differing starting salaries and offer some different benefits are actually competing for the same applicants (Seidner and Thompson, 2009). From the viewpoint of the applicant, decentralization can lead to increased burden, frustration, and perceptions of unfairness.

Federal hiring has been characterized by dramatic pendulum swings between the two extremes (Ban and Marzotto, 1984). In the last 30 years, the federal government has moved to a highly decentralized hiring model, in which agencies are delegated the authority to do their own hiring, using a variety of authorities and selection methods (US MSPB, 2008). Most federal managers and HR directors have strongly supported this trend, arguing that it enables them to tailor their hiring specifically to people with the training and experience they needed.

In 2010, the pendulum has begun to swing back again, as the Office of Personnel Management (OPM) has reintroduced centralized hiring registers for a limited number of occupations. Their use is free and optional for agencies, and managers can interview and hire immediately candidates referred from them. They are being touted as a way to speed up the process through economies of scale and use of sophisticated technology, but the central question for their acceptance is the perceived quality of candidates. John Berry, the director of the U.S. OPM, acknowledged this, when he frankly said, "If you ask for a register and you [interview] candidates . . . and you say, 'Oh my God, these were really crappy candidates,' let us know, because we will fix them" (Losey, 2010a).

NARROW OR WIDE ROLE FOR MANAGERS

When the civil service was first established, in 1883, its goal was to professionalize the public workforce by eliminating political patronage and nepotism, putting in place a scientific system designed and managed by professional personnel specialists. Managers themselves were excluded from all but the very final step, as they could not, at least in the eyes of the personnelists, be trusted to make these decisions, so they were not permitted to review all the applications and to decide who should be a finalist. Instead, their final choice was limited in the traditional civil service system by the "Rule of Three." Under this rule managers are given a list of the top three scorers (based on a written test or on a review by an HR professional of the candidates' qualifications) and must make their appointment from that narrow group (US MSPB, 1995). Today, there is increased acceptance of the value that "recruitment should be recognized as a management function, not solely an HR function" (US MSPB, 2004, p. 21), and, in many cases, subject matter specialists are now directly involved in reviewing initial applications. Further, the federal government has gradually moved away from the rule of three and is poised to eliminate its use altogether as part of Obama's new reform, discussed below.

An alternative to the rule of three is category rating, first tested by the U.S. Department of Agriculture (USDA) in a demonstration project begun in 1990 (Ban, 1992). Instead of receiving numerical scores, the finalists who meet qualifications are placed into two or more categories (typically, highly qualified and qualified). Managers can then select from the entire pool of those ranked highly qualified, rather than from only the three top scorers. If the quality group (i.e., those highly qualified) has only one or two candidates, those in the next category may also be referred to the hiring official. While this demonstration obviously abandoned the rule of three, it did not suspend veterans' preference; in fact, it gave veterans in the quality group absolute preference (US OPM, 1992). In 2002, Congress made the flexibilities tested in the Department of Agriculture demonstration program available to all agencies. Yet agencies have been surprisingly slow to adopt them. The Government Accountability Office reported that "a majority (13 of 22) [of Chief Human Capital Officers] . . . said that their agencies were using category rating to 'little or no extent'" (US GAO, 2004b, p. 4). The barriers most often mentioned were "lack of agency policies and procedures" and "lack of OPM guidance" (US GAO, 2004a). As J. Christopher Mihm reported to Congress, the limited use of category rating was "somewhat unexpected," since many human resources directors had reported earlier that numerical ranking and the rule of three were "key obstacles in the hiring process" (US GAO, 2004b, p. 3). According to HR specialists in the federal government, even in 2010, agencies were still reluctant to adopt category rating, in part because of veterans' preference.

MERIT VERSUS SOCIAL GOALS

We use the term "merit system" to describe civil service systems because they are meant to embody the core value that staff are selected based on their merit, rather than on other characteristics, especially political connections, friendships, or family relationships. But at the same time, governments have balanced the goal of merit with that of ensuring that specific groups are represented in government. That raises two linked issues: Should specific groups be favored and, if so, how? And how do we define merit?

WHAT GROUPS SHOULD BE REPRESENTED? Most people think the issue of representation of specific population groups is a new one, but, in fact, it is as old as the civil service, which from its creation required that positions be apportioned by state, territory, or District of Columbia, based on population (Mosher and Kingsley, 1941). Even though this was seen as conflicting with the value of merit, it endured until well into the second half of the twentieth century. The issue of giving preference to applicants based on race or gender has been a controversial one, and, except when a court orders redress as a result of proven discrimination, diversity programs cannot impose quotas, nor can they give extra points on civil service examinations.

The one group that gets quite formal favoritism in the competition for federal jobs is veterans. Veterans' preference actually dates to 1865, in the aftermath of the Civil War (Mosher and Kingsley, 1941). Under the current law, veterans, their widows or widowers, or the spouses of disabled veterans or mothers of individuals who lost their lives while serving in the armed forces are all eligible for veterans' preference under certain circumstances. Veterans have points added to a passing score on an examination: All veterans receive 5 points; disabled veterans have 10 points added, and disabled veterans with service-related disabilities of 10 percent or more "float to the top," that is, they are listed first on registers or lists of eligibles (US MSPB, 1995, Appendix 2).

When category rating is used, "[v]eterans' preference is absolute within each quality category" (US OPM, 2008, p. 14). In other words, if the qualified candidates are placed into two groups, any veteran who is in the most qualified group would have to be hired, or the manager would need to justify passing over that person by documenting his or her lack of qualifications for the job and to get formal permission to look at other people on the list. In some cases, this can result in candidates who are minimally qualified "blocking the register," because managers are reluctant to hire the person but have not received permission to look at other applicants. One HR specialist was quite vocal in discussing this problem: "I have seen real travesties. It continues to astonish me. If you have a compensable vet who has only minimum quals who blocks the register, that is a travesty. That's dumb."

Veterans' preference has had a profound impact on the demographics of the federal workforce. According to a senior expert on federal hiring, interviewed in May, 2010, 25.5 percent of federal staff are veterans, compared to 8.3 percent in the workforce as a whole. There is significant variation across agencies: Almost 50 percent of Air Force civilian employees are veterans, compared, on the low end, to the National Science Foundation (staffed primarily with PhDs and MDs), with only 5.6 percent veterans. The Obama administration unequivocally supports veterans' preference and, in 2009, launched a major veterans' employment initiative with an executive order creating an interagency Council on Veterans Employment as well as Veterans Employment Program offices in all agencies (White House, 2009). Certainly, the government has the right to pursue legitimate social goals, such as providing advantages to veterans, but how to do so without compromising the value of merit remains a challenge.

HOW TO SELECT THE BEST CANDIDATE: IS THE BEST THE ENEMY OF THE GOOD?

The tension between the technical, political, and managerial imperatives is most clear when one examines the actual processes used to screen candidates. Technical experts on testing have developed a whole science of selection and use complex methods to assess which approaches are more valid (i.e., which do a better job of predicting future job performance). But these formal selection methods may be quite time consuming to both develop and administer, and they may raise political objections if they are seen as having adverse impact. Indeed, the conflict over selection methods has been playing out in the federal government for close to 30 years.

Before 1981, selection was very straightforward, relying on a centralized written test. In the mid-1970s, the government introduced the Professional and Administrative Careers Examination (PACE), which was used for entry-level hiring for 118 occupations (Ban and Ingraham, 1988). That system defined merit in a narrow way, as a score on a single test. This had the advantages of simplicity for applicants and of economies of scale, since the government acted as a single employer. Further, the test was subjected to extensive validation. Typically, the number of applicants was far greater than the number of positions available, which meant that, although a 70 was, in theory, a passing score, people who scored lower than the high 90s were rarely selected for jobs. PACE had a significant drawback, in that blacks and Hispanics were far less likely even to reach the 70 percent passing level than white test takers (US MSPB, 1987), let alone to attain scores in the high 90s that might actually lead to being selected. Legally, an organization can use a test that has adverse impact on a specific population group, if the test has been properly validated. But, politically, doing so is untenable, and as a result, when the test was challenged in court (*Luevano v. Campbell*, later *Luevano v. Devine*), in 1981, OPM chose to sign a consent decree agreeing to abandon the use of the PACE (Martinez, 2008).

Now, in a decentralized environment, most agencies now develop their own selection processes but are faced with the same challenges, that is, the most valid selection methods are expensive to develop, and many agencies lack the resources to do this kind of work. Further, they may themselves be subject to court challenge. The court did require OPM to develop an alternative series of examinations to take the place of PACE. Although OPM spent a great deal of time and effort validating the six Administrative Careers with America (ACWA) examinations, ACWA as a system was largely a failure. Managers found it too slow, were dissatisfied with the quality of applicants (US GAO, 2004a), and proceeded to use every route possible to avoid hiring via ACWA. OPM then replaced the tests with a new version of ACWA, relying on a biodata approach—a lengthy questionnaire about the applicant's background and experience, but hiring officials did not see this as a significant improvement. In fact, a number of reports have called for terminating both the use of ACWA and the consent decree itself (NAPA, 2001; Partnership, 2004; US MSPB, 2000).

ASSESSING APPLICANTS OR END-RUNNING THE PROCESS? THE CURRENT STATE OF PLAY Currently only about half of entry-level hiring in the federal government is based on what is formally known as competitive examining, which requires that the position be posted on USAJobs and be open to all applicants. According to experts on test validity, the four assessment methods with the highest validity scores are work sample tests, structured interviews, general mental ability tests, and job knowledge tests (Schmidt and Hunter, 1998), but, because of the problems discussed above, these methods are used far less often than a review of the applicant's training and work experience or educational background, both of which are, as currently conducted, relatively weak predictors of job performance.

The first step in the process, for an applicant, is to go to the Web site www.USAjobs.gov to find out what agencies are currently hiring. OPM maintains the Web site, so at least at this point of the process there is a centralized recruitment tool that presents the federal government as a unitary employer. OPM reports that this Web site has been a major success, with thousands of hits a day and almost 77 million unique visitors in FY 2006 (US OPM, 2008). Individuals can fill out applications online, but, in fact, at this point the image of a unitary employer breaks down, as agencies may use different forms, so the process is far from seamless. And, unlike the private sector, where the first step in applying for a job is usually simply to send a resume, many agencies have required applicants to fill out a lengthy questionnaire or to complete essays documenting that they have the knowledge, skills, and abilities (KSA) required for the job. From the standpoint of HR staff, this provides important information used in ranking the candidates, but some applicants see it as unduly burdensome and off-putting. As discussed below, the Obama administration is now directing agencies to stop requiring these essays from the initial application phase.

Agencies and individual managers continue to avoid these problems by using a number of excepted service appointment authorities, which have less stringent requirements for open competition because the person hired does not initially have full civil service status. Currently, the most popular such hiring method is the Federal Career Intern Program (FCIP). Introduced in 2000, it allows agencies to hire entry-level staff for two-year internships, most often at grades GS 5, 7, or 9, after which they may be eligible for permanent positions (US OPM, 2008). The term "internship" may be a misnomer, as this is not a program providing temporary positions to students who will then return to school (Palguta, 2010). Rather, the FCIP allows for relatively rapid hiring since it allows agencies to tailor assessment tools to their needs and to "target" their recruiting by considering applicants only to certain locations, for example, selected colleges where they have recruiting teams (Palguta, 2010; US MSPB, 2006). It is important to note that, while excepted service appointments may not require completely open recruiting, candidates do need to go through a systemic review process, and so there is a real competition, and veterans' preference is applied. FCIP also in effect creates a two-year probationary period, during which the individual hired should receive formal training. This two-year period allows both sides to determine if the person is a good fit for the position, after which the person can be converted noncompetitively to a permanent position.

Use of the FCIP has increased steadily, and in 2008, fully 50 percent of new hires into entry-level professional and administrative jobs were via FCIP (US MSPB, 2010). But the FCIP has been criticized, as well. As the Merit Systems Protection Board (MSPB) points out, there is a trade-off between efficiency and openness, and narrowing the applicant pool can "potentially lead to perceptions of unfair, arbitrary, or inequitable treatment" (US MSPB, 2006, pp. 33–34). FCIP is already being challenged in court by a disabled veteran (Lunney, 2009). Federal unions have objected to the use of the FCIP, arguing that it is being used in ways that are quite different than the original intent and is, in some agencies, replacing competitive examining, which they see as undermining the concept of fair and open competition. As we will see below, the Obama administration is taking their concerns quite seriously (Newell, 2010a).

GOING OUTSIDE THE CIVIL SERVICE SYSTEM Managers who need staff for short-term assignments can hire people on temporary appointments, for up to one year, or on term appointments, for up to four years, but both require use of the competitive process. They can also bring on consultants, on excepted service appointments for temporary or intermittent work (US OPM, 2008). Often, however, the route chosen is simply to contract out the entire function. While doing so requires going through the federal procurement process, which is itself not easy, the private-sector employer may be able to use simpler and faster methods for hiring and will certainly have more flexibility on salaries than would the government agency.

The increased use of contractors has mirrored the decline in the number of federal employees. In fact, the size of the federal workforce has been politicized for at least

30 years. Ronald Reagan's first act as president, in 1980, was to sign a retroactive hiring freeze (later found to be illegal), and Clinton's reinvention of government focused as much on shrinking the size of the federal workforce as on improving the management of government. In fact, "[f]rom January 1993 to January 2000, the Federal Government civilian workforce was reduced by 384,000 employees" (US OPM, 2000). But, especially in the Clinton administration, this desire to take credit for reducing the size of government was not linked to a political vision of a smaller role for government, so there was no parallel reduction in the number or scope of federal programs. The result was, in effect, a shell game, in which federal ranks shrank while the number of employees working for the federal government as contractors continued to swell (Light, 1999).

While use of contractors has been going on for decades, the Bush administration greatly increased reliance on contractors, in part for ideological reasons—the assumption was that the private sector could almost always do the work faster, better, and cheaper than the government. So, for example, when Bush created the Office of Homeland Security, a massive reorganization of multiple governmental functions, much of the HR functions for parts of the new agency, in particular the Transportation Security Administration (TSA), were contracted out. Relying on contractors has also been used as a way to limit the impact of the federal unions, as contractor workforces are often not unionized.

In sum, the federal government has struggled to balance conflicting values and the requirements of the *Luevano* consent decree. The system that has resulted is highly decentralized and has been criticized as not applicant friendly, not making the best use of technology, not communicating effectively what is exciting about federal employment, and not using the most valid selection methods. The traditional system is still too slow and unwieldy, leading to increased use of excepted service authorities such as FCIP, as well as to reliance on temporary staff or contractors. These are the challenges addressed by current reform efforts.

REFORM IN ACTION

CAN TECHNOLOGY SOLVE THE PROBLEMS?

Technology holds great promise, in effective recruitment, ease of application, and in facilitating reviews of applicants' qualifications, but the federal government has not been at the forefront in its use. As mentioned earlier, OPM has introduced a government-wide Web site, USAJobs, to provide a single point of entry for applicants, which has attracted a large number of potential applicants. But the system has been hampered by both the extreme fragmentation of the federal personnel system and "a system of competing contractor interests" (Llorens and Kellough, 2007, p. 218). In fact, OPM does not have the authority to require all agencies to use a standard software for automated recruitment compatible with the Recruitment One-Stop system used on USAJobs, so applicants may have to reenter data or provide different information for applications to several agencies.

Technology can play an important role not just in recruitment but also in assessment, but, according to the MSPB:

> [F]ew agencies have taken full advantage of the potential of technology. Although automated hiring systems can administer or support high-quality assessments, such as objective tests and structured interviews, most agencies have instead simply automated existing training and experience-based

assessments. In other words, they have paved the cow path, but did not necessarily improve it. Second, those existing assessments are often dated, deficient, or over-extended. The result is that, in many agencies, technology has not improved the ability of the hiring process to predict future performance. (US MSPB, 2006, p. 43)

According to one expert interviewed, while this remains largely true, some agencies, notably the Internal Revenue Service (IRS), Drug Enforcement Agency (DEA), and Customs and Border Protection (CPB, part of the Department of Homeland Security), have successfully employed technology to assess applicants. Other agencies may be limited not by a lack of interest or creativity but rather, especially for small agencies, by a lack of financial and human capital resources.

THE SHIFT FROM BUSH TO OBAMA AND A NEW EXECUTIVE ORDER

The main thrust of change under President Bush was in two directions: even greater decentralization of the personnel system, which went so far that it could be considered dismantling the common civil service system, and greater emphasis on contracting out, both of key agency activities and of the personnel function itself. Under Bush, the trend of moving agencies out of the traditional civil service system (referred to as Title 5 based on the section of the U.S. Code) and letting them develop their own systems accelerated rapidly, assisted by the willingness of Congress to tailor civil service legislation to specific agencies rather than for the entire executive branch. This was particularly the case for the newly created Department of Homeland Security and for the civilian side of the Defense Department. Both departments introduced new pay systems, moving away from traditional position classification to broadbanding, which, at least in theory, gave agencies more flexibility to design entry-level positions with clear potential for growth and gave managers greater flexibility in setting entry-level pay. But the new systems were also designed to curtail the power of labor unions and the number of employees who had the right to join a union.

Clearly, the Obama administration is moving in the opposite direction, responding to criticisms that balkanization of the civil service has gone too far and that, far from benefiting from economies of scale by cooperating, agencies are actually competing in hiring. A number of the separate pay systems—most notably the National Security and Personnel System in the Department of Defense—have been abolished, and staff are transitioning back to the traditional pay system.

In addition, the movement to contract out everything possible has also been reversed. This does not mean that all functions will be brought back in-house. Rather, shortly after taking office, President Obama asked agencies to analyze carefully what functions are "inherently governmental" and should definitely be done in-house, what activities can be done more efficiently or effectively by outside contractors, and how to strike an appropriate balance.

The latest effort by the Obama administration has been specifically in the area of recruitment and hiring. On May 11, 2010, President Obama issued a presidential memorandum entitled "Improving the Federal Recruitment and Hiring Process" (White House, 2010). Developed through a close working relationship between OPM and the Office of Management and Budget (OMB), the memorandum responds to pressure to streamline the hiring process. That pressure comes primarily from the projections of massive future retirements as well as the need to fill new jobs created, particularly the Departments of Defense, Homeland Security, and Veterans Affairs.

For some time, there have been warnings about the large number of federal employees, and especially senior staff, who are already eligible to retire or who soon will be (Partnership, 2007). The rhetoric on this subject has become more and more heated, with recent commentators warning of a coming "retirement tsunami," citing projections that "three-fifths of the 1.8 million (nonpostal) workers will be eligible to retire during the next ten years" (Seidner and Thompson, 2009, p. 186). That tsunami has not yet hit, in part because some have delayed planned retirements in response to the financial crisis. But at whatever rate people retire, it is clear that the federal government is in a growth phase, as it increases staff to manage new programs (such as health care) and as it brings some activities that were previously contracted out back in-house. One expert interviewed in the spring of 2010 estimated hiring of approximately 600,000 new staff in the next three to four years.

Not surprisingly, agencies faced with massive hiring have concerns about making the process both faster and more user-friendly, and the presidential memorandum responds to those concerns quite concretely. As we saw earlier, currently, many agencies require applicants to submit essays demonstrating they have the necessary background and experience (KSAs). Those essays did provide useful information that enabled agencies to screen applicants, but they were so off-putting that they undoubtedly dissuaded some people from applying. And knowing how best to write such an essay was not always apparent, which engendered a whole industry of consultants who help applicants tailor their essays. (I should note that, in the past, the federal government used a standard application form, the SF-171, which also required insider knowledge to complete correctly, so these consultants have been around for many years.) Obama has decreed that, by November 1, 2010, agencies may no longer require these essays when people initially apply and must take applicants' resumes instead. Agencies can also ask for some additional information from applicants, but the clear intent is to make the process more "applicant friendly," as are the requirements for better communication with applicants as they go through the process and for making job announcements shorter and easier to understand.

The presidential memorandum also requires agencies that have not already done so to move to category rating. As discussed earlier, category rating has been legally available on an optional basis since 2000, but now the administration is taking advantage of the law to say that all agencies will now "choose" to adopt it.

The memorandum also calls for speeding up the hiring process. Although the exact time is not mentioned in the memorandum, the plan is to "cut hiring time to about 80 days from the date a vacancy is announced to the point a candidate is hired. In some agencies, it can [currently] take up to 200 days to process a hire, and 140 days is not uncommon" (Davidson and O'Keefe, 2010). Managers have long complained that they often lose the best candidates due to the slowness of the process, and, indeed, some applicants have reported taking other jobs during the long wait (Davidson and O'Keefe, 2010). The memorandum also requires "managers and supervisors with responsibility for hiring [to be] more fully involved in the hiring process including . . . engaging actively in the recruitment and, when applicable, the interviewing process."

The presidential memorandum and accompanying memorandum from John Berry, director of the U.S. OPM, on implementation of what is billed as "Comprehensive Recruitment and Hiring Reform" (Berry, 2010) do not force dramatic centralization of the process, but they do move the pendulum back somewhat from the current extreme decentralization in several ways. The presidential memorandum calls for an evaluation of "the effectiveness of shared registers used in filling positions common across multiple agencies" and requires OPM to "develop a strategy for improving agencies' use of these shared registers form commonly filled Government-wide positions," and it also calls on OPM to continue to strengthen USAJobs. Perhaps even more important, it sets up a stronger accountability system at all levels. At the lowest level, it requires holding individual managers "accountable for recruiting and hiring highly qualified employees and supporting their successful transition into Federal service," and it mandates training on effective hiring for all hiring managers. From a top–down perspective, the memorandum calls upon OPM to set up a "Government-wide performance review and improvement process" and to put into place "a goal-focused, data-driven system for holding agencies accountable for improving the quality and speed of agency hiring . . ." Berry's implementing memorandum reinforces this objective, stressing "monitoring agency efforts to improve the speed and quality of hiring and the satisfaction of managers and applicants with the hiring process" (Berry, 2010).

While the reform is very specific at the initial application stage (e.g., agencies must accept resumes rather than requiring long essays), it respects the spirit of decentralization in continuing to allow agencies to tailor the actual selection process to their own needs. At the same time, it provides extensive technical support to help agencies improve their processes, starting with a Web site (www.opm.gov/HiringReform/Index.aspx) and providing training on techniques such as job analysis, structured interviews, occupational questionnaires, and category rating. It is also offering the direct assistance of seven mobile assistance teams, each specializing in one part of the reform. And, according to one of the people I interviewed, it plans shortly to introduce "cutting-edge online assessments for 12 occupations across the federal government."

As we have seen earlier, one of the more popular current methods of hiring is the FCIP, which already meets one of the goals of the president's hiring reform, since it allows for a faster hiring process. But, as discussed, it is also controversial, as the unions, in particular, have argued that it violates the merit system principle of open recruitment and also gives inadequate weight to veterans' preference and creates, in essence, a two-year probationary period. One expert interviewed found the union position a bit disingenuous, since the unions are not responsible for representing veterans, and actually veterans groups have not been as outspoken in their criticisms. Unions have also raised concerns about abandoning the rule of three, and it would appear that their underlying concern is giving what they see as too much power to managers.

The president's memorandum takes a cautious approach to the question of use of FCIP: It calls for an evaluation of the program by OPM, to be delivered within 90 days. As part of that review, OPM is charged with proposing "a framework for providing effective pathways into the Federal Government for college students and recent college graduates." The unions clearly would have liked more decisive action, either eliminating or cutting back on the use of FCIP, and that has colored their response to Obama's memorandum (Davidson, 2010b). OPM Director John Berry has responded by reiterating the administration's commitment to veterans' preference (Newell, 2010b). OPM is, in fact, caught in a difficult situation, as it must come up with a report on FCIP in a short time, and it faces pressures on the one side from managers who do not want to abandon a hiring method they have found extremely useful and on the other side from strong opponents of its continued use.

While the issue of veterans' preference has been hotly debated, the importance of broader representation is given only a glancing reference in the president's memorandum, which calls, rather vaguely, for OPM to "develop a plan to promote diversity in the Federal workforce, consistent with the merit system principle . . . that the Federal Government should endeavor to achieve a workforce from all segments of society." The limited focus on racial diversity may reflect the fact that, except for Hispanics, the federal workforce is now representative of all segments of society.

While the president has already issued his memorandum, Congress is also trying to play a role in reform of hiring, in many ways paralleling the president's initiatives. In May 2010, the Senate passed S 736, the Federal Hiring Process Improvement Act. Sponsored by Senators Daniel K. Akaka (D-Hawaii) and George V. Voinovich (R-Ohio), a longtime advocate of improvement in the civil service system who is currently in his last term, the bill calls for use of resumes for initial application, a speedier hiring process, and better communication with job candidates and plain-language job announcements. It also calls for agencies to keep an inventory of all applicants interested in employment in other federal agencies (Losey, 2010b). The bill has not yet been scheduled for consideration by the House of Representatives.

Conclusions

The Obama reforms of hiring are not quite as dramatic as billed, but they hold considerable promise for improving the efficiency and effectiveness of federal hiring. They also illustrate the extent to which all of the five conflicts discussed earlier in this chapter are still central to the debate and how the government continually struggles to find the right balance. In the conflict over open competition versus speed, the reforms stress speed, but at the same time want to encourage open competition. Exactly how that can be done is not yet clear, and there is not even a clear consensus over what is required to meet the open competition standard. In the conflict over centralization versus decentralization, the government is continuing the recent trend away from total decentralization while trying to strike a balance and not to swing all the way to the other extreme. The issue of a narrow or wide role for managers is also clearly central, and here the movement is toward a wider role for managers, both in reviewing applicants' qualifications and in making the final selection from a wider array of candidates. The administration also continues to try to strike the right balance between hiring based strictly on merit (however defined or measured) and social goals such as diversity or providing special advantage to veterans. Finally, while the presidential memorandum mandates that initial application be by resume, it provides no detail on how agencies can best screen their applicants to ensure selection of those with the best skills and experience for specific positions, so the technical conflicts continue over how to design valid selection methods that are also cost-effective and fast.

It will take at least two years before we can assess the impact of these reforms, but the result is likely to be positive, at least in terms of the initial experiences of job applicants, who will, hopefully, find clearer and more compelling job announcements, simpler initial application processes, better communication on where they stand in the process, and quicker decisions. What will require careful evaluation is whether those hired actually meet high standards of quality and motivation. Given the projections of very high numbers of people to be hired in the near future, getting hiring right means bringing in to the federal government those who can meet immediate needs and who also have what it takes to be the leaders of the federal government in the future.

References

Ban, Carolyn. 1992. "Research and Demonstrations under CSRA: Is Innovation Possible?" In Patricia W. Ingraham and David H. Rosenbloom, eds. *The Promise and Paradox of Civil Service Reform.* Pittsburgh, PA: University of Pittsburgh Press.

Ban, Carolyn, and Patricia W. Ingraham. 1988, May/June. "Retaining Quality Employees: Life After PACE." *Public Administration Review* 48(3): 708–718.

Ban, Carolyn, and Toni Marzotto. 1984. "Delegations of Examining: Objectives and Implementation." In Patricia W. Ingraham and Carolyn Ban, eds. *Legislating Bureaucratic Change: The Civil Service Reform Act of 1978.* Albany, NY: State University of New York Press.

Berry, John. 2010, May 11. *Memorandum for Heads of Executive Departments and Agencies: Comprehensive Recruitment and Hiring Reform, Implementation of the President's Memorandum of May 11, 2010.* Washington, D.C.: US Office of Personnel Management.

Davidson, Joe. 2010b, May 20. "OPM Head Takes 'Hostile Fire' on Hiring, Intern Program." *Washington Post.*

Davidson, Joe, and Ed O'Keefe. 2010, May 11. "Obama Wants Federal Agencies to Hit the Gas on Hiring." *Washington Post.*

Light, Paul. 1999. *The True Size of Government.* Washington, D.C.: The Brookings Institution.

Llorens, Jared, and J. Edward Kellough. 2007 "A Revolution in Public Personnel Administration: The Growth of Web-Based Recruitment and Selection Processes in the Federal Government." *Public Personnel Management* 36(3): 207–221.

Losey, Stephen. 2010a, April 19. "OPM Expands Role in Hiring: Efforts Could Speed Process by 5 Weeks." *Federal Times.* http://www.federaltimes.com/article/20100418/PERSONNEL01/4180309/1053/PERSONNEL02.

Losey, Stephen. 2010b, May 20. "OPM Pushes Bill to Allow Agencies to Share Job Candidates." *Federal Times.* http://www.federaltimes.com/article/20100520/PERSONNEL03/5200301/1053/PERSONNEL02.

Lunney, Kellie. 2009, August 19. "MSPB Says Vet's Case Against Federal Internship Program Has Legal Merit." *Government Executive.* http://www.govexec.com/dailyfed/0809/081909m1.htm?oref=rellink.

Martinez, J. Michael. 2008. "The *Luevano* Consent Decree and Public Personnel Reform." *Public Personnel Management* 37(3): 327–338.

Mosher, William E., and J. Donald Kingsley. 1941. *Public Personnel Management.* New York: Harper and Brothers Publishers.

National Academy of Public Administration (NAPA). 2001. *The Quest for Talent: Recruitment Strategies for Federal Agencies.* Washington, D.C.: NAPA.

Newell, Elizabeth. 2010a, May 14. "Hiring Reform Could Signal End of Federal Internship Program." *Government Executive.* http://www.govexec.com/story_page.cfm?articleid=45281&oref=todaysnews.

Newell, Elizabeth. 2010b, May 19. "Vets Preference Tops List of Concerns about Hiring Reform." *Government Executive.* http://www.govexec.com/story_page.cfm?articleid=45306&dcn=todaysnews.

Palguta, John. 2010, April 29. Testimony prepared for the Senate Committee on Homeland Security and Governmental Affairs, Subcommittee on the Oversight of Government Management, the Federal Workforce and the District of Columbia.

Partnership for Public Service. 2004. *Asking the Wrong Questions: A Look at How the Federal Government Assesses and Selects its Workforce.* Washington, D.C.: Partnership for Public Service.

Partnership for Public Service. 2007. *Federal Human Capital: the Perfect Storm: A Survey of Chief Human Capital Officers.* Washington, D.C.: Partnership for Public Service.

Schmidt, Frank, and John Hunter. 1998. "The Validity and Utility of Selection Methods in Personnel Psychology: Practical and Theoretical Implications of 85 Years of Research

Findings." *Psychological Bulletin,* the American Psychological Association, Inc. 124(2): 262–274.

Seidner, Rob, and James R. Thompson. 2009. "Building Relationships to Fix the Federal Talent Pipeline: An Innovative Approach in Chicago Provides a Model for Recruitment Success." In Hannah S. Sistare, Myra Howze Shiplett, and Terry F. Buss, eds. *Innovations in Human Resource Management: Getting the Public's Work Done in the 21st Century.* Armonk, NY: M.E. Sharpe.

U.S. General Accounting Office. 2004a, June. *Human Capital: Additional Collaboration Between OPM and Agencies is Key to Improved Federal Hiring.* GAO-04-797.

U.S. Government Accountability Office. 2004b, July. *Human Capital: Increasing Agencies' Use of New Hiring Flexibilities* (statement of J. Christopher Mihm). GAO-04-959T.

U.S. Government Accountability Office. 2009, April. *Human Capital: Sustained Attention to Strategic Human Capital Management Needed.* GAO-09-652T.

U.S. Merit Systems Protection Board. 1987. *In Search of Merit: Hiring Entry-Level Federal Employees.* Washington, D.C.: MSPB.

U.S. Merit Systems Protection Board. 1995. *The Rule of Three in Federal Hiring: Boon or Bane?* Washington, D.C.: USMSPB.

U.S. Merit Systems Protection Board. 2000. *Restoring Merit to Federal Hiring: Why Two Special Hiring Programs Should be Ended.* Washington, D.C.: USMSPB.

U.S. Merit Systems Protection Board. 2004. *Managing Federal Recruitment: Issues, Insights, and Illustrations.* Washington, D.C.: USMSPB.

U.S. Merit Systems Protection Board. 2006. *Reforming Federal Hiring: Beyond Faster and Cheaper.* Washington, D.C.: USMSPB.

U.S. Merit Systems Protection Board. 2008. *Federal Appointment Authorities: Cutting through the Confusion.* Washington, D.C.: USMSPB.

U.S. Merit Systems Protection Board. 2010. "Fast Fact: the FCIP Continues to Grow." *Issues of Merit,* February. Washington, D.C.: USMSPB.

U.S. Office of Personnel Management. 1992. *U.S. Department of Agriculture Personnel Management Demonstration Project: First Annual Evaluation Report.* OS92-7. Washington, D.C.: USOPM.

U.S. Office of Personnel Management. 2000, September 30. *Federal Human Resources Management for the 21st Century: Strategic Plan.* FY 2000-FY 2005.

U.S. Office of Personnel Management. 2008. *Human Resources Flexibilities and Authorities in the Federal Government,* January. Washington, D.C.:USOPM.

The White House. 2009. President Obama Launches Major Veterans Employment Initiative, Press release, November 9. http://www.whitehouse.gov/the-press-office/president-obama-launches-major-veterans-employment-initiative.

The White House, Office of the Press Secretary. 2010, May 11. Presidential Memorandum—Improving the Federal Recruitment and Hiring Process. http://www.whitehouse.gov/the-press-office/presidential-memorandum-improving-federal-recruitment-and-hiring-process.

Endnotes

1. My thanks to John Crum, of the U.S. Merit Systems Protection Board, and John Palguta, of the Partnership for Public Service, for their review of an earlier draft.

12

THE CHALLENGES OF SUCCESSION PLANNING IN TURBULENT TIMES

Heather Getha-Taylor

Heather Getha-Taylor is an assistant professor in the Department of Public Administration at the University of Kansas. Her research considers the forces transforming public governance and the associated implications for effectively managing human resources. She is a graduate of the Maxwell School of Citizenship and Public Affairs, Syracuse University.

The transformation of human resource management to a strategic force in public organizations is notable, promising, and a work in progress. A critical component of strategic focus is a commitment to workforce planning. The ability to plan effectively, however, rests on an organization's ability to forecast trends and act accordingly. According to Pynes, organizational competitiveness depends on the ability to "anticipate, influence, and manage the forces" that have an impact on organizational effectiveness, including succession (p. 32). The key to doing this, says Pynes, is by adopting a strategic planning approach that considers short-term needs and long-term objectives concurrently. By doing so, organizations "are better able to match their human resource requirements with the demands of the external environment and the needs of the organization" (Ibid.). The author reminds us that budgeting and human resources are linked, and this interdependence must be considered throughout the planning process. The current economic recession illustrates this connection prominently.

A shared priority for public organizations at the federal, state, and local levels is excellent performance. As noted in the Winter Commission report of 1993, "the human dimension of public service" should be reflected in personnel decisions that contribute to creating high-performance public organizations. While performance is the ultimate goal, capacity is necessary, and human resources are critical building blocks of capacity. A key challenge for human resource managers then, says Pynes, is to "demonstrate on a continuing basis how HRM activities contribute to the success and effectiveness of the organization" (2009, p. 34). While cost savings achieved via retirements, voluntary separations, and reductions in force (RIF) may seem to indicate improved organizational efficiency, a broader understanding of how these "savings" will impact the remaining members of the workforce and the organization's long-term performance objectives is in order.

When the term "succession planning" is considered, it is most readily associated with internal vacancies created by retirements and the associated efforts to fill such vacancies with qualified individuals. Retirement eligibility records and employee surveys can help human resource managers effectively anticipate upcoming vacancies and identify/develop the needed competencies to fill the gaps. However, workforce trends that result from external forces, such as budget cuts, introduce unexpected turbulence into the traditional definition and provide an opportunity for reconsideration. "Succession planning," then, can be broadened in this context to include efforts to restructure work, capture knowledge, and focus on the needs of current employees who are left behind as a result of these unexpected vacancies.

Klingner and Nalbandian (2003) detail the variety of tools available for human resource planning and forecasting but are careful to consider the external forces that ultimately affect the usefulness of those resources. According to the authors, political and economic constraints impede the ability to "make rational and reflective choices" (p. 91). In times of rapidly shifting expectations, severely decreasing resources, and uncertain demands for the future, choices may not be made strategically, but reactively. Stanton (2004) cautions managers against this approach by noting that "numbers-driven downsizing can simply hollow out the wrong parts of an agency and reduce its ability to provide public services, either directly or through third parties" (p. 229). Stanton continues to note the importance of planning prior to cuts "to ensure that a government agency can maintain or increase its service levels while reducing the number of employees needed for certain tasks" (p. 230). However, this requires skills that may be in short supply in many organizations. According to Brown and Brown (2005), the human resource manager is uniquely positioned to guide strategic planning as someone who "leads and supports the activities of the organization as it moves from a vision and mission to goals and objectives, from tasks and responsibilities to outcomes and solutions" (p. 649). In sum, succession planning is an important component of strategic human resource management, which, says Daley, "takes *what is* and develops ideas of *what should be* along with plans for how to get there" (2006, p. 164).

Romzek and Ingraham (1994) foreshadowed the challenges facing state and local governments caught in a time of economic turbulence. State and local governments, said the authors, "must find ways to solve new problems in an era of shrinking resources" (p. 325). The authors emphasized the need to cultivate learning organizations that are "flexible enough to predict and provide for new levels of complexity and uncertainty" (Ibid.). This is not accomplished, however, through the loss of organizational capacity. Staff cutbacks and the associated loss of expertise alongside increased demand present an unbalanced picture of capacity. "Regardless of the specific functions and services government retains, it will be imperative that government develop strategies that allow it to keep a skilled, expert, and motivated work force" (Romzek and Ingraham, 1994, p. 326). The future vision of the organization becomes blurred when resources, including human resources, are insufficient to meet expected demand. Thus, the key question considered in this chapter is: *What does it mean to practice effective succession planning during times of turbulence?*

The example of South Carolina is used here to illustrate key concepts and challenges associated with workforce planning in turbulent times. South Carolina experienced severe implications of the economic downturn (including almost a full quarter cut from its annual budget) yet was distinguished as a leader among states in its workforce planning efforts. In 2008, South Carolina was recognized by the PEW Center's Grading the States for its excellent human capital planning efforts. The following were the criteria: (1) linking state, department, and employee goals, (2) recognizing and rewarding high performers, (3) regularly encouraging and utilizing employee feedback, and (4) addressing employee performance/behavior weaknesses and terminating for cause in a timely and fair manner. Lessons from this example provide guidance to practitioners and scholars alike who together share a commitment to understanding the best ways to consider the ways in which external forces affect internal capacity and future planning.

SUCCESSION PLANNING IN SOUTH CAROLINA

In South Carolina, human resource management is decentralized to state agencies, but the state's Office of Human Resources (OHR) partners with the 75 agencies "to create excellence in human resources." The primary customers of the South Carolina OHR include the state Budget and Control Board, the General Assembly members/staff, agency HR directors/staff, state employees, state agencies, job applicants, and the public at large. The organization's vision is: "To be recognized by agencies and the South Carolina General Assembly as human resources experts and leaders in applying human resources best practices and innovations to make South Carolina state government an employer of choice." The organization focuses on creating excellence in five key areas: (1) talent acquisition and development, (2) human capital management, (3) organizational development, (4) alternative dispute resolution, and (5) human resources information technology.

In 2001, South Carolina's OHR engaged in a statewide workforce scan that indicated that 29 percent of the workforce would be eligible to retire by 2006. Noting this, along with the aging of the workforce (the majority of workers in the 50–54 age bracket) the OHR had cause for concern regarding succession planning. "Considering that a significant number of these employees were in key leadership jobs, agencies were encouraged to develop succession plans and knowledge transfer approaches among other workforce planning strategies" (South Carolina Workforce Plan, 2009). However, the unexpected economic forces that occurred six years after the workforce scan presented unexpected concerns. Fortunately, the careful planning efforts that took place in the years prior meant that the impact was minimized as much as possible.

In 2009, the state of South Carolina employed approximately 71,000 of the nation's 3.8 million state employees (U.S. Census Bureau, 2009). According to the most recent data available from the South Carolina OHR, the average pay for all employees is $53,358. The average age is 45 years, and the gender composition is 41 percent male and 59 percent female. The average tenure with the state is 11 years. Education, health, and corrections employees comprise approximately 72 percent of the total workforce, with transportation, social, regulatory, executive, conservation, and public safety employees comprising the remaining 28 percent. South Carolina's state budget for fiscal year (FY) 2007–2008 totaled approximately $6.7 billion. Steeply declining state revenues as a result of the economic downturn propelled the state's General Assembly to authorize multiple budget reductions, which resulted in an overall budget cut of approximately 22 percent since FY 2007–2008 (OHR, South Carolina Budget and Control Board, 2009a, 2009b).

The cuts necessarily resulted in employment consequences for individuals working in the state's 75 agencies. The South Carolina OHR mobilized immediately to provide guidance and assistance on the available cost-saving options. The OHR held

Table 12.1	FY 2008–2009 Cost Savings by Category	
Category	**Details**	**Cost Savings**
Mandatory Furloughs	42 out of 75 agencies utilized mandatory furloughs; average furlough length was six days	**$30,251,116**
Separation Programs	11 out of 75 agencies utilized voluntary separation programs; 137 employees elected voluntary separation. 10 out of 75 agencies utilized retirement incentive programs; 102 employees participated	**$11,625,732**
Reductions in Force	13 out of 75 agencies engaged in reductions in force; 233 employees were separated	**$9,105,072**
Other Separations	27 out of 75 agencies separated employees who were without grievance protection; 295 employees without grievance protection were separated	**$10,430,802**
	Total Savings	**$61,412,722**

Source: South Carolina Office of Human Resources (2009a, 2009b).

regular advisory meetings and provided virtual resources to address the variety of cost-saving tools available, including furloughs, job sharing, teleworking, position cost sharing between agencies, retraining or reassigning employees, retirement incentive programs, restricted activities such as travel and overtime, hiring freeze, hiring temporary employees, voluntary separation, termination of employees without grievance protections, and RIF. Agencies worked with OHR to identify the best options for their organizations; RIF were minimized by electing other available cost-saving tools. According to OHR, the cost savings for FY 2008–2009 totaled $61,412,722 as a result of agencies' combined efforts. While the cost savings are remarkable, so too is the relative impact of the RIFs. In 2008, approximately 300 state employees (0.4 percent of total employees) were separated as a result of RIFs. Fourteen were rehired by other state agencies. Table 12.1 presents South Carolina's cost savings by category.

Despite the drastic required budget cuts, the state maintained its leadership as one of the nation's leaders in workforce planning efforts. Its example illustrates the U.S. Office of Personnel's workforce planning model (2005), which centers on the following focus areas:

1. Strategic direction
2. Workforce analysis

3. Plan development
4. Implementation
5. Evaluation

South Carolina's agencies, together with the state's OHR, engaged in efforts that illustrate the steps in the process, which are detailed in the following sections, and address the associated challenges, skills needed, and innovations resulting from this process.

CHALLENGES OF SUCCESSION PLANNING IN TURBULENT TIMES

Interviews with state leaders in the South Carolina OHR identified many challenges associated with effectively balancing the required budget cuts with existing human resource management priorities and activities. The process of succession planning typically involves an extended time frame and includes decisions based on assumptions grounded by multiple data sources. The conditions created by the rapid succession of budget cuts in South Carolina created an environment of urgent change. The OHR acted as a resource and guide for agencies as they worked through the accelerated process of framing (or reframing) future direction, analyzing current and future workforce capacity, developing a plan, implementing that plan, and evaluating the results of the decisions.

To begin, strategic direction and workforce analysis were considered on an individual agency basis and complicated by the expectation of no new hires in the immediate future. To help address this complication, the South Carolina OHR provided workforce planning guidance via their Web site and through regularly scheduled advisory meetings. Information provided included examples of workforce plans, demographic information, retirement trends, and overview of current initiatives and tools for cost savings.

Plan development included input from experienced human resource management professionals as well as agency employees. South Carolina's OHR requested that all state agencies appoint a "Workforce Planning Champion" to attend educational meetings as the organization's representative and "promote workforce planning" in their respective agency. While the plans were developed, current performance expectations were not abandoned. Strategic human resource management is often relegated to the back burner due to the pressing need to focus on the functional aspects of human resource management. In this example, the two priorities were balanced.

Implementing the required plan while maintaining some aspects of "business as usual" presented complications. Addressing the cost-saving needs while maintaining meaningful reward and recognition programs was a significant challenge. State employees who went without raises found reward in other ways. Agencies were encouraged to be creative in recognizing achievement during this time of transition. One important component of this effort centered on providing more feedback on employee performance. Especially when workload is redistributed to remaining employees, valuable feedback and job redesign can be helpful tools in providing recognition.

Evaluation is ongoing, and the results of each agency's efforts will be considered in the years ahead. According to OHR leaders, linking employee and organizational goals will be a priority for the future and can serve as a metric for judging success in answering the question: *Are we aligning employee capacity and organizational performance?* In addition, considering the ways in which the efforts met the needs of those who were separated as well as the "survivors" of the cost-saving measures serves as a metric for evaluation. The OHR worked to assist those affected by RIFs and also those who remained. The state utilized an online RIF applicant pool to allow individuals to access local resources, including those devoted to resume development and interviewing skills. For those who remain with the organization, "survivor guilt" can be a debilitating force that will affect morale and productivity. Acting with a commitment to open communication can speak to these trends. The National Academy of Public Administration advocated for this emphasis in their 1995 report, which noted the need to attend to the concerns of all affected employees—including survivors–to ensure continued organizational performance.

SKILLS FOR MANAGING THROUGH TURBULENCE

Lawler et al. (2006) provide some promising evidence to suggest that HR managers are occupying a more strategic role in organizations to align human resource practices with the vision for the future of the organization, but work remains: "HR can and should be more of a strategic partner" (p. 107). The authors contend that in order for this to happen, new skills are necessary. This case illustrates that prescription as well. In order to effectively navigate the workforce planning cycle, the lessons from South Carolina suggest that public personnel managers should develop and practice a set of skills that may not have been emphasized previously.

1. Human resource managers should develop both their **critical thinking skills and their creative thinking skills** to envision and anticipate multiple, unexpected scenarios that may not have been considered previously. Part of this skill building relies on an attention to external trends that affect internal organizational function.
2. A continued attention to **developing metrics** that illustrate the contributions of people to organizational performance is a necessity. The Return on Investment (ROI) of human capital remains intuitively obvious to most managers, but data to support this position will further the strategic position of human resources. Technology offers promise in advancing this goal.
3. The example of South Carolina illustrates the importance of **excellent communication skills** to effectively convey organizational needs, environmental constraints, and associated plans to balance concerns of employees at all levels. Part of this mastery centers on utilizing new technologies as appropriate to reach all members of the workforce. South Carolina's OHR utilized a variety of social media tools, including Facebook and Twitter, to communicate with employees and the public.
4. Finally, the South Carolina example illustrates that human resource managers must carefully consider the practical, emotional, and legal **implications of all available workforce planning tools**. The OHR provided agencies with regular updates on important legal issues associated with RIF and other cost-saving measures. Also, the state effectively balanced the need for cost savings along with a commitment to considering the morale of the workforce by addressing "Survivor Syndrome" in state agencies.

INNOVATIONS AS A RESULT OF SUCCESSION PLANNING IN TURBULENT TIMES

As noted by Sandler and Hudson (1998), public organizations, and those who work within them, must operate with the understanding that change is a way of life. Specifically, the authors contend that change, including budgetary changes, can serve as a force to revitalize organizations. "Government agencies—and all organizations—must operate on the principle that change is not a win–lose proposition but an opportunity to express individuality and creativity that will aid the organization in accomplishing its mission most effectively" (p. 32).

As noted previously, the State of South Carolina is notable in its efforts to respond to the needs of those left behind as a result of cuts and RIF. The state OHR led an effort to address "Survivor Syndrome" across state agencies. This syndrome is characterized as the feelings of overwork, frustration, and even guilt for those individuals who are left when their colleagues retire, resign, or are cut from the organization. Resources provided through the OHR are expected to continue in order to respond appropriately to "surviving" employee needs.

Further, the budget cuts and associated adjusted workforce plans propelled South Carolina to invest even more in efforts to modernize workforce planning information systems to help make informed decisions for the future. In this case, technology advances that span the OHR programmatic areas serve as aids to identify the best ways to address both short-term and long-term needs and goals.

Finally, the cost-savings efforts that were necessitated by state budget cuts highlighted the need to prioritize knowledge transfer in the years ahead. The South Carolina OHR is currently working with agencies to help identify appropriate techniques to capture and transfer knowledge (including job shadowing, open forums, knowledge inventories, learning games, lessons learned debriefing, mentoring, and structured training). The plan rests on a careful consideration of current knowledge, future needs, and the most appropriate transfer methods. To be truly effective, knowledge transfer programs must be linked to succession plans and must also be considered important enough to elicit full participation of key employees. Only then will organizations be able to recruit where needed, retain critical skills, and develop employees to meet agency needs.

Conclusion

South Carolina's state workforce planning efforts were noted as exemplary even amid environmental turbulence, and the state's OHR has no plans to reverse course. The OHR plans to continue to prioritize workforce planning in the years ahead. In addition to focusing on important functional areas as recruitment, compensation, training, and information technology, the OHR will work with state agencies to collect data, identify and disseminate best practices, help agencies develop workforce plans, and consider ways to minimize turnover (Office of Human Resources Strategic Plan, 2009a). As noted by OHR Director Samuel Wilkins, doing more with less "is the new normal" and illustrates the interdependence of government departments, including the department of revenue. This requires improved communication and collaboration to address the current and future challenges of public management.

In addition, practitioners must learn to balance proactive planning with flexibility. Strategic planning, including succession planning, requires a systems approach that considers the variety of forces that impact organizational planning. As noted by the South Carolina Office of Human Resources (2002), "workforce planning is not an exact science." Although the SC OHR recommends a process that relies on data collection and analysis from multiple sources, the organization is careful to note that projections and predictions are not always accurate. For researchers, considering the ways in which public organizations plan for the future holds potential for studies that consider the most appropriate tools and metrics for decision making. The guidance resulting from such studies will serve as an invaluable resource for public organizations at all levels and their leaders.

The implications of the economic downturn were evident in the nation's rising foreclosure rate, shocking unemployment numbers, and also in public employment decisions. Considering the complex interplay that exists between public budgets and workforce planning is a necessity. Noting this, public personnel managers must be proactive but also adaptable. They must consider the needs of both the organization and the individual. They must follow and anticipate internal and external forces that affect the workforce, and ultimately, the ability of public organizations to deliver high-quality public services.

Delivering excellent public service is a priority of public organizations but is only a motto when resources, including human resources, are unable to meet demand. Public personnel managers must work together with their colleagues to balance capacity and demand, while the former is in decline and the latter is climbing. This impossible task is the requirement and challenge of succession planning in turbulent times. In the words of Dwight Waldo, who in 1969 was also considering the impact of turbulent times on public organizations: "In the present time of turbulence, we in public administration will be hard put indeed to make prudent decisions about the proper balance between or combination of stability and change. This will be true not only because of confusion and disagreement about the direction and rate of change, but because we know too little of the effects of our actions—or inactions" (p. 275).

References

Brown, R. G., and M. M. Brown. 2005. "Strategic Planning for Human Resource Managers." In S. E. Condrey, ed. *Handbook of Human Resource Management in Government*, 2nd ed. San Francisco, CA: Jossey-Bass.

Daley, D. M. 2006. "Strategic Human Resource Management." In N. M. Riccucci, ed. *Public Personnel Management: Current Concerns, Future Challenges*, 4th ed. New York: Longman.

Klingner, D. E., and J. Nalbandian. 2003. *Public Personnel Management: Contexts and Strategies*, 5th ed. Upper Saddle River: Prentice Hall.

Lawler, E. E., III, J. W. Boudreau, and S. A. Mohrman. 2006. *Achieving Strategic Excellence: An Assessment of Human Resource Organizations*. Stanford, CA: Stanford Business Books.

National Academy of Public Administration. 1995. *Effective Downsizing: A Compendium of Lessons Learned for Government Operations*. Washington, D.C.: National Academy of Public Administration.

Office of Human Resources (OHR), South Carolina Budget and Control Board. 2009a. OHR's 3-Year Strategic Plan (FY 2009-2012).

Office of Human Resources (OHR), South Carolina Budget and Control Board. 2009b. South Carolina Workforce Plan 2009.

Pynes, J. E. 2009. *Human Resources Management for Public and Nonprofit Organizations: A Strategic Approach*, 3rd ed. San Francisco, CA: Jossey-Bass.

Romzek, B. S., and P. W. Ingraham. 1994. "Conclusion: The Challenges Facing American Public Service." In P. W. Ingraham and B. S. Romzek, eds. *New Paradigms for Government: Issues for the Changing Public Service.* San Francisco, CA: Jossey-Bass.

Sandler, M. W., and D. A. Hudson. 1998. *Beyond the Bottom Line: How to Do More with Less in Nonprofit and Public Organizations.* New York: Oxford.

Stanton, T. H. 2004. "Program Design and the Quest for Smaller and More Efficient Government." In T. H. Stanton and B. Ginsberg, eds. *Making Government Manageable: Executive Organization and Management in the Twenty-First Century.* Baltimore, MD: Johns Hopkins.

U.S. Census Bureau. 2009. South Carolina State Government Employment Data. Annual Survey of State and Local Government Employment and Payroll. http://www.census.gov/govs/apes/ (accessed June 21, 2010).

U.S. Office of Personnel Management. 2005. OPM's Workforce Planning Model. http://www.opm.gov/hcaaf_resource_center/assets/Sa_tool4.pdf (accessed June 21, 2010).

Waldo, D. 1969. "Some Thoughts on Alternatives, Dilemmas, and Paradoxes in a Time of Turbulence." In D. Waldo, ed. *Public Administration in a Time of Turbulence.* Scranton, PA: Chandler.

13

PUBLIC SECTOR PENSIONS AND BENEFITS: CHALLENGES IN A NEW ENVIRONMENT

Albert C. Hyde and Katherine C. Naff

Albert C. Hyde is currently an advisory consultant for the U.S. Department of Interior and U.S. Forest Service on strategy development. From 1992 to 2008, he was a senior consultant for the Brookings Institution's former center for public policy education in Washington. His academic experience includes directing public administration programs at San Francisco State University and the University of Pittsburgh.

Katherine C. Naff is a professor of public administration at San Francisco State University. Her teaching specialties include human resource management, public law, and diversity issues in public administration. Her research interests include the impact of the Supreme Court on public policy and the theory of representative bureaucracy as implemented in the United States and South Africa.

Students of human resource management may find this chapter on public sector pensions and benefits somewhat curious. They may think they've stumbled into a public budgeting or finance textbook by mistake. But as the chapter hopes to make clear, pensions and benefits (the deferred compensation systems provided by government entities) are as much about financing as they are about employee retention and performance strategies. And at this critical juncture, the financial crises that many governmental entities now confront are as much about shortfalls in revenues (hopefully temporary) as they are about structural deficits caused by financial commitments they can no longer meet in their postemployment systems. Those commitments include pensions and benefits.

Consider for example the following cases of budget and labor negotiations illustrating what is happening across the country in 2010:

> The City of Oakland, CA after negotiating with its police union for wage concessions to meet a 30 million dollar deficit, sent out lay-off notices to 80 of its over 775 police officers. The City is asking the union to agree to make employee contributions of 9% to the pension fund. Currently, police officers are the only group of city employees who don't pay an employee contribution. Police union officials point out that while firefighters now

pay an employee contribution, they were given a pay raise to cover that. While the City Council is eager to maintain current police force levels given that it has the 4th highest crime rate among major cities, the City Administrator noted that there is nowhere else to run for spending cuts since the Police and Fire departments account for over 75% of the City budget and the Fire Department's union contract has a no lay-off clause. (Kuruvilla, 2010)

The Governor of California reported that his administration has reached an agreement with four of the State's unions that represent 23,000 of the state's 170,000-union member employees ("Sanity in the Offing," 2010). At the center of the deal are new pension arrangements for all newly hired employees that increase their employee contribution for pensions and other benefits and move their eligible retirement date back. In previous agreements, some employees like highway patrol officers were able to retire at 50 with 90% of their salary level in their last year of employment. Perhaps feeling the pressure of how that is being perceived in a state still mired in recession with a 12% unemployment rate, a week later the union representing the Highway Patrol officers signed an agreement increasing their pension fund contribution to 10% and changing the base year for determining the pension payout to the last 3 years. (Neumann, 2010; "Sanity in the Offing," 2010)

The State Legislature of New Jersey passed legislation early this year significantly altering new government workers' benefits. The three bills passed and were signed by a newly elected Governor who campaigned on reforming pensions, require all employees to make pension fund contributions and also increases the amount of their contribution for health care insurance. Another part of the legislation attacks pension spiking—the controversial though legal practice of applying unused sick leave and vacation time and other cashable allowances to increase the final year of salary to be used as a basis for determining pension payments. (Chon, 2010)

Behind these three cases are the current strategies for pension and benefits reform. Reform in this case is mostly about renegotiating previous agreements with unions and other employee groups. While the primary objective now is to meet current budget shortfalls, there is a larger goal of bringing public sector pensions back into budgetary alignment, to tamp down what is referred to as the "crowding-out effect." This occurs because, for most government entities, personnel costs account for a majority share of the total budget, sometimes reaching as much as 70 percent. Within those costs is a substantial share for what are referred to as full fringe benefits: what each employer pays for insurance, retirement, Medicare, and other costs outside of salary. While this varies greatly, a useful benchmark is the federal fringe benefit rate. Periodically, as part of its competitive contracting process, the Office of Management Budget (OMB) updates these payments as a cost factor. Thus, in fiscal year 2007, the total cost of benefits as a percentage of salary, what is known as the civilian position full cost, fringe benefit cost factor was as follows (US OMB, 2006):

Clearly, salary and benefit costs are significant factors in resolving budget imbalances. In past decades, governments facing cutbacks have frozen hiring, encouraged employee turnover with incentive payments for early retirement, and occasionally resorted to layoffs and furloughs. They have not reduced overall

Insurance and health benefits	6.7 percent
Civilian retirement benefits	26.6 percent
Medicare benefit	1.5 percent
Miscellaneous fringe benefits	1.7 percent
Total fringe benefit cost as percentage of salary	36.45 percent

job salaries for the most part and have been even more hesitant to delve into benefits. But as the cost factor above shows, at some point if the budget crises deepen, there are fewer places to look for cost reductions, as the cases described earlier attest.

But first, some background on how public sector benefits came to this current state of affairs.

A SHORT HISTORY OF RETIREMENT SYSTEMS

The history of public pensions has been well documented. Olivia Mitchell and Edwin Hustead's 2001 edited book, *Pensions in the Public Sector*, from the Pension Research Council is an excellent source covering most of the basic systems at federal, state, and local government levels. They note that when the over 12 million state and local workers covered by pension plans are added with the 2.5 million federal workers and another 3 million military personnel, there are close to 20 million public sector employees covered by retirement systems.

Traditionally most of these workers started and still remain in some form of defined benefit pension system. A better term for these systems is deferred compensation. The concept is that employees pay some portion of their current compensation or forego payment as part of their wage agreement matched with some form of payment by the government employer to set up a payment fund upon their separation. Defined benefit systems are in contrast to defined contribution systems where payment upon separation is based on the employee's own savings matched by an employer contribution (Cayer, 2003; Gale, Shoven, and Warshawskey, 2005). A core premise for establishing defined benefit retirement systems in the public service was to appeal to workers who were interested in a career with government where a stable long-term stream of compensation was more important than highly variable pay in a more dynamic and competitive setting such as the corporate enterprise. Of course, much has changed since the earliest retirement systems were put in place in the mid-1850s. In terms of origins, Hustead and Mitchell note that the first municipal system was created in 1857 in New York City to cover police officers injured in the line of duty. That system was extended 30 years later to pay a pension based on 50 percent of the police officer's final salary to anyone with more than 20 years of active service. Various pension or retirement payments systems would be established over the next half century—but the real development of public pensions systems started following the Social Security Act in 1935 (Hustead and Mitchell, 2001).

Hustead and Mitchell's (2001) assessment of the growth of state and local retirement systems has three phases or eras:

> *1930–1950 Social Security Exclusion Era.* Because of congressional concerns that taxing state and local governments for inclusion under Social Security would be unconstitutional, state and local governments were excluded. Plans

established by larger state and municipal governments set up a two-part retirement benefit based roughly equally on (1) annuitized payments on what the employee had contributed and (2) an employer payment based on salary and years of service.

1950–1980 Social Security Inclusion Era. Congressional amendments after 1950 allowed state and local governments to opt in to Social Security and, in that process, a significant number (perhaps as much as a third of the larger entities) set up "split benefit" payment system. Under this arrangement, a lower benefit rate was applied to the first $4,200 of salary (this was pegged to the Social Security ceiling rate) and a higher rate applied to the portion of salary above that. This meant the lower-paid workers received benefits that were disproportionally less than higher-paid employees. Concerns about the retirement system significantly underpaying lower-salary workers led to pressures for system reform.

1980–2000 Growth and Investment Era. Growing recognition (coupled with considerable expansion of state and local government workforces) that pensions could be managed with a diversified investment strategy of accumulated assets and confidence in financial markets led to development of the current defined system. Governments realized that investment returns (i.e., earnings on investments) could allow for more generous payments to beneficiaries without raising either employee or employer contribution levels and causing undue fiscal stress on governments. Hustead and Mitchell point to the increase in investment earnings from 58 percent of all receipts in 1986 to 71 percent by 1997.

If one appends a new period to the Hustead–Mitchell historical overview, one might summarize the twenty-first century as a *Return to Fiscal Realities Era.* When the full history of U.S. state and local government compensation and labor relations is written, many will point to agreements reached during the 1980s and 1990s with unions to exchange increases in deferred compensation for its workforce members for current wage and salary givebacks to help states and cities cope with the two major recessions and to balance severe budget deficits. As public salaries lagged behind private sector compensation from 1980 to 2005, pensions and benefits were the primary vehicles used to keep public workforce turnover rates low. Human resource management continued to debate the merits of pay for performance even when survey results affirmed that job security and benefits were more important to most public workers than high variable pay systems, bonuses, and the like.

All this would change as quickly as the federal and state budget surpluses, bolstered by surging financial and real estate markets, began to evaporate. The first warning came in 2001 with the dot-com bust of 2000–2003 when the S&P 500 index plummeted from above 1,400 to 800. Along with it, as the National Association of State Retirement Systems Association (NASRA) (2008) reports, the aggregate market value of state and local government pension funds dropped from $2.3 trillion to $1.9 trillion—a decline of 20 percent over three years. Pension assets quickly recovered and rose to $3.2 trillion at the financial peak of the market in 2007. When the S&P dropped by half again in just 13 months, pension assets dropped more than $1 trillion. NASRA rightly reports that pension fund assets have recovered from each of these periods of market declines before and will likely do so again. The question this time is when?

But before concluding this section, it is important to include the federal retirement system into this historical overview. Developments in the federal government are instructive because, in 1987, the government switched from a defined benefit plan to a hybrid plan that has defined benefit and contribution elements. In terms of equivalency, the new plan—the federal employment retirement system (FERS)—paid about the same in benefit levels as the old civil service retirement system (CSRS) after Social Security is factored in. Table 13.1 highlights the differences and illustrates the key features of retirement system plans.

In the old system, CSRS, the pension payment based solely on increasing percentages of salary tied to longevity, providing incentives to stay in the workforce. Under CSRS, federal retirees' pension could reach as much as 80 percent of the three highest salary years (what is commonly referred to as their "high three") if they stayed for more than 20 years and worked past the age of 62. The FERS reduces the pension payment to a maximum of 1.1 percent of their high three but adds a matching 401k savings plan where employees can manage their savings in different funds in a federal "thrift savings plan." This type of defined contribution segment, which combines employee and employer contributions into a fund that provides a lump-sum amount upon retirement or separation, provides incentives for workers who don't intend to spend their careers in the federal service. In the private sector, the majority of retirement systems use some form of defined contribution system (though many firms also provide stock options) to be competitive in attracting future employees who view themselves as more mobile and thus more interested in taking their retirement accounts with them.

As the 30-year mark looms, the federal government is closing in on its transition to a total FERS workforce. (FERS was established in 1987 and applied to any unvested

Table 13.1 Federal Retirement Systems

	Civil Service Retirement System (Hired before 1983)	Federal Employees Retirement System (Hired after 1987)
Defined benefit eligibility and provision formula	Vested after 5 years 1.5 percent employees' highest 3 years of salary for first 5 years 1.75 percent high three for 5–9 years 2 percent high three after 10 years Maximum—80 percent highest 3 years of salary	Vested after 5 years 1 percent employees' highest salary for 3 years times total years of service 1.1 percent employees' high three if 20 years of service and retiring after 62
Defined contribution	N/A	Thrift savings plan vested after 3 years (Basically a 401k savings plan) Government contributes 1 percent of base pay Individual can contribute 10 percent and government matches 100 percent for first 3 percent and 50 percent for 4 percent to 5 percent

Source: Torregrosa, Elliot, and Musell (2008).

workers at the time, as well as those hired after 1983.) In terms of converting a retirement system, it stands as an exemplary model in that it is a hybrid system. Other government entities that are considering major change are pursuing a single-system approach, mainly putting all new employees in total defined contributions system that is augmented only by Social Security. It should be pointed out, however, that is not what was assumed as the guiding premise for defined contribution systems. As pension expert Alicia Munnell noted in her testimony to Congress in early 2009, 401k savings plans as the predominate mode of a defined contribution system were designed as supplements to systems that included either a pension or a profit-sharing plan (Munnell, 2009). But between 1983 and 2007, Munnell estimates a drop among all employers offering defined benefit systems from 62 to 17 percent, whereas the proportion of employers with defined contribution systems (410k plans) grew from 17 to 63 percent. Hybrid systems among employers also dropped slightly from 26 to 19 percent (Munnell, 2009).

Munnell's concerns are more systemic in terms of what this switch in systems portrays. She and other experts warn about the dangers inherent in defined contribution systems not providing adequate financial security from investment sources alone because "Evidence indicates that people make mistakes at every step along the way. They don't join the plan, they don't contribute enough, they don't diversify their holdings, they over invest in company stock, they take out money when they switch jobs, and they don't annualize at retirement" (Munnell, 2009, p. 1). As a result, she estimates that nationally the percentage of "households unprepared for retirement" increased from 31 percent in 1983 to 44 percent in 2006. That share increases to 61 percent if health care costs are included.

The purpose of this long digression on the issues surrounding defined contribution systems is not to bemoan the inevitability of this conversion trend; it is what it is. But governments are now realizing that their ability to fund pensions systems over the long run is not sacrosanct (Reddick and Coggburn, 2008). They too may be said to have been overly reliant on investing strategies. Rather the issues noted above speak to the task of human resource managers who must do more than simply point employees to booklets or Web sites explaining their retirement options. New-generation human resource managers must add to their work portfolios how to help employees make appropriate decisions about participation, contribution, and even investment in their benefit packages so that they better enable themselves when they retire to maintain the standard of living they had when they were working.

RETIREMENT SYSTEMS BY THE NUMBERS AND DOLLARS

Before delving into the financial state of affairs of current public retirement systems, it would be useful to provide some larger statistics enumerating who is involved and at what cost. The U.S. Census reports annually on state and local governments that have retirement systems. As Table 13.2 illustrates, there are just over 2,500 systems in the nation. This number has been stable since the 1980s (there were slightly over 2,400 systems in 1986). Furthermore, while there have been some minor shifts among local governmental units, the total numbers of members have increased by about 11 percent during the last decade. The beneficiaries ratio (i.e., the number of retired employees receiving payments against the number of active members) has increased slightly from 45 to 51 percent.

Table 13.2	State and Local Retirement Systems in the United States 2000–2008				
State and Type of Local Government	**Number of Systems**	**Membership (Total)**	**Membership (Active)**	**Membership (Inactive)**	**Total Beneficiaries Receiving Periodic Payments**
United States (totals)					
2000	2,209	16,833,698	13,916,705	2,916,992	6,292,329
2005	2,656	18,012,078	14,193,043	3,819,035	6,946,309
2008	2,550	19,097,226	14,701,442	4,395,784	7,553,373
States (totals)					
2000	218	15,077,009	12,281,004	2,796,005	4,786,433
2005	222	16,207,122	12,569,872	3,637,250	5,846,393
2008	218	17,215,183	13,073,495	4,141,688	6,405,199
Local (total)					
2000	1,991	1,756,689	1,635,702	120,987	1,505,896
2005	2,434	1,804,956	1,623,171	181,785	1,099,916
2008	2,332	1,882,043	1,627,947	254,096	1,148,174
County					
2000	145	512,866	462,962	49,904	220,036
2005	161	527,196	464,832	62,364	249,727
2008	160	576,572	483,239	93,333	274,556
Municipality					
2000	1,617	1,068,587	1,015,566	53,021	1,101,872
2005	1,749	1,100,725	1,002,889	97,836	754,523
2008	1,659	1,148,991	1,005,863	143,128	777,903
Township					
2000	156	32,353	29,567	2,786	18,788
2005	401	36,998	34,632	2,366	21,248
2008	395	38,634	35,116	3,518	21,930
Special District					
2000	59	57,866	51,539	6,327	126,319
2005	110	53,430	48,266	5,164	29,861
2008	106	45,777	41,620	4,157	28,700
School District					
2000	14	85,017	76,068	8,949	38,881
2005	13	86,607	72,552	14,055	44,557
2008	12	72,069	62,109	9,960	45,085

Source: U.S. Census (2000, 2005, 2009).

What the general membership statistics don't show are demographic patterns: average age of beneficiaries, life expectancy, and age at retirement. These lead to issues that are very much at the heart of pension reforms being touted across the country because they affect long-term cost obligations. Pension reform at this critical time is being driven by the dramatic change in finances emanating directly from the dramatic crash of the financial sector in 2007–2008 and a still very precarious recovery underway currently. Table 13.3 shows that dramatic change of fortune from the market heights of 2000 to the depths of 2008.

Employee retirement system finances are based on a three-pronged investment strategy. First, employees make contributions to their retirement system. The second prong is the governmental employer's contributions. The level of contribution is determined in actuarial terms as to what will be needed to maintain the payment stream to beneficiaries in the future. Actuarial projections are required to estimate average life spans for these payments.

While the largest part (or prong) of the investment strategy is based on invest-ment income, it should be kept in mind that these earnings on investment come from the accumulated pool of funds in the system built up over a period of years. In a sense, government and employee contributions are part of the maintenance and accu-mulation of capital strategy for the retirement fund, while earnings income will hinge on the state of the financial markets and the level of diversification within the funds. So, Table 13.2 shows clearly how easy it was in the past to sustain over 100 percent funding of the projected benefits payments. In 2000, investment returns were at over $230 billion compared to $100 billion needed for payments. Fast-forward to 2008, earnings on investments were now a negative—minus $40 billion. A closer look at the table shows just how dependant state and local retirement systems are on "market equities." While total worth of these systems exceeded $3 trillion compared to just $2 trillion in 2000, in 2008 corporate stocks were at 45 percent, corporate bonds at 21 percent, and foreign equities, 19 percent, while government securities accounted for less than 9 percent of investment holdings. Compared to 2000, this is really only a slight shift in investment emphasis.

The rise and fall of asset worth of pension funds was driven by a cycle of market bubbles and collapse. Defenders of the current system point to rapid recovery following the dot-com bust in 2000–2003 as the guideline. Critics however see something funda-mentally different in market conditions and ask the more sobering question: What if pension funds don't return to 8 percent to 10 percent annual investment earnings return levels (Wilshire, 2009)? In early 2010, in California, a fiery debate erupted when CALPERS (the state public pension system) announced that it expected 8.8 percent returns from the market for the future. Critics charged this was an overstatement follow-ing the previous year's disclosures of massive market losses that will necessitate increased contributions from California state workers.

Whatever happens in terms of market recovery and a recovering employment rate that is impacting current state and local budgets, the current pension debate is about a term called "unfunded liability." This measurement is produced by valuing the amount of pension benefits guaranteed against fund assets to meet those payments. In short, as the Pew Center on the States asks in recent reports, do public pension systems have the money to pay the bills coming due? Pew's first major study—aptly titled "Promises with a Price" (2007)—revealed that the cost of that bill was at $2.73 trillion— $2.35 trillion for pensions and another $381 billion for health care and other benefits

Table 13.3	Summary of State and Local Government–Employee–Retirement System Finances: Comparing 2000–2008 (Thousand dollars. Detail may not add to total because of rounding)			
	2000		**2008**	
	Amount	**Percent**	**Total**	**Percent**
Total receipts	$297,049,657	100	$79,649,581	100
Employee contributions	$24,994,468	8.4	$36,929,944	46
Government contributions	$40,155,114	13.5	$81,996,539	103
State government contributions	$17,547,408	5.9	$36,261,593	46
Local government contributions	$22,607,706	7.6	$45,734,946	57
Earnings on investments	$231,900,075	78.1	–$39,276,902	–49
Total payments	$100,457,883	100	$193,808,914	100
Benefits	$91,274,292	90.8	$175,423,416	90.5
Withdrawals	$4,431,876	4.4	$4,634,335	2.4
Other payments	$4,751,715	4.7	$13,751,163	7.1
Total cash and investment holdings end-FY	$2,168,643,033	100	$3,190,072,194	100
Cash and short-term investments	$121,142,060	5.6	$91,188,031	2.9
Total securities	$1,873,843,223	86.4	$2,674,888,614	83.9
Governmental securities	$271,551,952	12.5	$226,774,621	8.5
Nongovernmental securities	$1,602,291,271	73.9	$2,448,113,993	91.5
Corporate bonds	$342,679,425	15.8	$519,686,464	21.2
Corporate stocks	$787,748,623	36.3	$1,118,138,665	45.7
Mortgages	$21,288,457	1.0	$9,588,453	.4
Foreign and international	$286,278,390	13.20	$468,133,959	19.1
Other nongovernmental	$164,296,376	7.58	$259,914,837	10.6
Other investments	$173,657,750	8.01	$423,995,549	13.2
Real property	$47,189,167	2.18	$90,155,487	3.7

Source: U.S. Census (2000, 2005, 2009).

(Pew Center on the States, 2007). Their report noted that 85 percent of the pension bill, leaving a shortage of $361 billion, was covered, but less than 3 percent of health care and other benefits was funded.

Pew's next report (2010) raised that figure, noting that the gap was now at $1 trillion (and this was before the full brunt of the financial markets meltdown is factored in). Illinois was the unfunded liability leader, at just 54 percent and a daunting $54 billion shortfall. While the dependency on collapsing investment income was the major driver, Pew noted that 21 states failed to make their "mandatory" contributions to their funds on average over the last five years to cover 90 percent levels of funding.

Unfunded liability will be increasingly difficult for governmental entities to bypass and postpone to the future. First off, the general accounting and management principle in a retirement system remains that each generation of workers (and their employers) are responsible for the cost of the benefits they are to receive (Munnell, Aubrey, and Quinby, 2009). States may skip payments, but the liability remains on the books. So accounting standards are moving to make pension liability more transparent and to obligate governments to reveal what that value/cost is.

Enter the Government Accounting Standards Board (GASB), which in 2006 began work on amendments to its GASB statements no. 25, *Financial Reporting for Defined Benefit Pension Plans and Note Disclosure for Defined Contribution Plans,* and no. 27, *Accounting for Pensions by State and Local Governmental Employers* that would require . . . "full disclosure of the current funded status of the plan as the most recent actuarial valuation date" (GASB, 2006). As the GASB standards move to promulgation (currently planned for 2013), government entities would have to display the "missing amounts" of their contributions and include the result in their financial statements. Obviously this would have a major impact on what the annual budget imbalance would be along with affecting credit ratings.

In its continuing pronouncements, GASB issued another statement in 2010 that makes the impact even more compelling. First they noted that while it is the pension fund that is responsible for any unfunded liability, the employer government is also responsible, should the pension fund fail to pay its benefits. In GASB's view, the taxpayers of the governmental unit would be on the hook to make good any net pension liability. This is not to say that there won't be resistance. Several states are resisting the GASB requirements on the grounds that the financial consequences are too severe for an area like health care liability, which is not all that well understood. The Texas legislature passed a bill in 2007 (HB 2365) basically exempting its major cities from GASB standards, if they deemed it appropriate (Walsh, 2007), which Governor Rick Perry signed into law on June 15. The state of Connecticut is also considering even harsher legislation (Hyde, 2008).

Given this, it might be important to examine briefly the legal dimensions inherent in public sector pensions and benefits, and add in another variable: What happens if the governmental entity declares bankruptcy?

THE LEGAL UNDERPINNINGS OF PUBLIC PENSIONS

Public pensions were once considered a "gratuity" that could be modified or withdrawn by the state at any time. Monahan's (2010) recent analysis of state pension case law found that, presently, in nearly all states and localities pensions are protected by law.

(In Indiana, involuntary plans are still considered a gratuity.) Also, in nearly all states, courts consider pensions to be either a contract between employees and retirees and the state or local jurisdiction or as "property," protected by the Fifth and Fourteenth Amendments to the Constitution. (An exception is Minnesota, which protects pensions under a theory of promissory estoppel.)

Some states have an explicit constitutional provision protecting public pensions, while others have clear statutory language. Where this is not the case, courts have still found a contractual obligation implicitly in legislative history or through other circumstances (e.g., inclusion in collective bargaining agreements). When the public entity attempts to modify pension benefits by, for example, changing the benefit formula, beneficiaries frequently challenge that action. The courts then must decide if a contract exists when it took effect and whether that revision is consistent with the explicit or implicit contract. A substantial "impairment" usually may be justified if it is considered "reasonable and necessary to achieve an important public purpose" (Monahan, 2010, p. 18). However, this can be a high standard to meet, and even jurisdictions facing dire financial straits have failed this test. Beyond that, the extent to which benefits can be tampered with varies from state to state. In most, retirees can consider their benefits safe, but the rights of current employees are unclear. In some states, only past benefit accruals are protected, while in others, future accruals are as well; in others it remains unclear.

In some states, where courts have been unable to find the existence of a contract, they instead consider them property. Under the Fifth and Fourteenth Amendments, this means they cannot be impaired without due process of law. Moreover, in theory, if that property is "taken," the employee must be provided with just compensation under the Fifth Amendment. However, this theory provides less protection for employees than the contract theory, because as long as the state can provide a rational reason for a change in benefits (such as a financial crisis), those changes may be justified. Challenges under the takings clause seeking just compensation are rarely successful.

Unfunded pension liabilities can be a significant factor in driving a locality to declare bankruptcy, in which case U.S. bankruptcy law comes into play. Vallejo, California, was the first to declare its union contracts, including their pension provisions, null and void as part of the bankruptcy process. Most unions were able to renegotiate their contracts with the city. But in an unprecedented decision that caught nationwide attention, U.S Bankruptcy judge Michael McManus issued a decision on March 13, 2009, voiding the contract of the holdout union.

The bankruptcy statute includes a section (1113) that requires entities filing bankruptcy under chapter 11 to follow certain requirements prior to rejecting collective bargaining agreements. However, Judge McManus ruled, Congress did not extend this provision to chapter 9 bankruptcies, which applies to municipalities, and so they are free to jettison collective bargaining agreements (*In re City of Vallejo* (08-26813-A-9) (Eastern District of California)). This ruling was subsequently affirmed by a U.S. District Court judge ("Judge Affirms Rejection," 2010).

In short, public employees and retirees enjoy at least some legal protection from having their benefits reduced or modified in some other way that adversely affects them, though the amount of protection varies from state to state. However, government employers are not above finding ways to skirt those protections, as Vallejo did in filing bankruptcy, when faced with dismal financial circumstances.

THAT OTHER PUBLIC PENSION AND BENEFITS ISSUE-OPEB

Of course, employers offer other forms of deferred compensation, that is, other postemployment benefits (OPEB). Health care insurance has long been one of these benefits that governments provide. Indeed, many of these plans are so well administered that state legislatures have considered adding to the public sector agency health care rolls different categories of high-need citizens. The range of plans and coverage in public sector health benefits is wide and diverse. Basic health care insurance can be augmented with vision and dental care and increasingly heath care savings accounts. And while health care costs have increased rapidly over the last decade, governments have more flexibility to cope with rising costs, although they can work to the disadvantage of employees (Reddick and Coggburn, 2007).

For current employees, health care and other insurance options can be affected in three ways. Most systems require some form of premium payment for insurance, enabling governments, like their private sector counterparts, to pass on a portion of cost increases to the employee each year. That is one option. A second option is to pass onto employees other costs through raising deductibles, limiting coverage, raising copayments for services, and so on. These adjustments are an attractive means for employers seeking to share cost increases and also provide an incentive for employees to stay healthy. A third option combines elements of both but is done by changing the menu of health providers. Government units regularly contract with health care insurers and health maintenance organizations. The ideal is to provide a range of providers with different cost structures and benefits so that employees can make choices during what is commonly called "open season." As costs continue to escalate and health care organizations merge and consolidate, a less noticeable, but increasing, trend is to reduce the number of available choices.

Obviously, health care benefit programs will now be affected greatly by recent passage of the health care reform legislation, but it is too soon to know what the impact will be on public employers. While they should be slight, given that public programs are largely model programs, the looming challenge will be reducing health care cost escalation. If this doesn't occur over the decade, then human resource managers will themselves be pressed to provide the breath of choice and value that have been hallmarks for government programs for decades.

The challenge for providing programs for retired employees is greater, especially as life spans continue to increase. The options for managing increasing costs are fewer. Retirees generally enjoy greater legal protection from significant reductions in benefits or increases in premiums. Many retirees are on plans that require no premiums. As retirees are covered by Medicare and the prescription drug program of 2006, there will be increased confusion as to costs and likely dissatisfaction with levels of choice. But the big issue is that state and local systems have not addressed the funding liability of these programs in any serious way.

Further complicating the situation, potentially on an exponential scale, are new requirements that state and local governments now account for OPEB, primarily health care insurance (U.S. Federal Reserve Bank of Chicago, 2006). The December 2006 GASB standards (nos. 43 and 45) state that all state and local governments must show in their annual (audited) fiscal statements health care expenses and future liabilities. In addition, GASB stipulates that governments must shift from a pay-as-you-go system for health care to one that estimates and funds future costs. The GASB addressed this OPEB area because most government entities fund OPEB on a pay-as-you-go basis, shifting the real cost burden to the future as life spans increase. But unlike pension fund obligations, most government entities do not make OPEB investments on some form of prefunding basis.

Hence the Pew Center's ominous warning that the real time bomb in rising retirement system costs is the nearly $600 billion in OPEB costs, for which only 7 percent is fully funded. Pew's final comment in their 2009 report is that only two states, Alaska and Arizona, have as much as 50 percent of the funding set aside for their OTEB funding liability.

A CONCLUDING NOTE: LURCHING TOWARD REFORM

Testifying before a California commission looking into pension reform, benefits expert and *Governing* magazine columnist Girad Miller offered the following prediction about the choice confronting reform efforts: "Without significant structural reforms to the defined benefit system however, it will inevitably collapse under its own weight, and the disparity between public pensioners and the taxpayers who support them will worsen to the point that a severe backlash could ensue" (Miller, 2010, p. 7). Miller's comments contain two significant elements. The first is contextual—that the public will turn against public employees (as they have toward Wall Street executives) because of a reward system that they feel is lavish. It is a system that they do not understand and which does not correspond well to their own vision of current and future financial situations in a nation still in the midst of severe economic recession and sluggish recovery. The second is that the gap toward closing current levels of pension funding liability is more a chasm and unlikely to be resolved with slight changes or tinkering in retirement system formulas. Miller's charge for significant structural reform is really a call for moving further away from defined benefit systems all together.

In assessing the direction and momentum of reform efforts, Table 13.4 highlights the usual current options being pursued across the states and municipalities. Current employees and soon to be retirees are most likely to be affected by efforts to remove the opportunities for legal, but media deplored, pension spiking. The major reform impact of payment solutions is most often directed at new and future hires. Clearly, over time that will make a difference, especially with a strong market recovery, but it does violate the norm mentioned earlier. That is that the responsibility for each generation of employees and retirees lies within that generation. It also inserts into the public service work contract equation a potential disturbing trend toward the bimodal workforce. That is that new employees are offered a less valuable pension and benefit than current employees. It is a trend that may be perceived by new employees as establishing a compensation dichotomy between the privileged, better paid and the less privileged and underpaid. One can only guess how fundamental values and core constructs like public sector motivation, commitment, and engagement would be affected.

So, the real issue is whether a new era is coming into place, centered on the demise of the defined benefit system. This would constitute fundamental change, unlike the other steps where, via negotiation, reforms are basically premised on an intergenerational basis. Assuring real budget transparency would be the real death knell of defined benefit and likely lead to the type of reform accomplished by Oregon in 2006, where the state rolled up its pension liabilities for old employees into a bond measure and walled off its defined benefits system from new hires. Human resource managers will no doubt be in thick of the battles and confrontations to come over fiscally strapped budgets, layoffs, and pay and benefit negotiations and how to get out of the trillion dollar "hole" of net pension liabilities that current retirement systems have amassed. The direction of reform is very much uncertain, but one thing seems clear—former OMB director and member of Congress Leon Panetta's rule of holes will apply. Panetta is reputed to have said, "The first rule of holes is if you're in one, stop digging."

Table 13.4 Benefits Reform Dimensions

Impact on Payments (Contributions)	New Hires	Current Employees	Retirees
	Fundamental Reform or Change at the Margins		
Level of employee contribution	Current trend	Increasing trend—especially when there are differences across employee groups as to making minimum contributions	Not applicable—although there are cases where retirees are being pressed to make higher contributions for health care insurance and OPEB
Change retirement eligibility (usually extend minimum retirement age)	Current trend	Infrequent trend—though there are some cases trying to limit pension pyramiding	Not applicable
Change basis for determining benefits contribution (pension spiking, etc.)	Current trend	Emerging trend especially in efforts to deter pension spiking	Not applicable
Change system from defined benefit to defined contribution	Emerging trend—placing new hires in a defined contribution system or cash balance system instead of defined benefit plan	Only one state has made the conversion so far. In Nebraska, which established a cash balance plan for new hires in 2003, current employees were given the option of joining	Not applicable
Impact on Benefits (Payments)			
Lower benefits paid or rescind payments	Not applicable	Bankruptcy cases—i.e., Vallejo, California, where bankruptcy court has voided contracts with labor unions, requiring renegotiation of what payment levels will be	No major public sector precedent (although there are numerous private sector cases, usually associated with bankruptcy, in which pension benefits are predetermined usually by the Pension Benefit Guaranty Corporation (PBGC))

References

Cayer, N. Joseph. 2003. "Public Employee Benefits and the Changing Nature of the Workforce." In S. W. Hayes and R. C. Kearney, eds. *Public Personnel Management: Problems and Prospects* (pp. 167–179). Engelwood Cliffs, NJ: Prentice-Hall.

Chon, Gina. 2010, March 22. "New Jersey Cuts Workers Benefits." *The Wall Street Journal.*

City of Vallejo. 2010, June 15. "Judge Affirms Rejection of IBEW Collective Bargaining Agreement." Press release. Retrieved June 21, 2010 from http://www.ci.vallejo.ca.us.

"Sanity in the Offing- California's Public Sector Unions." 2010, June 26. *Economist* 395(8688): 35–36.

Gale, William G., John B. Shoven, and Mark Warshawskey, eds. 2005. *The Evolving Pension System: Trends, Effects, and Proposals for Reform.* Washington, D.C.: The Brookings Institution Press.

Governmental Accounting Standards Board (GASB). 2006, December 15. Summary of Statement No. 25, *Financial Reporting for Defined Benefit Pension Plans and Note Disclosures for Defined Contribution Plans.* http://www.gasb.org/st/summary/gstsm25.html (accessed October 1, 2010).

Hustead, Edwin C., and Olivia S. Mitchell. 2001. "Public Sector Pension Plans: Lessons and Challenges for the Twenty-First Century." In Olivia S. Mitchell and Edwin C. Hustead, eds. *Pensions in the Public Sector* (pp. 5–10). Philadelphia, PA: University of Pennsylvania Press.

Hyde, Albert C. 2008. "The Changing Environment of State and Local Government Public Pensions." In Christopher G. Reddick and D. Coggburn Jerrell, eds. *Handbook of Employee Benefits and Administration.* Boca Raton, FL: CRC Press.

Kuruvilla, Matthai. 2010, June 25. "Oakland Votes to Lay Off 80 Police Officers." *San Francisco Chronicle.*

Miller, Girard. 2010, April 22. *Testimony Regarding California Public Pension and retirement Plan reforms.* Sacramento, CA. http://www.lhc.ca.gov/studies/agendas/Apr10.html (accessed June 2010).

Mitchell, Olivia S., David McCarthy, Stanley C. Wisniewski, and Paul Zorn. 2001. "Development in State and Local Pension Plans." In Olivia S. Mitchell and Edwin C. Hustead, eds. *Pensions in the Public Sector* (pp. 11–37). Philadelphia: University of Pennsylvania Press.

Monahan, Amy. 2010, March 17. "Public Pension Plan Reform: The Legal Framework." *Education, Finance & Policy* 5; Minnesota Legal Studies Research No. 10-13. Available at SSRN: http://ssrn.com/abstract=1573864

Munnell, Alicia, Jean Pierre Aubrey, and Laura Quinby. 2009. "The Funding of State and Local Pensions." Center for Research at Boston College. http://crr.bc.edu/briefs/the_funding_of_state_and_local_pensions_2009-2013.html.

Munnell, Alicia. 2009, February 24. "The Financial Crises and Restoring Retirement Security." Testimony before the Committee on Education and Labor, U.S. House of Representatives. http://edlabor.house.gov/documents/111/pdf/testimony/20090224Alicia Munnell Testimony. pdf (accessed June 2, 2010).

National Association of State Retirement Associations. 2008, December. "Market Declines and Public Pensions." http://www.nasra.org/resources/NASRA_NCTR_ISSUE_BRIEF0812.pdf.

Neumann, Jeanette. 2010, June 29. "State Workers, Long resistant Accept Cuts in Public Benefits." *The Wall Street Journal*, p. A-9.

Pew Center on the States. 2007. "Promises with a Price: Public Sector Retirement Benefits." www.pewcenteronthestates.org.

Pew Center on the States. 2010. "The Trillion Dollar Gap: Underfunded State Retirement Systems and the Roads to Reform." www.pewcenteronthestates.org.

Reddick, Christopher G., and Jerrell D. Coggburn. 2007. "State Government Employee Health Benefits in the United States." *Review of Public Personnel Administration* 27(1): 5–20.

Reddick, Christopher G., and Jerrell D. Coggburn. 2008. *Employee Benefits Administration Handbook of Employee Benefits and Administration.* Boca Raton, FL: CRC Press.

Torregrosa, David, Cary Elliot, and Mark Musell. 2008. "An Overview of Federal Retirement Benefits." In Christopher G. Reddick and Jerrell D. Coggburn, eds. *Handbook of Employee Benefits and Administration* (pp. 121–140). Boca Raton, FL: CRC Press.

U.S. Federal Reserve Bank of Chicago. 2006. "OPEB—The 800 Pound Gorilla in the Room." Conference on Public Pensions. Civic Federation of Chicago and Federal Reserve Bank of Chicago. http://pensionconference.chicagofedblogs.org.

U.S. Office of Management and Budget (OMB). 2006, October 31. "Memorandum M-07-02: Update to Civilian Position Full Fringe Benefit Cost Factor." http://www.whitehouse.gov/sites/default/files/omb/assets/omb/memoranda/fy2007/m07-02.pdf (accessed June 2, 2010).

Walsh, Mary Williams. 2007, May 18. "Auditing Rule is Put at Risk by Texas Bill." *The New York Times*, p. C-1.

Wilshire Consulting. 2009. "2009 Wilshire Report on State Retirement Systems: Funding Levels and Asset Allocation." http://www.wilshire.com/BusinessUnits/Consulting/Investment/2009_State_Retirement_Funding_Report.pdf (accessed June 2, 2010).

U. S. Census. 2000, 2005, 2009. "National Summary of State and Local Government Employee-Retirement System Finances." http://www.census.gov/

14 | MANAGING HUMAN RESOURCES TO IMPROVE ORGANIZATIONAL PRODUCTIVITY: THE ROLE OF PERFORMANCE EVALUATION

J. Edward Kellough

J. Edward Kellough is Professor and Head of the Department of Public Administration and Policy at the University of Georgia. Dr. Kellough specializes in public personnel management, public administration, and program evaluation. Recent books include *Understanding Affirmative Action: Politics, Discrimination, and the Search for Justice* (Georgetown University Press, 2007); *The New Public Personnel Administration*, 6th edition, with Lloyd G. Nigro and Felix A. Nigro (Thomson/Wadsworth, 2007); and *Civil Service Reform in the States: Personnel Policy and Politics at the Sub-National Level*, edited with Lloyd G. Nigro (State University of New York Press, 2006). His research has also appeared in numerous academic journals.

Organizations are established when people are brought together, form authority relationships among them, are given material resources, and are charged with the responsibility for performing specified tasks. There are obviously numerous aspects of organizations that are worthy of systematic study, including hierarchical arrangements, environmental influences, and strategies for development, but we should always bear in mind the fact that the work of organizations is performed by people. For this reason, human resources are an organization's most valuable assets. The productivity of an organization's human resources, that is, the employees within the organization, is essential if we are to achieve organizational productivity. Although this observation may seem obvious, it is a point we can easily lose sight of in examinations of organizational performance.

Neglect of the human resource impact on organizational performance may occur because there are so many other factors that can affect performance, both positively and negatively. Among these are structural concerns, networking problems, and shortages of material resources or authority. None of these variables, however, can make up for a workforce that is unproductive. Today there is great interest in efforts to improve organizational performance in the public sector. Many scholars and practitioners of public management have focused increased attention on the issue of performance management (see, e.g., Bouckaert and Halligan, 2007; Heinrich and Lynn, 2000), and in much of the academic literature, effort has been made to identify organizational characteristics or management styles that facilitate the improvement of performance at the organizational level (O'Toole and Meier, 2000; Sandfort, 2000), but less attention is paid to the contribution made by individual employees. While it is certainly possible that the efforts of an effective workforce may be stifled (or augmented) by structural or other organizational characteristics, it is inconceivable that an organization can be productive when its workers, collectively, do not perform.

Given the potential impact of workers on organizational effectiveness, it is imperative that we have a well-developed and accurate means of evaluating the performance of employees, including each person's individual contribution. With this in mind, reconsideration and elaboration of essential points in employee performance evaluation, and the uses of those evaluations, are in order. Of course, a concern with employee performance evaluation is not new, since it has been a key human resources management function for years, but the importance of evaluating employee performance should be emphasized in the context of current discussions of organizational productivity. As Nigro and Nigro (2000, p. 134) have argued, a "key to improving productivity and quality services in the public sector is accurately measuring and controlling the performance of each worker."

This chapter examines the concept of individual-level performance appraisal in the public sector by focusing on the following questions: (1) What precisely is appraised? (2) More generally, how are appraisals conducted? The discussion then shifts to mechanisms to improve individual performance and, by extension, organizational performance, including the role of employee motivation and the structure of incentives. Special attention is also given to the popularity of pay-for-performance systems and the difficulties with such systems. The chapter concludes with a list of practical recommendations for public managers.

ASSESSING EMPLOYEE PERFORMANCE: IDENTIFYING PERFORMANCE CRITERIA AND STANDARDS

If we are interested in measuring job performance, our *criteria* for assessment should ideally reflect critical work outputs. That is, we should concentrate on what it is that the worker is responsible for producing. Such a focus will require, however, a knowledge of job content, developed through systematic job analysis—a time-intensive, but essential, personnel management task. Job analysis provides insight into the work essential for the job, and work outputs can be defined in terms of those tasks. Output-oriented measures could possibly examine such matters as the number of projects completed, the number of forms processed, or the number of clients served. Work output measures by themselves, however, are of limited utility. Allowance must be made for variation in the quality of products or services delivered and variation in the level of difficulty of specific tasks. As a result, the selection of criteria for performance evaluation is only half of the problem. The other half is determining appropriate *standards* of performance for each specified task. These standards should reflect reasonable expectations of what is actually possible in terms of the quality and extent of accomplishments. Those kinds of expectations, however, require an understanding of the nature and context of the jobs under analysis that has been developed through long experience and the documentation of previous levels of output quality and quantity (Carroll and Schneier, 1982, pp. 131–134; Murphy and Cleveland 1995, pp. 154–156).

Clearly, the development of performance appraisal systems based on output -oriented criteria and well-conceived performance standards is not easily accomplished.

In some instances, meaningful work outputs at the level of individual employees are difficult to identify. What, for example, should be specified as measurable work output for a highway maintenance crew worker whose specific tasks vary from day to day and are, at least in part, a function of weather and a variety of other factors that may not be easily predictable? Work products of numerous other types of employees in the public sector may also be difficult to ascertain. Consider, for example, a clerk in a tax commissioner's office or a receptionist in an agency whose specific duties will vary with fluctuations in public demand for the services of their respective units. Similarly, consider individuals who often work in teams such as a budget analyst or program auditor. What work outputs are appropriately specified for their individual jobs when the fact is that much of what they do is dependent upon the work of others? Certain products or services may be identified for which the individual employee may be held accountable in each of these instances, but those outputs may not capture the full extent of the responsibilities of the individual, and in addition, reasonable performance standards may prove to be illusive, especially when the nature of particular tasks vary in unpredictable ways. In such circumstances, appraisal may be skewed toward the assessment of work outputs that are most easily measured even if they are not necessarily the most meaningful. Performance appraisal based on the quality and quantity of work outputs produced by an individual are best developed when the individual's tasks are relatively routine and focused on the production of tangible work products. Performance criteria and standards for individual employees whose tasks are diffuse, whose work depends on the actions of numerous other individuals, and whose effort is directed toward the production of less-than-tangible services or products may not always be readily identifiable.

For these reasons, performance appraisal is often based on other types of criteria that may not represent actual work product or outputs but are nonetheless judged to be prerequisites for successful performance. Certain employee behaviors deemed to be essential for effective performance are used as such criteria. For example, the timely completion of required paperwork or reports; efforts to assist coworkers; respectful, courteous, timely, and tactful interaction with agency clients; and the ready acceptance of direction and feedback from supervisors are all examples of behavioral criteria that could form the basis for the performance appraisal of individual workers. The advantage of behaviorally based performance assessment systems is that for many jobs, specific criteria, that is, presumably effective job behaviors, are more easily identified than are work products or results for which the individual can be reasonably held accountable. It is also likely that similar behaviors may be relevant to a number of jobs so that separate criteria will not need to be developed for every distinct job, and employee behaviors should be relatively easy to observe and evaluate. A focus on behavior is not the same thing, however, as a focus on work product or actual employee accomplishments in terms of outputs, and that is the major disadvantage of behavior-based criteria. An employee may complete a report on time, but that obviously is not a productive activity if the report contains errors or is otherwise of poor quality. In other words, the presence of desired behaviors by themselves may not be sufficient if the connection between those behaviors and productive results is tenuous. Nevertheless, behavior-based approaches to performance appraisal are common.

Another approach to developing criteria for employee performance is to specify particular traits or personal characteristics presumed to be associated with effective performance. Employees may be evaluated, for example, on the basis of traits such as "dependability," "cooperativeness," "honesty," "diligence," or "initiative." Such evaluation systems are easily developed. It is not difficult to identify a set of presumably positive traits that are desirable as characteristics of employees. Trait-based approaches have been widely used in the past, and they can be used across a wide range of jobs, but their use is discouraged because the linkage between apparent possession of particular traits and actual performance on the job may be quite weak, and the determination of the extent to which an individual employee exhibits an individual trait is highly subjective (Carroll and Schneier, 1982, p. 37; Tompkins, 1995, pp. 252–253). In addition, trait scales do not provide the kinds of specific information necessary to structure effective employee training and development efforts (Latham and Wexley, 1994, p. 38). Actual job behaviors and work outputs (if they are specified) will better identify training and developmental needs.

CONDUCTING THE APPRAISAL

While there are a variety of specific approaches for conducting performance appraisals, including narrative essays written by supervisors and ranking or comparison methods (Cardy and Dobbins, 1994, pp. 64–67), performance appraisals are most often accomplished through the use of a rating scale upon which the person conducting the evaluation indicates the observed level of performance, generally by simply placing a check mark in an appropriate box. For each performance criterion specified, for example, four or five performance levels may be identified. It is not uncommon to find performance levels defined as "unsatisfactory," "minimally satisfactory," "satisfactory," "highly satisfactory," "outstanding," or some variation of that scheme. The performance levels specified are assumed to reflect relevant standards for performance, but obviously, the actual definition or meaning of those standards will be determined by the judgment of the raters involved and that judgment may well vary from one person to another. In other words, "satisfactory" performance on a particular criterion or job dimension may, to a considerable extent, rest in the eye of the beholder. To the degree that this is the case, an employee's appraisal can be as much a function of the rater's attitude and perception as it is actual performance.

To reduce this problem, it is necessary that performance levels be accompanied by at least brief narrative definitions. Trait- and behavior-based rating scales, for example, often utilize performance levels tied to behavioral anchors. Behaviorally anchored rating scales (BARS) do not rely simply on ambiguous performance levels defined as "satisfactory" or "unsatisfactory" and various other gradients thereof. Instead, each level of performance is defined in terms of clearly articulated behaviors that are intended to be easily observable and are relevant to the particular job being performed. This procedure narrows somewhat the range of interpretative discretion exercised by the rater and thus helps to ensure consistency or uniformity in the application of the rating scale, although some discretion will necessarily remain in the hands of the evaluator. In instances where job outputs or results are utilized as performance criteria, specific standards representing different levels of quality and quantity of work product should be identified. As noted earlier, these standards should be unique to the tasks associated with each job and developed through an analysis of the nature of the job and experience with the kinds of levels of productivity that are possible. But even in instances where meaningful individual-level work products and performance standards tied to those outputs can be defined, some judgment exercised by the rater will remain.

In many or perhaps most organizations, individual performance ratings are conducted on an annual basis, although other schedules are certainly possible. Regardless of the schedule, however, the results must be reported back to the employee. This communication can be accomplished simply by distribution of a copy of the rating sheet, but it is far more desirable to take advantage of the opportunity that this stage of the process provides for counseling and direction from the employee's supervisor designed to provide the employee with information, not only about how well he or she performed but also about what might be changed or altered so that performance can be improved (Carroll and Schneier, 1982, pp. 177–181; Daley, 1992; Klein and Snell, 1994). These appraisal interviews or briefing sessions may, in fact, be the most crucial aspect of the appraisal process. It is here that the supervisor can explain the basis for judgments made in the evaluation and offer suggestions for employee improvement. In some systems that are grounded on the concept of management by objectives (MBO), the supervisor and employee will set goals to be achieved during the upcoming performance cycle (Carroll and Schneier, 1982, p. 143). The individual goals are based on previously articulated organizational objectives, and it is assumed that directing employee efforts toward specific job-related goals tied to those objectives is one way of effectively promoting organizational productivity. Additionally, a substantial body of literature suggests that employee participation in the establishment of realistic yet challenging goals will enhance employee commitment to the organization and motivation to perform (Locke, 1983; Locke and Latham, 1984; Murphy and Cleveland, 1995, pp. 215–224; Roberts and Reed, 1996). Ultimately, however, the effectiveness of the goal-setting exercise and the appraisal interview itself will hinge on the skill, ability, and commitment of the supervisor involved.

It should be clear, then, that there may be a number of obstacles to effective performance appraisal. The process can never be entirely objective. Judgment must be exercised in the selection of criteria for appraisal, the definition of performance standards, and the application of those standards to individual employees. A substantial commitment from the organization is necessary for performance criteria and standards to be adequately defined and supervisors to be adequately trained in the proper application of the system. It is also important that sufficient time be allowed for effective counseling of employees during the performance briefing or interview, although that may be difficult to accomplish when supervisors are confronted with numerous other pressing demands on their time. In short, substantial organizational resources must be devoted to the performance appraisal process if it is to be made effective.

COMBATING ERROR

Because rater judgment is such a critical aspect of the appraisal process, it is useful to review the sources and significance of error in the exercise of that judgment. To begin, we should remember that performance ratings may be biased. Bias occurs when ratings are altered to conform with the rater's personal views of an individual employee that are unrelated to work productivity. Bias can obviously be the product of prejudice based on factors such as race, ethnicity, gender, age, or disability, and such considerations should have no place in the appraisal process. In addition to this kind of bias, however, error can occur as a result of less invidious but still unacceptable processes. A supervisor, for example, may have friends or "favorite" employees who are rated more generously than others. Several other common errors are identified in the literature and are widely known (see, e.g., Cardy and Dobbins, 1994, pp. 27–33; Carroll and Schneier, 1982, pp. 39–41; Latham and Wexley, 1994, pp. 100–104). It is useful here to consider briefly the most important of these inaccuracies.

THE HALO EFFECT

Evaluators will often rate an employee who performs well on one dimension of a job high on all other aspects of the job. In this situation, it is as if the employee can do no wrong–hence the label "halo effect," but the process can also operate in the opposite direction. For example, poor performance in one area of work may lead the rater to judge the employee harshly in other areas. In general, the problem occurs whenever a rating in one dimension or aspect of a job (whether good or bad) is generalized to other dimensions.

THE FIRST-IMPRESSION ERROR

Raters, especially supervisors, may base subsequent performance appraisals on the impressions they form of an individual employee when that person first comes to a job. In other words, initial impressions, whether favorable or unfavorable, influence subsequent evaluations of performance. Information that is not consistent with the first impression formed is suppressed or discounted. For example, if during the first month on a job an employee had difficulty and performed poorly, the impression such behavior leaves with a manager may lead that manager to give the employee low performance ratings during later evaluations even though the employee's performance improved.

THE SIMILAR-TO-ME EFFECT

Performance evaluators may tend to judge employees more favorably whom they perceive as exhibiting behaviors or values similar to their own. As Latham and Wexley (1994, p. 103) observed, "the more closely the employee resembles the rater in terms of attitudes or background, the stronger the tendency of the rater to judge that person favorably."

COMPARISON OR CONTRAST EFFECTS

It may frequently be the case that employees are evaluated relative to each other rather than to actual job performance standards. An employee who is quite good, for example, may be rated as average simply because he or she is compared to others who are exceptional performers. Alternatively, an employee who is only average in performance may be rated highly because, by comparison, he or she looks good next to his or her mediocre colleagues. In either situation, an error occurs because performance is not judged relative to the actual requirements and standards set for the jobs at issue, but the reliance on employee contrasts or comparisons as a basis for performance appraisal is driven in part by the view of some managers that the appraisal process should produce a distribution of ratings that resemble a normal or bell-shaped curve (Lane, 1994; Latham and Wexley, 1994, p. 101).

THE CENTRAL TENDENCY ERROR

This error is one of the most common in performance appraisal. It occurs when the rater judges all or most employees as "average" or "slightly above average." This problem may have the effect of limiting the usefulness of performance appraisal for some purposes, but the dynamics of the appraisal process often lead managers or supervisors into this difficulty. Typically there is no particular incentive in the process for a rater to judge a subordinate extraordinarily high. If such judgments are made in a few cases, the supervisor risks alienating the bulk of his or her employees who may feel resentment that some are favored at their expense. If higher ratings are given to numerous employees, upper management will question the rater's judgment and demand documentation to support that judgment. Alternatively, if employees are rated below satisfactory, the supervisor will risk the hostility of affected employees and will again need substantial documentation to support the judgment when it is challenged. In this situation, the path of least resistance for raters is to judge most employees as satisfactory or slightly above satisfactory unless truly extraordinary circumstances occur. As a result, there may be little variation in ratings among large numbers of employees, and actual scores will not reflect gradations in the quality of performance.

While bias and error may never be completely eliminated from the appraisal process, they can be reduced if raters are adequately trained in the application of the appraisal system and sensitized to the kinds of problems that can occur and when clearly defined behavioral or results-oriented performance standards are established (Latham and Wexley, 1994, pp. 104–107). Additionally, error may be minimized when appraisal information is collected from a variety of sources. That is, supervisory appraisals may be supplemented with information from self-appraisals as well as with ratings by an employee's subordinates, peers, or customers (Campbell and Lee, 1988; deLeon and Ewen, 1997; Edwards and Ewen, 1996; Lathan and Wexley, 1994, pp. 79–98; Murphy and Cleveland, 1995, pp. 133–142). Because these multirater approaches involve the collection of data from a number of points of view relative to the employee being evaluated, they are often referred to as 360-degree evaluations (Bracken et al. 1997; Tornow and London, 1998). Ratings by subordinates, peers, and customers and self -appraisals can provide useful supplements to the judgment of a supervisor who may not always be sufficiently familiar with an employee's work or who may not observe an employee often enough to render an informed judgment (Murphy and Cleveland, 1995, pp. 123–124). Of course, the expansion of the appraisal process to include other evaluators in addition to a supervisor can make the process more cumbersome, time consuming, and expensive.

MANAGING PERFORMANCE: THE PROVISION OF INCENTIVES

Performance appraisals are conducted because it is believed that their results will be helpful in the process of improving individual employee performance and ultimately organizational performance. As noted above, the appraisal interview, if conducted effectively, provides an opportunity for the supervisor to guide employee behavior in productive ways. When an appraisal uncovers areas of performance that need improvement, those areas can be pointed out to employees, and instructions as to how to improve can be provided (Roberts and Reed, 1996).

But before individual performance can be improved, it is important to identify and remove the obstacles that have blocked good performance. To do so, managers should recognize that the performance of employees can be affected by several factors (see, e.g., Steers, 1988, pp. 200–202; Pinder, 2008, pp. 16–19). For example, employees cannot be expected to perform well if they do not understand what it is that they are supposed to do. It is the task of managers to ensure that their subordinates know precisely what is expected of them, and they must communicate those expectations clearly and consistently. This does not mean that employees have no discretion, or that management speaks to every detail, but it does require that management tell workers what is required for high performance in their (the employees') jobs.

In addition, it is necessary that employees also accept the directives of management (Steers, 1988, p. 202). Of course, in the long run, employees who fail to accept managerial directives may be removed from the workforce, but this assumes that we will always know when employees reject direction. There are innumerable ways for employees to disguise their true dispositions and to delay, misdirect, or frustrate specific projects while at the same time appearing to work assiduously on their assigned tasks. They may, for example, give the supervisor only part what is requested, or they may claim that they are working on it, but it is simply taking longer than expected. In these situations, it can be difficult for a supervisor, who is already pressed for time, to be able to fully uncover the truth. As a result, it is imperative that employees not only understand what is required but also agree with those requirements. Management can facilitate that agreement by ensuring that employees know the rationale or reason for doing the work. Employees should also be reminded of how the work fits into the overall context of the organization.

It is also obvious that employees must have the ability to perform, if we are to expect them to do so, and it is the responsibility of management to ensure that employees have the requisite ability (Steers, 1988, p. 201). This responsibility manifests itself initially during the employee selection process. Care must be taken to ensure that selection is based primarily on the ability or potential of a job applicant to actually perform the job at issue. In addition, however, management must also provide all necessary training in specific job tasks or responsibilities. Too often, we devote insufficient attention to employee training programs. During tight budget times, for example, training is often one of the first organizational activities to be cut.

It is also necessary that employees be given an opportunity to perform, if we are to expect them to perform (Steers, 1988, p. 202). This observation may seem rather banal, but it is worth our attention, nevertheless, because it is so important. It is always the responsibility of management to ensure that employees have the resources they need, especially in terms of the requisite tools, equipment, authority, and time to do the jobs expected of them.

Finally, we must recognize that knowledge of the tasks required, acceptance of those tasks, the ability to perform, and the opportunity to perform, while all necessary, will still be insufficient for satisfactory performance, if the employee is unmotivated. Motivation is the inner drive that propels workers to achieve. Research on motivation theory is vast and multifaceted. However, much of that work addresses issues of incentives and how they are structured within organizations (see, e.g., Steers, 1988; Latham, 2007; Pinder, 2008). As is commonly understood, incentives may be either intrinsic to the job or extrinsic. Intrinsic incentives are derived from the nature of the work itself and the satisfaction employees have from doing the work. To the extent that management can enrich the work experience by providing responsibility, recognition, and opportunity for achievement and advancement, employees may be more motivated to perform the work. Intrinsic motivation may also be increased to the extent that employees believe they provide an important and valuable public service.

Extrinsic incentives, alternatively, are derived from the context within which work is accomplished. Here, we expect that working conditions, the quality of supervision, interpersonal relationships on the job, and organizational policies are important factors. If these factors are unsatisfactory, research suggests that employees may be dissatisfied and less productive than they would be otherwise (see, Herzberg, Mausner, and Snyderman, 1959; Herzberg, 1968). Therefore, to the extent that managers can manipulate these factors in a positive manner, employees may perform better, and organizational performance may also increase as well.

One factor not mentioned up to this point is employee compensation. Obviously, pay is essential. While there is some dispute within the literature regarding the impact of pay on job satisfaction and motivation to perform, it must be present at a reasonable level, if we are to prevent employee dissatisfaction and a concomitant suppression of employee work effort. In general, public sector pay should be competitive with what similarly qualified employees can make in the private sector, and it should be grounded on a systematic analysis and evaluation of job requirements. This approach ensures that employees are treated fairly relative to those outside of government and relative to each other. Often, we also see today more explicit efforts to connect pay, or pay increases, to individual employee performance. Because pay-for-performance systems are popular as a personnel management innovation or reform, and because they are also quite problematic, we turn now to a fuller discussion of their use as a means to incentivize performance.

PAY FOR PERFORMANCE AS AN INCENTIVE SYSTEM

Since the 1980s, pay-for-performance systems have enjoyed enormous popularity in the public sector (Ingraham, 1993; Kellough and Lu, 1993; Kellough and Selden, 1997). The most common of these systems, known as merit pay, requires that annual pay increases be tied to the outcomes of individual-level performance appraisals, although other systems distribute pay incentives in the form of bonuses and/or make distributions on the basis of work group productivity. At a basic level, the concept of pay for performance is appealing. The logic is simple: One must simply determine which employees are superior performers and reward them with increased pay. Such a policy would presumably keep the best employees satisfied while simultaneously providing an incentive for poorer performers to improve their levels of productivity.

The argument for merit pay fits closely with the principles associated with a set of ideas about worker motivation known as equity theory (Adams, 1965; Mowday, 1983; Rainey, 1997). According to that perspective, individual employees will adjust their behaviors at work depending on their perception of how equitably they are being treated. In other words, employees' perceptions of equity at work will affect their levels of motivation. A superior performer who receives the same compensation as a much less productive coworker would perceive inequity, for example, and would overtime adjust his or her output downward until that inequity is no longer present. Such an employee could easily question why the extra effort necessary to achieve higher levels of productivity should be sustained if it is not recognized and rewarded (Schay, 1988). In fact, equity theory would suggest that the best way to ensure that top performers will continue to be productive is to find ways to acknowledge their higher levels of productivity—such as pay differentials.

Additional theoretical support for pay-for-performance systems is found in expectancy theory (Porter and Lawler, 1968; Vroom, 1964). This theory specifically addresses the psychological or cognitive processes associated with the development of motivation rather than questions of what incentives or motives are most effective. According to this view, individuals will be motivated to behave in productive ways when they expect that (1) their efforts will lead to higher levels of performance (the effort–performance expectation), (2) higher performance will lead to specified outcomes (the performance–outcome expectancy), and (3) the outcomes are desirable or valuable. Since higher pay would appear to be valuable to most, if not all, employees, proponents of pay for performance suggest that to enhance employee motivation to perform management must simply offer financial incentives, encourage employees to believe that they can perform, and demonstrate that performance will be recognized. It sounds like a good idea, but in practice it has not worked well.

In the early 1990s, after more than a decade of experimentation with pay for performance in government, examinations of the empirical literature could find little evidence that employee motivation or productivity was actually enhanced by such systems (Kellough and Lu, 1993; Milkovich and Wigdor, 1991). In fact, difficulties with the concept of pay for performance arise in a number of ways. Consider, for example, the argument from expectancy theory that employees must believe that their levels of effort will lead to effective performance if they are to be motivated to perform. In some circumstances it will be difficult for management to promote that view among workers. Employees typically do not labor in isolation. Organizations are systems in which workers' efforts must be coordinated, and it is often the case that there are interdependencies among employees. A given individual's level of performance will, therefore, frequently depend upon the productivity of others in the organization. Other employees may make decisions or perform a variety of operations that will influence a specified individual's task difficulty and probability of success. Individuals in such situations will recognize this dilemma and will perceive that when this occurs, their own level of effort may make little difference in their ability to perform.

It is also essential, again from the view of expectancy theory, that employees perceive that performance is explicitly linked to pay, if pay-for-performance systems are to motivate workers. The issue referred to here is the performance–outcome expectancy. The trouble at this point is largely in the performance appraisal process. As demonstrated earlier, individual-based performance appraisal is never entirely objective. Ultimately, the appraisal process rests on rater judgment. Employees recognize this characteristic of the process, and as a result, there is a tendency for employees to often question the accuracy of appraisal outcomes, especially when their performance is not rated as highly as they think it should be rated (Hamner, 1983). Efforts to base pay on the outcomes of performance appraisal have the effect of raising the stakes and increasing employee sensitivity to appraisal outcomes. Ego involvement and a desire to rationalize unfavorable ratings may be more than sufficient to lead employees to question rater judgment, especially when pay is affected. Because employee perceptions are important determinants of employee motivation, that is, expectancy theory requires that employees perceive that good performance is recognized in order for the performance–outcome expectancy and subsequent motivation to be high, perceptions that the appraisal process is less than fair will undermine the motivational potential of pay for performance.

Clearly, the dynamics of performance appraisal can exacerbate this difficulty. As we have seen, it is often the case that raters, especially supervisors, are reluctant to draw sharp distinctions between employees. Low and high ratings may each require increased levels of justification. The rater must be prepared to defend the judgments rendered, and such effort will divert time and energy away from what may be seen by managers as tasks more instrumentally associated with the organization's mission. As a result, variation in appraisal outcomes is constrained and the perceived legitimacy of the process is further undermined. Efforts to link pay to the outcomes of such a process may invite more employee alienation than motivation.

An additional problem is associated with the often meager pay increases or bonuses offered under pay-for-performance systems. The assumption that higher pay (as opposed to lower pay) is valued by public employees seems reasonable on its face, but the motivational potential of pay is linked to the size of increases or bonuses offered, and governments are usually reluctant to make substantial amounts of money available for employee pay increases. This fact, combined with the reality that there is typically little variation in the outcomes of performance appraisal processes, means that most employees receive pay-for-performance awards that are not much different than they would have received under an across-the-board distribution. Very few are denied increases, and few receive substantial increases. In some organizations, outstanding ratings are actually rotated among employees in order to counter this problem, but, of course, that further undermines the perceived legitimacy of the system. It should be acknowledged also that even if pay-for-performance mechanisms could succeed in increasing employee motivation, improvements in employee and organizational productivity may not follow. For example, pay for performance may lead to dysfunctional activities among employees. Effort might be directed toward tasks that are most easily measured, regardless of their relevance to organizational outcomes, and competition among employees for performance-based incentives may undermine teamwork and cooperation necessary for organizational success. Additionally, we should remember that motivation alone may not be sufficient to boost productivity. Employees must also, as observed earlier, have (1) an understanding of what is expected, (2) the opportunity to perform, and (3) the ability to perform. Shortcomings in any of these areas can undermine individual productivity regardless of the level of employee motivation.

RECOMMENDATIONS FOR PUBLIC MANAGERS

Performance appraisal is intended to be a tool through which management can direct individual behavior within organizations into productive channels. Appraisal outcomes are used as the basis for a number of administrative decisions regarding training, promotions, adverse actions, and sometimes even pay. From the foregoing analysis, it is possible to draw several practical suggestions for public managers:

1. Public organizations should have a carefully devised system for evaluating the individual performance of every employee.
2. Attention and thought must be given to specifying appropriate criteria upon which performance is to be assessed. The criteria should focus on tangible work products whenever possible. If tangible outputs are not identifiable, the focus should be on appropriate work behaviors. Usually, some combination of work outputs and work behaviors can be utilized. Trait-based systems should be avoided.
3. Explicit standards should be developed to identify superior and inferior performance on each criterion.
4. Supervisors must be thoroughly trained in the application of the performance appraisal process so that common errors can be avoided. They must also be given adequate time to evaluate subordinate employees' performance. Supervisors should meet with each employee they evaluate in order to discuss performance.
5. Efforts to link individual performance appraisal outcomes to pay should be approached cautiously, given their problematic nature.
6. Superior performance should be incentivized primarily through job enrichment strategies that enhance intrinsic incentives associated with responsibility, recognition, and opportunity for achievement and advancement. Extrinsic incentives must be provided at levels that prevent employee dissatisfaction.
7. Managers must be certain that they communicate clearly and consistently all job requirements and expectations to employees. Managers must also make certain that employees understand those instructions and accept them. In addition, it is management's responsibility to ensure that employees have the ability to perform and are given the opportunity to perform.
8. Repeated poor performance should trigger a progressive disciplinary process that will ultimately culminate in separation of the offending employee from the organization.

References

Adams, J. Stacey. 1965. "Inequity in Social Exchange." In Leonard Berkowitz, ed. *Advances in Experimental and Social Psychology*. Orlando, FL: Academic Press.

Bouckaert, Geert, and John Halligan. 2007. *Managing Performance: International Comparisons*. London: Routledge.

Bracken, David W., et al. 1997. *Should 360-Degree Feedback Be Used Only for Developmental Purposes?* Greensboro, NC: Center for Creative Leadership.

Cardy, Robert L., and Gregory H. Dobbins. 1994. *Performance Appraisal: Alternative Perspectives*. Cincinnati, OH: South-Western Publishing Company.

Campbell, Donald J., and Cynthia Lee. 1988. "Self Appraisal in Performance Evaluation: Development Versus Evaluation." *Academy of Management Review* 13(2): 302–314.

Carroll, Stephen J., and Craig Eric Schneider. 1982. *Performance Appraisal and Review Systems: The Identification, Measurement, and Development of Performance in Organizations*. Dallas, TX: Scott, Foresman, and Company.

Daley, Dennis M. 1992. *Performance Appraisal in the Public Sector*. Westport, CT: Quorum Books.

deLeon, Linda, and Ann J. Ewen. 1997, Winter. "Multi-Source Performance Appraisals." *Review of Public Personnel Administration* 17(1): 22–36.

Edwards, Mark R., and Ann J. Ewen. 1996. *360° Feedback: The Powerful New Model for Employee Assessment & Performance Improvement*. New York: American management Association.

Hamner, W. Clay. 1983. "How to Ruin Motivation with Pay." In Richard M. Steers and Lyman W. porter, eds. *Motivation and Work Behavior* (pp. 264–275). New York: McGraw-Hill.

Heinrich, Carolyn J., and Laurence E. Lynn, Jr., eds. 2000. *Governance and Performance: New Perspectives*. Washington, D.C.: Georgetown University Press.

Herzberg, Frederick. 1968, January/February. "One More Time: How Do You Motivate Employees?" *Harvard Business Review* 46(1): 53–62.

Herzberg, Frederick, Bernard Mausner, and Barbara Bloch Snyderman. 1959. *The Motivation to Work*. New York: John Wiley and Sons.

Ingraham, Patricia W. 1993, July/August. "Of Pigs in Pokes and Policy Diffusion: Another Look at Pay for Performance." *Public Administration Review* 23(3): 348–356.

Kellough, J. Edward, and Haoran Lu. 1993, Spring. "The Paradox of Merit Pay in the Public Sector." *Review of Public Personnel Administration* 13(2): 45–64.

Kellough, J. Edward, and Sally C. Selden. 1997, Winter. "Pay for Performance in State Government: Perceptions of State Agency Personnel Managers." *Review of Public Personnel Administration* 17(1): 5–21.

Klein, Howard J., and Scott A. Snell. 1994. "The Impact of Interview Process and Context on Performance Appraisal Interview Effectiveness." *Journal of Managerial Issues* 6: 160–175.

Lane, Larry M. 1994, Summer. "Public Sector Performance Management: Old Failures and New Opportunities." *Review of Public Personnel Administration* 14(3): 26–44.

Latham, Gary P. 2007. *Work Motivation: History, Theory, Research, and Practice*. Thousand Oaks, CA: Sage Publications, Inc.

Latham, Gary P., and Kenneth N. Wexley. 1994. *Increasing Productivity Through Performance Appraisal* (2nd ed.). Reading, MA: Addison-Wesley Publishing Company.

Locke, Edwin A. 1983. "The Ubiquity of the Technique of Goal Setting in Theories of and Approaches to Employee Motivation." In Richard M. Steers and Lyman W. porter, eds. *Motivation and Work Behavior* (pp. 81–90). New York: McGraw-Hill.

Locke, Edwin A., and Gary P. Latham. 1984. *Goal Setting: A Motivational Technique that Works*. Englewood Cliffs, NJ: Prentice-Hall.

Milkovich, George T., and Alexandra K. Wigdor, eds. 1991. *Pay for Performance: Evaluating Performance Appraisal and Merit Pay*. Washington, D.C.: National Academy Press.

Mowday, Richard T. 1983. "Equity Theory Predictions of Behavior in Organizations." In Richard M. Steers and Lyman W. porter, eds. *Motivation and Work Behavior* (pp. 91–113). New York: McGraw-Hill.

Murphy, Kevin R., and Jeanette Cleveland. 1995. *Understanding Performance Appraisal: Social, Organizational, and Goal-Based Perspectives.* Thousand Oaks, CA: Sage Publications.

Nigro, Lloyd G., and Felix A. Nigro. 2000. *The New Public Personnel Administration* (5th ed.). Itasca, IL: F. E. Peacock Publishers.

O'Toole, Laurence J., Jr., and Kenneth J. Meier. 2000. "Networks, Hierarchies, and Public Management: Modeling and Nonlinearities." In Carolyn Heinrich and Laurence E. Lynn, eds. *Governance and Performance: New Perspectives* (pp. 263–291). Washington, D.C.: Georgetown University Press.

Pinder, Craig C. 2008. *Work Motivation in Organizational Behavior* (2nd ed.). New York: Psychology Press.

Porter, Lyman W., and Edward E. Lawler, III. 1968. *Managerial Attitudes and Performance.* Homwood, IL: Dorsey Press.

Rainey, Hal G. 1997. *Understanding and Managing Public Organizations* (2nd ed.). San Francisco, CA: Jossey-Bass.

Roberts, Gary E., and Tammy Reed. 1996, Fall. "Performance Appraisal Participation, Goal setting, and Feedback." *Review of Public Personnel Administration* 16(4): 29–60.

Sandfort, Jodi R. 2000. "Examining the Effect of Welfare-to-Work Structures and Services on a Desired Policy Outcome." In Carolyn Heinrich and Laurence Lynn, eds. *Governance and Performance: New Perspectives* (pp. 140–165). Washington, D.C.: Georgetown University Press.

Schay, Bridgette W. 1988. "Effects of Performance-Contingent Pay on Employee Attitudes." *Public Personnel Management* 17: 237–250.

Steers, Richard M. 1988. *Introduction to Organizational Behavior* (3rd ed.). Glenview, IL: Scott, Foresman, and Company.

Tompkins, Jonathan. 1995. *Human Resource Management in Government: Hitting the Ground Running.* New York: Harper Collins.

Tornow, Walter W., and Manuel London. 1998. *Maximizing the Value of 360-Degree Feedback: A Process for Successful Individual and Organizational Development.* San Francisco, CA: Jossey-Bass Publishers.

Vroom, Victor H. 1964. *Work and Motivation.* New York: John Wiley and Sons.

15

PRIVATIZED PRISONS AND UNIONS: PERSONNEL MANAGEMENT IMPLICATIONS

Trina M. Gordon and Byron E. Price

Dr. Trina Gordon is currently an assistant professor at UHV and Director of the Counseling Psychology Program at the University of Houston-Victoria. She obtained her Ph.D. in clinical psychology (Psychology and Law track) from University of Alabama. She has worked as a staff psychologist for the Bureau of Prisons. She has published articles and conducted presentations regarding juror decision-making patterns, use of victim impact statements in capital cases, expert witness testimony, and attitudes toward victims. Her research interests include forensic assessment/evaluation issues, mentally ill and female criminal offenders, dual diagnosis in offender populations, prison reentry issues, and cognitive factors associated with juror decision making in legal cases.

Byron E. Price (Ph.D., Mississippi State University) is an associate professor of political science in the Barbara Jordan-Mickey Leland School of Public Affairs at Texas Southern University (TSU) in Houston, Texas. He also serves as the executive director of the SOAR Center.

Privatization is not a new concept for the United States. Since the beginning of its inception, the United States has roots in privatization that relates to its economic, political, and societal well-being. Privatization by its very definition is "the contractual transfer of a combination of ownership, operation, or responsibility for government functions to private actors" (Austin and Coventry, 2001). The 1980s brought a wave of prison privatization unlike any other period before. The prison privatization was fueled by the war on drugs, and "get tough on crime" campaigns centered in the social and political atmosphere of antigovernment populism. This served as the impetus for the prison privatization movement during the Reagan administration (Price and Riccucci, 2005).

As a function of governmental management, the United States has gone through numerous phases of governmental outsourcing of public services, such as housing and health care facilities, and correctional agencies were not excluded (Selman and Leighton, 2010). This means that privatization in a correctional setting can be viewed as an intersection between private business and the criminal justice system, using a business model for correctional operations. Second, prison privatization has an economic vantage point. Lastly, political ideologies often help to shape the role of privatization in a correctional setting. This chapter will focus on the origins and history of prison privatization and its impact on human resources within the correctional environment. The role of unions will factor prominently in this discussion.

HISTORY OF PRISON PRIVATIZATION

The origins of prison privatization dates back to the beginning of the United States. The first-known traces of correctional privatization appear shortly after the first English settlers arrived in Virginia in 1607 (Feeler, 1991). During the time when new settlers arrived, convicted felons were also sent to America as a condition of pardon to be sold into servitude (Austin and Coventry, 2001). Private entrepreneurs sent felons to America; thus, we see the first sign of private individuals being directly involved in criminal justice matters. The overseas transportation of felons was considered "innovative" and expanded the power of the state to impose sanctions and being of low cost to the government due to private (nongovernmental) entity transporting the prisoners (Austin and Coventry, 2001).

As American history evolved, it often followed the traditions of English law and policies (Gittler, 1984). The same notion is true for the American correctional history. In England, during the middle ages, it was commonplace for a private individual to initiate criminal prosecution by hiring private prosecutors (Shichor, 1995). A focal point of Andrew Jackson's presidency was his belief and encouragement of the "ordinary person" to become involved in "all aspects" of government, which included criminal justice. It was during this time private police were created (Shichor, 1995). During the colonial and post-Revolutionary War periods, many crime victims would often prefer to settle restitution with the offenders directly rather than the fines paid directly to the courts (Shichor, 1995). In the colonial days, crime was seen as an offense against the individual, not society as it is viewed today (Shichor, 1995). Victims were often required to apprehend and require restitution from the offender on their own. In fact, victims during that time were required to pay the sheriffs, prosecutors, and attorneys on their own (Shichor, 1995).

According to Shichor and Gilbert (2001), one of the "greatest historical revolutions of the eighteenth and nineteenth centuries was the increased involvement of government in criminal justice" (p. 4). It was not until the eighteenth century, when the presence of modern-day prisons in the United States emerged (Austin and Coventry, 2001). It is at this point when American society opted to place criminal offenders in contained environments rather than receive the death penalty or serve a life of servitude (Shichor, 1995). The initial contained environments were modeled after the jail system in medieval England, which were operated and created by private entrepreneurs. In the medieval times, the jails, which were known as "gaols," were operated by private entrepreneurs, who hired county sheriffs to guard the offenders and felony suspects for a fixed fee to the state (Shichor, 1995). The gaols were not only a place for custody and holding but also used for punishment (Pugh, 1968). The gaolers (jailers) made their money by charging a fee to prisoners. The gaol keepers often made additional money by charging prisoners for special accommodations and family visits, and selling beer, wine, and tobacco to prisoners (Shichor, 1995). The privately operated jails often employed prisoners as "cheap laborers" and craftsmen in private-sector activities (Austin and Coventry, 2001). To say the least, early American jails were viewed as exploitive.

During the 1800s, prisons were among the largest structures in the United States (Selman and Leighton, 2010). After the signing of the Declaration of Independence in 1776, increased urbanization led to increases in criminal activities, thus forcing a governmental change to handling its offender population (Shichor, 1995). Due to this increase in inmates and burden of cost associated with housing and caring for offenders, the government and state legislators turned to nongovernmental ways to deal with the problem. During this time, private providers relentlessly tried to convince state officials that privately ran correctional facilities would be more cost-efficient and less corrupt than if the control was given to the government (Austin and Coventry, 2001). The debate since the incorporation of private entities in the correctional system has always centered on the economy and economic necessity. After a number of scandals and corrupt behavior in privately run facilities, states eventually gave control of these facilities back to the government. However, even after states relinquished control of the correctional facilities to the government, they continued to experience corruption and mismanagement of facilities. At this point, the states viewed the operations of correctional environments burdensome and costly.

By the early 1900s, government had begun a period of decentralization and localized criminal justice entities to private prison entrepreneurs once again (Shichor, 1995). By 1885, 13 colonial states had contracted private entities to control correctional facilities and lease out prison labor (McCrie, 1993). In the 1850s, San Quentin Prison in California was the first facility constructed and operated by a private provider in the state (Austin and Coventry, 2001). As, the number of prisons grew, so did the notion of using prisoners to create a "prison industry." This influx of prison labor appeared to coincide with the Industrial Revolution (Selman and Leighton, 2010). An early example of prison privatization and inmate labor was in the "Convict Lease System" used in the Southern States during the Reconstruction period. The main purpose of the "Convict Lease System" was that prisons would "lease-out" their inmates to work as laborers for large plantations and railroads (Zito, 2003). As a condition of the leasing system, private companies paid the state for inmate services. In addition, they would also be responsible for lodging needs, security, and daily care of the inmates (Wells, 1893, as cited in Zito, 2003). After the Civil War, there was an increasing need for more labor in the Southern states due to the abolishment of slavery and depletion of cheap labor source (Price, 2006; Shichor, 1995). Ironically, during the Reconstruction period, a large number of individuals were sent to prison, and this was seen as a "derivative of antebellum slavery" without the label of having a "master-slave" relationship (Shichor, 1995, p. 36). States began leasing out their offender population for profit, thus creating a greater likelihood of corruption, inmate mistreatment, and greed. By the early 1900s, the deplorable conditions of privately run facilities and increasing allegations of cruelty led to increased reforms regarding inmate labor. The beginning of the decline of inmate labor occurred in 1905 when President Theodore Roosevelt signed an executive order banning the use of "convict labor" for federal projects (Austin and Coventry, 2001). In 1929, the Hawes-Cooper Act was passed by Congress, which allowed states to ban the importation of inmate products made outside of the state where the inmates were housed (Ammon, Campbell, and Somoza, 1992). Also, during the time of the Great Depression, various legislative bills were passed that further closed the door to the use of inmate labor in the private sector (Austin and Coventry, 2001). The use of private entities custody of state and federal inmates remained in effect in the United States until 1923 when the "lease system" was phased out (Shichor, 1995).

MODERN HISTORY AND REBIRTH OF PRISON PRIVATIZATION—"THE AGE OF LESS GOVERNMENT"

The issue of prison privatization was reintroduced during the 1980s. Many scholars began asking the question as to what caused the United States to build more prisons between 1980 and 2000, which was more than in its entire history (Selman and Leighton, 2010). Many factors helped the resurgence of privatization of prisons due to the increase in the offender population. In addition, the government's use of outsourcing services reemerged and continues to shape the continued use of private prisons today (Selman and Leighton, 2010). To help answer this question, one must understand the dynamics of political policies and "Reaganomics" during the 1980s. President Ronald Reagan was a strong believer in "less government." He declared that too much government was the problem, and his goal was to outsource and privatize as many government functions as possible, including privatizing prisons and correctional facilities (Selman and Leighton, 2010).

During the 1980s, there were a number of legislative policies that helped to increase the prison population. For example, the state and federal prison population more than quadrupled between 1980 and 2008, going from approximately 320,000 inmates to more than 1.5 million inmates (Selman and Leighton, 2010). The rise in the inmate population can be attributed to the relentless "tough on crime" initiatives that led to an increase in harsher penalties and punishments for crimes that were once seen as minimal. Offenders who entered the criminal justice system during the tough-on-crime era of the 1980s and 1990s were often new offenders caught in the drug enforcement crackdown (Bloomberg and Lucken, 2000). The war on crime became a "mass mobilization" of resources aimed at low-level drug offenders and street criminals (Bloomberg and Lucken, 2000). In addition, the war on drugs also helped to contribute to the inmate population due to these harsher sanctions for drug crimes. As Reiman (1990) so eloquently stated, as the rich became richer, the poor became inmates. Due to this increase in inmates, prisons were often faced with overcrowding. The overcrowding led to lawsuits filed by inmates claiming their Eighth Amendment right against cruel and unusual punishment was being violated. Faced with the economic realities and shrinking state and federal budgets, policy makers began looking for new and innovated ways to handle their growing incarceration population (Price, 2006). The pressures of increased prison and jail population and rising inmate costs helped to further encourage reintroduction of privatization of correctional institutions. As time continued, the "follow the money" trend tended to encourage the increase of private prison expansion (Selman and Leighton, 2010). As a result, the government felt it was its duty to control the situation of overcrowding and increasing correctional costs by outsourcing inmates to private prisons. Although private prisons are not responsible for the "incarceration binge," they contributed to the "binge" by supporting legislation that enforces tough-on-crime initiatives.

As crime rates began to decrease, why did the funding and constructions of new correctional facilities continue to rise? For example, in 1994, the state legislators of Mississippi called a special meeting to address the issue of overcrowding. Approximately $73 million was allocated for capital outlays for new and expanded prisons; however, $45 million was actually used to build for-profit prisons (Shichor and Gilber, 2001). The concept of low-cost prison operation costs is based on the economic theory of the free market (Shichor, 1995). According to Shichor (1995), this notion of laissez-faire economics often leads to the decentralized role of government and its function in the private prisons industry. As the state and government needs for more prisons increased, more money was being allocated to criminal justice initiatives and taken away from other state services such as public education and health care. Many of the privately run prisons operated under a business model that looks for growth opportunities, and when you apply a business model to private corrections, rehabilitation is no longer the focus. As criminal justice policies, such as the "3 strikes" law and mandatory minimum sentence, toughened, the prison population grew larger and, the reliance on private prisons also grew. Private prisons promised more jobs in the area where new prisons would be built and less cost to the taxpayers because the cost to the state, government, or county would be lower, and many cash-strapped states bought into the idea of leaving the responsibility of inmate care to someone else. The idea and enthusiasm surrounding private prisons was the prospect of more cost-efficient prison operations. The promise of the private prisons was that they would build in small towns, pledging to bring more economic growth to the area by the creation of new jobs.

The private prison industry is one of the fastest growing industries in the United States (Selman and Leighton, 2010). The United States has the most individuals incarcerated in comparison with the rest of the world. There are presently over 2.3 million individuals incarcerated in prisons and jails throughout the United States (West and Sabol, 2009). Approximately 7 percent of inmates are housed in privately run correctional institutions (West and Sabol, 2009). Presently there are 13 American companies managing private correctional facilities for adults out of the 17 known entities (Zito, 2003). Thirty-one states have incorporated the use of private prison entities (Zito, 2003). Prison industries once again were seen as "big business" opportunities. In 1983, Corrections Corporation of America opened its first privately run correctional facility in Texas to assist the U.S. Immigration and Naturalization Service (INS) by housing undocumented immigrants. Corrections Corporation of America's federal contract for inmates helped to turn the problem around, and this transaction marked the rebirth of incarceration for profit (Shichor, 1995). The first county-level private prison contact was signed in 1984, between Hamilton County, Tennessee, and the Corrections Corporation of America. Shortly thereafter, in 1985, the first state-level contract was signed, between the Commonwealth of Kentucky and the U.S. Corrections Corporation, who opened a 350-bed prison in St. Mary's, Kentucky, to hold sentenced prisoners for the state (NCPA, 1995). However, in the late 1990s, this notion of overexpansion almost "bankrupt" the private prison entities due to lack of contracts with state and federal agencies to help fill bed spaces and incidences of increasing violence in and escapes from the institutions (Bernstein, 2008). The rising stock prices began to fall until the government imposed stricter federal laws under the "RICO Act," federal drug sentencing laws, and a tougher stance and sanctions for illegal immigrants (Bernstein, 2008). As a result of the addition of these new policies, the prisons once again were faced with the issue of overcrowding and turned to private prison corporations to help alleviate the problem. There are presently three major private prison corporations within the United States: Corrections Corporation of America, the GEO Group, Inc., and Cornell Companies.

Corrections Corporation of America is America's oldest and largest private prison company (CCA, 2003). They house approximately 75,000 inmates from the state, federal, and local prison and jails in more than 60 facilities (CCA, 2003). They have partnerships with federal agencies such as the Bureau of Prisons, U.S. Marshals Service, and Immigration and Customs Enforcement Agency (CCA, 2003). The second largest private prison provider in the United States is the GEO Group, Inc., which was founded in 1984. The GEO Group, Inc., currently has correctional facilities in six countries, including the United States, South Africa, and the United Kingdom (TGG, 2010). They operate approximately 47 facilities in the United States, with over 53,000 beds in 15 states (TGG, 2010). The third private prison corporation is Cornell Companies, which currently has 70 facilities in 15 states. The mission and philosophy of Cornell Companies focuses on a "unique" blend of rehabilitative treatment, as well as detention (CC, 2009).

By 1992, there were more than 500,000 correctional employees nationwide, which was more than most Fortune 500 companies with the exception of General Motors (Beckett, 1997). Private prisons are also able to keep their costs low by paying correctional officers at the rate of security guards rather than the higher salaries correctional officers at state and federal institutions receive (Camp and Gaes, 2002). In addition, the administrators for the private prisons claim that paying their correctional officers at the rate of security guards saves millions in overhead (Selman and Leighton, 2010). The story that is seldom told by administrators of private prisons is that there are often high attrition rates due to the low staff salaries, unsafe environments, inadequate training, and staff-to-inmate ratios (Camp and Gaes, 2002). According to Camp and Gaes (2002), in order for private prisons to work more effectively in regard to staff retention and lower assault rates, private prisons may need to adopt innovative strategies regarding custody practices or modify personal practices to help attract and retain experienced employees. The Walsh-Healey Public Contract Act of 1939 set restrictions on laborer rights for any government contract over 10,000 (Camp and Gaes, 2002). According to the Walsh-Healey Public Contract Act, correctional employees are entitled to minimum wage pay comparable to the locality median wage for the same job and overtime compensation. The act also sets specific standards, such as job sanitation and safety requirements for all contract employees.

The prison industries also made a comeback in the 1980s and 1990s. As America became more commercial and industrialized, so did the prison system through the presence of the "Prison Industries." Today, inmates are no longer making license plates for the states, but furniture and goods, which are provided all over the United States. Inmates housed in private prisons are no exception. Prison industry is an additional source of profit-generating business from the use of inmate labor. Offenders are often required to work for extremely low wages and do not usually have the same labor protections as one would if they worked for a company with a labor union. As private prisons gained widespread support and attention, lawmakers began changing regulations regarding the use of inmate labor to help decrease inmate labor mistreatments of the past. The Justice System Improvement Act of 1979 and, later, the Justice Assistance Act of 1984 created the "Prison Industry Enhancement Certificate Program," which allowed inmate-made goods to trade across state lines if certain conditions were met (Selman and Leighton, 2010). The Justice Assistance Act of 1984 was in direct conflict with the Hawes-Cooper Act of 1929. At least 37 states have legalized the use of inmate labor to private corporations with the stipulation that they must conduct their operation within the prison setting where the inmates are completing the labor. Due to the creation of the acts, employers were now able to take advantage of low-wage labor and keep the "Made in America" label and thus benefited from tax breaks (Selman and Leighton, 2010).

As a result of these trends, growth in the private correctional industry's revenues has been explosive: from about $650 million in 1996 to about $1.7 billion in 2008 (Berestein, 2008). By outsourcing inmate housing and care to private prison operations, the government's spending on corrections is reduced by as much as 15 percent of the

Bureau of Prison's budget (Chen, 2008). In addition, stock prices of the three major publicly traded private prison corporations (CCA, the Geo Group, Inc., and Cornell Corporations) have traded quite high, thus providing these companies with enough revenue to finance further expansion (Berestein, 2008).

In summary, prison privatization has a long-standing history within the United States. It has undergone numerous changes in the face of economic realities and will continue to be viewed as a viable solution to prison overcrowding and shrinking state and federal budgets. Research on prison privatization has been both positive and negative. Although contracting out inmates has provided fiscal relief for many states, it has not been without its problems. It is suggested that the government needs to have more accountability and a well-designed contract administration policy, along with a monitoring system to ensure quality and accountability from the contract awardees (Donahue, 1989).

UNION OPPOSITION TO PRISON PRIVATIZATION

For as long as private prisons have been around, opposition from public employees has been effective in thwarting attempts to privatize prisons. Furthermore, the convict leasing system in the 1800s saw the galvanization of the labor movement to protest the use of convict labor to suppress wage levels and break strikes. As a result of these protests, the labor movement effectively forced many states to abandon the practice of using prison labor for profit.

As it was in the past, so it is today; the labor movement objects to the privatization of prisons because of the perceived impact it has on public sector employees. This claim is reinforced by Fernandez, Rainey, and Lowman (2006), who contend that the main impetus of their opposition to prison privatization is its impact on public sector employees. Other inimical effects that galvanize unions to come out against prison privatization, according to Donahue (1989), is the fact that privatization fosters wage depression for correctional officers and employees, an erosion of benefits and working conditions and the penultimate issue. Chang and Thompkins (2002), who cite Donahue (1989), contend that prison privatization "threatens union power by displacing unionized correctional employees in the public sector" (p. 52). Thus, prison privatization is vehemently opposed by unions because it erodes union strength in the public sector. Organizations like the AFL-CIO and its associate organization American Federation of State, County, and Municipal Employees (AFSCME) are leading advocates against privatization. Their advocacy against prison privatization comes in the form of public statements opposing privatization, position papers challenging the claims of privatization being superior to public management, tracking problems private prisons have managing the facilities, and providing a newsletter to disseminate the findings, and grassroots organizations are spun off to attack the merits of prison privatization. Successful campaigns by the Tennessee State Employees Association (TSEA), Tennessee Bar Association, and Tennessee Trial Lawyers have emboldened many union organizations' efforts to stop prison privatization. The California Correctional Peace Officers Association (CCPOA) has also provided a heuristic for other unions committed to halting prison privatization in their states. CCPOA is one of the wealthiest and most organized labor entities in the country. It has a strong lobbying arm and very healthy financial resources and has been a pioneer in thwarting prison privatization efforts. States such as Alaska, Minnesota, New Mexico, and New York, to name a few, have orchestrated successful union challenges to prison privatization using CCPOA's heuristic for lobbying against prison privatization. Additionally, AFSCME has been instrumental in supporting union efforts across the country to stem the trend to privatize prisons. Given how organized AFSCME is, it is a formidable opponent of prison privatization. Considering that its Web site asserts that the organization represents 83,000 correctional officers, the recent successes of unions to thwart prison privatization appear to bear out the belief that AFSCME is a formidable foe to privatization.

Another challenge for unions opposed to prison privatization is the fact that when jobs are transferred to the private sector, it is much more difficult to unionize; thus, any potential benefits gained through employment opportunities in the public sector because of rising incarceration is undermined when the job becomes private. They also fear that if employees are retained by the private firms, they will have to take severe salary reductions and lose fringe benefits.

There is very little empirical research on the implications and the impact of prison privatization on public sector employees. Given that private prisons have been around since 1979, there should be more research on the issues of how prison privatization impacts job security, wages, and benefits. There is research on the implications and impact of privatization on public sector employees, but not specifically on the aspect of prison privatization. The current climate may render this debate mute, given the shedding of jobs since 2008.

PRIVATIZING PRISONS, UNIONS, AND THE FUTURE

The current economic meltdown and the dire straits many states budgets are in should bring future efforts to privatize prisons. For instance, in New York City, Mayor Michael Bloomberg has hired the former mayor of Indianapolis Stephen Goldsmith as his chief deputy of operations. Mayor Goldsmith was big on competitive bidding and privatization. The New York State budget is in shambles just like that of many states across the country. Governor Christie of New Jersey is exploring privatization; thus, these two cases illustrate that unions will need to continue their vigilance to protect public sector employees' jobs. Both states are negotiating with unions that have come out strongly against privatization efforts. Prison privatization efforts have leveled off at the state level, but federal and community corrections privatization is on the increase.

Unions have matched the efforts of private prison corporations to facilitate prison privatization across the United States. Much of their success has been achieved when the economic climate has been robust. The likelihood of unions continuing to win this battle may become difficult given the fiscal strain many states are under. Public prisons as well as other government agencies are more open to the criticisms advocates of privatization lodge against them, such as they are inefficient, ineffective, bloated, and lack incentive to perform because public sector agencies are not subject to the market mechanism. Although many point to Wall Street as the culprit for the current economic maelstrom, government agencies have become the targets because of public agencies' inability to generate revenues and demonstrate results. New public management and the tenants' concomitant with this new paradigm have opened the public sector up to criticisms. Since unions protect public sector employment, they are seen as a part of what is ailing the economy. Unfairly or not, the future climate for public sector unions to protect wages, benefits, and job security will become more difficult with the current deficit and antiunion sentiment pervading the political landscape. In summary, unions will have to show results if they are to stave off privatization efforts in the future.

References

Ammon, D., R. Campbell, and S. Somoza. 1992. *The Option of Prison Privatization: A Guide for Community Deliberations.* Athens, GA: University of Georgia.

Austin, J., and G. Coventry. 2001, February. "Emerging Issues on Privatized Prisons." *Bureau of Justice Assistance: Monograph NCJ 181249.* http://www.ncjrs.gov/pdffiles1/bja/181249.pdf.

Beckett, K. 1997. *Making Crime Pay: Law and Order in Contemporary American Politics.* New York, NY: Oxford University Press.

Bernstein, L. 2008, May 11. "Private Prison Industry Experiences a Boom." *Copley News Service.* http://www.infowars.com/private-prison-industry-experiences-boom.

Bloomberg, T., and K. Lucken. 2000. *American Penology: A History of Control.* Hawthorne, NY: Aldine Transaction.

Camp, S. D., and G. G. Gaes. 2002. "Growth and Quality of U.S. Private Prisons: Evidence from a National Survey." *Criminology & Public Policy* 1(3): 427–450.

Chang, T. F. H., and D. E. Thompkins. 2002, Spring. "Corporations Go to Prisons: The Expansion of Corporate Power in the Correctional Industry." *Labor Studies Journal* 27(1): 45–69.

Chen, S. 2008, November 19. "Larger Inmate Population Is Boon to Private Prisons." *The Wall Street Journal.* http://online.wsj.com/article/SB122705334657739263l.

Cornell Companies, Inc.-CC. 2009. http://cornellcompanies.com/index.html.

Corrections Corporations of America-CCA. 2003. http://www.correctionscorp.com/about/.

Donahue, J. D. 1989. *The Privatization of Decision: Public Ends, Private Means.* New York, NY: Basic Books.

Feeler, M. M. 1991. "The Privatization of Prisons in Historical Perspective." *Criminal Justice Research Bulletin* 6(2): 1–10.

Fernandez, S., H. G. Rainey, and C. E. Lowman. 2006. "Privatization and Its Implications for Human Resources Management." In N. M. Riccucci, ed. *Personnel Management: Current Concerns, Future Challenges* (4th ed.). New York: Longman.

GEO Group Inc.—TGG. 2010. http://thegeogroupinc.com/index.asp.

Gittler, J. 1984. "Expanding the Role of the Victim in Criminal Action: An Overview of Issues and Problems." *Pepperdine Law Review* 11: 117–182.

McCrie, R. D. 1993. "Private Correction: The Delicate Balance." In G. Bowman, S. Hakim, and P. Seidensta, eds. *Privatizing Correctional Institutions* (pp. 19–32). New Brunswick, NJ: Transaction Publishers.

National Center for Policy Analysis-NCPA. 1995, November 21. *Private Prisons Succeed.* http://www.ncpa.org/pdfs/ba191.pdf.

Price, B. E. 2006. *Merchandizing Prisoners: Who Really Pays for Prison Privatization?* Westport, CT: Praeger Publishers.

Price, B. E., and N. M. Riccucci. 2005. "Exploring the Determinants of Decisions to Privatize State Prisons." *American Review of Public Administration* 35(3): 223–235.

Pugh, R. B. 1968. *Imprisonment in Medieval England.* Cambridge, UK: Cambridge University Press.

Reiman, J. 1990. *The Rich Get Richer and the Poor Get Prison.* New York: Macmillan.

Selman, D., and P. Leighton. 2010. *Private Prisons, Big Business, and the Incarceration Binge.* Lanham, MD: Rowman and Littlefield Publishers Inc.

Shichor, D. 1995. *Punishment for Profit: Private Prisons/Public Concerns.* Thousand Oaks, CA: Sage Publications.

Shichor, D., and M. J. Gilbert. 2001. *Privatization in Criminal Justice: Past, Present, and Future.* Cincinnati, OH: Anderson Publishing Co.

Reinman, J. 1990. *The Rich Get Richer and the Poor Get Prison.* New York, NY: MacMillan Publishing.

Wells, Ida B. 1893. "The Reason Why the Colored American Is Not in the World's Columbian Exposition." http://digital.library.upenn.edu/women/wells/exposition/exposition.html.

West, H. C., and W. Sabol. 2009. Prisoners in 2008 (NCJ 228417). http://bjs.ojp.usdoj.gov/index.cfm?ty=pbdetail&iid=1763.

Zito, M. 2003, December 8. *Prison Privatization: Past and Present.* http://www.ifpo.org/articlebank/prison_privatization.html.

16

HUMAN RESOURCES MANAGEMENT IN NONPROFIT ORGANIZATIONS

Joan E. Pynes

Joan E. Pynes is a professor of public administration at the University of South Florida, Tampa, Florida. She is the author of *Human Resources Management for Public and Nonprofit Organizations: A Strategic Approach* (2009), published by Jossey-Bass, Inc., and coauthor of *Human Resources Management for Health Care Organizations* (in press). Her research interests are public and nonprofit management.

Charitable nonprofits are private organizations that serve a public purpose. Because of their nondistribution constraint, they cannot pay dividends on profits to members or other individuals. If for some reason they must dissolve and no longer operate, their remaining assets must be distributed to a nonprofit organization. For those reasons, it is believed that they possess a greater moral authority than for-profit organizations. Nonprofits often perform public tasks that have been delegated to them by the state or those tasks for which there is a demand that neither government nor for-profit organizations provide. They provide a myriad of services such as helping the disadvantaged, providing medical services, supporting museums and cultural activities, preserving the environment, and funding medical research. Similar to government in many respects, nonprofits define themselves according to their missions or the services they offer and are responsible to multiple stakeholders. Nonprofits are primarily responsible to supporters, donors, clients, interest groups, and government sources that provide funding and impose regulations, whereas public agencies are primarily responsible to their respective legislative and judicial branches, taxpayers, interest groups, political appointees, citizens, the media, and other levels of government.

Many nonprofits are the recipients of government contracts and grants; therefore, government has some influence on them through the conditions it may place on agencies and programs that receive public funds.

There are, however, some interesting differences between public and nonprofit organizations in regard to issues that may influence human resource management (HRM) practices. This chapter will discuss some important differences in HRM for nonprofits; the rights of nonprofits given their status as voluntary associations, permission to discriminate on the basis of religion, collective bargaining and labor relations, and the rights and responsibilities of nonprofit organizations in the management of volunteers.

THE VOLUNTARY AND LOCAL NATURE OF NONPROFIT ORGANIZATIONS

Nonprofits are often referred to as voluntary organizations because they receive much of their financial support from private contributions and depend on volunteers to contribute their time and energies to serve charitable purposes. Because of their voluntary nature, which is reinforced by the First Amendment's protection of the freedom of association, nonprofits were often considered exempt from the application of nondiscrimination laws. The behavior and activities of voluntary associations were considered to fall within the sphere of private activity (Rosenblum, 1998, p. 161).

This changed in 1984, when the U.S. Supreme Court ruled in *Roberts v. United States Jaycees* that local chapters of the Jaycees could admit women. The local St. Paul and Minneapolis chapters of the Jaycees sued their national organization. The national Jaycees had threatened to revoke the local charters because the local chapters had voted to admit women, a violation of the national organization's bylaws. The national Jaycees claimed that requiring them to admit women as regular members violated its organization's constitutionally protected freedom of association. By ruling in favor of the local chapters, the U.S. Supreme Court expanded the scope of "public accommodation" to include voluntary associations like the Jaycees and limited their freedom of association when in conflict with the state's compelling interest to eradicate discrimination (*Roberts v. United States Jaycees*, 1984).

Examples of public accommodations include, but are not limited to, hotels, restaurants, shops, hospitals, theaters, libraries, camps, swimming pools, meeting place, amusement and recreation parks, colleges, and universities. Three specific exemptions to public accommodations in most nondiscrimination laws are organizations that are "distinctly private," a religious institution or "an educational facility operated and maintained by a bona fide religious or sectarian institution," or the right of a natural parent, or the *in loco parentis* exception (in the place of a parent; acting as a parent with respect to the care and supervision of a child).

An organization's "expressive rights of association" refer to the right to associate for the purpose of engaging in those activities protected by the First Amendment: the right to speech, assembly, petition for the redress of grievances, and the exercise of religion. Any government intervention to regulate an organization's internal operations, such as membership or personnel policies, must be balanced against the organization's expressive rights of association. Nondiscrimination laws that force organizations to accept members whom they may not desire violate an organization's freedom of expressive association if the organization can demonstrate that these new members would affect in a significant way the group's ability to carry out its mission and express its private viewpoints (*Board of Directors of Rotary International v. Rotary Club*, 1987; *Hurley v. Irish-American Gay Group of Boston*, 1995; *New York State Club Association v. City of New York*, 1988).

Another important characteristic of nonprofit organizations is their local orientation. Most social service agencies, schools, libraries, hospitals, museums, theaters, advocacy groups, foundations, clubs, and other common types of nonprofit organizations focus primarily on local constituencies and local issues. Even nonprofits linked with national organizations such as the American Red Cross are coordinated and run through local chapters with substantial local discretion. They raise and spend most of their money and employ most of their staff and volunteers through the local chapters (Oster, 1992; Young, 1989, p. 103).

Because of their local orientation, nonprofit managers must walk a thin line when defining and defending their membership and HRM policies. The complex environment that nonprofit administrators must operate in became exacerbated when the U.S. Supreme Court in a 5-4 decision held that the application of New Jersey's public accommodation law to the Boy Scouts violated its First Amendment right of expressive association (*Boy Scouts of America and Monmouth Council v. Dale*, 2000). The Boy Scouts argued successfully that, as a private organization, it has the right to determine criteria for membership. The Supreme Court heard this case on appeal from the Boy Scouts of America (BSA) in response to the New Jersey Supreme Court's decision against its position (Hostetler and Pynes, 2000a, 2000b).

The New Jersey Supreme Court held that the BSA is a place of "public accommodation" that "emphasizes open membership" and therefore must follow New Jersey's antidiscrimination law. The court further held that the state's law did not infringe upon the group's freedom of expressive association (*Dale v. Boy Scouts of America and Monmouth Council Boy Scouts*, 1998, 1999). The court reasoned that the New Jersey legislature, when it enacted the antidiscrimination law, declared that discrimination is a matter of concern to the government and that infringements on that right may be justified by regulations adopted to serve compelling state interests.

The New Jersey Supreme Court noted the BSA's historic partnership with various public entities and public service organizations. Local BSA units are chartered by public schools, parent–teacher associations, firehouses, local civic associations, and the U.S. Army, Navy, Air Force, and National Guard. The BSA's "learning for life" program has been installed in many public school classrooms throughout the country. Many troops meet in public facilities. The BSA in turn provides essential services through its scouts to the public and quasi-public organizations. This close relationship underscores the BSA's fundamental public character.

Nonprofit administrators must stay current with the changing and sometimes contradictory community norms and legal requirements across a diverse set of local communities and reconcile them with mandates from the national/parent organization. This is especially true for sexual orientation discrimination. When confronted with sexual orientation discrimination, nonprofit managers find themselves in a complex legal environment. No federal legislation has been passed defining a national standard; thus, nonprofit managers face a patchwork of state and local laws, executive orders, and judicial and commission decisions barring such discrimination. The organizations that have withdrawn their support from the Boy Scouts have clearly stated that they cannot fund or support organizations that have policies that conflict with their own antidiscrimination policies. Despite the U.S. Supreme Court's ruling supporting the BSA's exclusionary policy, the stand of the Boy Scouts' National Council to refuse local councils to determine local policy has jeopardized their funding and support from *their* local communities (Hostetler and Pynes, 2000a, 2000b).

The New Jersey Supreme Court's analysis of the public nature of the Boy Scouts is shared by many. The BSA's decision to exclude homosexuals became controversial. The State of Connecticut dropped the Boy Scouts from the list of charities that receive donations through a state employer payroll deduction plan. The Boy Scouts sued the state, saying that the ban was unconstitutional; it lost in two federal court decisions, and the U.S. Supreme Court declined to hear the case, letting the lower court rulings stand (*Boy Scouts of America v. Wyman*, 2003, 2004). Connecticut has banned the scouts from using public campgrounds or buildings. Many school districts across the country restricted access to their schools for meetings and events, prompting the passage of the Boy Scouts of America Equal Access Act, 20 U.S.C. § 7905 (2003). The act prevents public schools and local educational agencies that receive federal funds from denying equal access and fair opportunity to meet or discriminating against groups officially affiliated with the BSA or any other youth group listed in title 36 of the U.S. Code as a patriotic society for reasons based on the membership or leadership criteria or oath of allegiance to God and country (Pynes, 2009).

On November 15, 2004, the Defense Department agreed to end the direct sponsorship of Boy Scout Troops in response to a religious discrimination lawsuit brought by the American Civil Liberties Union (ACLU). The ACLU of Illinois charged that the BSA required troops and pack leaders and in this case government employees to compel youth to swear an oath of duty to God. The ACLU charged that the Boy Scouts policy violates the religious liberty of youth who wish to participate but do not wish to swear a religious oath and that direct government sponsorship of such a program is religious discrimination. The settlement does not prohibit off-duty public employees from sponsoring Boy Scout troops on their own time, and the Boy Scouts will still have access to any military facilities that are currently made available to other nongovernmental organizations.

There is presently a disagreement in the City of Philadelphia, Pennsylvania. The city has requested that a local chapter of the BSA, the Cradle of Liberty Council, to publicly renounce its membership against people who are openly homosexuals or atheists if it wishes to remain in its headquarters on city-owned land. Failure to do so would require the chapter to pay $200,000 a year "fair-market rent," instead of the yearly lease of $1. The city told the scouts that its policy of discrimination against homosexuals and atheists violates the city's antidiscrimination fair-practices law. The local council maintains it has used a "don't ask, don't tell" practice but cannot change the policies without violating their charter from the national organization (Pynes, 2009; Slobodzian, 2007; Urbina, 2007). In May 2008, the Cradle of Liberty Council filed a lawsuit against the city to stay in the city-owned space. The federal suit accuses the city of censorship for targeting the scouts but maintaining free or nominal leases with other groups that limit membership such as the Baptist and Roman Catholic Church groups and the Colonial Dames of America (Dale, 2008; Hinkelman, 2008; Pynes, 2009; Slobodzian, 2008). On November 20, 2009, the U.S. District Court ordered the city to "immediately cease and desist" efforts to evict the council from its headquarters while the federal lawsuit was pending. The ruling does not prevent the city from pursuing similar claims in the federal suit. On June 23, 2010, a federal jury decided that the City of Philadelphia violated the Boy Scouts' First Amendment right by using its antigay policy as a reason to evict them from the city-owned offices (Gorenstein, 2010). The Cradle of Liberty Council has no tests for prospective members but noted that it must follow the national policy. The issue may still not be resolved. Under the ordinance that leased the property, the city has the right to evict groups without giving any reason at all. There were also inconsistencies by the jury to 11 questions on the verdict sheets, indicating that the potential exists that the verdict was flawed. The city stated that it is exploring its options (Gorenstein, 2010; United Press International, 2010).

What does this mean? The U.S. Supreme Court upheld the right of voluntary associations to discriminate in regard to their employees and volunteers. The most appropriate policy, however, is for national nonprofit organizations to permit local chapters that are sensitive to their community norms to formulate their own nondiscriminatory policies. Other nonprofits such as the Girl Scouts of America have deferred to the norms of each local community and let each troop decide how to handle this potentially divisive issue.

LAWS THAT ADDRESS RELIGIOUS DISCRIMINATION

TITLE VII OF THE CIVIL RIGHTS ACT OF 1964

Most of us are aware that Title VII of the Civil Rights Act of 1964 forbids any employer to fail to hire, discharge, classify employees, or discriminate with respect to compensation, terms, conditions, or privileges of employment in any way that would deprive any individual of employment opportunity due to race, color, religion, sex, or national origin. However, there are exemptions to Title VII that specifically state employers may discriminate on the basis of sex, religion, or national origin if the characteristic can be justified as a "bona fide occupational qualification [BFOQ] reasonably necessary to the normal operation of the particular or enterprise" (Title VII Sec. 703e).

Nonprofit organizations that provide secular services but are affiliated with and governed by religious institutions are exempt from the law under Section 702 of the Civil Rights Act of 1964, which states: "This title shall not apply to an employer with respect to the employment of aliens outside any State, or to a religious corporation, association, educational institution, or society with respect to the employment of individuals of a particular religion to perform work connected with the carrying on by such corporation, association, educational institution, or society of its activities" (as amended by P.L. 92-261, eff. March 24, 1972).

Section 702 of Title VII permits religious societies to grant hiring preferences in favor of members of their religion. It states: "this title shall not apply to an employer with respect to the employment of aliens outside any State or to *a religious corporation, association, educational institution, or society with respect to the employment of individuals of a particular religion to perform work connected with the carrying on by such corporation, association, educational institution, or society of its activities*" (As amended by P.L. 92-261, eff. March 24, 1972).

Section 703(e)(1), (2) provides exemptions for educational institutions to hire employees of a particular religion if the institution is owned, controlled, or managed by a particular religious society. The exemption is broad and is not restricted to the religious activities of the institution.

In *Corporation of the Bishop of the Church of Jesus Christ of Latter Day Saints v. Amos* (1987), the U.S. Supreme Court upheld the right of the Mormon Church to terminate a building engineer who had worked at its nonprofit gymnasium for 16 years, because he failed to maintain his qualification for church membership. The Court claimed that the decision to terminate was based on religion by the religious organization and thus exempted from the Title VII prohibition against religious discrimination. The Section 703(e)(2) exemption is broad and is not limited to the religious activities of the institution.

Although the language of Title VII allows religious or faith-based organizations to discriminate on religious grounds only, courts have interpreted the religious exemptions to Title VII more broadly and have allowed religious organizations and affiliated nonprofits to discriminate against applicants or employees not only on the basis of religion or religious beliefs but also in regard to gender and conduct that is inconsistent with the tenets and teachings of the religious institution.

Pedreira v. Kentucky Baptist Homes for Children (2001) was a federal district court case that addressed the personnel policies of a religiously affiliated nonprofit organization that provides government-funded social services. Americans United for the Separation of Church and State and the ACLU filed a lawsuit in the Federal District Court in Kentucky against the Kentucky Baptist Homes for Children (KBHC) alleging religious discrimination in violation of Title VII of the Civil Rights Act of 1964, the Kentucky Civil Rights Act for terminating Alicia Pedreira, who was identified as a lesbian, and on behalf of Karen Vance, who, as a lesbian, felt deprived of the opportunity to apply for work at KBHC because its policy against hiring homosexuals was well known. The U.S. district judge ruled that KBHC was not guilty of religious discrimination when it fired Pedreira nor was it guilty because its hiring policy discouraged Vance from applying for work. The judge found that any discrimination practiced against Pedreira was due to her sexual orientation, not her religion, and rejected the argument that because her dismissal was motivated by KBHC's religious tenets, it constituted discrimination on the basis of religion. KBHC did not, the judge noted, establish any religious tests for its employees, nor are they required to attend religious services or be members or believers in any particular religion or religious group. The decision stated that Title VII "does not forbid an employer from having a religious motivation" for discharging somebody because of some other trait or conduct not covered under the law. "While KBHC seeks to employ only persons who adhere to a behavioral code consistent with KBHC's religious mission, the absence of religious requirements leaves their focus on behavior, not religion. KBHC imposes upon its employees a code of conduct which requires consistency with KBHC's religious beliefs, but not the beliefs themselves; the civil rights statute protects religious freedoms, not personal lifestyle choices" (*Pedreira v. Kentucky Baptist Homes for Children*, 2001, pp. 4–5).

The courts have also read a "ministerial exception" into Title VII under the Free Exercise Clause that allows religious organizations to discriminate on gender, race, and age. In some cases, the courts have expanded the definition of clergy to include lay employees of religious institutions whose primary duties consist of teaching, spreading the faith, governance, supervision of religious order, or supervision or participation in religious ritual and worship. What this means is that civil courts have ruled that the First Amendment prevents the civil courts from applying civil rights law to the relationship between a church and a minister. There have been mixed holdings in recent court cases in regard to the ministerial exception. Some have upheld it, while others have not (*Coulee Catholic Schools v. Lab & Ind Review Comm*, 2009; *Petruska v. Gannon University*, 2006a, 2006b; *Tomic v. Catholic Diocese*, 2006).

An often-cited case is *McClure v. The Salvation Army* (1972). In this case, a female officer took the Salvation Army to court after she was discharged for complaining that she received less compensation than did male officers of equal rank. The U.S. Court of Appeals for the Fifth Circuit ruled that the Salvation Army was a religious organization and that Congress did not intend for Title VII to regulate the employment relationship between a church and its minister. The employment of ministers was not subject to gender discrimination suits under the Civil Rights Act, even though the statute itself contained no such exemption.

Why should the compensation practices of sectarian nonprofits be a concern to public administrators? One needs to question if a greater influence of religious institutions in the provision of social/human/educational services will disadvantage women. As it now stands, women significantly contribute to their families' income, despite weekly earnings of only 80 percent of what men are paid (U.S. Department of Labor, 2010). In 2009, women held 49.83 percent of the nation's 13.2 million jobs. Women tend to be employed in the service sectors, which are where the majority of job growth is anticipated through 2016 (U.S. Department of Labor, 2010). One needs to question whether or not the increased participation of religious organizations in the provision of social or educational services will further depress the salaries of women working in the nonprofit sector (Steinberg and Jacobs, 1994), as well as attempt to restrict certain employer-provided benefits they are entitled to.

The California Supreme Court ruled in 2004 that Catholic Charities must offer birth control coverage to its employees. This ruling is consistent with 20 states that have concluded that private employee prescription plans without contraception benefits discriminated against women (Elias, 2004). In 2006, the New York Court of Appeals upheld a decision by a lower court that religious charities, hospitals, and schools in New York must abide by the Women's Health and Wellness Act (WHWA), which requires that employers cover workers' birth control costs if they offer health insurance for other prescriptions, even if the organizations consider contraception sinful (Hughes, 2006). The law made an exception for religious organizations, but did not find that schools, hospitals, and social service providers met the definition of "religious employer" established by lawmakers because they did not primarily hire or serve people of their own faiths, nor did they have religious indoctrination as their purpose. The New York law was modeled on the California statute (Hughes, 2006).

CHARITABLE CHOICE AND THE PERSONAL RESPONSIBILITY AND WORK OPPORTUNITY RECONCILIATION ACT OF 1996 (PRWORA)

The Personal Responsibility and Work Opportunity Reconciliation Act (PRWORA) of 1996 was passed to "reform welfare as we know it." "Charitable choice" was passed as part of the act. States could enter into funding relationships with any faith-based institution to provide social services using federal TANF (temporary assistance for needy families) dollars. Charitable choice permits religious organizations or faith-based organizations to receive federal funds for use in providing social services to their communities. As recipients of federal funds, they still retain their autonomy as independent organizations, while remaining in control of their religious mission and their organizational structure and governance. Faith-based organizations have a right to display religious art, scripture, and icons and retain their right to use religious criteria in hiring, firing, and disciplining employees (Gossett and Pynes, 2003). However, none of the funds received to provide services may be "expended for sectarian worship, instruction, or proselytization." Like their secular counterparts, faith-based service providers are subject to financial audits for the funds received under government grants and contracts. Under charitable choice, clients are given the right to choose among religious and nonreligious providers and cannot be refused services on the basis of their religion, religious beliefs, or religious practices. Charitable choice explicitly prohibits participating faith-based organizations from denying services to people on the basis of religion, a religious belief, or refusal to actively participate in a religious practice. Clients who feel they are discriminated against can bring civil suits against providers (De Vita, 1999).

Congress passed additional legislation involving charitable choice provisions, including the Welfare-to-Work (WTW) program (1997); the Community Services Block Grant program funded by the Health and Human Services Reauthorization Act (1998); and drug treatment programs funded by the Substance Abuse and Mental Health Services Administration (SAMHSA) (2000).

Public monies are allocated in a variety of ways. TANF funds are provided through block grants, which are distributed in lump sums to states, which can choose to administer the funds at the state or local levels or at both levels. For CSBG programs, the states are required to pass through at least 90 percent of their federal block grant allotments to primarily community action agencies to provide services directly or subcontract them out. Substance Abuse Prevention and Treatment (SAPT) funds are block grants distributed to states that have broad discretion on how they distribute the funds, as long as the funds are passed on to a public or nonprofit entity. WTW has two funding streams: 75 percent of its funds are distributed to states through formula grants to pass on to local workforce boards though subgrants; the remaining 25 percent are designated for competitive grants, which are distributed at the federal level by the Department of Labor directly to local applicants. Because federal funds are disbursed at multiple levels and to a variety of contractors, it is difficult to track the pervasiveness of faith-based services (GAO, 2002; Montiel, Keyes-Williams, and Scott, 2002).

FAITH-BASED INITIATIVES

To further expand the use of religious organizations and religious affiliated nonprofits in the delivery of public services, President George W. Bush signed executive orders requiring executive branch agencies to identify and remove barriers that served as a deterrent to faith-based organizations in participating in executive agency programs. These executive orders are referred to as "faith-based initiatives." He first signed Executive Orders 13198 and 13199 in January 2001, followed by Executive Orders 13279 and 13280 in December 2002, and Executive Order 13342 was signed in June 2004 requiring executive branch agencies to *eliminate regulatory, contracting, and other programmatic obstacles to the participation of faith-based and other community organizations in the provision of social services.* The final Executive Order 13397 was signed on March 7, 2006, creating a new Center for Faith-Based Initiatives in the Department of Homeland Security. The executive orders established the White House Office of Faith-Based and Community Initiatives, as well as offices in more than 10 government agencies. The initiatives have also been promoting other government agencies and quasi-government entities–established offices in areas ranging from citizen service to homeownership and business development to energy conservation (Farris, Nathan, and Wright, 2004; Wright, 2009). In 2007, the Bush administration's Office of Legal Counsel (OLC) in the Department of Justice prepared a memo arguing that federal statutes prohibiting faith-based hiring could not be applied to religious groups because of the Religious Freedom Restorative Act (RFRA), which prohibits the federal government from placing "substantial burdens" on religious groups and practices.

While the faith-based initiatives address a number of issues, in the context of HRM, the executive orders now allow federally funded religious or faith-based organizations to consider religion in the selection of employees where the jobs to be performed are sectarian or not. While faith-based service providers are permitted to require applicants to be a member of a particular denomination in hiring personnel, they are still prohibited from discriminating on the basis of race, gender, disability, or national origin.

Another reason why public administrators should pay attention to the adoption of faith-based initiatives is the increase in litigation that often accompanies their introduction. In a lawsuit filed in the U.S. District Court, Southern District of New York, it was alleged that the Salvation Army had unlawfully discriminated on the basis of religion with respect to its professional employees working in child welfare services funded by New York State and New York City. The plaintiffs charged that the Army's New York division tried to force them to sign forms revealing the churches they had attended over the past 10 years, name their ministers, and agree to the Army's mission "to preach the Gospel of Jesus Christ." The employees felt forced to violate their professional obligations and codes of ethics. For example, the children assigned to receive foster care and other social services include sexually active teenagers who are at risk for HIV, sexually transmitted infections, and unintended pregnancy. However, the Salvation Army condemns nonmarital sexual relations, contraceptive use outside of marriage, homosexuality, and abortion (*Lown v. The Salvation Army, Inc.; Commission, New York City Administration for Children Services and others*, 2004). In 2005, the U.S. District Court Southern District of New York ruled that the Salvation Army did not unlawfully discriminate on the basis of religion with respect to its professional employees working in child welfare services funded by New York State and New York City. The court held that religious entities are exempted by Section 702 of the Civil Rights Act of 1964, and on comparable exemptions in the law of most states. The court concluded that the exemption represented a reasonable accommodation, within the discretion of Congress, of the interests of religious entities in their employment-centered exercise of religion, and the reasoning in the *Corporation of the Bishop of the Church of Jesus Christ of Latter Day Saints v. Amos* (1987) extends fully to comparable state law provisions protecting the right of faith-based organizations to engage in faith-selective hiring for some or all positions (*Lown v. The Salvation Army, Inc.; Commission, New York City Administration for Children Services and Others*, 2004, 2005; Lupu and Tuttle, 2005).

The Civil Rights Act of 1964 and the executive orders allow federally funded religious or faith-based organizations to consider religion in the selection of employees whether the jobs to be performed are sectarian or not, even when the religious affiliated or faith-based nonprofits are operating under contracts from the government. While faith-based service providers are permitted to require applicants to be a member of a particular denomination in hiring personnel, they are still prohibited from discriminating on the basis of race, gender, disability, or national origin.

On February 5, 2009, President Obama signed *Amendments to Executive Order 13199 and Establishment of the President's Advisory Council for Faith-Based and Neighborhood Partnerships* to help address the country's social problems by strengthening the capacity of faith-based and community organizations. The executive order does not reverse President Bush's policy that allowed federal agencies to award contracts to faith-based organizations that discriminate in their hiring processes based on religious status, marital status, or sexual orientation. In fact, President Obama has taken hits from the ACLU and the Coalition Against Religious Discrimination for backing down from his pledge during the campaign to reverse faith-based employment discrimination in publicly funded programs (ACLU, 2010); however, conservatives are pleased with the direction the White House is taking (Wallsten, 2010).

Nonprofit organizations have been at the forefront of many HRM issues such as developing fair employment practices, the hiring and promotion of women and minorities, and providing domestic partnerships benefits to their employees. What might be the societal implications for services for disenfranchised groups if secular nonprofits lose out on public monies to provide services to faith-based organizations? What might happen if the practices of some faith-based organizations diminish the role of women and their contributions to society or choose to neglect certain social problems like domestic violence, homelessness, and services to individuals with HIV and AIDS? This is not hypothetical; in February 2010, the Washington D.C. Catholic Archdiocese transferred its foster care program to another provider because the city council voted to legalize same-sex marriage. Under the city's law, religious organizations would not have to perform or make space available for same-sex weddings, but they could not discriminate against homosexuals. The church claimed that adhering to the law would be impossible because it opposes same-sex marriage (Boorstein, 2010; Craig and Boorstein, 2009; Urbina, 2009). As a result, beginning March 2, 2010, Catholic charities have not been offering benefits to spouses of new employees or those of current employees not already enrolled in its plan (Wan, 2010).

LABOR RELATIONS AND COLLECTIVE BARGAINING

Nonprofit labor relations and collective bargaining are governed by the same laws that govern for-profit private sector labor–management relations. They fall under the provisions of the National Labor Code, which consolidated the National Labor Relations Act of 1935, the Labor-Management Relations Act of 1947, and the Labor-Management Reporting and Disclosure Act, 1959. The National Labor Relations Board (NLRB) is the administrative agency responsible for enforcing the provisions of the laws. Until the 1970s, the NLRB excluded nonprofit employees from coverage. In 1974, Congress amended the National Labor Relations Act to bring nonprofit health care institutions under the law's coverage (P.L. 93-360, 88 Stat.395). The health care amendments indicated that Congress had no objection to bringing nonprofit employers under federal labor law. In 1976, the NLRB began to treat nonprofit and charitable institutions in the same way it treated businesses operated for profit. If a nonprofit employer has revenues that exceed certain amounts, then the NLRB can become involved in labor–management disputes. The NLRB has established a table of jurisdictional standards that provides the dollar amounts required for nonprofit organizations to come under its jurisdiction (NLRB, 1997). For example, symphony orchestras fall under the NLRB's jurisdiction if they have gross annual revenues of $1 million or more. Employers who provide social services come under the NLRB standards if their gross annual revenues are at least $250,000; nursing homes, visiting nurse associations, and related facilities come under the NLRB standards if their gross annual revenues are at least $100,000.

There are, however, some exceptions. In the case *NLRB v. Catholic Bishop of Chicago* (1979), the U.S. Supreme Court ruled that schools operated to teach both religious and secular subjects are not within the jurisdiction of the National Labor Relations Act. It held that "there would be significant risk of infringement of the Religion Clauses of the First Amendment if the Act conferred jurisdiction over church-operated schools and neither the language of the statute nor its legislative history discloses any affirmative intention by Congress that church-operated schools be within the NLRB's jurisdiction, and, absent a clear expression of Congress' intent to bring teachers of church operated schools within the NLRB's jurisdiction, the Court will not construe the Act in such a way as would call for the resolution of difficult and sensitive First Amendment questions" (pp. 499–507).

Other court decisions have held that an educational institution organized as a nonprofit and the school, college, or university must be "religiously affiliated" (*Universidad Central Baymon v. National Labor Relations Board*, 1986; *University of Great Falls v. National Labor Relations Board*, 2002). The criteria used to exempt an institution are if it (a) holds itself out to students, faculty, and community as providing a religious educational environment; (b) is organized as a "nonprofit"; and (c) is affiliated with, or owned, operated, or controlled, directly or indirectly by a recognized religious organization, or with reference to religion (*Universidad Central Baymon v. National Labor Relations Board*, 1986, pp. 399–403).

Unlike federal government employees and some state and local public employees, nonprofit employees are permitted to negotiate over wages. They can also negotiate over hours and working conditions. Also, unlike many public employees, nonprofit employees are permitted to strike. In January 2010, members of the Cleveland Orchestra went on strike over salaries. The leadership of the orchestra asked the musicians to take a 5 percent pay cut this year, go back up to their present salaries the next year, and accept a 2.5 percent raise the following year. Administrators and staff have taken pay cuts. The players proposed freezing their salaries for this year and reexamining their salaries in the summer. Benefits may also have to be cut (Wakin, 2010).

Hospital employees including respiratory therapists, radiology technicians, licensed practical nurses, nurse assistants, pharmacy technicians, paramedics, secretaries, dietary workers, and housekeepers working at Norwood Hospital in Boston voted to join the Service Employees International Union (SEIU). This was the third hospital in the Caritas Christi Health Care system that voted to unionize this year. The president of SEIU, George Gresham, stated "during these difficult economic times, it's clear that hospital workers across Massachusetts have made the decision to come together to protect the quality of care they provide, the economic health of their hospitals, and their communities" (cited in Weisman, 2009).

The uncertainty of many workplace changes has shaken the confidence of many employees that their jobs are secure and their wages will remain competitive. Professional employees are the fastest growing group in the labor force, and unionization has been viewed as a mechanism to defend professional autonomy and improve working conditions. Unions have stepped up efforts to organize them. The old line unions that historically represented blue-collar workers have realized that, if they are to remain viable, they must follow the job growth. The projected job growth is in the service sector for both higher-paid technical and professional positions and low-paid service workers such as custodians, nursing assistants, and child care workers.

The impact of competition and organizational restructuring has become an issue in nonprofit organizations. Contracts have called for employers to notify employees of impending layoffs and to offer voluntary leaves of absences to employees before reducing their hours. In other circumstances, unions have been called on to defend professional autonomy and improve working conditions. Unions have sought to expand the scope of bargaining to include such issues as agency-level policy-making, agency missions, standards of service, and professional judgment. Other negotiated topics have included coverage for malpractice and professional liability insurance, legal representation of workers, workload issues, provision of in-service training, financial assistance for licensing examinations, and remuneration for enhanced education.

As more and more public services become privatized and former public employees enter nonprofit agencies, nonprofit managers can expect to see an increase in union activities. If nonprofit organizations wish to keep adversarial labor–management relations at bay, nonprofit administrators and boards of directors must work with their staffs to develop progressive and relevant human resource polices that respect employees. Employees must feel that their jobs are important and that they are contributing to the mission of the agency. Performance evaluations, promotions, and merit pay systems must be administered in an equitable and consistent manner. Career enrichment opportunities must be provided. Organizations that provide employees with the opportunity to participate in the decision-making process tend to have less labor strife (Peters and Masoka, 2000; Pynes, 2009).

MANAGING VOLUNTEERS

There is a tradition of volunteerism in this country that began with religious affiliated organizations and local government councils. Today a wide range of nonprofit organizations provide a variety of volunteer opportunities ranging from serving as board members of nonprofit organizations to serving on local government boards and commissions. Volunteers are used to assist employees in meeting their agency's mission and thus become an important part of strategic HRM and planning. In 2006, 26.7 percent of the U.S. population said they had volunteered during 2005, resulting in 61.2 million volunteers. The volunteer hours were equivalent to 7.5 full-time employees, and assuming those employees would have earned the average private nonfarm hourly wage, they would have earned $215.6 billion in 2006 (Wing, Pollak, and Blackwood, 2008, pp. 69–70).

Recruiting volunteers can be difficult as there has been an increase in competition among public and nonprofit agencies for volunteer talent. Contributing to the difficulty in recruiting volunteers is the nature of today's society. Seventy-five percent of women work on a full-time basis, while 25 percent work part-time (U.S. Department of Labor, 2010). The United States ranks among the highest on a global scale in the percentage of employees working 50 hours per week or more. Many workers are finding it difficult to balance job and family demands. As a result, nonprofits need to develop volunteer recruitment strategies to reach individuals whose interests and skills are likely to match the needs of the organization. Internet volunteering is a way to fit volunteering into their busy and sometimes unpredictable schedules. Virtual volunteering has become more common. Virtual volunteering is the use of information and communication technology to permit some part of the volunteering process to be carried out at a distance from the organization (Murray and Harrison, 2005, p. 31). Virtual volunteering has been used to conduct research on the Web, track relevant legislation, give specialist advice, design a Web site or newsletter, create databases, provide translation, and provide telephone or e-mail mentoring (Pynes, 2009).

Other nonprofits are rethinking the assignments they give to volunteers in terms of time, location, and length of commitment. Many communities have established volunteer banks where volunteers can be assigned to projects that do not require a long-term commitment to the agency or require volunteers to work scheduled hours each week. This is referred to as episodic volunteering (Macduff, 2005).

To facilitate intelligent staffing decisions, key staff should be involved in the development of the job descriptions for the volunteers they will supervise. This information will enable the agency to match the interest and skills of the volunteers with the positions in the organization. For example, a volunteer who wants to interact with other individuals would be unhappy working in isolation. Taking the time to match volunteer interests and skills with the needs of the agency in advance of their placement should help to minimize frequent turnover or absenteeism. The turnover rate and absenteeism of volunteers are some of the greatest challenges facing nonprofit administrators. Volunteers, like employees, should also receive training on how to perform their tasks and on the performance standards of the agency.

The research on why individuals volunteer indicates that both intrinsic and extrinsic rewards motivate them. Intrinsic rewards include satisfaction, a sense of accomplishment, and being challenged, which result from the work itself. Extrinsic rewards are benefits granted to the volunteers by the organization. Many individuals use volunteering as a means for career exploration, others to develop skills that may enhance their paid positions. Some people volunteer because it provides them with the opportunity to meet new people. Some volunteer as a way to contribute and give back to the community. Others volunteer because they value the goals of the agency, and still others volunteer because they desire personal growth or external recognition (Pynes, 2009).

There is no one reason that individuals volunteer. Therefore, the volunteer experience should attempt to provide satisfying and interesting opportunities and some form of external recognition. Nonprofit agencies need to recognize the different needs of volunteers and be flexible in developing volunteer assignments and working hours.

Attention should be paid to the recruitment, selection, training, evaluation, and management of volunteers. While volunteers can be tremendous assets to any organization, they also present new HRM challenges. Administrative responsibilities are increased as agencies must keep records and extend their liability insurance and worker's compensation policies to volunteers. Managing volunteer programs requires the development of personnel policies and procedures to assist with the integration of volunteers into the everyday operations of the agency. Paid staff, unions, and board members need to support the use of volunteers; oversight needs to be provided so that volunteers are properly utilized; and strategies need to be developed to motivate and retain volunteers (Pynes, 2009). Five reasons identified as to why volunteers may not return are when agencies do not match volunteers' skills with assignments, failing to recognize volunteers contributions, not measuring the value of volunteers, failing to train and invest in volunteers and staff, and failing to provide strong leadership (Eisner, Grimm, Maynard, and Washburn, 2009).

One group of very important volunteers in nonprofit organizations is the governing board, often referred to as the board of directors or board of trustees. The governing board is responsible for developing policies relating to the nonprofit's management. It is the responsibility of the board of directors to make sure that the public purpose of the nonprofit organization is implemented. Some of the basic responsibilities of nonprofit boards include determining agency mission and purposes, selecting the executive director and evaluating her or his performance, participating in strategic and long-range planning, establishing fiscal policy and oversight, monitoring the agency's programs and services, promoting the agency in the community, and participating in the development of personnel/HRM policies and strategies. Governing boards should not be involved in the day-to-day activities of the nonprofit, but instead develop policies to guide the agency and provide oversight to ensure that it is fulfilling its public purpose. Because of the variety of knowledge and skills needed by nonprofit boards, agencies must make an effort to recruit board members who can assist the organization. The recruitment strategy includes seeking board members with diverse backgrounds and professional expertise. Nonprofit boards should be sensitive to the community and organizations they are serving. When possible, there should be a distribution of ages, gender, color, and representatives of the constituency being served by the organization. Expertise is needed in the following areas: personnel/HRM, finance, law, fund-raising, and public relations.

Volunteers are critical to the success of most nonprofit organizations. Agencies should develop volunteer recruitment strategies to reach individuals whose interests and skills are likely to match the needs of the organization. To facilitate good staffing decisions, key staff should be involved in the development of the job descriptions for the volunteers they will supervise. This information will enable the agency to match the interest and skills of the volunteers with the positions in the organization. Taking the time to match volunteer interests and skills with the needs of the agency in advance of their placement should help to minimize frequent turnover or absenteeism. The turnover rate and absenteeism of volunteers are some of the greatest challenges facing nonprofit administrators. Volunteers, like employees, should also receive training on how to perform their tasks and on the performance standards of the agency.

FUTURE CHALLENGES

The economy has changed dramatically. The U.S. economy is in the midst of a serious recession. Public, for-profit, and nonprofit employers have furloughed and laid off employees. In January 2010, the U.S. Labor Department noted that 15.3 million people were out of work and that job seekers outnumber openings by more than six to one (U.S. Department of Labor, 2010).

Despite the high unemployment rates across most of the country, one area that is anticipated to have higher employment growth is the provision of health, human, and social services, which are heavily concentrated in the nonprofit sector. Nonprofits currently employ about 10 percent of the workforce (Urban Institute, 2010), and if the Senate's proposal for a job creation tax credit is passed, it is estimated that the credit could generate between 10,000 and 23,000 nonprofit jobs (The Washington Insider, 2010), making it critical that nonprofit organizations implement HRM policies and practices that emphasize fair wages and salaries, offer family-friendly policies and flexible work hours, and develop practices to enhance job satisfaction and quality.

References

American Civil Liberties Union. 2010, February 4. "White House Must Reform Faith-Based Initiative, says ACLU: Faith-Based Office Continues to Raise Civil Liberty concerns." http://www.aclu.org/religion-belief/coalition-letter-president-obama-reform-faith-based-office.

Board of Directors of Rotary International v. Rotary Club. 1987. 481 U.S. 537, 544, 107 S.Ct. 1940, 1945, 95 L. ED. 2d 474, 483–84.

Boorstein, M. 2010, February 17. "Citing Same-Sex marriage Bill, Washington Archdiocese Ends Foster-Care Program." *The Washington Post*, p. B01.

Boy Scouts of America Equal Access Act. 2003. 20 U.S.C. § 7905.

Boy Scouts of America v. Dale. 2000, June 28. 530 U.S. 640. http://supct.law.cornell.edu/supct/html/99-699.zo.html

Boy Scouts of America v. Wyman. 2003. 335 F. 3d 80, 90 2d Cir. 2003.

Boy Scouts of America v. Wyman. 2004, March 8. 03–956.

Civil Rights Act of 1964, Title VII, Sec. 70.

Colliver, V. 2009, December 8. "Nurses Unions Join Together for More Clout." *San Francisco Chronicle*, p. A–1.

Corporation of the Bishop of the Church of Jesus Christ of Latter Day Saints v. Amos. 1987. 483 U.S. 327.

Coulee Catholic Schools v. Lab & Ind Review Comm. 2009, July 21. Wisconsin.

Craig, T., and M. Boorstein. 2009, November 12. "Catholic Church Gives D. C. Ultimatum: Same-sex Marriage Bill, as Written, Called a Threat to Social Service Contracts." *The Washington Post.* http://www.washingtonpost.com/wp-dyn/content/article/2009/11/11AR2009111116943_pf.html.

Dale, M. 2008. "Scouts Sue After Philly Demands Rent or New Policy." *Philadelphia Daily News.* www.philly.com/philly/apwires/apnews/nation/20080527_ap_scoutssueafterphilly demandsnewpolicy.html?asString=ph.news/nation;!category=ntion;&randomOrd=05280 8121033.

Dale v. Boy Scouts of America and Monmouth Council Boy Scouts. 1998, March 2. A-2427-9573, N.J. Super. Ct. http://lawlibrary.rutgers.edu/courts/supreme/a-195-97.opn.html.

Dale v. Boy Scouts of America and Monmouth Council Boy Scouts. 1999, August 4. A-195/196-97, N.J. Sup. Ct. http://lawlibrary.rutgers.edu/courts/supreme/a-195-97.opn.html.

De Vita, C. J. 1999. "Nonprofits and Devolution: What Do We Know?" In E. T. Boris and C. E. Steuerle, eds. *Nonprofits and Government: Collaboration and Conflict* (pp. 213–233). Washington, D.C.: The Urban Institute Press.

Eisner, D., R. T. Grimm, Jr., S. Maynard, and S. Washburn. 2009. "The New Volunteer Workforce." *Stanford Social Innovation Review* 7(1): 32–37.

Elias, P. 2004, March 2. "Calif. Justices: Catholic Charity Must Cover Birth Control." *The Washington Post.* Retrieved from washingtonpost.com, http://washingtonpost.com/ac2/wp-dyn/A20797-2004Mar1?laanguage=printer.

Farris, A., R. Nathan, and D. Wright. 2004, December. *The Expanding Administrative Presidency: George W. Bush and Faith-Based Initiatives.* Albany, NY: The Roundtable on Religion and Social Welfare Policy.

Gorenstein, Nathan. 2010, June 23. "Federal Jury Decides in Favor of Scouts." *The Inquirer.* http://www.philly.com/philly/news/breaking/20100623_Federal_Jury_Decides_in_Favor_of_Scouts.html.

Gossett, C. W., and J. E. Pynes. 2003. "The Expansion of 'Charitable Choice' and 'Faith-Based Initiatives'—HRM Implications for Nonprofit Organizations." *Review of Public Personnel Administration* 23(2): 154–168.

Hinkelman, M. 2008, May 28. "Scouts Sue the City to Stay in $1 HQ." *Philadelphia Daily News.* http://www.pphilly.com/philly/hp/news_update/20080528_Scouts_sue_city_to_stay_in1_HQ.html?asString=ph.news/update;!category=news_update;&randomOrd=081 208115620.

Hostetler, D. W., and J. E. Pynes. 2000a. "Sexual Orientation Discrimination and How It Challenges Nonprofit Managers." *Nonprofit Management & Leadership* 11(1): 49–63.

Hostetler, D. W., and J. E. Pynes. 2000b. "Commentary: Sexual Orientation Discrimination and How It Challenges Nonprofit Managers." *Nonprofit Management & Leadership* 11(2): 235–237.

Hughes, C. 2006, October 24. *Religious Service Providers Included in Birth Control Law, New York Court Rules.* Albany, NY: The Roundtable on Religion and Social Welfare Policy.

Hurley v. Irish-American Gay Group of Boston. 1995. U.S. No. 94–749.

Lown v. The Salvation Army, Inc. 2004, June 21, U.S. District Court, Southern District of New York. http://www.justice.gov/crt/religiousdiscrimination/lown_opinion.pdf (accessed June 2010).

Lupu, I. C., and R. W. Tuttle. 2005. Legal Update: *Lown v. The Salvation Army, Inc.; Commission, New York City Administration for Children Services and others.* http://www.religionand socialpolicy.org/legal/legal_update_display.cfm?id=38.

McClure v. The Salvation Army. 1972. No. 71–2270, 460 F.2d 553; 1972 U.S. app. LEXIS 10672.

Montiel, L. M., J. Keyes-Williams, and J. D. Scott. 2002, September. *The Use of Public Funds for Delivery of Faith-Based Human Services.* Albany, NY: The Roundtable on Religion and Social Welfare Policy.

Macduff, N. 2005. "Societal Changes and the Rise of the Episodic Volunteer." In J. L. Brudney, ed. *Emerging Areas of Volunteering* (pp. 49–61). Indianapolis, IN: ARNOVA.

Murray, V., and Y. Harrison. 2005. "Virtual Volunteering." In J. L. Brudney, ed. *Emerging Areas of Volunteering* (pp. 31–47). Indianapolis, IN: ARNOVA.

National Labor Relations Board. 1997. *A Guide to Basic Law and Procedures Under the National Labor Relations Act.* Washington, D.C.: U.S. Government Printing Office.

New York State Club Association v. City of New York. 1988. 108 S.Ct. 2234.

NLRB v. Catholic Bishop of Chicago. 1979. 440 U.S. 490.

Oster, S. M. 1992. "Nonprofit Organizations as Franchise Operations." *Nonprofit Management & Leadership* 2: 223–258.

Pedreira v. Kentucky Baptist Homes for Children. 2001. 186 F.Supp.2d 757 (W.D.Ky.).

Personal Responsibility and Work Opportunity Reconciliation Act of 1996 (PRWORA, Section 104 of P.L. 104–193).

Peters, J. B., and J. Masaoka. 2000. "A House Divided: How Nonprofits Experience Union Drives." *Nonprofit Management and Leadership* 10(3): 305–317.

Petruska v. Gannon University. 2006a, May 24. 3rd Cir.

Petruska v. Gannon University. 2006b, June 20. 3rd Cir.

Pynes, J. E. 2009. *Human Resources Management for Public and Nonprofit Organizations: A Strategic Approach* (3rd ed.). San Francisco, CA: Jossey-Bass, Inc.

Roberts v. United States Jaycees. 1984. 468 U.S. 609, 104 S.Ct. 3244, 82 L.Ed. 2d 462.

Rosenblum, N. 1998. *Membership and Morals: The Personal Uses of Pluralism in America.* Princeton, NJ: Princeton University Press.

Slobodzian, J. A. 2007, December 4. "Scouts Ignore Gay-policy Deadlines: They Held Off on Lifting a Ban Also Barring Atheists. The City Said It Would Look for a New Tenant for Their Logan Headquarters." *Philadelphia Inquirer*, p. B01.

Slobodzian, J. A. 2008, May 24. "Boy Scouts Sue City in Building Dispute." *Philadelphia Inquirer*, p. B01.

Steinberg, R. J., and J. A. Jacobs. 1994. "Pay Equity in Nonprofit Organizations: Making Women's Work Visible." In T. Odendahl and M. O'Neill, eds. *Women and Power in the Nonprofit Sector* (pp. 79–120). San Francisco, CA: Jossey-Bass.

Tomic v. Catholic Diocese. 2006. 442 F.3d 1036.

United Press International. 2010, June 14. "Boy Scout Council Faces Eviction Over Gays." http://www.upi.com/Top_News/US/2010/06/14/Boy-Scout-council-faces-eviction-over-gays/UPI-29351276544222/.

Urban Institute. 2010. *Nonprofits.* http://www.urban.org/nonprofits/index.cfm.

U.S. General Accounting Office (GAO). 2002, September. *Charitable Choice: Federal Guidelines on Statutory Provisions Could Improve Consistency of Implementation*, GAO-02-887. Washington, D.C.: U.S. General Accounting Office.

U.S. Department of Labor. 2010. *Quick Stats on Women Workers, 2008.* www.dol.gov/wb/stats/main.htm.

Universidad Central Baymon v. National Labor Relations Board. 1986. 793 F.2d 383.

University of Great Falls v. National Labor Relations Board. 2002. U.S. Court of Appeals for the District of Columbia Circuit, No. 00–1415.

Urbina, I. 2007, December 6. "Boy Scouts Lose Philadelphia Lease in Gay-Rights Fight." *New York Times.* http://www.nytimes.com/2007/12/06/us/06scouts.html?ei=5070&en.

Urbina, I. 2009, November 13. "New Turn in Debate over Law on Marriage." *The New York Times*, p. A17.

Wakin, D. J. 2010, January 9. "Strike in Cleveland Points to Classical music Woes." *The New York Times*, p. A1.

Wallsten, P. 2010, February 4. "Keeping Faith, Courting Conservatives." *The Wall Street Journal.* http://online.wsj.com/article/SB10001424052748703357104575045623785996294.html.

Wan, W. 2010, March 2. "Same Sex Marriage Leads Catholic Charities to Adjust Benefits." *The Washington Post*, p. A01.

Washington Insider. 2010. "Senate Job Creation Tax Credit Could Generate 10,000 to 23,000 Nonprofit Jobs." http://unca-acf.org/insider/?p=271.

Weisman, R. 2009, October 7. "Hospital Staffers Vote Yes on Union." *The Boston Globe*. www. boston.com/business/healthcare/articles/2009/10/07/hospital_stafferss_vote_yes.

Wing, K. T., T. H. Pollak, and A. Blackwood. 2008. *The Nonprofit Almanac 2008*. Washington, D.C.: The Urban Institute.

Wright, D. J. 2009. *Taking Stock: The Bush Faith-Based Initiative and What Lies Ahead*. Albany, NY: The Nelson A. Rockefeller Institute of Government.

Young, D. 1989. "Local Autonomy in a Franchise Age: Structural Change in National Voluntary Associations." *Nonprofit and Voluntary Sector Quarterly* 18(2): 101–117.

17

ETHICS MANAGEMENT AND TRAINING

Jonathan P. West and Evan M. Berman

Jonathan P. West is a professor of political science and director of the graduate public administration program at the University of Miami. He has published eight books and over 100 scholarly articles and book chapters. His research interests include human resource management, productivity, local government, and ethics. He teaches undergraduate and graduate courses in American politics, public policy and management, and human resource management. He is the managing editor of *Public Integrity* journal. He taught previously at the University of Houston and University of Arizona.

Evan M. Berman is University Chair Professor at the National Chengchi University in Taipei (Taiwan), Doctoral Program in Asia-Pacific Studies, and the Department of Public Administration. He is the editor—chief of American Society for Public Administration's (ASPA) Book Series in Public Administration & Public Policy (Taylor & Francis), and senior editor of *Public Performance & Management Review*. He is a Distinguished Fulbright Fellow. His recent books include *HRM in Public Service* (2009, with West, Bowman, and Van Wart) and *Public Administration in East Asia* (2010).

Ethics is defined as the standards by which actions are determined to be right or wrong (Kazman and Bonczek, 1998). Interest in ethics has grown in recent decades, fueled by political corruption cases in cities like Miami and Providence and debacles at Enron, WorldCom, and elsewhere (Bowman, West, and Beck, 2010; Cox, 2009; Huberts, Maesschalck, and Jurkiewicz, 2008; Menzel, 2007, 2010; Richter and Burke, 2007; Svara, 2007; West and Berman, 2006). As these examples suggest, the challenge is to get individuals in organizations to adopt a common, shared set of standards that is consistent with organizations doing the "right" thing and avoiding wrong actions that cause harm to them and others.

Institutionalizing ethics in public organizations requires collaborative leadership. Human resource (HR) managers are in a strategically advantageous position to work with others in creating and maintaining an ethical organization. These individuals can help increase ethical awareness, cultivate ethical reasoning, encourage ethical action, and exercise ethical leadership. HR managers' responsibilities in the areas of hiring, orientation, compensation, training, performance appraisal, employee assistance programs, and adverse actions provide leverage points for introducing the ethics factor into decisions. Ethical implications for human resource management (HRM) are also evident in diversity initiatives, union–management relations, HR information systems, health, safety, and accessibility issues, pension plans, family/work relations, productivity and quality, and privatization (West, 2009). Together with others on the management team, HR managers can assist in shaping and implementing HR systems and processes that reinforce an ethical workplace.

There are many different sources of ethical behavior in organizations. One such source is *professional conduct*, from which norms develop regarding standards for professional knowledge and skills, having a constructive, professional attitude about working with others, and promoting excellence. A second source is *serving the public interest*, from which norms are derived about respecting democratic processes and the roles of citizens and elected officials in those processes, making decisions that best promote the public interest, and promoting fairness and justice, including due process. A third source is *personal honesty and integrity*, from which norms arise about telling the truth, following through on what has been promised, taking responsibility for one's mistakes, and serving as a model of ethical leadership. A fourth source stems from *knowing and respecting the law*, such as avoiding discrimination, conflicts of interest, taking bribes, and other prohibited activities. Each of these examples is a widely recognized source of ethics.

It is often noted that ethical behavior and legal behavior are not necessarily equivalent. Generally, ethical norms concern a broader class of conduct. What is illegal is usually unethical, though the converse is not always true. For example, leaving work a few minutes early each day is not illegal, but it is unethical, because it violates norms of personal integrity and fails to serve the public interest. Also, while there is an ethical obligation to avoid the appearance of conflict of interest or discrimination, the legal standard often is narrower, namely, to avoid committing specific acts, which are often carefully circumscribed and defined by law. Because ethics concerns a broader class of actions than just legal ones, legal woes can often be avoided by attention and commitment to ethics. Attention to ethics often gives a margin of error, of safety, in avoiding unintentional legal missteps.

But two of the greatest challenges today are getting organizations to (i) articulate and (ii) manage a set of common, specific values and standards. It is not so much that organizational leaders are unaware of the importance of ethics in organizations. They hear and read the news, just like everyone else. Indeed, often their organizations have identified many of the broad values stated above. But leaders, especially those in HR, need to inform members of their organizations about the specific forms of conduct that are either prohibited or especially welcomed. For example, what exactly does promoting the public interest mean in the context of doing a background check on a prospective employee? Specifically, how much time and money should the organization spend? Or, in the interest of promoting professionalism and excellence, exactly how much training should be given to employees and in which areas? These are very important practical questions that require specific, detailed answers; broad values alone do not provide operational clarity and, as such, do not suffice.

Another problem is consistency and follow-through. Organizations and their leaders cannot realistically expect good results if they do not devise and manage those activities through which standards of specific conduct are set. Managers and employees need to be informed of these expectations and also to be expected to put them into practice. Performance in these areas needs to be monitored and measured, and individuals should receive feedback and experience consequences of their behaviors in a systematic way. That is, there needs to be management of these expectations (Cozzetto, Pedeliski, Tomkins, and West, 2009). Some time ago, we called this "ethics management," and this term is now frequently used (Berman, West, and Cava, 1994; Menzel, 2007; West, 1995). While most organizations could do a better job of managing ethics, many institutions are laying the groundwork, and quite a few have even made substantial gains in this area.

This chapter begins by identifying and briefly discussing six principal elements of a systematic strategy of ethics management. Second, the current state of the art of ethics training in U.S. cities, an important HRM activity, is reported in greater detail. Third, the purpose of ethics training, the breadth and depth of topics covered, pedagogical approaches to instruction, and the correlates of training are considered. Finally, a simultaneous equations model is presented depicting the impact of ethics training and the factors affecting its use.

ETHICS MANAGEMENT

The need to manage an organization's values is no different from that of other resources, such as technology or money, but it does take on its own form. The main ingredients are leadership, assessment, articulation, training, feedback, and consequences.

Leadership is the cornerstone of the moral foundation of organizations. This is a historic truth. Leaders set the tone, and through their actions and conduct they model this behavior for everyone else. As noted by an interviewee in one of our studies: "there is truth to the old saying 'a fish stinks from the head down.' If there is mediocrity at the top, it permeates the organization" (Berman and West, 2003). The same holds true for moral corruption. It is certainly no coincidence that leaders of morally corrupt organizations are often prosecuted for specific, illegal acts that they committed. Conversely, when we asked several years ago about sources of ethical leadership in organizations, the most frequent response by senior managers was "exemplary moral leadership" (West, Berman, and Cava, 1993). There is no doubt that leaders set the tone of the organization. If ethics is to be taken seriously, it must start at the top (see Van Wart, 2006; Northouse, 2006; Kaptein, Huberts, Avelino, and Lasthuizen, 2005). This is reflected in their specific actions ("don't do as I say, do as I do"), as well as in their commitment to ensuring ethical standards throughout the organization, by their own commitment to the activities discussed below.

Of course, no amount of ethics management can avoid any and all forms of ethical wrongdoing. To expect this is to be truly naïve. Additionally, selection processes in HRM are uncertain at best. When it comes to ethics, we know very little about the ethical philosophies and practices of those whom we hire. However, undertaking ethics management reduces the risk and amount of ethical wrongdoing. This system will sometimes catch unethical action at an early stage before even more damage is done, while in other instances the system will entirely preempt it. Ethics management also provides a shield for organizations, enabling them to better distance themselves from the unethical acts of individuals. It is better to have to acknowledge having had one or two bad apples in the barrel than to appear as though the barrel is half full of them.

If the purpose of ethics management is to increase ethical conduct, then managers need to know the current state of ethics in their organizations (Berman, 2003; Bonczek, 1998; West and Berman, 2006). They need to know what is working well and what is not. They need to know what is important, but not yet on the radar screen of employees and managers. This proactive approach is called *assessment*, and there are several ways in which this is done. Leaders can rely on their own sense of what is lacking, informed by broader discussions in society and reinforced through conversations with others in the organization. This allows them to gauge the sense of ethics in both general and specific terms. For example, leaders may find that matters of personal integrity and professionalism receive little emphasis in personnel appraisals, or that ethics is a minor factor in promotion decisions—both crucial HR functions. They may also discover a surprising lapse in knowledge concerning major provisions of law, or a rash of ethics violations. Some organizations also conduct employee surveys that may include such items as "My department has a defined standard of integrity, and I know what it is" or "My supervisor encourages me to act in an ethical manner." Responses to such statements can be quite illuminating.

After assessing the ethical climate and conduct, the next step is to clearly *articulate* what is expected. This is often contained in codes of ethics or standards of conduct that are found in many jurisdictions and offices (ICMA, 1998). These documents usually contain general statements, such as "we are committed to honesty and integrity in all of our actions" or "we are committed to providing the highest level of customer service." Numerous examples of these standards and codes can be readily found on the Internet. However, as stated above, managers will need to operationalize these generalities in order to provide guidance for specific situations that their employees encounter. Employees are rightly skeptical of ethics plaques that are not buttressed with specifics. As Payne (1996, p. 313) notes, "ethical knowledge is not only 'knowing that' a particular conduct is wrong but also 'knowing how' to cope with one's responsibility in regard to such conduct."

For example, in an HR department, specific ethics standards would relate to procedures for protecting the confidentiality of employee information, proactively assisting employees to ensure that their benefits selection is in their best interest, ensuring that recruitment and selection is done in ways that promote organizational interests, informing managers of sources of possible litigation and procedures to avoid, and requiring that managers instruct their employees about provisions in the code of ethics and standards of conduct. Such specific measures go beyond generalizations such as "serving as role models for maintaining the highest standards of ethical conduct" or "being ethically responsible for promoting and fostering fairness and justice for all employees and their organizations," which are found in the Society for Human Resource Management's "Code of Ethical and Professional Standards in Human Resource Management." In order to be effective, the principles actually must be applied.

Ethics management can never entirely foresee the myriad ways in which ethics principles need to be applied. People are challenged on a daily basis to make ethical decisions. Some of these are new and lack precedents. For example, what about the manager who wants to go to a conference in Las Vegas but stays an extra day at public expense to enjoy the sights? What about the employee who spends half an hour everyday surfing the Internet pursuing his or her own personal interests? While job applications should identify the most important candidate qualifications, *ethics training* helps to both ensure a broad sensitivity to matters of ethics and provide employees with a process for identifying and dealing with thorny ethical dilemmas. Most ethics training includes processes of identifying warning signs and cultivating moral reasoning skills. When in doubt about ethical matters, it is often helpful to raise the issue and discuss it with others.

Organizations vary greatly in the extent and depth of their ethics training. There is substantial room for improvement. Beyond training, another aspect of ethics management is the monitoring of performance and provision of feedback. Today, monitoring is seldom a systematic activity, and often episodic, based on whether or not lapses in ethics judgment have become apparent. However, one systematic approach involves use of an ethics "scorecard" with various measures for assessing ethical conduct in different areas. This is clearly a cutting-edge concept that is yet to be mainstreamed. Rather, supervisors are more likely to "monitor" by becoming informed when something has gone wrong, such as when a client, employee, or staff person in another department brings to their attention some questionable behavior or conduct.

This information, then, affords the opportunity for supervisors to provide feedback and consequences. *Feedback* is important because it is the starting point of human learning and change. People need to know that what has been done is wrong. While some unethical acts are intentionally committed, it is usually more common that unethical behavior is either conducted unknowingly or by people who simply make bad judgments in difficult situations. Perhaps these individuals were unaware of standards or of the options available to them in dealing with a particular situation, and feedback can provide a genuine learning opportunity for avoiding such problems in the future. Feedback can be provided in meetings between employees and their supervisors. Such sessions can provide a summary of the facts of what has occurred, the nature of the unethical conduct, the standards that apply, and a statement of more desirable actions and decisions. For example, one of our managers shared this experience:

> We had an incident whereby a manager hung some of her colleagues out to dry by blaming them for a problem and thereby deflecting her responsibility for a mistake. In counseling with her, I used the GFOA Code of Ethics to explain why her conduct violated a provision of the professional code. She recognized the problem, and there has been no recurrence of unethical behavior. (Berman and West, 2003, p. 36)

Consequences are the next step of ethics management. Reinforcement matters. All organizations send strong signals about ethics, and consequences are a powerful message. For example, when unethical conduct is known to constitute a disqualification for salary raises and promotion, a signal is sent that ethics matter. When individuals are punished (negative consequences) for unethical acts, a similarly strong signal is communicated. When leaders praise individual and organizational acts of ethical leadership and exemplary conduct, the importance of ethics is reinforced. Consistency of consequences, whether positive or negative, shapes both managers' and employees' perceptions about what is expected, what they need to do, and what to avoid. By contrast, when organizations are inconsistent or unclear regarding consequences, employees may conclude that ethical conduct is not very important, especially compared to other things that receive greater emphasis.

Ethics management, then, is a systematic approach to managing the values and actions of the organization's members. It consists of leadership, assessment, articulation, training, feedback, and consequences. Beyond consequences, the cycle is closed through a renewed leadership assessment of the current situation regarding ethics, and so on. Ethics management can shape conduct and thereby reduce the amount of failure, in the process helping organizations to deal with unethical situations that may develop. Yet, while the desirability and vision for it is clear, the practice of ethics management is still variable and underdeveloped. This is because the notion of ethics management is new and many leaders fail to make ethics an important priority. Others may agree that ethics management is important, but view it as a matter of personal responsibility and therefore not an appropriate organizational concern. Ironically, failing to make ethics management a priority increases the risk of a serious ethics failure, thereby making it an urgent priority when failure does occur. Ethics management initiatives are likely to increase in the future, as ethical conduct continues to be a salient societal issue. The remainder of this chapter focuses on a crucial component of ethics management: ethics training.

ETHICS TRAINING

Ethics training has become a centerpiece of corporate and government compliance and values-oriented initiatives (Berman, West, and Cava, 1994; Bruce, 1996; Wells and Schminke, 2001; West, Berman, Bonczek, and Kellar, 1998). It sharpens participants' awareness and competence in dealing with a myriad of issues that often arise in the work life of employees and managers. Ethics training is part of an integrated view of ethics management. Of course, it can also be viewed and studied as a form of workforce training, focusing on skills and abilities in matters of ethics and ethical decision making.

An important contribution to the literature on ethics training in the public sector was the recent publication of a two-volume symposium edited by Don Menzel on "Ethics Education and Training," appearing in *Public Integrity* journal (Vol. 11, 3 and Vol. 12, 1, 2009–2010). The dual goals of the symposium were to assess education strategies that help to foster ethical behavior and practices and to spur thought regarding cultivation of ethical competencies; both goals are relevant to HR managers. The symposium consisted of six research articles and two commentaries. The lead article by Robert Peters and Anna Filipova (2009) highlights the value of cognitive dissonance theory to encourage learners to think critically regarding values that may or may not be aligned with public service concerns. They consider five instructional techniques, including counterattitudinal advocacy, hypocrisy induction, remedying belief perseverance, structured controversy, and instructing the conscience. The authors maintain that each of these ethics training approaches is useful in ethics instruction. Don Menzel's article focused on another popular instructional strategy: training with cases to cultivate ethical reasoning. He shows the utility of the case approach whether instructors rely solely on cases, use them in combination with lectures, or use them in an online format. Nancy Matchett's (2009–2010) contribution to the symposium examines cooperative learning, critical thinking, and character to cultivate ethical deliberation. She sees cooperative learning as a way to assist learners in assessing the two perspectives of "simplistic subjectivism" and "anything-goes relativism," stressing the inherent weaknesses of these perspectives. She demonstrates the utility of cooperative learning, whether in ethics classrooms or workshops, as a way to assist learners in developing abilities to articulate and defend nuanced positions on ethical issues.

Three symposium articles also highlight training issues for those in specific professional roles, including HRM, city management, and law enforcement. Education for ethics and its links to HRM is explicitly addressed in Jeremy Plant and Bing Ran's (2009) article that examines a three-course sequence on HR offered in the graduate public administration program at Penn State University/Harrisburg and highlights the ethical issues in HR. The authors emphasize the value of this approach in contrast to the single stand-alone ethics course that may be either required or optional at other institutions. Greg Streib and Mark Rivera (2009–2010) focus on the ethical knowledge of city managers by analyzing results from the International City Management Association (ICMA) Applied Knowledge Assessment. Results confirm ICMA's success in ensuring that city managers are knowledgeable regarding the Code of Ethics and that such knowledge influences their professional managerial role. Heather Wyatt-Nichol and George Franks (2009–2010) give attention to ethics training in law enforcement agencies. They report results of a study of ethics training based on a survey of police chiefs in cities with populations of 100,000–500,000. Findings show positive results in reinforcing the organization's mission and adherence to policies and procedures as well as helping individuals to recognize and resolve ethical issues. Finally, the two symposium commentaries dealt with both high school education in ethics and distance learning. Jason Giersch laments the relative absence of ethics education in high schools and makes a spirited case for more moral education in American secondary schools. The opportunities to provide ethics training via distance learning are addressed in Manfred Meine and Thomas Dunn's (2009–2010) commentary. They advocate a more vigorous leadership role for American Society for Public Administration (ASPA) as a potential provider of ethics training for public service organizations.

In the context of training, a valuable decision-making tool, with philosophical roots, is the "ethics triangle" (Svara, 2007). It enables trainees and managers to critically assess and resolve ethical problems by drawing on the three principal schools of thought: expected results of action (consequentialism), reliance on rules (deontology), and character (virtue ethics). Svara (1997, 2007) has used this tool to analyze several managerial decisions. Bowman and West (2007, 2009) applied it to the analysis of such contemporary HRM issues as at-will employment and reform of the federal Hatch Act (a 1939 law restricting the political activities of federal workers). Managers seeking to make an ethically justifiable decision could be aided by applying the triangle to consider results, rules, and virtues. Ethics trainers could use it to help learners think through issues, decisions, and actions from a normative perspective.

Another valuable decision-making framework assists in weighing ethical principles and economic imperatives (see West and Bowman, 2008). Using this approach, choices can be viewed in terms of both their ethical right and wrong and their economic good and bad (Bowman, 1995). This results in a 4-by-4 decision matrix, which categorizes different ways to address an issue. Decisions can be ethically correct and economically efficient, ethically correct but economically inefficient, ethically deficient but apparently economically efficient, and ethically incorrect and economically inefficient. West and Bowman (2008) applied this framework, together with others, to analyze a variety of employee benefits from both an ethical and economic perspective. This tool, together with the ethics triangle, could be introduced and usefully applied in an ethics training seminar.

Managers who decide to undertake ethics training have various additional tools and resources at their disposal. For example, in 1998, ICMA published "Ethics in Action," which provides a participant's handbook and leader's guide. This publication contains situational exercises, icebreakers, presentation slides, and ethics definitions and applications. Topics include corruption, conflict of interest, disclosure, and fairness of treatment, for example, as well as strategies for decision making. There is also an additional collection of professional articles on ethics and a CD-ROM with interviews and further exercises. These materials were updated in the mid-2000s and comprise a training package together with ICMA's book, *The Ethics Edge* (2006). Many other professional organizations have also developed materials for their members that deal with situations they are likely to face. Generally, it would appear that a broad range of training materials are available. It should also be noted that there are a vast number of organizations and consultants that offer to provide ethics training.[1]

The focus will now shift from a selective review of recent literature and resources on ethics training to report findings from a particular study done by the authors. Specifically, the remainder of this chapter is adapted from our article, "Ethics Training in Cities" (West and Berman, 2004), which is the most comprehensive examination to date of ethics training and its use in local governments.[2] It should be noted that our survey focused on the use of ethics training in cities generally and was not limited to HR managers or their departments.

We find that 64.1 percent of jurisdictions offer training that meet our definition of "activities that increase participants' knowledge of the standards of conduct within an organization (and) deals with what is right and wrong, giving both guidelines and specific examples for identifying and addressing issues of ethical concern." Only about 36.8 percent of respondents call this training "ethics training." Use does not vary significantly by region or form of government; however, large cities are more likely to offer ethics training. Among those that offer training, about one-third (37.3 percent) provide it as mandatory training for all employees, and 43.5 percent offer it as voluntary. Most of the remainder includes that which is offered only to managers, new staff, or violators. Thus, there exists considerable variation in the use of ethics training.

The purposes of ethics training are now widely accepted to include a "high" road and a "low" road (Bowman, West, and Beck, 2010; Paine, 1994). The low road (which is also sometimes referred to as "defensive") focuses on legal compliance and helps organizations avoid the embarrassment associated with allegations of legal wrongdoing. The high road (which is sometimes called "aspirational") includes efforts to develop employees' capacity to identify, articulate, and resolve ethics issues. Such training often includes additional efforts to increase openness, communication, and accountability. Many authors view this as a desired state to promote ethical conduct, and others additionally view it as a way to increase organizational productivity.

Our findings support the view that ethics training supports both purposes. Regarding the "low road," reducing the frequency of unethical conduct is widely mentioned by 82.5 percent of respondents, as is heightening familiarity with key legal requirements (77.3 percent), avoiding litigation (75.2 percent), and reducing the legal liability of the jurisdiction (74.6 percent). Among cities that use training, 84.8 percent mention at least one of these defensive purposes. But ethics training also serves aspirational purposes, or at least has aims beyond narrow, legal concerns. Two-thirds of the respondents state that a purpose of ethics training is to encourage critical thinking about ethics and three-fourths mention that a purpose is to offer practical guidance. Also, 43.3 percent use ethics training as a means of transforming the organizational culture, and 82.5 percent view it as a means of reinforcing the organizational culture. Eight in ten respondents mention at least one of these purposes. Also, 77.0 percent use training to communicate and discuss ethical standards and expectations, which can be used for either reinforcing or transforming organizational culture.

The topics of ethics training reflect these purposes. Some topics emphasize general awareness of ethical principles and decision making, whereas other topics provide specific applications of ethics in specific areas of administration or ethical situation. By and large, respondents state that many topics are covered "in-depth" or "adequately," such as being a good role model (82.1 percent), making decisions that are fair and just (84.8 percent), due process (80.7 percent), respect for individual rights (80.4 percent), and how to decide whether something is unethical (73.2 percent). Additionally, 82.7 percent also state that they deal with ethics issues in specific areas such as law enforcement in adequate or in-depth ways, as do 79.1 percent of respondents with regard to explaining what "conflict of interest" is in operational terms, and "personal honesty" (65.1 percent). Somewhat less frequently addressed are potentially perplexing problems for busy public managers, such as: detecting warning signs of unethical behavior (63.4 percent), dealing with inadvertent mistakes (53.2 percent), and balancing legal and ethical considerations (67.9 percent). Ethics audits, however, are only rarely covered in ways that are in-depth or adequate (11.7 percent). Many authors find this a significant omission (Van Wart, 1998; White and Lam, 2000).

However, the median duration of voluntary ethics training for employees is only about 4 hours per year and about 3 hours for training that is mandatory. Although this is a very modest amount of training (about two half mornings a year), it frequently occurs in conjunction with other forms of ethics management activities, which also help clarify what is expected of employees. For example, among those that provide ethics training, 58.3 percent state that they also monitor adherence to a Code of Ethics, 51.3 percent also use ethics as a criterion in hiring and promotion, 52.5 percent regularly communicate with employees on matters of ethics, and 57.5 percent require financial disclosure. Also, among those that require training, 82.8 percent also state that "exemplary moral leadership" by senior managers is used as a strategy for ensuring an ethical climate. Further analysis suggests that ethics training is often one of several activities in an overall ethics strategy.

With so little time devoted to ethics training, a reasonable question arises: What is the depth of coverage? Jurisdictions that offer 2 or more hours of mandatory training agree frequently that these topics are covered more thoroughly than jurisdictions that provide less than 2 hours. For example, whereas 44.8 percent of respondents with 2 or more hours of mandatory training agree that "warning signs of unethical behavior are covered thoroughly or in-depth," only 15.0 percent of those who offer less than 2 hours of mandatory training agree. Likewise, the percentages regarding "dealing with inadvertent ethical missteps" are 25.0 percent and 5.0 percent; explaining what "conflict of interest" means in operational terms, 41.4 percent versus 17.9 percent; and examples of professional conduct, 42.9 percent versus 22.5 percent. In short, respondents report that more training allows for a more thorough (deeper) coverage of the topics. It is important to note that training is not the only source of information on these topics in organizations (interdepartmental memos, presentations by top managers, on-the-job discussion, and hiring/promotion decisions), and in this sense the purpose of ethics training is to clarify and strengthen ethics expectations and procedures established by managers and their organizations.

Because in-service training involves adult learners, adapting training to adult learning styles is important. Several learning considerations and instructional methods need to be considered in designing an effective program. Best practices for ethics training have been summarized by Larry Ponemon (1996), who identifies a dozen features crucial to success: live instruction, use of a professional trainer, a powerful message from the manager, small class sizes, at least 4 hours of training, a decision-based focus, significant group interaction, realistic case materials, comprehensive involvement of employees, separate course for compliance areas, follow-up communications, and new employee programs. Although authors may differ in their assessment of essential features, the literature reflects a clear preference for reality-based, varied, active learning adapted to the needs of adult trainees, thus allowing sufficient time for digesting information, encouraging trainee participation, using experiential teaching techniques to supplement traditional lecture methods, and emphasizing competency-based learning applicable to workplace decisions (Knowles, 1973; LeClair and Ferrell, 2000; Menzel, 2007, 2010; Svara, 2007; Van Wart, Cayer, and Cook, 1993; West and Berman, 2006).

Ethics training in cities often is reality based and practical and includes hypothetical scenarios (82.5 percent), case materials (80.9 percent), and role plays or short exercises (67.89 percent), and has a decision-based focus (57.5 percent). These methods are consistent with most descriptions of best training practices (see Ponemon, 1996) and with knowledge concerning adult learning styles. The schedule for training often involves different points in time (84.1 percent), and training is delivered with optimal class sizes (81.7 percent with 30 or fewer trainees). The training is tailored to the needs of the jurisdiction (79.6 percent) and delivered in ways that minimize time away from the job (81.6 percent). Professional trainers or outside consultants are used in most cities (64.3 percent), and the lecture format is the primary means of delivery (61.4 percent). Posttraining materials for later reference are provided (81.4 percent), and in-class evaluation of training is conducted (72.3 percent). These results clearly reflect that ethics training has become, in many ways, "professionalized." Most training is offered in the form of live instruction with very limited use of Web-based or other forms of electronic instruction (9.6 percent).

Correlates and Impact. Why do some cities provide broad coverage and use numerous methods of ethics training while others do not? To examine this question, some factors mentioned in the framework above are considered. Having adequate resources for training is associated with use of more ethics training, even controlling for the size of the jurisdiction. Training is also associated with respondents' perceptions that their jurisdiction frequently develops new, innovative programs. However, perceptions of the amount of litigation or employee grievances are not associated with the use of ethics training. Such perceptions may be related to other, nonethics factors. Ethics training is (weakly) associated with using ethics as a criterion in hiring and promotion: It stands to reason that employees need to be informed and trained in that for which they are held accountable.

The above associations are stronger for more targeted ethics training efforts. Consistent with the model of adult learning, a six-item index variable was made of training content that emphasizes warning signs of unethical behavior, the importance of getting facts, dealing with inadvertent ethical missteps, addressing ethical complaints, consequences of ethical violations, and ethical issues in specific areas (such as law enforcement). This broad measure is more strongly associated with using ethics as a criterion in hiring and promotion. It is also associated with monitoring adherence to the Code of Ethics.

To examine the impact of training, an index variable of revitalized "organizational culture" was developed, measured as a construct of the following items: "in our city, people are strongly supported to put forth their best effort," "our organizational culture encourages creativity and new ideas," "our organization encourages open and constructive dialogue," "our organization rewards passionate commitments to accomplishment," and "in our city, people are encouraged to take on rather than avoid new challenges." In the sample, 51.8 percent agree or strongly agree with these statements. Ethics training is significantly associated with improvements in the organizational culture. Among jurisdictions offering training, 67.2 percent report having a revitalized organizational culture, compared to only 29.0 percent of those that do not do ethics training. Similarly, among jurisdictions that have applications-oriented ethics training discussed above, 79.6 percent report having a revitalized organizational culture compared to only 25.0 percent of those that do not do such training.

These associations do invite questions of causality: for example, does ethics training cause improvements in the organizational culture, or are revitalized organizational culture more likely to use ethics training? Moreover, is the impact direct or indirect, caused by other intervening variables? Such questions of causation and immediacy are explored in Figure 17.1, a simultaneous equations model (SEM) of the impact of ethics training, and factors affecting its use.[3] A variety of conclusions can be drawn from this model. First, the model uses the applications-oriented measure of ethics training; a general measure of ethics training often is not associated with the following paths that are significant for the measure of targeted ethics training efforts. Thus, this corroborates the above emphases on targeted measures of training. Second, the model shows that although the relationship of ethics training to citizen trust and employee productivity is complex, training is significantly associated with improvements in the organizational culture and positive labor-management relations. However, the relationship between ethics training and the outcomes is indirect; no direct relationship is significant, and it is therefore not shown.

Third, it can be calculated that the effect of ethics training on perceptions of employee productivity is about the same as the effect of moral leadership by senior managers on employee productivity, though both effects are less than the direct effects of organizational culture and having positive labor-management relations.[4] Fourth, Figure 17.1 also shows that, interestingly, the moral leadership of senior managers also does not directly affect perceptions of employee productivity and citizen trust (those paths are not shown, because they are insignificant). The use of ethics training is affected by moral leadership of senior managers, monitoring of employees' adherence

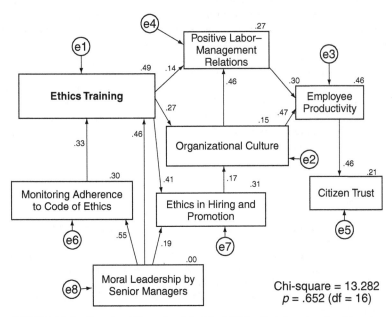

FIGURE 17.1 **Structural Equation Model of Ethics Training, Leadership, and Outcomes**

to the code of ethics (if an organization has one), and using ethics as a criterion in hiring and promotion. In sum, Figure 17.1 clearly shows the complex, but real, relationship of ethics training in connection with other ethics activities, leadership, and important organizational outcomes.

CONCLUSION

Ethics is defined as the standards by which actions are determined to be right or wrong and ethics management as those activities through which organizations define and implement such standards and thereby affect the conduct of employees and managers. As a concept, ethics management is more than a decade old, but it has been catching on in recent years. The main ingredients of ethics management are leadership, assessment, articulation, training, feedback, and ensuring consequences.

Ethics training is thus one of several strategies through which leaders manage their organization's ethics. Based on our study, about 64 percent of cities offer some form of ethics training, although only 36 percent call it "ethics training." This training covers a broad range of topics that include both legal aspects and broader concerns that help employees to recognize instances of questionable ethics and adopt appropriate responses to such situations. We also found that training is associated with fostering organizational cultures of openness, accountability, and performance that, in turn, is associated with increased employee productivity. This study further reveals considerable variation in the extent of ethics training and in the depth with which different topics are covered. The results also suggest that the perceived effectiveness of training is greatest when it is applied to specific problems and when managers monitor ethics implementation.

While ethics training has been substantially "professionalized" in the last decade, progress is still needed. The depth of training is modest at best, about a half day or so a year. Although ethics training is not the only source of ethics-related information and priorities in organizations, it is important from the perspective of reinforcing management priorities. Why is more not being done? The usual reasons still exist in some organizations, such as managers considering ethics to be a private or confidential matter for individuals to resolve or perceiving that addressing ethics can be construed as an affront suggesting that coworkers are deficient in some way. In others instances, the need for ethics management and training has not yet surfaced on the radar screens of managers and leaders. Paradoxically, the lack of adequate attention to ethics increases the risk of ethics failure and, hence, ensures that ethics will require greater attention in the future.

References

American Society for Public Administration. 1998. *Applying Standards and Ethics in the 21st Century*. Washington, D.C.: ASPA.

Berman, E. 2003. "Implementing Ethics." In Jack Rabin et al., eds. *Encyclopedia of Public Administration and Public Policy* (pp. 461–464). New York: Marcel Dekker.

Berman, E., and J. West. 2003, December. "Solutions to the Problem of Managerial Mediocrity: Moving Up to Excellence (Part 2)." *Public Performance & Management Review* 27(2): 28–50.

Berman, E., J. West, and A. Cava. 1994. "Ethics Management in Municipal Government and Large Firms: Exploring Similarities and Differences." *Administration & Society* 26(2): 185–203.

Bonczek, S. 1998. "Creating an Ethical Work Environment." In E. Berman, J. West, and S. Bonczek, eds. *The Ethics Edge* (pp. 77–79). Washington, D.C.: International City/County Management Association.

Bowman, J. 1995. "Ethics and Quality: A 'Right-Good' Combination." In J. West, ed. *Quality Management Today* (pp. 64–72). Washington, D.C.: ICMA.

Bowman, J., and J. West. 2007. "Lord Acton and Employment Doctrines: Absolute Power and the Spread of At-will Employment." *Journal of Business Ethics* 74: 119–130.

Bowman, J., and J. West. 2009. "To 're-Hatch' Public Employees or Not? An Ethical Analysis of the Relaxation of Restrictions on Political Activities in Civil Service." *Public Administration Review* 69(1): 52–63.

Bowman, J., J. West, and M. Beck. 2010. *Achieving Competencies in Public Service: The Professional Edge*. Armonk, NY: M. E. Sharpe.

Brattebo, D., and E. Malone, eds. 2002. *The Lanahan Cases in Leadership Ethics & Decision Making*. Baltimore, MD: Lanahan.

Bruce, W. M. 1996. "Codes of Ethics and Codes of Conduct: Perceived Contribution to the Practice of Ethics in Local Government." *Public Integrity Annual*, pp. 23–29.

Cooper, T. 2001. *Handbook of Administrative Ethics*. New York: Marcel Dekker.

Cox, R., ed. 2009. *Ethics and Integrity in Public Administration*. Armonk, NY: M. E. Sharpe.

Cozzetto, D., T. Pedeliski, J. Tompkins, and J. West. 2009. "Employee Responsibilities: Setting Expectations." In S. Freyss, ed. *Human Resource Management in Local Government* (3rd ed., pp. 213–236). Washington, D.C.: International City/County Management Association.

Gueras, D., and C. Garofalo. 2002. *Practical Ethics in Public Administration*. Vienna, VA: Management Concepts.

Giersch, J. 2009. "Lessons in Ethics in American High Schools." *Public Integrity* 11(3): 251–260.

Huberts, Leo W. J. C., Jeroen Maesschalck, and Carole L. Jurkiewicz, eds. 2008. *Ethics and Integrity of Governance: Perspectives Across Frontiers*. Cheltenham, UK: Edward Elgar Publishing, Inc.

International City Management Association. 1998. Code of Ethics with Guidelines, as adopted by ICMA Executive Board. Washington, D.C.: International City/County Management Association.

Kaptein, M., L. Huberts, S. Avelino, and K. Lasthuizen. 2005. "Demonstrating Ethical Leadership by Measuring Ethics." *Public Integrity* 7(2): 299–311.

Kazman, J., and S. Bonczek. 1998. *Ethics in Action*. Washington, D.C.: International City/County Management Association.

Knowles, M. 1973. *The Adult Learner: A Neglected Species*. Houston, TX: Gulf Publishing.

LeClair, D. T., and L. Ferrel. 2000. "Innovation in Experiential Business Ethics Training." *Journal of Business Ethics* 23: 313–322.

Local Government Institute. 1995–1998. *Honesty and Fairness in the Public Service*. Tacoma, WA: LGI.

Matchett, N. 2009–2010. "Cooperative Learning, Critical Thinking, and Character: Techniqust to Cultivate Ethical Deliberation." *Public Integrity* 12(1): 25–38.

Meine, M., and T. Dunn. 2009–2010. "Distance Learning and Ethics Education and Training." *Public Integrity* 12(1): 51–59.

Menzel, D. 2007. *Ethics Management for Public Administrators*. Armonk, NY: M. E. Sharpe.

Menzel, D. 2009. "Teaching and Learning Ethical Reasoning with Cases." *Public Integrity* 11(3): 239–250.

Menzel, D. 2010. *Ethics Moments in Government: Cases and Controversies*. Boca Raton, FL: CRC Press.

National Conference of State Legislatures. 2003. *The State of State Legislative Ethics*. Denver, CO: NCSL.

Northouse, P. 2006. "Leadership Ethics." In J. West and E. Berman, eds. *The Ethics Edgen* (pp. 46–54). Washington, D.C.: ICMA.

Paine, L. 1994. "Managing for Organizational Integrity." *Harvard Business Review*, pp. 106–117.

Pasquerella, A., X. Killilea, and M. Vocino, eds. 1996. *Ethical Dilemmas in Public Administration*. Westport, CN: Praeger.

Payne, S. L. 1996. "Ethical Skill Development as an Imperative for Emancipatory Practice." *Systems Practice* 9(4): 307–316.

Peters, R., and A. Filipova. 2009. "Optimizing Cognitive-Dissonance Literacy in Ethics Educatino: An Instructional Model." *Public Integrity* 11(3): 201–219.

Plant, J., and B. Ran. 2009. "Education for Ethics and Human Resource Management: A Necessary Synergy." *Public Integrity* 11(3): 221–238.

Ponemon, L. 1996, October. "Key Features of an Effective Ethics Training Program." *Management Accounting*, pp. 66–67.

Richter, W., and F. Burke, eds. 2007. *Combating Corruption, Encouraging Ethics* (2nd ed.). Boulder, CO: Roman and Littlefield.

Streib, G., and M. Rivera. 2009–2010. "Assessing the Ethical Knowledge of City Managers." *Public Integrity* 12(1): 9–23.

Svara, J. 1997. "The Ethical Triangle: Synthesizing the Bases of Administrative Ethics." In *Public Integrity Annual* (pp. 33–41). Lexington, KY: Council of State Governments.

Svara, J. 2007. *The Ethics Primer for Public Administrators in Government and Nonprofit Organizations*. Boston, MA: Jones and Bartlett Publishers.

Thompson, W., and J. Leidlein. 2009. *Ethics in City Hall*. Boston, MA: Jones and Bartlett Publishers.

Van Wart, M. 1998. *Changing Public Sector Values*. New York: Garland Publishing, Inc.

Van Wart, M. 2006. "An Ethics Based Approach to Leadership." In J. West and E. Berman, eds. *The Ethics Edge* (pp. 39–45). Washington, D.C.: ICMA.

Van Wart, M., N. J. Cayer, and S. Cook. 1993. *Handbook of Training and Development*. San Francisco, CA: Jossey-Bass.

Wells, D., and M. Schminke. 2001. "Ethical Development and Human Resources Training: An Integrative Framework." *Human Resources Management Review* 11: 135–158.

West, J. P., ed. 1995. *Quality Management Today*. Washington, D.C.: International City/County Management Association.

West, J. P. 2009. "Ethics and Human Resource Management." In S. Hays and R. Kearney, eds. *Public Personnel Management: Problems and Prospects* (pp. 275–289). Upper Saddle River, NJ: Prentice Hall.

West, J. P., and E. Berman 2004. "Ethics Training Efforts in U.S. Cities: Content and Impact." *Public Integrity* 6(3): 189–206.

West, J. P., and E. Berman. 2006. *The Ethics Edge*. Washington, D.C.: International City/County Management Association.

West, J. P., E. Berman, and A. Cava. 1993. "Ethics in the Municipal Workplace." *The Municipal Yearbook 1993* (pp. 3–16). Washington, D.C.: International City/County Management Association.

West, J. P, E. Berman, S. Bonczek, and E. Kellar. 1998. "Frontiers of Ethics Training." *Public Management* 80(6): 4–9.

West, J. P., and J. Bowman. 2008. "Employee Benefits: Weighing Ethical Principles and Economic Imperatives." In C. Reddick and J. Coggburn, eds. *Handbook of Employee Benefits and Administration* (pp. 29–53). Boca Raton, FL: CRC Press.

White, L., and L. Lam. 2000. "A Proposed Infrastructural Model for the Establishment of Organizational Ethical Systems." *Journal of Business Ethics* 28: 35–42. www.aspanet.org/ethicscommunity/compendium.

Wyatt-Nichol, H., and G. Franks. 2009–2010. "Ethics Training in Law Enforcement." *Public Integrity* 12(1): 39–50.

Endnotes

1. Other valuable ethics training resources that can complement instructional activities include ASPA (1998), Cooper (2001), Brattebo and Malone (2002), Cox (2009), Gueras and Garofalo (2002), Huberts, Maesschalck, and Jurkiewicz (2008), Kazman and Bonczek (1998), LGI (1995–1998), Menzel (2007, 2009), NCSL (2003),

Pasquerella, Killilea, and Vocino (1996), Richter and Burke (2007), Svara (2007), Thompson and Leidlein (2009), West and Berman (2006), and www.aspanet.org/ethicscommunity/compendium.

2. Data were collected as part of a 2002 questionnaire mailed to city managers and chief administrative officers (CAOs) in all 544 cities with populations over 50,000. Two hundred usable responses were received after three rounds of mailing, for a response rate of 36.8 percent. Survey respondents report having extensive government experience of 20 years, of which 11 are spent with their current jurisdiction. Respondents hold a variety of very senior positions, so we refer to the response groups as "senior managers." We also conducted in-depth telephone interviews among a sample of respondents.

3. Although path analysis can also be used to estimate this recursive model, the approach used here includes additional tests for the appropriateness (specification) of the overall model. Figure 17.1 satisfies the usual goodness-of-fit standards (chi-square=13.28, $p > .05$). See West and Berman (2004) for a complete discussion of other fit measures. Although this is not statistically the most parsimonious model, it does show the theoretically relevant linkages.

4. The respective effect sizes on employee productivity are .208 (ethics training), .191 (moral leadership), .608 (organizational culture), and .304 (labor-management relations). These are the beta coefficients. Indirect effects are calculated as the product of coefficients. For example, the indirect effect of organizational culture on productivity through labor-management relations is $.46 \times .30 = .138$. The direct effect is .47, hence, the total effect is .608. Other indirect effects are calculated in the same manner.

INDEX

A

absolute immunity, 106, 109, 110, 112
Acanfora v. Board of Education of Montgomery County, 64
ADA Amendments Act (ADAAA) of 2008, 85
Adam's equity theory, 129, 130
Adarand Constructors, Inc. v. Pena, 45, 107, 114
Administrative Careers with America (ACWA), 139
adverse impact, 5
Alexander v. Choate, 90
Americans with Disabilities Act (ADA), 61, 82, 83, 84, 85, 87, 89, 90, 91
Anderson v. Creighton, 110
Atwater v. City of Lago Vista, 108, 113
at-will employment, 8, 125
Aviation and Transportation Security Act (ATSA) of 2001, 98–100

B

baby boomers (boomers), 30, 31, 35
Bailey, Margo, 50
Ban, Carolyn, 135, 136, 137
Barr v. Matteo, 108
Battaglio, Paul R., 8
behaviorally anchored rating scales (BARS), 129, 176
Berman, Evan M., 2, 213, 214, 215, 217, 218, 220, 227n
Berry-James, RaJade M., 51
binding arbitration, 97
Bivens v. Six Unknown Named Federal Narcotics Agents, 109, 110
BMW of North America v. Gore, 111
Board of County Commissioners, Wabaunsee County v. Umbehr, 107
Board of Directors of Rotary International v. Rotary Club, 197
Board of Trustees of University of Alabama v. Garrett, 87
Bogan v. Scott-Harris, 112
bona fide occupational qualification (BFOQ), 66, 200
Bowman, James S., 2, 4, 22, 128, 213, 219
Boy Scouts of America and Monmouth Council v. Dale, 198
Boy Scouts of America Equal Access Act, 199
Boy Scouts of America v. Wyman, 199
Bragdon v. Abbott, 84, 85
Brentwood Academy v. Tennessee Secondary School Athletic Association, 115
Brewer, Gene A., 33
broadbanding, 142
Brosseau v. Haugen, 113
Brown, R. C., 31

Bush v. Lucas, 109, 112
Butz v. Economou, 112

C

California's Proposition 209, 42
career bands, 122–123
Carlson v. Green, 109, 110
Carroll, James D., 105, 108, 115
Cayer, N. Joseph, 159
central tendency error, 178–179
Chanin, Joshua, 105, 107, 108, 109, 111, 113, 115
charitable choice, 202
Choi, Sungjoo, 50
Chrysler v. DILHR, 90
City of Canton v. Harris, 115
City of Newport v. Fact Concerts, 105
City of Richmond v. Croson, 45, 107
Civil Rights Act of 1871, 104, 109
Civil Rights Act of 1964, 1, 5, 40, 44, 62, 63, 66, 200–202
Civil Rights Act of 1991, 46, 63, 66
Civil Service Commission, 6
Civil Service Reform Act of 1978, 1, 2, 6–7, 62
civil service retirement system (CSRS), 161
Cleavinger v. Saxner, 112
Cleveland v. Policy Management System, 83
Coggburn, Jerrell D., 162, 168
Collings v. Longview Fibre, 84
Collins v. Bender, 112
Commission, New York City Administration for Children Services and others, 204
compelling governmental interest, 40, 41, 42, 45, 46
Condrey, Stephen E., 2, 6, 8
Conley v. Village of Bedford Park, 84
Connecticut v. Teal, 5
contractors, 140–141
Cornwell, Christopher, 39
Corporation of the Bishop of the Church of Jesus Christ of Latter Day Saints v. Amos, 200, 204
Corrections Corporation of America, 190
Coulee Catholic Schools v. Lab & Ind Review Comm, 201
County of Sacramento v. Lewis, 113
crowding-out effect, 158
Crum, John, 55

D

Dale v. Boy Scouts of America and Monmouth Council Boy Scouts, 198
Daley, Dennis M., 5, 177
Davis v. Passman, 109
Davis, T. J., 128
Defense of Marriage Act of 1996, 69
Delaware v. Prouse, 107

deLeon, Linda, 179
Deming, W. Edwards, 127
demonstration projects, 6, 7
Disabled Veterans Act, 83
Doe v. City of Belleville, 67
Dolan v. City of Tigard, 107
domestic partnership benefits, 60, 68, 69
Don't Ask, Don't Tell, 73
due process rights, 111, 112, 121, 122, 128, 129, 133

E

Employee Assistance Program (EAP), 100
employee relations, 130–132
Employment Non-Discrimination Act (ENDA), 62, 63
Enriquez v. West Jersey Health Systems, 61
Equal Employment Opportunity Act of 1972, 5
Equal Pay Act of 1963, 67
equal protection, 107, 108, 114, 115, 118, 119n
ethical leadership, 213, 214, 215, 217
ethics training, 215, 216, 218–224, 227n
Ewen, Ann J., 179
Executive Order 11478, 62
Executive Order 13087, 62
Executive Order 13198, 203
Executive Order 13199, 203, 204
Executive Order 13279, 203
Executive Order 13280, 203
Executive Order 13342, 203
Executive Order 13397, 203
extrinsic incentives, 126, 127, 128, 130, 180, 183n, 208

F

Facer, Rex, 33
faith-based initiatives, 203–205
Farmer v. Brennan, 113
FDIC v. Meyer, 105
Federal Career Intern Program (FCIP), 140, 144
federal employment retirement system (FERS), 161
Federal Hiring Process Improvement Act, 145
Federal Labor Relations Authority (FLRA), 98, 99
Firefighters Local Union and Memphis Fire Department v. Stotts, 44, 46
Follett, Mary Parker, 125
42 U.S. Code Section 1983, 104, 109, 110, 119n
401k plan, 161, 162
free speech rights, 107, 118
free-agents, 33
Fullilove v. Klutznick, 44
furlough, 151, 158

G

Gabris, Gerald T., 128
gain sharing, 127–128
Garcetti v. Ceballos, 108
gender dysphoria, 61

gender identity disorder (GID), 61
generation X (Gen-Xers), 30, 31, 32, 34, 35
GeorgiaGain, 29
Gertz, S., 4
Givhan v. Western Line Consolidated School District, 113
globalization, 22
goal sharing. *See* gain sharing
Goins v. West Group, 71
Gossett, Charles W., 60, 62, 66, 67, 202
Government Accounting Standards Board (GASB), 166, 168
Gratz v. Bollinger, 41, 45, 114
Griggs v. Duke Power Company, 5
Grutter v. Bollinger, 40–41, 45

H

Hafer v. Melo, 105
halo effect, 177–178
Harley v. Schuylkill County, 113
Harlow v. Fitzgerald, 110, 111, 114
Hawes-Cooper Act, 188
Hawthorne studies, 125
Hays, Steven, W., 8
Health Care and Education Reconciliation Act, 80, 91
Heclo, Hugh, 7
Herzberg's two-factor theory, 129, 130, 180
Hess v. Allstate Ins. Co., 90
Hiibel v. Sixth Judicial District Court of Nevada, Humboldt County, 108
Holman v. Indiana, 67
Holzer, Marc, 21
Hope v. Pelzer, 111, 114
Hopwood v. State of Texas, 45
Hostetler, Dennis W., 68, 198
Hurley v. Irish-American Gay Group of Boston, 197
Hyde, Albert C., 166

I

impasse, 96, 97
Ingraham, Patricia W., 128, 139, 149, 181
inherently governmental, 142
Int'l Assoc. of Firefighters v. City of Cleveland, 45
intrinsic incentives, 126, 127, 130, 180, 183n, 208

J

job analysis, 174
Johnson v. Transportation Agency, Santa Clara County, 45
Julnes, Patria, 21
Jurkiewicz, Carol E., 31, 213, 226n
Justice Assistance Act of 1984, 191
Justice System Improvement Act of 1979, 191

K

Kearney, Richard C., 8
Kellough, J. Edward, 2, 15, 39, 51, 141, 181

Kettl, Donald, 17
Klingner, Donald, 2, 14, 15, 21, 22, 121, 149
Kolender v. Lawson, 107

L

labor-management partnerships, 8
Labor-Management Relations Act of 1947, 205
Labor-Management Reporting and Disclosure
  Act of 1959, 205
Lah, T. J., 7
Lawrence v. Texas, 61, 66
*Lebron v. National Railroad Passenger
  Corporation*, 115
Lee, Yong, 106, 109, 111, 118n
Lesage v. Texas, 45
Lewis, Gregory B., 62
Light, Paul, 141
Llorens, Jared, 2, 14, 141
Lown v. The Salvation Army, Inc., 204
Lu, Haoran, 181
Lucas v. South Carolina Coastal, 107
Luevano v. Campbell, 139, 141
Luevano v. Devine, 139, 141

M

Maffei v. Kolaeton Industry, 67
Malek Manual, 6
Management by Objectives (MBO), 121, 126,
  128, 129, 130
Martin v. Wilks, 45
Marzotto, Toni, 136
Maslow's hierarchy of needs, 129, 130
Mathews, Audrey L., 51, 54
McClure v. The Salvation Army, 201
McDermott v. Xerox, 90
Meier, Kenneth J., 55
Menzel, Donald C., 213, 214, 218, 222, 226n
merit pay for managers, 6
merit pay, 126, 128, 181. *See also* pay for
  performance
Merit Systems Protection Board (MSPB), 6, 112
Mesch, Debra J., 121
Michigan's Proposal 2, 40–42
millennials (Gen-Yers), 30, 31
ministerial exception to Title VII, 201
Miranda v. Arizona, 107
Miranda warnings, 107, 112
Missouri v. Jenkins, 108
Mitchell v. Forsyth, 110
Munnell, Alicia, 162, 166
Murphy v. United Parcel Services, Inc., 84
*Murray v. Oceanside Unified School
  District*, 67

N

Naff, Katherine C., 2, 4, 39, 51, 55, 105
Nalbandian, John, 2, 14, 15, 22, 149
narrowly tailored, 40, 41, 42, 47
National Labor Relations Act (NLRA) of 1935,
  96, 97, 98, 205
National Labor Relations Board (NLRB), 205

National Security Personnel System (NSPS),
  6, 8, 10
National Treasury Employees Union (NTEU),
  98, 99, 100
Naylor, Lorenda A., 41
Nebraska's I-424, 42
neutral professionalism, 14
new public management (NPM), 4, 8, 17
*New York State Club Association v. City of
  New York*, 197
Newland v. Dalton, 84
Newman, Meredith, 4
Nicholson-Crotty, Jill, 55
Nigro, Felix A., 2, 29, 174
Nigro, Lloyd G., 2, 15, 29, 174
NLRB v. Catholic Bishop of Chicago, 205
Norton v. Macy, 66

O

*O'Hare Truck Service, Inc. v. City of
  Northlake*, 107
O'Leary, Rosemary, 105, 107, 108, 109, 111,
  113, 115
Obama Administration, 9–10
Office of Personnel Management (OPM), 6, 62
Oncale v. Sundowner Offshore Services, 66
other postemployment benefits (OPEB),
  168–169
outsourcing, 3, 4, 8, 17, 114, 115, 186,
  189, 191
Owen v. City of Independence, 110, 111

P

Palguta, John, 140
patronage, 16
pay for performance, 126–127, 131, 174,
  181–183. *See also* merit pay
*Pedreira v. Kentucky Baptist Homes for
  Children*, 201
Peffer, Shelly L., 43
Pembaur v. City of Cincinnati, 105
Pendleton Act of 1883, 2, 6, 7
pension spiking, 158, 168, 170
performance management, 10
performance-based compensation. *See* pay
  for performance
Perry, James L., 4, 7, 17, 28, 33
personal liability, 105, 110
Petruska v. Gannon University, 201
Pickering v. Board of Education, 113–114
Pitts, David W., 50, 59n
Plant, Jeremy, 218
Plata v. Schwarzenegger, 111
Price Waterhouse v. Hopkins, 64, 67
Price, Byron E., 186, 188, 189
Professional and Administrative Careers
  Examination (PACE), 139
Protestant work ethic, 32
Public Safety Employer-Employee Cooperation
  Act (PSEECA), 97–98
Public Service Motivation (PSM), 33, 34

public trust, 104
Pynes, Joan E., 29, 68, 148, 198, 199, 202, 207, 208

Q

qualified immunity, 108–110, 111, 112, 113, 115

R

Rainey, Hal G., 50
Ran, Bing, 218
Raytheon Co. v. Hernandez, 87
reasonable accommodation, 83, 84, 85, 86, 87–89, 90, 91, 92
recruitment, 9, 29, 63–65, 208
Reddick, Christopher G., 162, 168
reductions in force (RIFs), 148, 151, 153, 154
Regents of the University of California v. Bakke, 40, 44
Rehabilitation (Rehab) Act, 82, 83, 84, 85, 86, 87, 89, 90, 91, 92
Religious Freedom Restorative Act (RFRA), 203
Returns on Investment (ROIs), 120
Ricci v. DeStefano, 39, 42–44, 47
Riccucci, Norma M., 2, 7, 8, 39, 51, 63, 66, 68, 105, 186
Rice, Mitchell F., 23, 50, 51
Richardson v. McKnight, 115
Roberts v. United States Jaycees, 197
Romzek, Barbara S., 149
Rosenbloom, David H., 41, 105, 107, 108, 109, 111, 112, 113, 114, 115
Rubaii-Barrett, Nadia, 57
rule of three, 9, 137, 144

S

Sabet, G., 21
Sandfort, Jodi R., 174
Scheuer v. Rhodes, 109
School Board of Nassau County v. Arline, 84
Schroer v. Billington, 65
Scott v. Harris, 113
searches and seizures, 107, 109, 118
Seidner, Rob, 136, 143
Selden, Sally Coleman, 33, 181
Senior Executive Service (SES), 6, 7, 51
seniority, 44, 46, 47
separate but equal doctrine, 107
sexual harassment, 66–67
Shahar v. Bowers, 65, 66
Sheehan v. Marr, 83
Sheet Metal Workers' International Association v. EEOC, 45
Shelton v. Tucker, 64
Shilts, Randy, 62
Simonton v. Runyon, 67
Sims, Ronald R., 5, 6
Singer v. United States Civil Service Commission, 66
Slack, James D., 82, 86
smart practice, 15, 17, 20, 24

Smith v. City of Salem, 64
Smith v. Wade, 110–111
Social Security Act of 1935, 159
sovereign immunity, 106
Sowa, Jessica E., 8
Spalding v. Vilas, 106
spoils system, 14
Stonewall rebellion, 62
strict scrutiny test, 40, 41, 45, 46
Stump v. Sparkman, 106
Sullivan v. River Valley School District, 84
Sutton v. United Airlines, 84
Svara, James, 213, 219, 222, 227n

T

Tanner v. Oregon Health Sciences University, 68
Tennessee v. Lane et al., 87
Terry v. Ohio, 107
Thompson, Frank J., 6, 7
Thompson, James R., 4, 136, 143
3 strikes law, 190
Title VII. *See* Civil Rights Act of 1964
Tobias, Robert, 10
Tomic v. Catholic Diocese, 201
Total Quality Management (TQM), 121, 127, 130
Tower v. Glover, 112
Toyota v. Williams, 84
traditionalists, 30, 31, 32, 34
training and development, 10, 129, 176
trait-based approach to performance, 175–176
Transportation Security Administration (TSA) screeners, 96, 98–100
Transportation Workforce Security Enhancement Act of 2009, 98

U

U.S. v. Paradise, 45
union membership, 95–96
United States v. James Daniel Good Real Property, 107
United States v. Lee, 106
United Steelworkers of America v. Weber, 44
Universidad Central Baymon v. National Labor Relations Board, 206
University of Great Falls v. National Labor Relations Board, 206

V

Van Riper, Paul, 2, 6
Van Wart, Montgomery R., 2, 213, 215, 222
veterans' preference, 137, 138, 140, 144
Victory Fund, 65
virtual volunteering, 207
Vroom's expectancy theory, 126, 129, 181

W

Walsh-Healey Public Contract Act of 1939, 191
Washington's I-200, 42
Waters v. Churchill, 114

West v. Atkins, 115
West, Jonathan P., 2, 4, 6, 8, 213, 214, 215,
  218, 220, 222, 227n
Western Weighing Bureau v. DILHR, 90
Weyer v. Twentieth Century Fox Film Corp., 90
whistle-blowing, 98, 107, 113
White, Harvey L., 51
Whren v. United States, 108
Wilkie v. Robbins, 113

Will v. Michigan Department of State Police, 105
Williams v. Widnall, 84
Winter Commission report, 148
Wise, Lois R., 28, 50, 59n, 121
Wood v. Strickland, 109
Woodford v. Ngo, 108
workforce planning, 148, 149, 150, 151, 152,
  153, 154
Wygant v. Jackson Bd. of Education, 44, 46, 47